Reading Hegel's *Phenomenology*

Reading Hegel's
Phenomenology

John Russon

INDIANA UNIVERSITY PRESS
BLOOMINGTON AND INDIANAPOLIS

This book is a publication of

Indiana University Press
601 North Morton Street
Bloomington, IN 47404-3797 USA

http://iupress.indiana.edu

Telephone orders   800-842-6796
Fax orders   812-855-7931
Orders by e-mail   iuporder@indiana.edu

The paper used in this publication meets the minimum require-
ments of American National Standard for Information Sciences—
Permanence of Paper for Printed Library Materials, ANSI
Z39.48-1984.

Manufactured in the United States of America

Library of Congress Cataloging-in-Publication Data
Russon, John Edward, date
Reading Hegel's Phenomenology / John Russon.
p. cm. — (Studies in Continental thought)
Includes bibliographical references and index.
ISBN 0-253-34421-2 (alk. paper) — ISBN 0-253-21692-3
(pbk. : alk. paper)
1. Hegel, Georg Wilhelm Friedrich, 1770–1831.
Phänomenologie de Geistes. I. Title. II. Series.
B2929.R86 2004
193—dc22
2004007631
1 2 3 4 5 09 08 07 06 05 04

Dedicated, with gratitude and
respect,
to my friend John Stuhr

Life negates itself in literature only so that it may survive better.

JACQUES DERRIDA, "EDMOND JABÈS AND THE
QUESTION OF THE BOOK"

We must go back to the things themselves.

EDMUND HUSSERL, *LOGICAL INVESTIGATIONS*

Contents

Contents

Religion

Absolute Knowing

Acknowledgments

This book was written over a period of about a decade, and most of the chapters were originally presented as public lectures. I am grateful to many excellent students at the University of Toronto and at Penn State University with whom I studied Hegel in this period, to my colleagues at Acadia University, the University of Toronto, Penn State University, and the University of Guelph, and to the many schools and conferences that gave me an opportunity to present my ideas publicly. Various versions of these chapters were presented at the University of Toronto, the University of Guelph, McMaster University, Trent University, York University, Brock University, Bishop's University, the University of Ottawa, St. Thomas More College, the New School for Social Research, Villanova University, the Pennsylvania State University, the University of California at San Diego, Northern Illinois University, and Bates College, and at annual meetings of the Canadian Philosophical Association and the American Philosophical Association. Earlier versions of chapters 2, 8, 11, and 12 were published in the *Southern Journal of Philosophy*, and I am grateful for their permission to reprint them here, as I am for permission to reprint chapter 13, an earlier version of which was originally published in *Sites of Vision: The Discursive Construction of Vision in the History of Philosophy*, David Michael Levin, ed., by MIT Press, and for permission to reprint chapters 6 and 7, earlier versions of which appeared respectively in *Interrogating the Tradition: Hermeneutics and the History of Philosophy*, Charles Scott and John Sallis, eds., by the State University of New York Press, and in *Hegel and the Tradition: Essays in Honour of H.S. Harris*, Michael Baur and John Russon, eds., by the University of Toronto Press. Many of my ideas were first aired publicly at a series of annual meetings organized by Hegel scholars from Ontario, Quebec, and the Northeastern States, which afforded me regular consultation with Jay Lampert, John Burbidge, David Morris, James Crooks, Bruce Gilbert, Graeme Nicholson, Peter Simpson, David Ciavatta, and many others. Throughout this time, I have also had the privilege to work on a number of dissertation committees, including those of David Ciavatta, Nathan Andersen, Brian Mackintosh, Cory Styranko, and Jennifer Bates, and this has been a great educational opportunity for me. I am also grateful to the participants in the first "Toronto Seminar" who went through the whole route with me: Scott Marratto, Alexandra Morrison, Kym Maclaren, David Cia-

Acknowledgments

vatta, Peter Costello, Maria Talero, David Morris, Graeme Nicholson, Bruce Gilbert, Joanna Polley, David Bronstein, Nicholas Storch, Dana Hollander, Susan Bredlau, Jessica Brotman, Daniel Brandes, and Kirsten Jacobson. I especially thank my friend William Roberts, who read through the whole manuscript and gave me many detailed and stimulating comments. Finally, I am grateful for the friendship and support of Peter Hill, Ron Davis, Ken Aldcroft, Arthur Goldstein, and Wayne Cass.

A revised version of John Russon, "Hermeneutical Pressure and the Space of Dialectic: What Hegel Means by 'Spirit,'" in Charles E. Scott and John Sallis eds., *Interrogating the Tradition: Hermeneutics and the History of Philosophy* (Albany: State University of New York Press, 2000), is here published as Chapter 6, reprinted with the permission of the State University of New York Press.

A revised version of John Russon, "Hegel's 'Freedom of Self-Consciousness' and Early Modern Epistemology," in Michael Baur and John Russon, eds., *Hegel and the Tradition: Essays in Honour of H.S. Harris* (Toronto: University of Toronto Press, 1997), is here published as Chapter 7, reprinted with the permission of University of Toronto Press.

A revised version of John Russon, "'For Now We See Through a Glass Darkly': The Systemantics of Hegel's Visual Imagery," in David Michael Levin, ed., *Sites of Vision: The Discursive Construction of Sight in the History of Philosophy* (Cambridge, Mass.: MIT Press, 1997), is here published as Chapter 13, reprinted with the permission of the MIT Press.

NOTE ON THE TEXT

This study focuses on G. W. F. Hegel's *Phänomenologie des Geistes* of 1807. All references to this Hegelian text will be to *Phänomenologie des Geistes*, hrsg. v. Hans-Friedrich Wessels and Heinrich Clairmont (Felix Meiner, 1988), and to *Phenomenology of Spirit*, translated by A. V. Miller (Oxford, 1977). Citations of this text and translation will be given as follows: reference to the paragraph in the Miller translation will be given first, as M, followed by the paragraph number, and reference to the page in the Wessels-Clairmont edition will follow as W/C, followed by the page number. Periodically, the page number of the German text will be followed by a decimal point and a number or numbers; this will indicate the precise line numbers of the passage under consideration (negative numbers indicating lines counted from the bottom of the page). Throughout I will cite Hegel's chapter numbers in Roman numerals, and give the title of the relevant chapter or section; I will refer to my own chapters using Arabic numerals. Unless otherwise indicated, English translations of the *Phenomenology of Spirit* are taken from Miller's translation.

References to Hegel's *Science of Logic* will be given as E followed by page number to refer to the English translation by A. V. Miller (New York: Humanities Press, 1976), and G followed by page number to refer to the two-volume German text edited by Eva Moldenhauer and Karl Markus Michel (Frankfurt am Main: Suhrkamp, 1986).

Reading Hegel's *Phenomenology*

Introduction

This volume is an interpretive study of Hegel's *Phenomenology of Spirit* as a whole. It is unlike other commentaries in two fundamental ways. First, I do not aim to discuss everything there is in the *Phenomenology*; I am concerned with Hegel's book only insofar as it is an argument. Other works have studied the language, the allusions, and the cultural context of Hegel's book, and these are all worthwhile and important studies. I, however, pay little heed to these matters, but attend primarily to the methods, premises, evidence, reasoning, and conclusions that Hegel is deploying in each of the major steps of the book and in the book as a whole. Second, I proceed by way of independent studies of particular sections. Other works have offered continuous commentary upon the book from start to finish. My approach, on the contrary, is to take each major section separately and pursue it as an independent argument. Thus this book is composed of a set of chapters, each of which is a study that can be read entirely on its own, but the whole of which forms an integrated study of the entire *Phenomenology of Spirit*. This method of proceeding by way of independent studies has two motivations, one in terms of the nature of Hegel's philosophy, the other in terms of the pedagogical needs of my readers.

Hegel's *Phenomenology* is typically thought to claim about itself that it is a step-by-step study of all the forms of human experience, orchestrated in a necessary developmental order. It is thought that each step leads to the next, and that all find their justification only in the conclusion of the book. Consequently, it is thought, if there is an error at any step along the way—and especially if there is a problem with the beginning or the end—the whole edifice (which is built upon its claims to absolute necessity) will crumble. There is some justice to these claims, to be sure. In my view, however, they provide far too simplistic a conception for the understanding of Hegel's massive, complex, and subtle work. I believe that it is only through a well-developed understanding of the specific content of the *Phenomenology* as a whole that one can come to understand the sense in which these familiar claims are true. I believe that interpretations that begin from this vision of Hegel's project typically miss most of what is important in Hegel's work and, worse, often substantially misconstrue the true form and method of Hegel's argument. My method takes each major section of Hegel's *Phenomenology* as a separate topic of study, and develops an argument to show both how this is a compelling interpretation of an aspect of human experience and how it fits into (supports) Hegel's overall philosophical position. In other words, whereas others have thought that each section of the book depends essentially upon the other sections of the book and can be understood only in terms of them, I argue on the contrary that each section stands alone and is capable on its own of developing from out of itself all the resources typically thought to be supplied by the other portions of the book. The net result of my work is to show that Hegel's interpretations of the various aspects of human experience are more independent and more compelling than they are often taken to be and to show that his overall position is much harder to refute than is typically believed.

The chapters in this book each work to explain some major section of the *Phenomenology of Spirit,* and to do so in a way that basically defends Hegel's project. The systematic, quasi-organic character of Hegel's project means that the identity of the whole should be present in each part, and to show how this is in fact so has been one of my primary objectives. I have tried to take the separate segments of Hegel's argument and show how each on its own is a good argument, and also to show how, from out of each, one can work out the larger implications of Hegel's argument as a whole. (Loosely, this means showing that "dialectical phenomenology" is the answer to all questions, ethical, epistemological, or metaphysical.) Each chapter is an independent "lesson" in how to read a major section of Hegel's book. Precisely what my chapters offer is an interpretation of the *point* of each of Hegel's sections: I identify clearly the familiar phenomenon Hegel is studying and make clear exactly what he wants to accomplish with it. These aspects of Hegel's book are often the hardest to discern—one finds the trees, but rarely sees the forest—and I consider being able to show how the arguments are rooted in familiar phenomena of everyday life to be one the major contributions of these studies.

Throughout the book I have tried to show how Hegel's arguments are also rooted in dialogue with the history of philosophy and with the philosophical movements that have emerged since Hegel's time. I do this not by looking to Hegel's comments on other philosophers, nor by looking at other philosophers' comments on Hegel, but by focusing on the arguments and the phenomena themselves, and showing how Hegel's lines of investigation cross paths with the lines of investigation undertaken by other philosophers before and since. One result of this (besides what is I hope its obvious result, namely, illuminating the nature of Hegel's work, primarily, and secondarily the works of others) is that Hegel's relationship to the history of philosophy appears somewhat differently than it is often portrayed by contemporary figures. This is especially so regarding Hegel's relationship to contemporary Continental philosophy. On my reading, it is by no means clear that there is a significant difference between the philosophical methods, goals, or results of Hegel's philosophy and the philosophies of such figures as Heidegger, Merleau-Ponty, and Derrida. It is most certainly not my intention in this work to defend that claim—my intention is to explicate Hegel's philosophy on its own—and so the reader will find only a few suggestive remarks about how such correlations might be made; but I hope that this book provides various materials from which such an argument could be made, and I especially hope it will do some work toward inhibiting the all-too-familiar facile characterizations of how Hegel stands in relationship to phenomenology, existentialism, and deconstruction. In this regard, I hope this book will contribute to a new tradition in Hegel scholarship.[1]

Most of all, however, this book is shaped by pedagogical motives. I have tried to write as a teacher, each separate chapter offering a lesson to someone who is reading through the *Phenomenology of Spirit* for the sake of understanding its argument. The form of my writing is intended to encourage certain interpretive practices and discourage others.

First, I want to encourage readers of Hegel to demand of themselves first that they understand the phenomenon of which Hegel's analysis is a phenomenology. One cannot, for example, understand Hegel's argument *about* understanding if one does not first understand what "understanding" refers to. I have aimed always to direct readers to thinking about the familiar nature of certain experiences, prior to launching into a study of Hegel's specific analyses of such experiences. Through this focus on the phenomena themselves, I have also tried to show that the lessons of the chapters are not just about Hegel's book, but about knowledge, about politics, about morality, and so on. While this is no doubt true to some extent of any commentary on Hegel, it is nonetheless usually the case that other commentaries remain "about" the book; I have tried, following Hegel, to remain focused on the phenomena, and I believe this "outward-directed" orientation produces a work that makes it easier to see the relevance of the philosophical conclusions.

Second, I want to break readers of too simplistic an interpretation of what it means to say that Hegel's chapters have a necessary sequence. The logic of Hegel's argument is subtle and complex, and has relatively little in common with the simple model of necessary logical progression often imputed to it. (This is not to say that there is no relevance to this notion.) I have, through my method of analysis, tried to encourage readers to see more of the implications of one section of Hegel's book for another by "skipping around," that is, reading one chapter in conjunction with another that is not continuous with it.[2] The good interpreter of Hegel must learn to read each section autonomously, and must learn to be able to see the implications of each for each other, rather than always interpreting each chapter only in light of those that immediately succeed and precede it. I have especially relied upon the analysis of the dialectic of recognition and of ethicality in my analyses of most other chapters of the book, because I believe these two sections most reveal the "point" of Hegel's philosophy. Other conjoinings would certainly be possible, however, and I hope that the style of analysis I have undertaken in these chapters will serve as a sort of prototype for the innovative readings of others.

Third, I have tried to deploy as much of the history of philosophy as I am able in my interpretations of these chapters in order to supply to many readers the simple familiarity with these other figures that they may lack on their own. Hegel's book is a book that responds to the philosophical work of others, and its message is largely unavailable to readers who are not familiar with the highly developed level of philosophical debate to which it is a response.

Fourth, I have tried to strike a balance between readability and textual explication. I try, as far as possible, to argue from the issues themselves, rather than from Hegel's text, tying the argument to the text by the analysis only of chosen key passages. I have tried to pick pivotal (and often otherwise opaque) textual sites for specific analysis, so that the reader is guided through the decisive textual moments, while counting on my larger conceptual analysis to guide the reader through those surrounding passages that I do not explicate specifically. I intend the arguments I give to be very close to the text, but typically I do not demonstrate this proximity except at the crucial moments.

And finally, beyond the unifying structure derived by following the movements of Hegel's own book, the volume is loosely guided by a unifying concern throughout—the notion of "reading." Throughout the book I have returned to the phenomenon of reading as exemplary of the logical relations with which Hegel is specially concerned. Many of the chapters offer some analysis of the phenomenon of making sense of an inscription, that is, of an aesthetically (sensibly, intuitively) presented material given as "to be understood." The result is that, as the reader progresses through the chapters, she accumulates a growing set of insights into the logical, epistemic, practical, social, and moral parameters of reading, of interpretation, and by the end of the book it becomes clear why this is appropriate as a central theme for Hegel's philosophy. Hence the title of the volume, *Reading Hegel's Phenomenology*: the title refers (1) to my (and the readers') practice of reading Hegel's book, (2) to the use of Hegel as a route through which other figures and phenomena become accessible (i.e., in studying other figures and phenomena, we are really reading Hegel's phenomenology), and (3) to the phenomenon of reading itself that is at the core of Hegel's volume (as if the title were *Reading: Hegel's Phenomenology*).

The sequence of essays is a single book, intended to be read in order from start to finish. Read in this fashion, the book essentially provides a full course in the interpretation of the *Phenomenology of Spirit* as a whole (and with just about the same number of chapters as there are weeks in a semester, making it, I hope, a good companion volume for a one-semester course on the *Phenomenology*). Nonetheless, any chapter of the book can be read entirely on its own. Each is a self-contained study of certain facets of Hegel's argument, and there is no necessity that any be read in a specific order or in conjunction with any others. If the reader should want to get to know quickly my overall interpretation of Hegel's book, she should turn to Chapter 11, "Selfhood, Conscience, and Dialectic," for in this chapter I most concisely state what I take to be the basic argument of the book. If the reader should want to get to know quickly my distinctive "hobby horses" in Hegel interpretation, she should turn to Chapter 5, "Reading and the Body." Beyond that, no chapters are especially privileged from the point of view of importance, though Chapter 2, "From Perception to Philosophy," Chapter 4, "Death and Desire in Hegel's Epistemology: The Form of Hegel's Argument," and Chapter 12, "The Ritual Basis of Self-Identity," are similarly effective in revealing my understanding of the comprehensive argument and import of Hegel's *Phenomenology* as a whole. Chapter 3, "Understanding: Things, Forces, and the Body," and Chapter 8, "Reason and Dualism," are the chapters I personally consider my greatest accomplishments with respect to the overall effort to decipher Hegel's difficult text.

Chapters 1 through 3 consider the separate chapters of Hegel's section called "Consciousness." In general, they each demonstrate that these "theoretical" postures are grounded in practical life (that is, they demonstrate how consciousness rests on self-consciousness), and I show in each case how Hegel's argument implies an essentially existentialist conception of humanity.

Chapter 1, "Sense, Time, and My Meaning," is a study of the "lesson" about the "now" in Hegel's "Sense-Certainty" chapter, the first section of his analysis of "Consciousness." My emphasis in this chapter is away from working through the steps of Hegel's analysis of the "now" (which is competently done by other commentators, and which is one of the easier portions of the *Phenomenology* to read and understand) and toward bringing out the significance of this argument. My effort is to establish what Hegel's (existential) point about time really is, and also to show that from these opening moves alone we could develop vastly important conclusions about the temporal nature of meaning, about the inseparability of subject and object, about consciousness and reality, and about the ineffaceable place of the body and language in experience. In short, Hegel's chapter on "Sense-Certainty" is shown to be implicitly a revelation of man's existential condition.

Chapter 2, "From Perception to Philosophy," begins from an explication of the basic conceptual argument of "Perception," Hegel's second chapter in his study of "Consciousness," and develops this into a study of the dialectical transformation of perception into understanding (science) and thence into existentialism (philosophy). This chapter does not specifically explicate texts from the *Phenomenology* beyond the chapter on perception (except for the crucial paragraphs that introduce the project of understanding), but instead shows how the argument launched in the analysis of perception plays itself out in the larger themes of Hegelian metaphysics—his "system"—arguing that the real import of this "system" is an essentially existential conception of man. Part of the goal of this chapter, though, is to prepare the reader for the interpretation of the chapter on "Understanding" that follows.

Chapter 3, "Understanding: Things, Forces, and the Body," clarifies the essential argument of Hegel's notoriously difficult chapter, "Force and Understanding: Appearance and Supersensible World." This chapter begins with a study of the tension in everyday life between the demands of perception and the demands of understanding (a theme initiated in the preceding chapter), and identifies conceptual inconsistencies in the foundations of familiar scientific endeavors. This analysis lays the ground for a discussion of Hegel's explicit study of the dialectic of understanding, and for understanding his technical notions of "the first supersensible world," "simple difference," and "the inverted world." This analysis leads us to the phenomena of learning and insight, the investigation of which allows us to develop a notion of the identity of subject and object and takes us backward to the Heraclitean "back-turning harmony," and forward to an existential conception of the body.

Chapters 4 through 7 focus on the specific themes in Hegel's "Self-Consciousness" chapter. In general, these studies show how practical life is inherently theoretical (that is, how self-consciousness is implicitly consciousness). In general, I use Hegel's analyses in the self-consciousness chapter to develop an Hegelian epistemology.

Chapter 4, "Death and Desire in Hegel's Epistemology: The Form of Hegel's Argument," considers the significance of the structuring of Hegel's book in terms of consciousness and self-consciousness, arguing that this structure plays out a modified version of Kant's Third Antinomy, but a version of it in which the antimony is resolved in a synthesis of consciousness and self-consciousness, of the theoretical and the practical. In particular, self-consciousness's encounter with its own death is shown to be central to the very project of knowledge, hence to the project of "Consciousness" in the opening three chapters of the *Phenomenology*.

Chapter 5, "Reading and the Body," considers the existential drama of the "Struggle to the Death," as the foundation of self-consciousness and intersubjectivity, and in particular shows that the dynamism of these latter two notions is rooted in the changing character of the lived body. Though Hegel does not himself thematize the body or language within the argumentative structure of the *Phenomenology*, this chapter shows that both body and language are central to the very core of the development of spirit. This larger significance of the notions of body and language is specifically demonstrated in relation to Hegel's analysis of "ethicality" in Chapter VI, "Spirit."

Chapter 6, "Hermeneutical Pressure: Intersubjectivity and Objectivity," studies the dialectic of master and slave, specifically to see how this dialectical relationship is to be understood in terms of something like the transcendental structures of experiential synthesis that are the subject matter of Kant's *Critique of Pure Reason*. Fundamentally, Hegel's analysis of master and slave completes the Fichtean incorporation of the demands of intersubjectivity into the Kantian analysis of objectivity. The Hegelian "hermeneutics" that is implicit in the phenomenology of master and slave leads us forward (as in the preceding chapter) into the analysis of ethical life, this time construed as an epistemological category, and into a cursory study of "Stoicism, Scepticism and the Unhappy Consciousness" as an analysis of the relationship between individual identity and tradition.

Chapter 7, "The 'Freedom of Self-Consciousness' and Early Modern Epistemology," turns directly to "Stoicism, Scepticism and Unhappy Consciousness" to extract an Hegelian epistemology. Stoicism and skepticism are shown to correspond to the epistemology of simple empiricism, while the logic of unhappy consciousness corresponds to a rationalist, and ultimately a transcendental idealist, epistemology by effectively introducing the distinction between the transcendental and the empirical ego. The analysis of this section of Hegel's dialectic of self-consciousness allows us to see how Hegel's own philosophical project is rooted in Cartesian rationalism but at the same time inverts and undermines the central dogmas of that rationalism, ultimately returning us to something like an Aristotelian empiricism of *epagōgē*.

Chapters 8 through 15 study the argument of the untitled Section C of Hegel's *Phenomenology*. Chapter 8 alone studies the argument of "Reason," Chapters 9 through 11 study "Spirit," Chapters 12 through 14 study "Religion," and Chapter 15 alone considers the argument of "Absolute Knowing." These sections of Hegel's text are the longest, richest, and most detailed in the *Phenomenology*, whereas his earlier chapters are short, dense, and terse. Inversely, whereas my earlier chapters seek to expand the presentation of the logic immanent in Hegel's early chapters, my later chapters seek to distill and simplify the presentation of Hegel's later chapters. This is a function of my overall intention to discern the argument of the *Phenomenology* as a whole. I have tried to keep my explication tightly constrained by the core argument of these various sections. My interest lies in what Hegel's argument is about reason as a whole, about spirit as a whole, about religion as a whole, and about absolute knowing overall. Consequently, my analysis bypasses detailed study of many valuable themes in these later chapters of the *Phenomenology*, such as the analysis of the forms of Greek religion, of the relation of church and state in medieval Christendom, and so on, generally focusing instead on the simple logical role that these analyses play in the larger arguments of these chapters.

Chapter 8, "Reason and Dualism," considers first how the stance of reason is an *Aufhebung*, a dialectical self-transformation, of the definitive moments of self-consciousness, and how it carries forward the epistemological program implicit in "The Freedom of Self-Consciousness." Reason is the immediate identification of the empirical with the transcendental ego, the immediate identification of myself with the universal and necessary structures of subjectivity as such. This immediate identification amounts to a kind of epistemological formalism that is simultaneously the source of reason's success and the mark of its essential limitation. This chapter shows that Hegel's analysis of reason fundamentally traces out the logic of its failure, the logic by which its formalist limitation comes to undermine its whole project. Hegel's explicit analysis of the failure of reason implies what it would take for its project to be rectified, and this is what is developed in the ensuing phenomenology of spirit.

Chapters 9 through 11 analyze the argument of the "Spirit" chapter. Chapter 9, "Spirit and Skepticism," begins with the problem of skepticism as it is raised in Hegel's chapter on self-consciousness. Hegel's analysis of the dialectic of skepticism is shown to be a defense of the phenomenological method, and the "Spirit" chapter is interpreted in this light as a phenomenology of our self-experience as a "we." The argument implied in Hegel's division of the "Spirit" chapter into "Ethics," "Culture," and "Morality" is shown to be the dialectical development through the experience of the "we" as it struggles with different aspects of its own reality—its universality, its particularity, and its singularity. The concluding moment, "Morality," is the moment in which the experience of the "we" itself is enacted in the form of the phenomenological method from which this analysis was launched.

Chapter 10, "The Contradictions of Moral Life: Hegel's Critique of Kant," focuses directly on Hegel's study of the moral spirit, the moment that marks the culmination of spiritual life. Morality is shown to have an internal dialectic of its own, in which it moves from a kind of Kantian formalism to an Hegelian phenomenological ethics in its culminating form as conscientious forgiveness.

Chapter 11, "Selfhood, Conscience, and Dialectic," uses this notion of conscience as an interpretive key to the argumentative structure of the *Phenomenology of Spirit* as a whole. The *Phenomenology* is shown to be structured by the dialectic of self-consciousness, the logical form of which has its completion in that relationship to one's situation that is conscientious, forgiving action. Absolute knowing is shown to be the name for this structure of conscientious forgiveness.

Chapters 12 through 14 focus on Hegel's analysis of religion. I have restricted my analysis of Hegel's text almost exclusively to Hegel's study of the "Revealed Religion" because this is the moment of the dialectic of religion that is essential to the argumentative structure of the book as a whole.

Chapter 12, "The Ritual Basis of Self-Identity," uses Hegel's dialectic of self-consciousness to determine what the nature of the phenomenon of religion in general is. Religion is seen to be the ritualized, communal activity of self-affirmation through traditionally determined processes of interpersonal recognition. Religion is effectively the language of a social order. Understood in this way, Hegel's dialectic of religion turns out to be a pluralistic affirmation of the necessity of multiculturalism and of cross-cultural dialogue.

Chapter 13, "Vision and Image in Hegel's System," uses the theme of visual imagery to take a comprehensive look at Hegel's systematization of the forms of human experience. The emphasis of this chapter is on developing the sense of the "concrete reason" that is definitive of Hegel's philosophy, that is, his answer to the formalism of the reason studied in Chapter 8, "Reason and Dualism." Reason understood concretely turns out to be the very substance of social life, and this in turn is to be understood as the arena of religion. This analysis concludes with a consideration of the relation between religion and philosophy in Hegel's system, to show why it is that philosophy is the appropriate *Aufhebung* of the "revealed religion."

Chapter 14, "Deciding to Read: On the Horizon (of Christianity)," looks specifically at what it means to consider the "Revealed Religion" as the *Vorstellung*, the "metaphor," as it were, for Hegelian philosophy itself. The phenomenon of reading is shown to be that which is imaged in the Christian images, and also to be the exemplary phenomenon of dialectical philosophy itself. Precisely what the metaphorics of the revealed religion suggest is a world that is always prospectively open—the arena of freedom itself—but that inherently demands that it be retroactively understood systematically: precisely the structure of reality articulated in Hegelian dialectical logic.

Finally, Chapter 15, "Absolute Knowing: The Structure and Project of Hegel's System of Science," concludes the analysis of Hegel's *Phenomenology of Spirit* with an interpretation of its notorious final chapter. Read by itself, this chapter is an interpretation and defense of Hegel's notion of absolute knowing as simply the counterpart of phenomenological method itself. Read as the conclusion of this series of studies, however, it also amounts to a systematic articulation of a set of ideas that have come up repeatedly throughout the book. Indeed, it is the goal of many of the independent chapters to develop and defend a version of absolute knowing from within the phenomenological analyses of specific other chapters. In a sense, this chapter does not contribute new content, but rather draws out the systematic implications of an idea that has already been developing throughout the book as a whole.

There are certainly other chapters I could have written that would fit the book equally well and other sections of Hegel's book to which I could have devoted greater emphasis. In other words, the particular set of analyses I have developed here do not constitute the "necessary" route through the *Phenomenology of Spirit*. I do believe, however, that, collectively, they constitute an interpretation of the book as a whole that is simultaneously original in its methods and results and yet faithful to the argument and the text of the *Phenomenology* itself. It is my best effort at reading Hegel's *Phenomenology*.

PART 1. CONSCIOUSNESS

one
Sense, Time, and My Meaning

1. Now Is the Time It Takes to Say "I"

I can put off the time when I will complete a project, but I cannot keep putting it off forever. Why? Because I will die, and the opportunity will be gone. While there is a significant range of variability to the "when" of any of my projects, ultimately the answer to "when" is always fixed for me: It must be while I *am*, it must be in the time of my existence. In this sense, all of my projects, insofar as they are mine, have "now" as their "when," that is, it is during *this* time, my time, the time of me, that they can be.

When is now? Now is the time of "mine," the time when I am I, the time when "there is," for me: when being, my being, is an issue for me.[1] Time is always the now of my being an issue for myself, the time marked by my mortality, my finitude. Time is being self-conscious in my mortality.

It is always now, for me. And yet, this now never fully arrives, nor was it ever fully absent. We await it, we retain it, it endures. Now, always already and always not yet, always now. Now stretches out for as long as it takes to say "I am I": now lasts a lifetime.

2. The Dialectic of the Now

If time is my life, how, then, is time lived? What is the experience of "now"? Let us follow Hegel's phenomenology of the "now" in Chapter I of the *Phenomenology of Spirit*, "Sense-Certainty, or, The This and Meaning." Let us take up the most obvious sense of "now" and see where it leads us. Consider this moment, now.

This moment, now, seems absolute. Initially, it seems to be the only time when I can truly claim to be, the only time when reality truly is. Other realities perhaps *were* or *will be*, but this is the only one that *is*. Similarly, this is the only me that actually *is*, the only experience I am actually experiencing. This is the immediate way in which the now appears, namely, as the absolute immediacy of knowing and being. It is immediacy itself, immediacy as absolute. The phenomenon of the now is, first, the phenomenon of the firstness of the now, the phenomenon of the nowness—the presence—of *is*.

This immediacy appears to be the very stuff of reality. Whatever *is* must ultimately be present in and as the now. It is surely this notion that lies behind the familiar positivist doctrines of empiricists from John Locke to A. J. Ayer.[2] The empiricist criterion of meaningfulness—that the significance of any experience must ultimately be "cashed out" in terms of the irreducible givens of immediate experience—surely draws on this idea that whatever is available to us must be available in the "now." And there surely is a great deal available to us: colors, sounds, smells. Indeed, there is a whole world. Whatever we say about the vast reality of the world of our experience, then, must, it seems, ultimately be a way of talking about what is immediately available to us in the now.[3]

So it seems that it is all there in the now. Whatever I say about my experience now—"there is a man sitting at that table"—will thus be a selective extraction from and decisive ordering of this all. I will ignore much of what is there and introduce hierarchies into the now, privileging this feature over that in what is noticed. It seems that it is only by the introduction of negation into this immediate all—the negation of exclusion and the negation of rank ("not equal to")—that I can specify and speak of this.[4] The now is thus like the Parmenidean *to eon*, "being,"[5] and whenever I speak of it I fail to do it justice by underexpressing it, by distorting it, by introducing negation, limitation, rank into a seamless, immediate all. And further, any terms I use to describe it—any language—will be language meaningful to another: it will involve comparisons of my experience—this "now"—with other nows, and with the experiences of others. All description will thus invoke terms with a meaningfulness beyond this experience, when I intend on the contrary to express its utter uniqueness. All description will integrate it into the larger, coherent realm of possible experience, whereas it seems that it is its insularity, its non-assimilability that needs to be communicated. The now, it seems, can never be adequately said. I must live it, be there, now, to grasp it, and this—the real meaning of now—is never captured in the speaking of it.[6]

Whatever I say of it, apparently, distorts and lessens the now. The real experience of the now—the experience of reality—must, then, not be in what I can express, but in what I live. I may well try to express to someone what I intuit, but my expression will not give them the thing itself, *die Sache selbst*, since "you have to be there." The truth of my words will *not* be what is ultimately *said*, that is, what the other can receive, but what I *meant* by them— the inexpressible immediacy of being there. But *can* I be there? Do I myself know that inexpressible immediacy?

What did/do I mean? (Indeed, what did/does "I" mean?) Both what I "meant" and what "I" meant is a seamless totality, no different in character from the seamless totality we considered under the name of "now" in the first place.[7] "I" just am the experiencing of this now, this meaning, and this meaning is just as inexpressible "to me" as it is to anyone else. When I initially fall back on "what I meant" to compensate for the way that language, through its negations and its determinacy, seems to distort the pristine character of the now, the implication is that "I" am somehow in possession of a truth beyond this language.[8] In fact, "my" grasp on this "I" who experienced is no different from that of the one to whom I speak—this "I" is as opaque to me as it is to you. If, after the fact for example, I want to know what I meant, that knowing of what I meant would be a specific articulation, a narration of determinacies rooted in the two sorts of negations I noted above. The "I" who might have meant something inexpressible cannot be the same "I" who takes note of this— that "pure I" is just as opaque to me as the "now" itself. Both the putatively pure now and the putatively pure I, then, are inexperienceable by me; they cannot, in fact, be meaningful elements of my experience.

To me, in other words, "there is . . . " only on condition that what is there be determinate, be articulatable. For it even to enter into *my* field, it must be able to be integrated with my other experiences; that is, it must be meaningful beyond its utter immediacy: it must be inherently open to comparison. Its uniqueness cannot be a richness that comes from isolation—that would actually be precisely *nothing*. Its uniqueness must be a uniqueness expressed and realized through the way this experience takes up possibilities open to other experiences, deploys terms and meanings available beyond its own specific actuality. Indeed, Hegel's phenomenology of the now precisely shows how it cannot be (present) *except* by comparison with other possible nows.[9]

It seemed that the truth of my experience of the now is the inexpressible immediacy of being there, but, we asked, can I truly be there? Is this actually something I can experience? To answer this, we have had to consider what are the demands of experience itself; that is, what is necessary in order for there to be something called experience? A long tradition of philosophers, including Descartes, Kant, Fichte, and Sartre, has made one point clear: experience requires awareness—consciousness—and that means there must be a noticing, there must be a happening "for" some recognizer. For there to be experience, one must be noticing (and we can leave aside for the moment the question of who this "one" must be). Let us ignore the concrete richness of the now, and consider simply what it takes to recognize "now" as such, to notice the now *as* now.

The now, according to what we had been understanding it to be initially, passes in an instant. Indeed, it is just this passing—there is no quantity of duration to it—it is just the instant. One can try to hold on to it—simply to "be here now." Yet, as soon as one tries to grasp it, it is gone. "Now." It is gone. "Now." It is gone. As soon as I try to hold on to *this* now, it has already passed, and this passing is what I notice—this is what it is to recognize the phenomenon of the now (which recognition is the hypothesis of this whole analysis, i.e., it is given by the form of consciousness itself that we are considering).

The now is experienced *as* passing. But to be experienced as passing, the now must be recognized as something that was, but is no longer.[10] And this notion of "was" can be recognized only in distinction from what is now "now." In other words, to recognize the now as passing, it must be recognized in a temporal context in which it is distinguished from and compared to other temporal moments.[11] The now that has passed can be recognized as past only by contrast with the current now. *This* now is then recognized as *now* in contrast to the now that *was* but is no longer. This now is meaningful *as* now only when held in a single experience of contrasting it with the past. Similarly, the now, in passing, is recognized as giving way to what is not yet. The now is recognized as now only by recognizing it in relation to a future that is already making its meaning felt in the now. In sum, the notion of now is inseparable from the notion of passage, of coming to be and passing away. But the notion of passage—a motion—is understandable only in relationship to a context of points from which and to which.[12] Time can only be experienced as a relation of past, present and future.

Since the now is experienced as "now" now, it follows that past, present, and future must all be present now. That is, *I must now still be experiencing what was* in order now to contrast it with now: I must *now* be both "here and there," so to speak; that is, one act of being conscious must be conscious both "now and then" in order *now* to experience the former now, that is, *now* to experience the now that is no longer so as to note its passing and to note that *this* now is not *that* now. Indeed, the present is experienced as something like an answer to the question posed by the former now, and it has its identity in how it carries forward the thread of that past. In an analogous way, I must now *already* be experiencing what *will* be in order to *now* contrast it with now: the now must be the posing of a question to which the future now will be the answer. I can experience now only because I am now *still* experiencing the no longer and now *already* experiencing the not yet. Every moment of a temporal experience must itself live *simultaneously* in past, present, and future. The temporal nature of our experience means that we never exist in the instant, but that we exist as stretched outside ourselves, as ec-static.[13] The now is experienced *as* "now" only to the extent that it is anticipating the new now that will surpass it (the future) and fulfilling the past now in which it had itself been anticipated. The now can thus be present only in the context of the not-now.[14]

> The present is, only because the past is not: the being of the now has the determination of not-being, and the not-being of its being is the future; the present is this negative unity. The not-being replaced by the now is the past; the being of not-being contained in the present is the future. If one considers time positively one can therefore say that only the present is, but the concrete present is the result of the past and is pregnant with the future.[15]

Here we see that the apparent independence and "positivity" of the now is really a product of dependence upon negations. It is only *as* not-the-no-longer and not-the-not-yet that the present is: these negations are inherent to its very identity as now, and thus the past and future are similarly inherent to the now itself.

So the now is not contained in the instant after all. The now exists only as a temporal whole. It exists only insofar as it is a constituent moment of a temporal continuity of past, present, and future—its existence cannot be severed from those, and they themselves do not exist just at their own moment, but are still and already existing now, even as they are no longer and not yet. The now, in other words, endures.[16]

The instant, in other words, in not a self-subsistent reality. It occurs only insofar as it is a moment *of* a larger temporal continuity, of which it is a partial presentation.[17] The instant does not bear its significance in itself—its meaning is how it is situated within the larger temporal reality of which it is a moment. This now plays its role in the gradual passage of day to night, this now plays its role in the gradual realization of my process of self-expression, this now plays it role in the slow process of developing a life with my partner. The now does not exist on its own but exists only in relationship to the retention of past events and the expectation of future events that constitute the contextualizing perspective in relationship to which it can be noticed, the background by negation of which it can stand out.[18] Now, in other words, is always the now *of* a larger now.

It had seemed earlier that the now possessed infinite riches in itself, and that through negation its significance was cut down into a determinate expression. Now, on the contrary, we can see that negation is what introduces significance to the now. The now isolated from negation can never be a meaningful element of experience; it cannot be—be "now"—at all. The now *is* only how it stands out in relationship to past and future, it *is* only the determinateness it receives by way of the negation of these specificities. But the past and future with which it resonates are the past and future of *my* experience, of my consciousness. The now is precisely how I am situated between who I have been and who I shall be. The larger now of which this now is a moment is the now of my situation, the time of my life. The now is not a disinterested theoretical recognition, but is a passing, developmental moment of the practical activity of being myself:[19] the now is just the way it reveals the emerging shape—the sense—of my reality. The now, as the revelation of my reality, stretched between my origin and my end, has as its meaning "myself"—the now is the showing to me of who I am. The meaning of the now can be determined only by determining what the nature of my reality is.

3. The Bodily and Linguistic Character of Time

Let us begin to approach the question of the nature of my reality by asking, "What is the nature of the sensing subject?" What does it take to be present, to be *here, now*? In a manner akin to that of Kant, we have pursued the transcendental conditions of this experience; that is, we have investigated the immanent structure that is the necessary condition under which this experience happens. We found the now always to be necessarily contextualized by past and future; that is, the now is *experienced in terms of* the not-now, the *then*. But we can also see that these transcendental conditions of the experience of the present are, as Marx might say, material as well. I can *experience* the present only by *being* present, which means I must *be* some *where* and some *when*: I must be *in* the world, determinately situated. I must be a spatial being, and a temporal one: I must be a body.[20] Though Hegel does not, in this chapter, pursue the question of the "who" or "what" of the sensing subject, we can ourselves pursue some of the implications of this position, drawing especially on Hegel's fundamental commitment to the untenability of ontological dualism.[21]

I must be in the spatial world in order to interact with that world. Were I (as subject) not of the same ontological character as the world (as object), there could be no relation, no interaction: this is the familiar problem of dualism. When reality is construed in terms of two essentially unrelated realities, there can, by definition, be no relation between them. Relationship presupposes community, ontological continuity. For one to be affected by the other, both must be of the same type: the same in genus, but different in species, as Aristotle says.[22] Such must be the case with subject and object, self and world: they can be defined as opposite to each other only because they are within the same ontological field, different species of a single ontological genus. I must be worldly—subject to the laws of space and time—in order to experience that world. I must be a spatial, temporal object—a body—in order to be a subject.[23]

Kant implies as much in his "Metaphysical Exposition of the Concept of Space," itself essentially a phenomenological description of our spatial experience.[24] In this exposition, Kant describes the form in which we experience space, in order to show that it has features that cannot be derived from experience but must instead be presupposed by experience. In the first of his four points, he writes:

> For in order that certain sensations be referred to something outside me (that is, to something *in another region of space from that in which I find myself*), and similarly in order that I may be able to represent them as outside and alongside one another, and accordingly as not only different but as in different places, the representation of space must be presupposed. (A23, B38; my emphasis)

Though Kant's interest is in the presupposed character of our "pure intuition" of space, his description makes a further point, namely, that our experience of space includes our experience of ourselves as spatial. Kant is here arguing that all experience of the "outer" is possible only on condition that the subject is so constituted as to experience things spatially in the first place, or, in Kant's language, the pure intuition of space is a transcendental condition of sensation. What his description should remind us of, though, is that if something is outside in relation to me then I too am defined in relation to the coordinates of that spatial system: it can be over there only if I am over here. My being here, now, then, means that I must be a spatial body, affected by other spatial bodies.

Notice, though, that I am not just any arbitrary kind of body. The subject must be a body that is itself a subject: the body must in its own nature as body be intentional. To be a "here" that is open to a "there" (as Heidegger says, to be *Da-sein*), my body must, by its nature, be sensitive to the form of the other.[25] Continuing our reflection on the demands of a non-dualistic position, we can see that the body as intentional must be such as to distinguish itself from others, to contrast itself here with there—with *its* there: the there with which it is consubstantial. The sensitive body, in other words, cannot just be placed within a world, but must be *of* that world, it must have an identity that straddles itself and its other: it must be, as Heraclitus says, a *palintropos harmoniē*, a "backturning harmony" that "differing with itself agrees with itself."[26] "There," in other words, cannot be simply substantially other to me, but must be present within my "here" as a potential. "There" must be a meaning *of* my body. But what is "there" as a bodily meaning?

To say that "there" is a meaning immanent to my body is to say that "there" is a spot I *do* not occupy but *could*: it is the locus of another possible me. As Hegel says:

> 'Here' is, e.g., the tree. *If I turn round*, this truth has vanished and is converted into its opposite: 'No tree is here, but a house instead.' (M98, W/C 72, my emphasis; cf. M104, W/C 72)

"There" is where I could be; it is a possibility already inherent to my existence here. Note that this also shows that "there" is an inherently temporal notion: it is the future of my bodily subjectivity. This shows, further, that hand in hand with the body's sensitivity to being here (which means sensitivity to the form of the other), is the body's capacity for motion. The future is essentially a notion for a *dynamic* body, that is, a meaning for a body that moves itself.[27] The experience of time, then, is the experience of a bodily significance, a significance for a mobile, sensitive inhabitant of the spatial, temporal world.

Let us consider a little further this bodily character to temporality in order to see further the nature of the now. We saw above that the now is contextualized by past and future in a dialectic of anticipation and fulfillment, of question and answer. The past that poses to me the question is my history, and the question it poses is the question of my life. In the now, I experience the things of my world as calling upon me to fix their significance, to settle what of the possibilities they offer will have had determining force. The now is thus the moment of decision in which I, through my action, interpret the sense of my world.[28] The future is the real realm of possibility, but it does not exist yet on its own, for it requires my bodily act to determine it into being. The present is the moment of decision in which I, by my action, crystallize the sense of the real. In acting, I take a stand on what is real and thereby enact it. The past is determinate, but has its sense in question, and it is by this, my act of interpretation, that I answer that question, allowing my act to show what its truth was.[29] In acting, then, I am self-expressive, self-assertive, just as I am given over to expressing the nature of the real. Indeed, this is the precise nature of the present: it is the moment of the identity or undecidability of subject and object, the point at which my passive undergoing of the real is my active expression of myself.[30]

We can still investigate further this notion of the present as decision and interpretation. Let us return to the place of negativity in the present. For any determinate *now* to be noticed, it must be distinguished from other possibilities: it must be distinguished from the others that are past and future, and (what amounts to a very similar notion, as we have seen in our discussion of the temporal character of "there") it must be distinguished from the not-this that is not being noticed, the not-this that is above, below, beside, or behind the *this* I notice. Noticing thus involves negation in that the present *this* must be (a) cut off from others and (b) cut off from me such that it can be before me, "for" me. Negativity goes yet further, though. To notice, I must notice *as* "this": such so-called indexical expressions as "this," "now," "here," and "I" cannot be done without in an experience of noticing. To notice is to notice *as* "now," *as* "this." Whether to another or to myself, I must, in other words, *point*.[31] I cannot simply be immersed in the other or I will fail to notice it, and I must thus identify it as "it," as "that one," or in some other way point it out, name it.

To point is to instill some determination (a finger, a sound, a mark) with the force of intending, of aiming, of naming. The pointer is a determination that does not present its own determinacy for notice, but rather gives itself as to-be-bypassed in favor of that to which it directs attention. Notice, then, that "to notice" does not simply involve the negation by which the noticed determination is differentiated from other possible determinations: it also rests on another determination being adopted as a pointer, which means (c) that pointer must be separated out and distinguished from others (an external negation), and especially (d) from that to which it points, and further (e) that pointer must be a determination that *negates itself* (an internal negation)—that is, it effectively says "not me, but it."[32] Noticing, then, rests, one might say, on the erection of a monument, that is, the severing of some determination from the normal circulation of being and investing it with the significance of signifying.[33] Noticing, then, rests on the establishing of a sign, a determination that distinguishes within itself between its determinacy *qua* being (its presence as a sensible thing, the signifier), and its determinacy *qua* pointer (the sense it intends, the signified). Something can be present—can be presented—only on the basis of (or in the context of) this complex system of negations, of non-presences and, in particular, the non-presence that is the sign.[34] The noticed determination, then, rests on the not-noticed determination that points to it; in other words presence presupposes some minimal writing, presupposes some minimal language. The "material conditions" of presence, then, extend beyond the organic body to writing: there is no present without body, and no present without writing. The decisive, interpretive character of the present is thus a bodily act and an inscription, a writing or saying of what is. Seeing, we could say, is always reading.

Who, then, is the temporal subject? The temporal subject is an interpretive body, a temporally finite, moving, sensitive body that lives the moment as the interpretation of the sense of its own life, and that functions with signs, which means functions in a world of language. Within the description of sense-certainty, then, we can already see the ferment that will lead us to the central themes of the rest of the *Phenomenology of Spirit*.

4. The Time of My Life

Though the *Phenomenology of Spirit* is a "ladder to the absolute," Hegel describes it as the "way of despair."[35] What this means is that our phenomenological attention to the dialectic of experience constantly results in the breaking down of our familiar sense of self-identity and the loss of our familiar foundations and guarantees within experience. This process is evident in the dialectic of sense-certainty, as we have studied it here. Experientially, we often resort to our "having been there" in some "now" as a guarantee of our own authoritative (authorial) stance on our experience or our self-identity. The dialectic of sense-certainty has revealed that we cannot automatically presume to speak authoritatively of ourselves simply by virtue of our supposed immediate presence to ourselves. On the contrary, our self-possession is always mediated by time, by interpretation, and, if my argument in this chapter is right, by our bodies and our language. Similarly, those (so-called empiricist) philosophies that seek to found all knowledge claims on the absolute guarantee of immediate sensory experience are similarly shown to be untenable. What the dialectic of the now has shown us is that we cannot evade the complex problems of meaning—of power, love, communication, or any other aspects of human meaningfulness—even in our attempt to grasp the sense of a single moment. The now is always the now "of" the whole of the event of "my meaning," and cannot have its sense comfortably secured in separation from the substantial themes that govern the flow of existence.

The now is always the now "of" some identity, the appearing—presenting—of a reality that exceeds and contextualizes the moment, while simultaneously being actual and real in the moment. The now is always the now of some "me" in some "reality," some setting: me responding to the world of feelings, pressures, things, forces, persons, laws, responsibilities. Specifically, the now is always the appearing of me precisely at the point where my reality joins reality as such: now is the identity of subject and object, the point at which the history of "it" and the history of "I" cannot be distinguished. The now is this moment of my identity with reality, equally the moment of my self-exceeding, and of reality's being known. The present—the "I," the "it is"—only is as my being outside myself in the world, and the world being realized in my experience of it. We might call this convergence of my reality with reality as such, "my situation." This convergence—this situation—is, as we see here and as we shall see in subsequent chapters, determinately spatial; it is historical, emotional, interpersonal. The now is the site of all happening; it is the very matrix of all becoming, itself always determinate, but always in flux beyond itself. The now is space and time and intersubjectivity, the very phenomenon, as Hegel will later call it, of "spirit," that is, the phenomenon of my experiencing of my involvement with others precisely in and through the determinate natural and historical realities—the bodies—that constitute "what is."[36]

How do I experience this now, this convergence of "I" and "it"? I experience now as the jointure of my accomplishments and my aspirations: the experience of the now is the experience of the meaning of my life, a fragile, mortal meaning. "Now" my world is this—*has become* this: I have become this person. These are the terms in which my time is meaningful to me—it is meaningful in terms of who I am, who I have become. Yet now does not get its meaning just by carrying within itself my past. "Now" is the occasion for. . . . Now is my opportunity, the doorway to my aspirations, to who I *shall be*. This is what appears to me "now," this is what appears to me *in and as the things of my world:* my freedom, my desire, my self-transcendence, and equally my determinacy, my limitation, my finitude.[37] Now is the appearing of the world as transcending itself—realizing its immanent dialectic—through my mortal freedom. Now is the time of choice, the time where I and it are one, the time where "I" and "it" will come to be. This now can appear as the *kairos*, the "moment of decision" (in either Aristotle's or Machiavelli's sense), the moment in which I answer to the way the determinacies of my situation call me to resoluteness, or as just one more moment in which I allow myself to drift into the future, to act automatically according to the tendencies and trajectories already set in place.[38] The now is the site of the determinate enactment of "I am I."

two
From Perception to
Philosophy

I want to start with a description of perception, and then show that the fact that our experience takes this form commits us to believing in Hegelian metaphysics whether we like it or not. Basically, by using the argument by which "Perception" is transformed into "Understanding" in the *Phenomenology of Spirit,* and by using the dialectic of "The Absolute Relation" in the *Science of Logic,* I will make a transcendental argument—an argument about what is necessary in order for us to experience the way we do—to show that the disparity between the form our experience takes and the concepts we use to analyze it inaugurates a dialectical advance through a commitment to a series of metaphysical views that have as their historical analogues the philosophies of Aristotle, Spinoza, and Leibniz, and finally to Hegel's own view that reality is the self-determining system of reason bringing about its own self-comprehension. This will show why Hegel's phenomenological project legitimately leads to the kind of systematic science he outlines in his *Encyclopaedia of the Philosophical Sciences,* and I will conclude by arguing that the metaphysical closure effected through Hegel's system is precisely the condition that makes it possible—and indeed necessary—for us to be open to others. In sum, the fact that we perceive things will show that we should all be absolute idealists of the hermeneutical pluralist variety.

1. Perception: Aristotle and the Phenomenology of Everyday Experience

In our day-to-day experience, we are occupied with things. This is where Aristotle begins, noting that it is things that we see, and not simple colors or other sense qualities, and it is such things that he makes the building blocks of his ontology.[1] What do I mean by a "thing"? I mean, for example, a woman, a book, a horse, a tulip. I can point them out: the man, the chair. If you ask, "which man?" or "which chair?" I can specify for you that I mean that tall, dark-haired man over there, or that hard chair by the wall. What needs to be noticed here is that (1) we recognize things as independent units, and it is these units that we take to be the fundamental "stuff" of our world, and (2) we can both recognize these independent units as independent units and differentiate them from one another by specifying their distinguishing features. Hegel's argument, in the chapter of the *Phenomenology of Spirit* entitled "Perception," is that this everyday attitude of perceiving things is self-contradictory, because these two actions of *identifying* unique things and *differentiating* them one from the other operate on two mutually exclusive conceptions of what a thing is, namely, an interpretation of the thing as active and an interpretation of the thing as passive. I want to show how this is so, first by considering the notion of a property, and then by considering two opposed notions of thinghood.

When I see the brown of that jacket over there, the brown is not seen as an independent quality, but is indeed given as being "of" the jacket. I see the brown that is proper to the jacket; that is, it is a property of the jacket, which is to say that I see the jacket when I see that brown. *Contra* seventeenth- and eighteenth-century epistemology, experience does not take the form of a subject first experiencing discrete informational data and then operating on them intellectually to form them into larger unities; on the contrary, the simplest experiential structures we are given are meaning-full relations, wholes. Whatever sensory information we receive is always given with a reference outside its immediate self to its context.

Now when I see the brown that is the brown of the jacket, it is "of" the same jacket that the wooliness is "of." All of the sensible features—the properties—of the jacket *are* really "the same thing," namely, the jacket. The thinghood of the thing is precisely this feature, namely, that all the multiple properties share the same ultimate identity: they are one and the same thing. This "one and the sameness" of the determinate multiplicity is the thinghood. It is, in Hegel's words, "the simple Here," where each property resides:

> All these many properties are in a single simple "Here," in which, therefore, they interpenetrate; none has a different Here from the others, but each is everywhere, in the same Here in which the others are.[2]

The weight of the jacket, the color, the scent, the texture—each of these properties is present throughout the totality of the jacket and is not localized into a discrete portion, separable from the others. The thinghood of the thing is this "simple togetherness" of the manifold of properties (M113, W/C 80). The thinghood is the fact that there can be one and the same identity maintained throughout the totality of different properties in such a way as to let each property characterize the whole, without any property affecting the others:[3] the salt, as Hegel says, "is white and *also* tart, *also* cubical" and so on (M113, W/C 81):

> The whiteness does not affect the cubical shape, and neither affects the tart taste, etc.; on the contrary, since each is itself a simple relating of self to self it leaves the others alone, and is connected with them only by the indifferent Also. (M113, W/C 81)

The "thinghood" is precisely the fact of this "also": it is the characteristic of being able to be a self-same unity in the context of an indifferent mutuality, an indifferent interpenetration, of a multiplicity of different determinations. So if we begin with a description of how sensible features are given to us in our day-to-day perception, we see that they are given as properties of things, and initially it seems that what this thinghood amounts to is the fact of the simple togetherness of these properties within a simple Here—a single identity—in which they completely interpenetrate without in any way affecting each other. A thing is the mutually indifferent coexistence of a multiplicity of differences.

If this is what a thing is, however, then there is a problem. A thing cannot be such an indifferent aggregate—an "also"—because the manifold properties in another sense *cannot be* indifferent to one another. Color is not mass, and this difference from mass is not indifferent to color: it is essential to color that it not be mass. Color by definition must actively resist being the same as any other property, and this means that its very determinateness as "this" property is implicitly a repelling, a negation, of any other property:

> for [the properties] are only determinate in so far as they *differentiate* themselves from one another, and *relate* themselves *to others* as to their opposites. (M114, W/C 81)

The other-relatedness of these properties is essential to them: they can be defined only *in terms of* what they are not, and *not being* those others—not sharing the same identity—is necessary to their determinateness. If the "also" is just the indifferent aggregate of properties—this and also this and also this and also this—then the mutual repulsion of properties means that there is no thing, but only a multitude of differences that have no coexistence, no shared identity:

> Yet; as thus opposed to one another they cannot be together in the simple unity of their medium. (M114, W/C 81)

If we settled for the conception of thinghood as an "also," then we would have the thing as only the passive result of the aggregation of properties, and, because of the mutual exclusivity of the properties, we would have no thing at all.

We must, then, have a better conception of thinghood, and it must be a conception of a unity that overrides the mutual exclusivity of the properties. Recognizing things, then, *which we do,* must indicate that we posit thinghood as active rather than passive. With the thinghood as an "also," we represent the thing as basically a plurality, a patchwork, but if this were the form that the objects of our experience took, we could never experience a *thing.* What we must recognize instead is that the thing is absolutely unique throughout: to recognize a thing is to recognize something that must not let itself be simply a product of what is outside itself but instead must be first and foremost *itself,* "this." Whether you touch my hand or my face or my knee, you touch *me*— each of these is really just me as a unique identity, a unique "self" or "itself." This is certainly what Aristotle means by a "thing," which he defines as that which can exist on its own and which has properties but is not itself the property of another:[4] independence is the key to the Aristotelian thing. For Aristotle the identity of the thing is the ground of its properties; that is, thinghood is primary, and the properties (and this is really the sense of saying the properties are "of" the thing) are derived on the basis of the thinghood; but *this is really the opposite of thinghood conceived as an "also"* for the thing as "also" is the passive product—the derivative—of the properties.[5] So, in place of a conception of thinghood as the way an aggregate is one and the same throughout—the "also"—we must have a conception of how the thing is through and through unique unto itself—how it is *self*-defined, the source of its own identity. This is the conception of thinghood as a "One."

This conception of thinghood as a self-sufficient "one" allows us to salvage the sense of thinghood as non-derivative, and thereby keeps the thing from falling apart through the opposition of its varied properties. We face a new problem, however. Now, to combat the loss of the sense of the integrity of the thing that came with the "also" and the other-definedness of the properties, we have the thing as a solely self-reliant "one"; but this exclusivity and absolute singularity makes the thing indefinable, for there is no way to express its determinateness without invoking terms that name properties, that is, that name determinate features of the thing that are different from one another and that also pertain to other things. If the thing is exclusively self-defined so as to exclude essential reference to others, there cannot be anything essential to it for which a relation to another is likewise essential. That means, however, that it cannot have any determinate properties, for any determinate property has its determinateness only by the essential exclusion of another. Color, as we already noted, *must* not-be weight; more seriously, red must not-be green. *Qua* necessarily related to other, then, none of the properties can belong to the thing. Their very determinateness, then, must not be intrinsic to the real thing, and this is the point Hegel makes when he initially defines the "One" in opposition to the "Also":

> the differentiation of the properties, in so far as it is not an indifferent differentiation but is exclusive, each property negating the others, thus falls outside. (M114, W/C 81)

Qua one, the thing does not have determinate properties; it is, so to speak, mute with respect to otherness. This muteness, however, undermines the very exclusivity of the thing, for the very notion of exclusivity is to be this one *and not that*; that is, it is only by being determinate, by being one among many, that it can be exclusive. Thus the very grounds of its self-determination *must be* other-determinedness.

Let us take stock of what we have seen. On the one hand, we require a sense of the uniqueness and self-definedness of the thing in order to do justice to our sense of the ontological primacy of thinghood over property-hood. This is the sense of thinghood we employ when we see "it," that is, our first experiential approach to the thing is toward it as an integral unit: a "One." When we are then asked "which," we resort to differentiating it from others by reference to shared, definitive properties, but in so doing we change our metaphysical stance and treat the thing as an "also," as a passive, derivative aggregate. And, indeed, this sense of thinghood as an "also" is obviously equally necessary for our experience of things, for this ability to differentiate things is essential to us. But these two conceptions of thinghood—the thing is a "one" and the thing is an "also"—*cannot both be true*, for as they stand they are contradictory: the first says that the thing is a self-defined, active unity, while the second says it is other-defined and passive. And indeed, while both are necessary, both equally show their inadequacy, the "also" by not being able to account for the unity of thing and the "one" by not being able to account for the determinateness. But the "also" *needs* to be able to account for the unity, for otherwise there is no "also," and the "one" needs to account for the determinateness, for otherwise it cannot be the exclusive, that is, the unique, one that it is.

In our day-to-day lives, then, we operate with two opposed metaphysical visions of thinghood. This is obviously inadequate *as a whole*, because self-contradictory, and the two accounts are each inadequate *singly*, for each fails to live up to its own needs (and it is precisely this failure that causes us to vacillate between the two, using each to mop up after the other). What happens is that we treat the essence of the thing as self-defined *as opposed to other-defined* or other-defined *as opposed to self-defined*, and we clearly fail both if we try to make the thing not other-defined and if we try to make the thing not self-defined. There must be something wrong with this whole way of setting up the alternatives: we must restructure our own conceptualizations. It must be possible for the thing to be both self-defined and other-defined: we need some synthesis of these notions.

The concepts we tacitly employ in day-to-day perception try to hold apart uniqueness and interaction, and this, we have seen, leads to contradiction; what this shows us is that we need to replace our original analysis with the notion of something the uniqueness of which comes *through* its dependence on others; this will be something that is self-defined only insofar as it enters into relations with others. The very idea of a thing was the idea of something that was this thing *and not that*, and so if we are driven to recognize that self and other *cannot* be dualized, that is, that self-relatedness is other-relatedness, then the very conceptual move that allows us to make sense of things is also going to be the move that pushes us beyond things by showing that perception's way of dividing up the world is inadequate. The idea of a *force* is the idea of something that is self-related only as an other-relatedness, and our use of the notion of force will both allow us to make sense of things and simultaneously push us to recognize that, *contra* perception's claims, things are not the ultimate building blocks of the world.

A force exists as a force only insofar as it is forcing, that is, insofar as it expresses itself. A force determines itself in relation to others, and has its selfhood defined only in terms of how it relates to others. For a force, to be itself and to interact with others are the same. This idea of force is, indeed, present in Aristotle's notion of a "natural" substance: a natural substance is a substance that is defined as the pursuit of some goal and that realizes this as a characteristic form of embodied behavior, wherein each determination of the embodiment is an organic *expression*—an organ—of the defining identity, the "indwelling form"; this form is essentially a force, a dynamic power. To return to my earlier example, when you touch my hand, you touch me, but the relation of me and my hand is not arbitrary: it is *necessary*, for the hand is what is required to realize the function (the force—*dunamis*) that defines my identity as, basically, a reasoning *animal*. The notion of the thing as *organism* is precisely the notion of a thing whose properties exist as *the expression of the internal necessity of the thing's definition*; and notice that these organs are precisely the points of contact with the larger environment of others *against which* and *in the context of which* the organism defines itself by doing its characteristic work, its unique function. This is the way we must conceive of things, and it is the only model that will allow us to overcome the contradictions of our initial approaches. Things, then, are neither uninterpretable metaphysical isolates nor coincidences of properties with no integrity: things are identities that exist only as processes of self-expression. The identity of a thing is how it shapes its relations with others, how it expresses a single message, a single "force," within a shared medium, within a universal language, so to speak. This notion of force allows us to reconcile the thinghood and the properties; it also shows us something about what it takes to recognize a thing.

Recognizing a single message, a single force, expressed in, expressed through, and expressed as a multiplicity is an act of *understanding*. We *understand* the single thing that is being said through a complex expression; understanding is precisely the power to recognize a multiplicity as a unity, to see a multiple being-for-other as the expression of a single being-for-self. Our recognition of things, then, is an act of understanding. In our day-to-day life we do not take ourselves to be thinking or interpreting when we look around, but we are: it is only insofar as we are doing this that we are able to recognize things. To see a thing is really to understand that a force is expressing itself: this was always implicitly the way we had to be interpreting our experience, but we did not initially realize that this is what we had to mean by "things." The contradictions within our familiar sense of *the perception of things* have thus led us to recognize *the understanding of forces* as being the real activity we are engaged in, in our daily lives. Let us look more explicitly at the understanding of forces.

2. Understanding: Spinoza and the Metaphysics of Substance

To recognize a thing—to recognize thinghood—requires understanding. That means, first of all, that only a being capable of operating with concepts, with universals, with ones-through-many, can perceive a thing. Without what Kant calls "the synthesis of recognition in a concept," in other words, there would be no experience of things.[6] We perceive a thing only when we see a multiplicity as the way features *had to be* in order for that single thing to be. To coherently posit the primacy of things it is thus required to posit the primacy of forces that express themselves, which means to posit the primacy of the relation according to which being-for-another is the necessary expression of being-for-self; that is, being-for-other is the way that a self exists for itself. But this principle that explains the *form* in which any thing exists also has consequences for explaining the very *content* of the world of thinghood in general.

Each thing is precisely *a* thing, *a* being, and as such each is a "property," is "of," being itself.[7] Just as it is a phenomenological truth that sensory determinations are given as "of" things—given as properties—so is it a phenomenological truth that things are given as "of" a world, of a single reality. What you touch when you touch me, or the chair, or the dog is *reality*, is being itself. We say of every thing that it "is," and by attributing is-hood to each, we posit its adherence to the law of non-contradiction, we posit the imperative that it integrate with all other things—all others that share is-hood—into a reality—an is— that is one.[8] The multiplicity of things is precisely the being-for-other through which the being-for-self of being itself is realized: they are the different ways that "what it is to be" shows itself, the modes in which reality appears.

Hegel makes this point as he explains the dialectical move from perception to understanding:

> the unity of 'being-for-self' and 'being-for-another' is posited; in other words, the absolute antithesis is posited as a self-identical essence. At first sight, this

> seems to concern only the form of the moments in reciprocal relation; but 'being-for-self' and 'being-for-another' are the *content* itself as well, since the antithesis in its truth can have no other nature than the one yielded in the result, viz. that the content taken in perception to be true, belongs in fact only to the form, in the unity of which it is dissolved. (M134, W/C 94)

The move here is really rather simple, but decisive. The essential idea of perception is the idea of the property, which is the idea that determinations point beyond themselves; they mark themselves off from some and they join with others, and they perform both of these functions by reference to a grounding context, and it is only through recognition of this context that the differentiation and organization of the determinations is possible; it is by belonging to a larger whole that differentiation—comparison, really—is possible. But that means equally that the differentiation of things one from another is also a differentiation within a common field, on a common ground. The fact that we can recognize that this thing is not that thing means that we are more fundamentally recognizing a shared field of being itself of which these particular things are determinations, or, we might say, properties: in recognizing things we have already projected ("posited") an horizon of "being," that is, *we commit ourselves* to the view that there is a comprehensive field that can be spoken of as a whole, a "one."[9] It is, in other words, only on the basis of a presumed understanding of a single shared ground, a shared medium, that we can recognize the identities of things.[10]

The move Hegel is making here is essentially the move from the textbook Aristotle to the textbook Spinoza. Aristotle defines a substance, roughly, as that which exists on its own and which has properties but is not the property of another, and this sense of the ontological primacy of the thinghood is what Spinoza states in Proposition 1 of Part 1 of the *Ethics*: "Substance is by nature prior to its modifications." Now Aristotle treats the individual man or horse as having properties but not being a property of anything else, and Spinoza's insight is to see that these Aristotelian "substances" really are properties of the one single substance of reality: what Spinoza recognizes is that Aristotelian substances do not exist independently but stand in relations of dependence to other things. Aristotle certainly recognizes that things depend on their others, as plants, for example, depend on food, but Aristotle does not make the further recognition that this means that what he posits as the ultimate ontological units are *not* ultimate but are *derivative* of the single total system of nature, the one substance.[11]

Now Spinoza himself is articulating the metaphysical foundations for natural science by showing how our very perception of things necessitates that there be a single unified system, and that the seemingly independent unities are only appearances that reflect the interplay of the real forces that define being itself. Natural science then has the job of finding out what are these universal forces, and the task of science has thus changed from a Aristotelian empiricism of the observation of natural, and irreducibly different, things to a bypassing of those things in favor of the otherwise invisible forces of which these things are the visibility, the appearances. Spinoza, like natural science, thus turns the world on its head and denies the reality of the *apparent* unities in our experience, which are things, and shows that the truth is the interplay of forces. Aristotle's common-sense metaphysics, which is based on the good phenomenological principle that we see things, is thus overturned, and we must recognize that these very phenomena exist only *because they are not* the ultimate terms of reality. *Experience tends to science as toward the fulfillment of its own efforts at consistency*: in place of a partial account of the assortment of identities that happen to appear to us and that we take for granted, we need a comprehensive and systematic account of the reasons why our experience is the way that it is.[12] This need for science—for an account that is comprehensive, necessary, and systematic—will not change; indeed Hegel's phenomenology is a version of such science. Nonetheless, the Spinozistic formulation of the metaphysics that experience requires is inadequate. I want to turn to the *Science of Logic* to show how this is so: I will discuss the dialectic of "The Absolute Relation" from the *Science of Logic*, in which Hegel describes the dialectical transformations within a metaphysics of substance.

We have already seen that the metaphysics of substance—the metaphysics that we tacitly endorse by engaging in the act of understanding—posits the one total substance as, to use a Platonism, the "really real," whereas the things of day-to-day perception are really the insubstantial modifications of that substance, which Spinoza calls "modes"; their identities are mere appearances. It is the same substance that appears everywhere and at all times, so the real identity of reality, it seems, is never-changing. All the particularities within the world of our experience, then, are mere contingencies that do not change the fundamental structure of reality. The same substance is, the same basic principles are, simply reenacted in ever-changing accidental forms. Hegel describes this substance:

> Absolute necessity is absolute relation because it is . . . *being* that is *because* it is. . . . This being is *substance*; as the final unity of essence and being it is the being in *all* being; . . . it is immediate actuality itself and this as absolute reflectedness-into-self, as a *subsisting* in and for itself.[13]

Hegel goes on to describe the accidents:

> The accidents as such . . . have no power over one another. They are the simply affirmative something[s], . . . existing things of manifold properties, . . . forces which require solicitation from one another and have one another for condition. In so far as such an accidental seems to exercise power over another, it is the power of substance which embraces both within itself. (E556–557, G221)

The point is that whatever happens within the realm of the contingencies of appearance is really the work of the one substance itself. The one substance is a self-causer; there is a single totality, and the substance is that totality *qua* causing, while the accidents are that totality *qua* caused.[14] Hegel's argument in the *Science of Logic* is that this metaphysical relationship, like the relationship of thing and property, is not adequate as it stands, but will dialectically transform itself.[15]

Now the key, recall, to the move to substance was the notion of force. The properties of a thing, we said, exist as the necessary expression of the force that is definitive for the essence of a thing. Plants, for example, are defined by their activity of self-nutrition and growth (to follow Aristotle's model here), and such a defining activity *requires* roots, xylem and phloem, and the like. These properties of the thing exist because they are the necessary way that identity expresses itself. Similarly, the move to the one substance is the move to the causal ground of all beings; that is, we are identifying substance as the ultimate identity that *necessitates* the forms of appearance.[16] Now initially this leads us to bypass the autonomy and integrity of things in favor of the universal forces that constitute them; things are for understanding, as they are for the scientist, contingent in themselves and only so many varied expressions of the same basic forces. But this very reasoning that leads us to bypass them also backfires on the attempt to overrule their autonomy: if it is in fact true that their condition is entirely accounted for by the necessities of force, then it is equally true to say that *they had to be in exactly the way they are*; that is, *they* are necessary *to the force*—it can realize itself only by producing *precisely these* appearances. The very structure of cause and effect that characterizes the essence of the substance-accident relation shows that the identity of the substance *is not* independent of the particularities of the accidents; that is, the substance can be itself only *through* the precise determinacies it causes. Thus, where we initially thought the one substance remained self-same in indifference to the contingent changes of nature and history, we now see that it is not indifferent at all, but must, in fact, be realizing itself in and through these changes. Each "mode," therefore, represents a necessary stage along the way to the substance's realization of its self, and each mode, then, represents the totality—the substance—from a particular stage, or from a particular point of view. Each mode is thus a Leibnizian monad.

To say first that everything about a thing was caused by something else seems to remove from it its autonomy, and this is the first move of understanding; yet if its condition really is a function of *necessity*, then the thing *has to be* exactly the way it is, and this is not just a necessity for it, but for the necessity itself, for the very identity of the substance. But if the substance *has* to produce such a thing under these precise conditions, then the substance needs this thing in order that the substance might be itself. Each "mode," then, is an expression of the identity of the substance. The substance, though, is the whole totality understood as a self-causing unity. It follows, therefore, that, inasmuch as each mode expresses the identity of the substance, each mode expresses the identity of the whole totality, which is why it is a monad, to use Leibniz's language.[17] Now if each monad expresses the whole totality, then each monad is intrinsically defined in relation to each other monad; that is, it is defined as related to every other determination. This absolute relativity is what Hegel means by reciprocity; that is, the total substance of reality is a system of reciprocal determinations:

> a reciprocal causality . . . [where] each is alike active and passive . . . in relation to the other. (E569, G238)

No one mode has primacy over any other, for each is really the same identity—each contains every other—from a determinate perspective.

Since every determination is necessary, each unique perspective is necessary, and thus we have flipped our world over again and returned to a situation of recognizing the integrity and the autonomy of something like individual Aristotelian substances, but the mediation of the Spinozistic metaphysics of understanding has made a crucial difference. Each monad is like an Aristotelian substance in that it is an integral, self-defined whole, but it is unlike an Aristotelian substance in that *it has this status only because it is a member participating in a system*, which means that an overarching unitary system of reality must be recognized as the necessary contextualizing ground for the identity of any thing: to return to the issues of perception, we could say that we can see things only because there is a self-determining system of reality that expresses itself as determinate, self-moving wholes: this metaphysics is *implicit in any experience of a thing*.

Leibniz begins his *Discourse on Metaphysics* with the proposition that "God does everything in the most desirable way," and this idea that all determinations are for the good is indeed an implication of the metaphysics of understanding as we have worked this out.[18] The key to the perspective of understanding is the idea that things happen for a reason. When someone says, for example, "Shouldn't that door be closed?" we give the reason why it is open to show that "open" is how it *should* be: to give the reason *is* to explain why it should have the form it does. To show that each determination of reality is an expression of the necessary demands of reality itself is likewise to show that things are as they should be: they are the way they have to be in order for the essence of being to work itself out, for reality itself to be real.[19] This Leibnizian account of metaphysics is, in principle, adequate. What we have still to do, though, is to work out more precisely some of the implications of this metaphysics, for our first image of what such a system is like is probably misleading; what we must see is that Leibniz's inversion of Spinoza has transformed the metaphysics of substance into a dialectic of subject.[20]

Now, if things are as they should be, that is, if things are the rational expression of what reality needs, that is, if everything is necessary, then the point of view that recognizes the whole must be as necessary to the whole as anything else. About anything, we should be able to answer the question, "why did this have to happen?" and that is equally true for the phenomenon of performing this philosophical analysis.[21] Thus this philosophical analysis cannot be concluded unless it recognizes its own necessity, that is, unless it recognizes that reality requires this argument to be made, and this vision to be achieved. Reality needs to be *seen as* a system, then, in order to actually fulfill itself as system. Reality therefore requires to be understood—being *is* "to be understood"—or is, we might say, "for consciousness," and in comprehending reality we are thus acting on behalf of reality. The truth of reality, then, is that it is reason comprehending itself; that is, reality is a process of realizing a goal of coming to comprehend itself as a process of coming to comprehend itself, and it is in our recognition of this that we are performing reality's truthful self-recognition. That reality is a systematic process of working to realize itself as self-comprehending reason is thus a view to which anyone who perceives things is committed.

But, now, if it is the case that we are being consistent with ourselves only insofar as we realize this, then we are at odds with ourselves to the extent that we do not. The imperative to realize the good by the performance of this comprehension—our moral imperative, the philosophical imperative—is thus the same as the logical demand to be consistent in our account of our own perceptual experience. Epistemology—epistemology as phenomenology—is thus the same science as ethics (as we will see more clearly in the final section of the chapter, and in later chapters): our moral imperative is to comprehend what we initially encounter as "other" in such a manner as to see it as a call to understand it, and to understand it in such a way that our comprehension of it is really the self-comprehension of the whole system of reality: since we know that anything is a monad in the sense of being a "moment" of the system of self-comprehending reason, then we know that we do not know the thing until we comprehend it in this way. We already saw that we truthfully describe our experience only when we describe the perceptual things as they are properly systematically contextualized, and now we have the concept for this context: to rightly recognize anything, then, will be to see where it fits within the system of self-comprehending reason.[22] This means that we must understand why it is rational that it in its concreteness should be the way that it is. This is precisely what Hegel's systematic science, does: the *Phenomenology* educates us to this point of view, the *Logic* works out systematically the dialectical categories for thus analyzing things, and the philosophies of nature and spirit work this out for the concrete determinations of actuality. The philosophical comprehension of the world of our experience is thus the highest fulfillment of our ethical responsibility: it is a duty.

We have essentially been engaged in a transcendental analysis: we have been asking what are the necessary conditions for the possibility of the experience of things, and we have answered that the object of our experience must take the form of a self-articulating system of self-comprehending reason that realizes itself through our realization of this necessity and of the necessity for our recognizing it. We have therefore been engaged in a study of the structures of subjective synthesis: here is how we must be engaged in interpreting in order that we might see things. A transcendental analysis of consciousness thus leads to metaphysics: Hegel teaches us what we have to believe reality to be if we are to be consistent with ourselves as perceivers of things.[23] This metaphysics, further, leads to an ethics, for it implies the duty of philosophical comprehension. Hegel has thus followed up Kant's transcendental project, but brought it to a radically different conclusion. I want to conclude this chapter by looking a little bit closer at this conjunction of philosophical method and ethics. Traditionally, Hegel's systematic closure of metaphysics has seemed to preclude an existential understanding of human life, and it has seemed at best that within Hegel's philosophy there is a tension between the systematic drive toward absolute knowing and the existential drive in his phenomenological analyses of human dramas. I believe this is a false opposition, and I want to conclude this chapter by considering how the systematic closure to metaphysics for which I have so far argued is precisely what is required to make an existential account of human life possible: it is, we might say, precisely the windowlessness of the monads that allows them to be open to others; that is, their absolute internality exists only as a self-externalization.[24]

3. Hermeneutic Pluralism: Windowlessness as Receptivity and Teaching

Now, if everything is reciprocally determined, that means that the identity of anything is inextricable from the identity of anything else. In the case of self-conscious agents such as ourselves, this universal involvedness shows itself most pointedly in what Hegel analyzes as the need for recognition. In our experience we recognize other selves; like the recognition of things, the recognition of other minds is a constant structure of human experience; that is, our world is automatically divided up into constellations of things and relationships with other persons. To recognize another person is precisely to recognize *within the field of one's own experience* another perspective: in recognizing another we recognize one for whom we ourselves count as another. To recognize another is to recognize that I have a being-for-other. The initial move that propelled us through the whole dialectical analysis of the metaphysics of consciousness was the recognition that the determinations of being-for-self and being-for-other could not be held apart, and the implication of that for the sphere of interpersonal dealings is that my own identity is not in my possession alone, but is dependent upon how I am recognized by others: who I am is who I show myself to be; that is, my identity is public property. We always exist in a social context, and it is how our self-expression—our action—impacts upon others that fundamentally decides who we are; this means our own identity can never be decided without determining who are the others amongst whom we act.[25]

From what we have said in this chapter so far, we know two things. First, we know that how we are for the other defines how we are. Second, we know that the other is rational. For us to be rational requires, thus, that we own up to the way we appear to others; that is, we must be responsible to the images of ourselves that we are creating. Now, the other to whom we appear is, in general, not an Hegelian philosopher, and, to the extent that it is only the Hegelian philosopher who has recognized (based upon the arguments I have made above) the adequate logical structures for recognizing the identity of the other, the others to whom we appear by and large do not perceive us adequately. Our situation, then, is that we are responsible for recognizing the rationality—the rightness—of others misrepresenting us, which is to say we are responsible for owning up to the misrepresentations of ourselves. Now this sounds paradoxical, for we seem to be saying that others make errors that are not errors. What I want to consider is how we can maintain this seemingly paradoxical attitude without simply contradicting ourselves or making ourselves schizophrenic.

Hegel's *Phenomenology* begins (in the preface and introduction) with the recognition of the necessity of honoring the point of view of the singular self-consciousness.[26] The *Phenomenology* must make a place within its argument for the particular point of view of each reading ego, and it must make its argument in such a way that it speaks to the (felt) needs of that ego. As Hegelian phenomenologists, we are called upon to do this same thing with respect to the other. Notice, though, that endorsing the legitimacy and rationality of the other's point of view does not entail portraying the other's view as right *simpliciter* or absolutely: precisely what the adequate recognition of the other entails (using the *Phenomenology* as our model) is seeing how the other view is responding to a legitimate demand, but also how (to the extent that it is not identical with the comprehensive, systematic, self-knowing, self-justifying Hegelian perspective) it is self-contradictory in its orientation. If it is not comprehensive, it cannot be absolute. We can sanction its being non-comprehensive, unforgiving, and exclusive, but to the very extent that it does that it is at odds (as we have shown a priori) with its own character as consciousness, and it therefore exists for us as a call to be led to reconciliation. Thus in one sense the other is always right, and in another sense the other can be wrong, and the imperative we are placed under is to be able to see how this is so concretely. To truly recognize the other concretely, then, naturally and necessarily produces the imperative to teach, but it is not teaching in the sense of imposing a doctrine; it is, on the contrary, teaching as providing a supportive environment in which the other can pursue her or his "own thing" so as to allow that other its own dialectical self-development.

This teaching, this concrete comprehension of others, is essentially an issue of action, of social relations. Whatever we do is an expression of who we are; it as a creative act in which we define an intersubjective space; it is a hermeneutical response in that it is a response to the perceived demands—the interpretation—of the situation; and it is a violent act in that it forces itself into the public sphere, demanding of all others that they recognize it.[27] Whether we like it or not, we are involved with others, and we are always performing in this violent, expressive way: our metaphysics of self-comprehending reason gives us the parameters for defining our responsibility in this situation. I have argued here that we can claim, as Hegelians, to know the absolute truth, and what this means ultimately is that we know we have a moral imperative to approach others phenomenologically, but this knowledge—*logically* concrete— remains *existentially* abstract, and always requires to be given life and embodiment by being enacted in a determinate interhuman space. It is always *this* situation that I am involved with and that I must respect. I know a priori that my other is the bearer of my own identity, but my own immediacy always presents itself to me as an opacity, an otherness that is not yet reconciled with my self, and so my situation always presents me with the particularities of my duties; *contra* Kant, the key to morality is to be able to make the universal bend to the contingencies of the particular situation.[28] But this bending, this comprehension of one's immediate situation, can be done only, as it were, at gunpoint, which means there is no room to step outside, but instead one is *already* wrestling with the situation.[29] Our transcendental analysis, and our concern for the autonomy and integrity of the self, have in fact led us back to Aristotle again, and his notion that ethical action is like navigation on the open sea:[30] *how* the a priori truths can be meaningful to *us*—to *this* us—has always to be worked out on the spot. To be a point of view then, to be a body—a consciousness of and involvement with things in a world—is to be faced always with the hermeneutical task of comprehending how *this* situation is rational.

There is no guarantee ever that one will reconcile oneself to the opacities of one's situation in such a way as adequately to comprehend and to sublate one's situation. Another can approach me and threaten my life. I can know without question that this other really is striving for recognition, and that this striving will not be satisfied by killing and would be satisfied by pursuing the path of self-knowledge that culminates in Hegelian absolute knowing. There is no guarantee, however, that I can use this a priori knowledge to perceive how the other is open to my discourse, and whether or not I die will depend on how successful I am at reading the situation. The other may kill me before I have a chance even to begin to think about it. Or I may hit the other, and this may be exactly what it takes to bring the situation to an end. Or I may hit the other and this may be what provokes the other to make the decision to go through with it and kill me. There is no a priori answer to this question accessible to us—the situation is *in itself* undecidable, and awaits our decision, our action. After the fact, and provided we have sufficient information, we can see why the affair went as it did; but from the position of the immediate embodied subject for whom her or his own otherness remains immediately opaque, no such deduction is possible. Hegel says in his lectures on the philosophy of history that history brings with it the presupposition that reason has operated in history, but that philosophy proves this, and we have here made this proof;[31] but even though we know it will turn out to be visible how reason is operative here and now, our situation as finite egos requires that we approach our dealings with others inductively and without guarantees.[32]

Sometimes a lie is better than the truth, ignorance better than knowledge, cowardice better than courage. We cannot prove the answer in any situation; but what we can know is the goal we are after, and that is the bringing to full self-consciousness of ourselves, of our own situation, and that means the bringing to full self-consciousness of others. We must maintain the goal of teaching, of providing a supportive environment for the self-development of others, but also we must engage in a teaching that must be constantly relearning the language of the social world in which it operates, for we face the hermeneutical task of interpreting *how* each situation *can* be supported. The Hegelian metaphysics thus implies an ethics of hermeneutical pluralism, according to which we must be struggling to comprehend a multiplicity of opaque others, all of whom (and because of this very opacity we are obviously also included automatically in this "all") are marks of the call to reconciliation that characterizes the world of embodied subjectivity.

In general and in sum, Hegel's system is the system that proves the a priori rationality of the other, and therefore brings with it the imperative to conform oneself to the demands of the other: the other appears to me as the moral imperative to give respect. The plurality of self-opaque monads is the necessary state of finite consciousness, but we are equally also potential possessors of the absolute truth; that is, we have, so to speak, the "innate idea of God," of the infinite reconciliation of all being, and we are thus split into infinite and finite selves, a transcendental and an empirical ego, an potential absolute knower and a finite self hermeneutically involved in a plural situation of opacity that calls for clarification. Our goal must be to learn the principles of truth, the Absolute Idea, and to lead others to see this through a conversation that we conduct by learning the language of the determinations of their situations (and that can equally be described as us leading our own immediate and opaque situation to self-consciousness). In other words, the very fact that we perceive things implies that we should be Hegelian philosophers in the form of multicultural pluralists.

three
Understanding: Things, Forces, and the Body

The chapter of Hegel's *Phenomenology* entitled "Force and Understanding: Appearance and Supersensible World" has long been notorious as perhaps the most difficult and obscure piece of writing in his corpus. The consequence of this situation is that interpreters of Hegel tend to work around this chapter, rather than work through its lessons with care. In fact the argument of this chapter is extremely important for Hegel's larger philosophical argument as well as extremely relevant to contemporary philosophical concerns; indeed, careful interpretation of the point of this chapter is, I think, one of the most valuable routes into overcoming traditional prejudices about Hegel (just as many of the traditional prejudices are reinforced by careless interpretation of this part of Hegel's argument). My intention here is to explain the basic argument of this chapter, and I will do this in three stages.

The first section of this chapter will be devoted to a simple explanation of the phenomenon of understanding and its dialectic. My intention here will be to make clear what the basic argument of the chapter is in terms of the central themes that pertain to understanding. The second section will revisit these same themes, but by reference to some of the technicalities of Hegel's discussion in the text of "Force and Understanding," and also by reference to some parallel materials from the *Science of Logic*. I will not exhaustively analyze the text, but I will bring out enough features to enable the reader to make sense of what Hegel is saying and especially to allow the reader to see how Hegel's text is studying the same issues I developed in different terms in Section 1. In the final two sections, I will explain some of the significance of this analysis of understanding. In particular, I will show (as in the preceding chapters of this volume) that Hegel's philosophy here leads directly into themes of twentieth-century existential philosophy, especially the philosophy of the body (in explaining which point I will draw on materials from the *Philosophy of Right*).

Overall, the goal of this chapter is to show that Hegel's description of the dialectic of understanding is clear and cogent, that in this analysis are contained the essentials of the Hegelian dialectical "metaphysics," and that the significance of Hegel's metaphysics is an existential conception of the human body.

1. The Perceptual World and the Project of Understanding

We do not typically recognize our projects of perception and of understanding as being opposed. We look at things and make decisions in terms of them ("I like the way this jacket looks," "I need to pick Mary up from school," "Those books are too heavy to carry"), and we are scientists, struggling to understand our world ("Why is there so much poverty?" "Why is my car running roughly?" "Why are these plants dying?"). Though we are quite capable of taking up both of these projects (and in that sense they "cohere"), these projects are in fact based upon fundamentally different presumptions about reality, and the presumptions of perception do not cohere with the presumptions of understanding.

Perception takes reality to be a diverse multiplicity of *things*: individual, self-subsistent realities, each the ground of its properties (i.e., we recognize the weight *of* the horse, the color *of* the book, the shape *of* the tree). Our perceptual life—the typical stance we adopt in our familiar experience—takes these things, these realities, to be ultimate, to be the truth. The desire to *understand*, however, is the desire to know why, the desire to find the ground, the reason, that some multiplicity is in fact a unity, the desire to know how a coherent sense is manifest throughout a range of differences: it is the desire to ascertain the cause of appearance. Understanding looks beyond the immediate, determinate multiplicity it encounters to find the single rationality that is manifest throughout this multiplicity. Understanding, therefore, operates with the presumption that behind any multiplicity there is a unity. Thus the perceptual realm of the multiplicity of things is not taken by understanding as ultimate, not as that which is the ground, but as something *to be explained*, an *explanandum*, something that itself rests on a further ground. There is thus a fundamental opposition between the premises of perception and of understanding.

The project of understanding, then, is to understand. It is unfulfilled when it does not understand. Anything that it must accept as simply given— simply immediate—is, for it, a frustration, a failure. Simply to know of something that "it is so" is not to understand it, but only to perceive it. As Aristotle expresses it, understanding must go beyond the "that" to the "why." Consequently, we are familiar with two ways in which understanding shows itself within our experience.

On the one hand, understanding is woven together with our perceptual life in our day-to-day experience in various local contexts. For our immediate purposes, typically it is enough to "understand" some situation not ultimately, but only proximately. I understand that the house is cold because I forgot to shut the window. I do not bother to understand fully "why" it is cold; that is, I do not seek to understand "cold" in itself, because I am not here pursuing understanding as such as my explicit project but am seeking only immediate practical knowledge, that is, what to do to change the temperature of the house. This is our day-to-day employment of understanding, in which we weave its activity around the things we perceive to be the anchors of reality in our world. Typically, that is, we rest our understanding on uninterpreted givens, and we operate entirely within the parameters set by the standards of the perceptual world. And, indeed, this process of understanding may be so familiar that it never really crosses the threshold into explicitly self-reflective consciousness.

On the other hand, we typically do pursue the project of understanding on its own terms. We really do want to understand reality, not just for some other purpose, but for the sake of understanding. This is the project of knowing—of science—that has shaped our culture and our learning throughout the entire range of our cultural and personal histories. The projects of the physicist, the logician, or the historian are not (are not supposed to be) constrained by local, practical goals, but answer the demands of understanding as such— the demand to trace all things back to their ultimate source, their ultimate explanatory ground: the demand for truth.

Now there are some problems within this project of understanding in both these forms. First, let us consider a little more carefully these projects of science, these projects that intend not to be merely local and practical, but to be universal and theoretical (i.e., to be in search of the truth on its own terms, the truth "in and for itself"). History, for example, seeks to understand human affairs as they have unfolded on earth through time. Yet history does not take as its task the understanding of time itself. "What is time?" or "Why should there be time?" is not its question. Rather, it presumes the reality of time, as it presumes the reality of the planet, the reality of the distinction between human and animal, the distinction between one person and another, and so on. The physicist, similarly, presupposes matter and energy, or motion, mass, and volume, and so on.[1] In each such "science," the very determinacy of the field marks the limits of that science and reveals it to rest upon non-understood perceptual givens; that is, each remains local and practical, rather than uncon-ditioned understanding proper.

Consequently, the promises of "science" or "understanding" made by these disciplines are always ultimately unfounded *according to their own charter principle, viz* to understand. The best these "sciences" offer is a simplification—a reduction—of the multiplicity of perceptual life to a statement of non-deduced (i.e. inductively established) regularities ("laws") that provide a sim-plified *redescription of* the given perceptual world. They only render a stable image of the flux of appearance and leave precisely *unexplained* the fundamen-tal premises that they draw upon to make their "science."[2]

But, second, this problem is a problem for understanding as such, and not just a problem of these particular approaches to understanding. We have seen that understanding divides reality into *explanans* and *explananda*: the multi-ple, perceptual determinacies—the *explananda*—are posited *in principle* as derivative. Yet, it is only from these that the project of understanding is given birth, for it is *these* that we want explained. In other words, it is the putative *explananda* that *define* the situation, and thus in an important sense the princi-ples of explanation will be *derived from* these *explananda*. It is *these things*, in other words, that are the ultimate arbiters of "reality," and it is to these that the principles of explanation must answer. These will always be the *measure of the truth of* the putative *explanans*.[3]

Let us look back for a moment. We saw that the explicit project of under-standing begins by inverting the world of perception, taking what, in our everyday perceptual experience, we consider to be original—the ground—and treating it instead as derivative, as not what is ultimately real, and it thereby affirms as real that which will explain the perceptual world. Hegel describes this as positing a "supersensible world" (M149, W/C 104–105). What our dis-cussion of the process of understanding has just now shown, though, is that in its actual practice understanding in fact treats this first "supersensible world," that is, the intelligible "ground" of the things of perception, as to-be-explained by the determinacy that actually appears. In other words, the initial super-sensible world that characterizes understanding has itself been inverted, and the world of appearance is now invested with ultimate meaningfulness; the *explananda* have become the *explanans*. This is the situation that Hegel re-fers to as the "second supersensible world" or the "inverted world" (M157, W/C 111).

By the explicit logic of understanding, this "inverted world" seems a puz-zle: appearances must be explained, but they also must be the source of mean-ing. To the usual project of understanding, this is simply a contradiction. Understanding proper would have to explain why there is a certain "this," but it would have to draw this explanation from "this" itself. This puzzle is not simply a "logical" exercise.

Notice first that this situation of the inverted world is exactly the situation one does encounter in the sciences I referred to above (history, chemistry, etc.). We really do follow something like this procedure when we come to understand. This is clearest, perhaps, in history, where we move back and forth between using events to explain the nature of "the Renaissance," and using the notion of "the Renaissance" to explain events, but it is also evident in a more problematic way in the natural sciences, where we constantly manipulate the theories to correspond to empirical life, despite the intention to have the theories be the explanatory grounds. But let us think, second, about what happens when we do come to understand.

Coming to understand involves a transition from a situation of not understanding to a situation of understanding. "Coming to understand" is a situation in which a manifold phenomenon comes to be seen in its unitary coherence, such that formerly disconnected elements are seen in their interrelation in such a way as to express themselves as the effect of a cause, the expression of a force, or in general the manifold presentation of a simple identity. We precisely move from a position of not understanding to a position of understanding through *learning* this cause or this force, this "why." Someone explains to us the relevant parameters of a situation and we "get it." Upon completing this process we can look to the same situation we were formerly in "with new eyes," so to speak, and we say "now I see what it is," or "now I see what it was all along."

According to the attitude of understanding, the situation that comes to be understood is *the same one* that formerly was not understood. Indeed, this is crucial, for it is precisely *that* that I want to understand. The understanding itself, however, has gone through a process—the process of explanation and, precisely, "understanding"—in which its "take" on the situation changed entirely. Indeed, how its object *appears* to it has changed utterly. But it is *the same object*. The difference [from not understanding to understanding] makes all the difference, yet there is no difference [in reality].

The object itself, apparently, has not changed—we have just come to see what it truly was all along—it is only its appearance that has changed. This is the sense of the inverted world; that is, it is *this realm of determinacy* itself that is now seen to be *the real world*, but it is the real world not in its immediacy for perception, but only in its having come to be seen as the manifestation of intelligibility (M147, W/C 103). The difference, then, seems to be *in the understanding itself*. The object now appears as what it was all along—only we have changed. It would seem, that is, that the process of understanding is really indifferent to the object, and the efforts of understanding are really answering to the needs of understanding, that is, to the nature of the subject, rather than responding to anything in the nature of the object.

Thus the necessity to go through the procedures of understanding was a necessity, apparently, only for us—a kind of prompting of us to see what was always there all along. The project of understanding, in other words, has really been answering to itself. Its switching back and forth between positing the simple unity as primary to explain the diversity (first supersensible world) and positing the diversity as primary to explain the unity (second supersensible world) is to be explained by its own limitations and needs, rather than by reference to the internal demands of the object.

Understanding, then, at this stage *understands* reality to be indifferent to it, and understands its own necessity to be shaping what appears. In other words, in its efforts to understand how this situation should be understood, the first move of the understanding here is to insist that the object is just there, independent of it, and that the process has entirely been within itself. To understand this situation, in other words, what appears to be required is to make this recognition about understanding. Understanding here asserts that reality stayed self-same, indifferent to the process of understanding, and that it is the process of understanding alone that explains why the object appeared in different forms at different times. The *object* did not change, and its differing *appearances* are caused by the inner necessity of the project of understanding.

But note what is said here, and remember that the whole project of understanding was to explain appearance! In having discovered that it is the process of understanding itself that explains appearance, understanding has actually shown that the necessity of the understanding itself *is the inner of appearance*. What causes reality to appear the way it does? The demands of understanding itself. Since the claim of understanding is that the necessity that things *appear* that way is really just a function of its own needs, this then entails that the necessity that is the inner of appearance—that is, what appears—is simply the understanding itself. In other words, by pulling the appearance to its own side, it does not *remove* its needs from the inner, but demonstrates that its needs *are* the inner. It is my desire to understand that has given form to the situation. This is the identity that has defined the whole situation. It is what has been appearing.[4]

Let us review the three steps we have taken in this section. First, we have considered the way the conflicting stances of perception and understanding are manifest in everyday experience, and have considered the logical tensions between these two stances, and what this entails for the project of understanding. Second, through working through the logical tensions within the project of understanding, we have come to see how its inherent commitments in fact return us to a kind of primacy of perception in that, in a way, one is always waiting upon the given: this is the point of the inverted world. But this new given of perception is different than either sense-data empiricists or Aristotelian empiricists would imagine. The given, rather, is one shaped by our involvement: it is a world in which we see our own selves, our own projects, reflected, so it is no longer the alien object of simple "consciousness." Thus, third, we can now anticipate that the very essence of the object is to be the "mirroring" object of an experience of "self-consciousness," that is, we can see that, in encountering its object, consciousness is really encountering the appearance of its own essence and it thus recognizes the truth of its situation when it recognizes that situation to be an activity of self-consciousness. We will go on in Sections 3 and 4 to see that this given perceptual world is our existential (bodily) situation, given with its whole range of hermeneutical pressures, drawing us forward ultimately into objectivity, into interpersonal life, into law, morality, and religion (as we shall see in subsequent chapters), but first let us go over this basic argument again with attention to more of the technicalities of Hegel's specific argument.[5]

2. Law, Simple Difference, and the "Inverted World" in Hegel's Argument

In his phenomenology of perception, Hegel shows that in our day-to-day life we vacillate between positing things as metaphysically autonomous "ones," or unique centers of reality that are solely self-defined, and positing things as "alsos," or coalescences of universal properties, such that thinghood is a derivative consequence of the coming together of other-defined properties. We vacillate, in other words, between defining the thing in terms of its essential being-for-self and defining the thing in terms of the common properties that constitute its being-for-other. The dialectic of perception reveals that this contradiction must be resolved by recognizing a reality that is self-related only by being other-related. "Force" is this concept of the identity of being-for-self and being-for-other, that is, a force only is itself insofar as it forces, insofar as it expresses or utters itself. It can realize its identity—its self-identity—only by entering into relation with others. Now a force is not an immediately perceivable reality. A force is only recognizable by going beyond the immediate and recognizing it *as* the "inner" of some multiple expression. To recognize a force is to *understand* that a single identity is manifesting itself through some total extent. Now, to the extent that the thinghood of a thing is itself such an "inner" of a sensible multiplicity (the properties), it is clear that the power of understanding must already be at play in effecting a recognition of thinghood. Understanding is thus implicitly at work, even in perception.[6] It is this same implicit power of perception that we take up explicitly when we endeavor "to understand" something. In such a situation we explicitly ask of some multiplicity, "how are you the being-for-other of some being-for-self?" that is, "how is this multiplicity the expression of some unitary force?"[7]

To take on this project explicitly, that is, to approach the world with the presumption of the identity of being-for-self and being-for-other, entails that the whole world of perception thus is now recognized as the being-for-other of some being-for-self. More exactly, it is precisely the being-for-other of being itself; that is, it is the being-for-other of the very identity of being-for-self and being-for-other, which has now been explicitly acknowledged as the nature of being itself. It is this identity of being-for-self and being-for-other that *appears* as the realm of perceptual existents (in the totality of their interactions). This whole realm of existence, then, has two sides to it: it has its character as the manifold perceptual diversity *and* it has its character *as* the appearing of the absolute essence (i.e., of the identity of being-for-self and being-for-other).

The realm of existence has two sides. Its truth, its essential side, is itself *as* the appearing of the absolute essence; its manifold diversity—its immediacy—is its inessential side, the side, that is, the recognition of which is precisely the failure to understand the truth of this realm. The absolute essence, the real identity of this realm, is its unchanging reality, the stable identity that produces despite, or in indifference to, the manifold inessential multiplicity.[8]

Yet it is this multiplicity that is to be understood. Indeed, this is the other side of the point that there is an identity of being-for-self and being-for-other: just as what appears must be the appearing of this essence, so must this essence itself appear, manifest itself. Therefore the determinacy of the manifold existence *must be understandable as* the manifestation of the essential identity. Hence the common project of understanding: identifying the *laws* that explain how a stable identity is being manifested in this manifold of perceptual existence.

The common phenomenon of understanding is this practice by which we identify laws that "explain" how a stable identity is being maintained within some manifold determinacy. To illustrate this common practice, Hegel uses the examples of electricity and gravity (M152–154, W/C 106–109). With electricity, there are two separate and opposed phenomena, positive charges and negative charges. We do not, however, leave them in our understanding as simply two different "things," but rather say that they are the necessarily opposed forms in which a single reality—the reality that is electricity itself—appears. Similarly, a rock tumbles down the hillside; a pen stays at rest on the table top; I have to exert effort to climb the stairs; rather than traveling off in a straight line into space, a moon travels around a planet in a regular orbit; and an apple falls on Newton's head; we understand all of these phenomena as revealing gravity in action. It is when we learn the law of gravity that we are able to understand why these bodies behave this way in relation to each other.[9]

In these common examples from the physical sciences, Hegel notices two different sides. On the one hand, the unity of the force is presupposed in order to explain the empirical opposition. On the other hand, the empirical opposition is presupposed to explain the unity of the force. What are positive and negative charges really? Electricity. What is gravity really? It is a constant quantitative relation between the product of the masses of the two bodies and the square of their distance. When we seek to "explain" the opposition, we posit the force. When we seek to "explain" the force, we presuppose the opposed elements (M152, W/C 106–108). The "necessity" of the law or force, that is, its ability to explain "why," rests on the presumption of a deduction of the empirical opposition from the nature of the explanatory unity. In fact, however, the law or force itself must presuppose those very *explananda* in order that it might be explained: the law becomes instead a redescription of those *explananda* in what is effectively an inductive recognition of a regularity that can be abstracted from the total phenomenon. The law, rather than expressing the essence of the related identities, becomes at best only a statement of their superficial (i.e., inessential) relation, inasmuch as each is presumed to be a self-contained reality metaphysically independent of the other (i.e., there is no essential relation of mass and distance, or time and space).[10]

(Hegel's own philosophy of nature, of course, shows otherwise, demonstrating how, for example, space and time are logically inseparable identities, and he thus shows how a full understanding of these determinations does not allow their appearance of mutual alienation to stand as the final word. Understanding works throughout with the positivistic presumption of the isolation of discrete identity. Indeed, this is the tacit presumption of the whole attitude of consciousness in general. It has not yet learned of the identity of identity and difference that characterizes Hegel's thinking—what Hegel calls "the infinite." It will soon be led to this recognition through its very attempt to resist this recognition.)

In its operations of explaining, understanding really operates with a kind of double standard. On the one hand, it operates on the notion that, in principle, the totality of perceptual existence is the coherent expression of the unity of being-for-self and being-for-other that is the simple essence of reality. (Or, more exactly, understanding operates with the presumption that reality is the appearing of its inner essence—it is our phenomenological description that has established the legitimacy of this stance but has done so by showing that it rests on the precise notion of the identity of being-for-self and being-for-other.) At the same time, the actual practice of understanding is to move from given determinacy and to move *from* this *to* the law that is to explain it. Understanding, in other words, is deductive in principle, but inductive in practice. The supersensible world was supposed to explain the multiplicity of perception, but instead it is the multiplicity of perception that sets the terms for what must be in the supersensible world: there is thus a manifold realm of laws to correspond to the manifold types of determinacy, a "supersensible world" that duplicates as its essential "image" the entire world of appearance (M149, W/C 104–105).[11]

What results, then, is a situation in which the putatively explanatory principles (the laws that describe the operation of the forces that constitute the [first] "supersensible world") are really abstractions from the total phenomenon they are to explain. The force is really just the "essential" aspect of the phenomenon. The world of appearance (inasmuch as its reality is the law within it) is *both* the "reality"—the actuality—of the supersensible realm *and* its inessentiality in addition: it contains *both* the essential content *and* the left over.[12] Understanding flips back and forth between presuming the given to explain the law and presuming the law to explain the given,[13] where this whole opposition of the supersensible and the sensible, *explanans* and *explananda* really does not do the cognitive work claimed for it, for in the end it rests on the ultimate given of appearance itself.

(That, at least, is how it immediately seems. And yet this appearance is now appearance *as* mediated by the very opposition of sensible and supersensible; that is, the ultimate given is the unity of appearance that contains this opposition within itself.[14] This—the appearance that is internally mediated by the opposition of sensible and supersensible—is what Hegel calls the "inverted world." We will see that, in fact, some work has been done through the effort of understanding.)

In seeing that the object it explains is really the self-same object with which it started, understanding takes the two separate processes ("deduction" and "induction") to have been only for its sake: explanation is how it brings itself to see what was there all along. Understanding takes itself to be preserving the principle of the identity of the object, by presuming the object to remain self-same (i.e., indifferent to the opposition of sensible and supersensible that has operated in understanding's own procedure) while positing the need to go through the opposed operations of explaining the opposition and explaining the principle ("deduction" and "induction") as answering only to the demands of its own identity, its own internal needs as understanding (M155, W/C 109–110). But note that, in so doing, understanding posits itself as a self-identity that is realized only through a self-opposition; that is, *it* is one action that must go through two opposed forms in order to be itself. Understanding's own process demonstrates an essence that necessitates its manifestation as two opposed actualities necessarily united/related. Its very attempt to preserve the pure identity of the object as indifferent to difference is what leads understanding to impute to itself the necessity for two opposed modes of self-realization; in so doing it thus produces for itself the concept of an identity that is itself an identity of identity and difference, that is, a "quiescent reality" that *is* only *as* the life of self-opposition. This is the concept understanding would need in order to make sense of appearance itself, and understanding is educating itself into this concept even as its actual practice carries over hypostasizing prejudices of "simple" unity as inert (and of opposition as therefore presupposing such inert, substantial realities as opposed to what Hegel calls a "simple difference," that is, an originary, rather than a derivative, differing).[15]

But what has understanding found except that its law is the law of appearance, that is, it itself is the inner. The very opposition of appearance and the supersensible world—the opposition that for understanding constituted the very nature of reality—has now been recognized to be only a reflection of understanding's own nature. Its nature is the ground of the very self-opposition of reality itself. In looking for the "inner," understanding must now understand that it was pursuing a reflection of its own demands, and its initial search for causes has led it to itself as the cause for that which it posits as the cause of things.[16] Appearance—and in its very appearance as the opposition of appearance and reality—is now the appearance of understanding's own nature, and understanding thus overcomes the difference of subject and object—of understanding and the inner—in the same move by which it tries to differentiate them: its logic of the identity of opposites overreaches (or "subsumes," so to speak) both itself and its putative opposite.

This notion of a reality—a unity or identity—that is the identity of itself and its appearance as opposed realities is the notion of the union of the supersensible realm and the world of appearance, which Hegel calls the "inverted world."[17] Here, it is recognized that reality itself is structured as a negative self-relation, or, the sides in appearance are a *simple difference*. There is not an inert identity opposed to an inert manifold diversity, but a *self-differentiating* reality that differentiates itself as the expression of its essential identity—the identity of being-for-self and being-for-others.[18] This is what is made *explicit* in the last move of understanding (the inverted world), that is, in the explicit recognition of what the nature of the "inner essence" was all along.[19] This recognition of *simple difference*, the self-differentiation of being into the identity of being-for-self and being-for-other, likewise implies that the subjectivity *for whom* reality appears is the fulfillment of its own essence.

In the inverted world, the project of understanding is complete. Understanding is ultimately led, by its project to understand, to understand the situation as the reflecting of its own nature as the object. In other words, in seeing its object it is seeing itself: the very difference of subject and object is thus itself a "difference that is not a difference," that is, a difference that is a self-differing. The culmination of the stance of *consciousness*, then, is its recognition that it is in reality *self-consciousness*.

3. Learning, Insight, and the Palintropos Harmoniē

Having followed out Hegel's dialectic of understanding, I want now to consider how this lesson is manifest in everyday experience. What is the vision of reality to which this Hegelian analysis of understanding—and specifically of the "inverted world," the "identity of subject and object"—leads? The key to this conception of understanding is that it must be understood in terms of the process of *learning*. This is what we typically forget when we study understanding. We model understanding on the grouping together of separate atoms in terms of some common principle or unifying theme, and we assume the object understood to be separate from us and the principle of understanding to be separate from the atoms understood. In fact, understanding is primarily a concrete phenomenon, an identification of the *inner* principle of things *in their identity with oneself*, and this identity is itself performed or realized through the very process of recognition. This process is the process of learning, the process by which that which was formerly alien comes to be that in which one finds oneself. I want in this section to address this issue by considering the familiar phenomenon of learning, of coming to understand, and to show how Hegel's themes are manifest here. This will allow me to conclude, in the final section of this chapter, with a consideration of the nature of the body.

When we truly approach some situation with understanding, our approach is not simply the repetition of a rule; rather, we demonstrate insight. This is the point Aristotle makes in his famous discussions of learning in the last chapter of the *Posterior Analytics* and the first chapter of the *Metaphysics*.[20] Truly coming to understand means grasping the first principle—the *archē*—of that which we are trying to understand, and this is no longer the situation of trying to subsume some puzzling specifics under some overarching rule, but is rather a situation in which we "see into" the thing itself and comprehend the details of the situation as the uniquely appropriate expression of the inner essence. This is what we call insight. Such an achievement of insight is most familiar to us in practical situations.

Imagine trying to understand what it is to be a chef. One could observe the chef in action, and wonder at her ability to produce such excellent meals. One might seek the rule being employed—such rules are precisely gathered in recipe books—but, when one follows such rules, one finds that one does not produce the same meals as the chef. The chef herself is not following such rules. If asked what guides her cooking choices, she might well say "the meal itself," or she might say that she does "what the dish needs." The chef has an insight into what it is that she is really working with. The recipes will lead an apprentice along the path, but they are not themselves understanding, and to rely upon such recipes in cooking is, in an important sense, not to understand cooking. One could make a similar point regarding the family cook. One must make meals for one's family. In trying to learn how to become such a cook, one will eventually have to come to the realization that the family cook must do what is necessary to answer to the nutritional needs and dining desires of the family members, and will have to construct the cooking activities out of this principle; yet in learning, one might think "I must do this on Tuesday," "I must serve this with that," and so on. Properly to be the family cook is not to apply the universal rules of family cooking to this particular instance of a family situation, but is, rather, to generate the appropriate cooking demands out of an insight into the family's needs.[21]

Such practical situations give us a good model for insight. Prior to achieving insight, we are left with a situation in which we must try to put together elements through the application of rules. We "understand" neither the elements nor the rules in the sense that we do not have insight into their inherent necessity but rather find them as the given materials we are to deploy. Upon attaining insight, however, we have the experience of a transformation of the situation and our relationship to it. Now we "see into" the elements, and our understanding of the situation allows us to recognize what is to be done. We no longer "apply" one structure to another, but instead respond intelligently to the immanent demands of the situation. In insight, precisely what we do is overcome our alienation from the object: we now see into the thing itself, and we need only to turn to ourselves—to our own understanding—to access the nature of the situation. In such situations of practical insight, we speak our own mind, and it is the essence of the thing.[22]

In such situations of understanding, one comes to recognize the "quiescent unity" that is the immediately changing multiplicity of appearance.[23] Now what is particularly striking when one understands a situation is how much someone who only repeats rules does not understand the situation. The one who applies rules to instances demonstrates thereby a *failure* to understand. But note that this attitude of rule-applying is precisely the attitude of understanding that we considered when we considered the positing of the first supersensible world. To the person with insight, in other words, the person operating with an opposition of supersensible and appearance is the one who has not understood, whereas the insightful understanding itself is precisely characterized by the overcoming of the alienation of the subject and the object, that is, by the attitude that posits the second supersensible world, or the inverted world. The very opposition of the first supersensible world to appearance, which seemed the zenith of understanding (because it was the refusal to rest with the immediately perceived, but the demand instead for the laws of intelligibility that structure this perceptible world), is its nadir, in that it is precisely the presumption of the alienation of subject and object and of appearance and supersensible world that simultaneously characterizes definitively the first attitude of understanding and is that which essentially inhibits its ability to understand.

Hegel stresses that the law of this inverted world is that "everything is its opposite," and we can now see how this is so. We have already seen this to be so in the most profound senses, namely, the identification of subject and object and the identification of the appearance and supersensible world in the experience of insight. These instances alone, however, would make Hegel's remark seem hyperbolic, which it is not. Rather, the reality of the inverted world of insight is that it is a situation characterized by the logic that Heraclitus names the "*palintropos harmoniē*," or "back-turning harmony."[24] Heraclitus's point is that self-identities are shaped by structures of self-opposition or internal negation: "differing with itself, it agrees with itself," says Heraclitus.[25] Such "back-turning harmonies" are precisely what we recognize in insight, that is, in understanding. I want to address this point by exploring further the topic of the identity of subject and object that we have already broached.

How is it that subject and object are the same identity? The key is that the object of experience takes different forms, even in relationship to the same putative "thing." At one point I see the thing "as" a set of properties, at another point "as" an independent and unique reality, at yet another point "as" an aspect of the appearing of reality itself. The same situation appears to me now as "red," now as "apple," now as "dinner." That which is the object *of the experience* changes, and the object changes as the subjective interest changes.

My object is a color when I look for sensible properties, my object is an apple when I look for things, my object is dinner when I try to understand what is appearing in the situation. The identity of that which appears cannot be separated from the subjective interest—the "intention"—for which it appears.

Indeed, the whole notion of an inner—a cause—exists only for one who understands, for without the challenge to the immediacy of appearance—without the *questioning* of experience—there would be no experience of anything beyond perception. In other words, it is only for a being that does not rest content with immediacy but instead desires that there be an answer to the question "why?" that there can be a supersensible world. And yet, the notion of the cause is not simply a subjective fabrication, or something arbitrarily imposed upon reality. On the contrary, having raised the question of cause, I must now turn to the thing itself for the answer to this question.[26] It is only for understanding that there can be a cause, and therefore the identity of the cause cannot be understood outside the context of understanding itself; at the same time, there is no understanding without the recognition of the cause as within the nature of the reality. Understanding is a subjective change, in that my desire to find a cause is satisfied, but this change is made possible only insofar as this change equally amounts to a realization of the determining essence of the thing itself. There is an identity of subject and object in that each reaches its truth—its fulfillment—through the change in the other, which it both depends upon and supports.[27] It is thus undecidable whether understanding is subjective or objective, whether the object responds to the subject or whether the subject responds to the solicitation of the object.[28] Understanding—unconditioned insight—is, rather, the upsurge or revelation of meaning that is the reality simultaneously of the subject and of the object. This is what it means to say that they share an identity.

What Hegel shows us in the opening chapters of the *Phenomenology of Spirit* is precisely *how* this mutual solicitation or sharedness of identity between subject and object is so. What we discover through our phenomenological description of the experience of consciousness is that with each changing mode of consciousness there is a changing character to the object. Reality *is* (*simpliciter*) *for* the attitude of sense-certainty. Reality is things *for* the attitude of perception. Reality is forces, and the comprehensive totality of these forces, *for* understanding. The dialectic of understanding reveals the formal truth that the nature of the object was shaped by the nature of the subject, and the phenomenology of consciousness overall has shown how this is true concretely.

Furthermore, what this dialectic of consciousness has repeatedly revealed is that an opposition that exists *for* consciousness is in fact the expression of a unitary principle operating *within* consciousness. Perception, for example, is plagued by the opposition of being-for-self and being-for-other in the thing, but these are reconciled in the notion of force; that is, we can see that either can be only if it is also implicitly the other. It has similarly shown that the theoretical and the practical—though seeming opposites—are in fact simply different

phases of the same single notion. As we have just seen, and as we shall reconsider below, the form of the object of consciousness is itself a result of what
consciousness *does*: knowing is a kind of doing, theory is a kind of practice.[29] In
another context, one could argue that rationalism and empiricism—seeming
opposites—are really just the two sides by which a unitary conception of the
human mind shows itself. Or, again, bourgeoisie and proletariat, though essentially opposed groups, are themselves the two necessary sides by which the
unitary logic of capitalism expresses itself. This is what it means to say that the
law of the inverted world is that each thing is its opposite.

To say that the inverted world is the world governed by the logic of the
palintropos harmoniē is to say that it is the world revealed through dialectical
phenomenology. It is the world in which subjectivity and objectivity are two
aspects of the same experiencing of meaning. It is the world in which things
project from themselves their own standards of self-interpretation and self-
criticism, and thereby propel themselves through processes of self-transcendence whereby their explicit opposition to some other is revealed to be implicitly an identification with that other. The law of the inverted world amounts to
the demand that one turn to appearance itself to learn how it projects its own
principles for its interpretation, or, in other words, how it needs our understanding to allow it to realize its identity. That which is, in other words, is not a
self-existent determinate substance, either in the sense of the thing of perception or of the fixed causal order of understanding. On the contrary, that which
is is a *gap* (*chaos* in Hesiod, "simple difference" in Hegel). That which is is that
which differs from itself, that which is both itself and the standard to which it
aspires, that which calls upon us to realize it, to complete it. Reality is not a
finished, fully determinate world, but is the very reality of dynamic appearing,
the reality of experience as the point of identification of subject and object in
the shared process of "making sense," of realizing meaning, in time: in world
history, in the process by which things come to themselves through a process of
self-criticism, and in lived temporality, in the constant answering of experience to the future it bears within itself. This gap, this differing from itself that
is the process of experience is, we will now see, first and foremost the body
as the fundamental reality of the subject-object identity as self-transcending
openness.

4. The Metaphysics of the Body

In Descartes, consideration of the nature of understanding leads us to
construe it as a reality diametrically opposed to the reality of the body. Hegel's
philosophy, on the contrary, leads us to see that this reality that is understanding is fundamentally realized as the body. By consideration of the phenomenon of insight, we have seen that understanding is properly to be understood as
the practice of coming to identify with the essence of things, that is, making
the essence of oneself and the essence of things one and the same essence.

This initially seemed appropriate for discussions of practical life, but we have now seen how it applies in principle for theoretical matters as well. I want now to look again at how this practical structure is indeed the proper structure for understanding understanding *simpliciter; that is,* our identification with things follows the same pattern as our identification with practices. We have seen that this understanding of understanding entails a entirely reconceptualized metaphysics. I want now to show how this new metaphysics is what I will call the metaphysics of the body.

Hegel does not devote a great deal of explicit text to the discussion of the body, but he does have powerful small studies in the early sections of the *Philosophy of Spirit* and, in particular, in his discussion of property in the *Philosophy of Right.* What we learn in the opening pages of the *Philosophy of Right* is that our body is not immediately "our own"—it must be "appropriated," that is, we must come to make it exist as the expression of our will.[30] Hegel's analysis here is reminiscent of psychological studies of early childhood development that study the ways in which the child gradually comes to feel "at home" in its body. In other words, the control of "its own" body, and the corresponding division between itself and others, is not an immediate given, but is a significance to its experience that must be accomplished. It is in this light that we must read Hegel's discussion of making our bodies our property. They become our own property—our "own" bodies, our "proper" bodies—by our coming to live through them. An initial resistance and alien opacity comes to be *our own* as we come to live through it, to find it the medium for the expression/realization of our will, our projects, ourselves.

This model of "making it oneself" that initially pertains to the appropriation of our original "alien opacity" is the same pattern we reproduce on a larger level when we develop habits of interaction with things and other people. Through our processes of habituation we come to establish a *home* in the world—a resistant, alien opacity comes to be the unresisting medium for our own self-expression and self-realization. It is in this way that we fundamentally "understand" the world: we live through it unreflectively. This founding relationship to "reality" is what Hegel will later analyze under the name "Ethicality," and I will not pursue that study in detail here. My point is only that consciousness's (understanding's) initial positing of the object as the metaphysically independent alien is in fact a biased and misrepresentative presentation. To be such an alien object is not the *essence* of reality; it is, rather, the form *our living situation* takes when it is *posited* as such an alien by our theoretical attitude: its "objecthood" is not its own, but is a status is has only *in relation to ourselves,* to our projects. Similarly, the involvement that we ultimately discover to be the essence of things does not speak of some mystical union with the secret essence of things beyond understanding. It rather points to the origin of "things" in our *situation,* our original "being-in-the-world," as Heidegger says.

It is through this consideration of our bodily reality that we can understand the Hegelian metaphysics, that is, the immanent result of the dialectic of understanding. We can see another side of this by considering our bodies in relationship to the notion of the *palintropos harmoniē* that we developed in our account of the inverted world.

If we think about this notion of habituation, and in general about the body as our living practical capacity for engagement with the world, we can notice that its very character is to be the magical power by which this identification with things is accomplished. The body is that by which *I am in contact with the not-I*; that is, it is the point (the "limit" point) that is both self and other, inner and outer, the "edge" between conscious interiority and spatial materiality. As the reality that is *in itself* this identity of self and other, it is the internal mediation—the way that inside is already outside, and *vice versa*—that is presupposed by external mediation, that allows any construction of a mediated relation between some particular inside and some other particular outside. It is precisely the prototype for all reconciliation of opposites, the prototype of the *palintropos harmoniē*, the *coincidentia oppositorum* that we take as the essence of the Hegelian *Aufhebung*, of dialectical self-overcoming. What is dialectical self-overcoming? It is the reality of the body. The body is that which transcends itself, that which reaches beyond to its own alien and thereby transforms both that alien and itself into a new harmony. Its self-transcendence is what lets there be a world that transcends me: it is my openness to. . . . The reality of the body is thus the process of dialectic: the self-opposing that has as its immanent norm the project of reconciliation, of understanding. Understanding, then, far from being the opposite of the body as Descartes claims, is, in fact, the very essence and fulfillment of bodily reality.

PART 2. SELF-CONSCIOUSNESS

four
Death and Desire in Hegel's Epistemology: The Form of Hegel's Argument

We have two experiences around which we typically orient ourselves. On the one hand, we are passive. On the other hand, we are active. The first is the experience we typically associate with knowledge, that is, the experience in which we are determined by objects. The second is the experience we typically associate with action, that is, the experience in which objects are determined by us. This is an old story, told most forcefully in one of the texts that functions as a sort of "key" for German idealism, namely, the third antinomy of Kant's *Critique of Pure Reason*.[1] I want to consider how this antinomy is a player in the structure and argument of Hegel's *Phenomenology of Spirit*, and in so doing show how death is the foundation—or the abyss—of meaning.[2]

My path may be a bit intricate, but I trust it will be clear enough. I will begin in the first section by looking at Hegel's account of the logical beginnings of consciousness and self-consciousness, that is, sense and desire respectively.[3] With each in turn I will consider why such a beginning makes sense, but also why it necessarily faces a problem. We will see that the problems are parallel, each complementing the other. The problems of each will be problems of the relation of immediacy and mediation in a context of negativity. In the second section I will sketch out the ways in which the problems that arise at these beginnings must be solved. In this section, I will show how the resolution of the problem of immediate consciousness and the resolution of the problem of immediate self-consciousness again parallel and complement each other, and, furthermore, we will see how the projects of consciousness and self-consciousness show themselves to be mutually interpenetrating, such that each project emerges at some point in the normal course of development of the other project. The development in each project here will revolve primarily around the problem of determinacy. Finally, in the third section I will look specifically at the place within self-consciousness of its own death, in order to show ultimately that both the project of consciousness and the project of self-consciousness are necessarily founded in the originariness of the desiring being's relation to its own death (and such a relation is the distinctive mark of "spirit"). This section will raise the themes of embodiment and responsibility, and will point the way to understanding why in principle spirit must complete itself as absolute knowing (but it will only point).

Let me begin, then, by developing the Hegelian version of the third antinomy, in order to follow out its dialectical development toward the primacy of the relation to our own death.

1. Sense-Certainty and Self-Certainty

When we speak of being, we typically have in mind that which is what it is by itself, it has its own determination—it *is*.[4] Being has commanding weight—it is reality. Being is that in relation to which we are passive. Being passive in relation to being is at the core of our experience. Indeed, this is close to a definition of experience: "there is," for us.

This is where Hegel's *Phenomenology of Spirit* begins, with "there is" (M91, W/C 69–70). But what is there? Initially, nothing specific: all we can really say of the most immediate structure of objectivity is "it is." This is the stance that Hegel calls "Sense-Certainty." For sense-certainty, there is, and there is nothing more to say.

Hegel's beginning with the analysis of our experience in sense-certainty echoes Kant's beginning of his phenomenology of experience with sensibility in the "Transcendental Aesthetic." Kant argues that experience must begin as a immediate relation to immediacy, as *Anschauung*, intuition.[5] Sense is our immediate contact with something meaningful, something that has a sense, a direction, a determinateness of its own. Both that to which we originally relate and our original relation itself must be immediate, for if the origin were not immediate it would presuppose another, and it would thus not be the origin but instead that other would be the real start (M90, W/C 69).[6] Our knowledge, then, begins as sense, as our immediate relation to immediate meaning.

The very structure of such a *relation to* immediacy, a *consciousness of* immediacy, entails, however, an opposition between the immediacy that characterizes the object and the form of the relationship itself: by virtue of being a relation, this consciousness is a *mediacy*, something that exists only through or by way of another. This mediation is the very form of conscious immediacy: sense consciousness is the immediacy of the "for"—a sense is there *for* me. This mediation that is the immediacy of consciousness is what Hegel calls "negativity," and what since the twentieth century we are more likely to call "intentionality."

Right off the bat, then, the nature of consciousness as negativity entails that how it intuits is out of step with how it is, for it intuits that what is is immediate, while its own nature is to be a situation of mediation. Consequently, we can narrate two stories about conscious negativity: we can narrate the immediacy of how it initially is—immediately negative (what Hegel calls "negative self-relation"),[7] the "for"—and we can narrate the immediacy of what it initially apprehends—immediate being, the simple "is." To describe consciousness adequately requires telling both the story of the "is" and the story of the "for."

So, to repeat, for sense-certainty, there is, and there is nothing more to say. This "nothing more to say" still amounts to something though: this nothing more is the "for"—*for* sense-certainty, there is. In the experience of "there is" what is not acknowledged is the very space of appearing; only what appears is recognized. Even in this simple, primitive experience, there is enough complexity for us to notice a disparity between its form and its content, its object and its relation to this object. The stance says "there is" and the stance itself is, and the "there is" that is said is not adequate to what is there, to the stance itself.

What seems right about the stance of sense-certainty is its stance of passivity: the stance of passivity acknowledges the determining character of being. At the same time, however, this bias toward the object fails to account for itself—for itself *qua* bias, *qua* perspective. The stance of passivity seems definitive of consciousness, but, inasmuch as this is a *stance*, it seems that consciousness cannot itself be strictly passive. Consciousness, in its stance of passivity, misrepresents itself; by seeming right-headed *qua* consciousness, immediate certainty seems wrong-headed as self-consciousness. Let us consider self-consciousness.

Kant's third antinomy draws our attention to the different ways we relate to our situations when we try to know and when we try to act. Kant calls this the distinction between the theoretical and the practical. Whereas in the theoretical stance we seem to be passive in relation to being, in practical life we seem active—the determination of the situation flows from us, from our choices, from our freedom. Whereas the theoretical stance starts with "it," the practical stance starts with "I." If you lift my arm from the table, I have not acted (though I may be conscious of the event). We say I have acted when I lift my arm, when the action is my own, when the movement expresses who I am, what my desires are. The key to action is initiative: the action is attributed to the one who did it, the one for whom the act announces "I." Action is the enacting of self-consciousness, the enacting of a sense of self. Our self-consciousness begins as the immediate experience of initiative, of ourselves as active. To be an "I" and to be active are inseparable. There is something fundamentally right—fundamentally inescapable—about the recognition of ourselves as active. Let us consider the original experience of ourselves as active.

There is a stance a person can adopt that denies that there is any passivity in experience. This is the stance that acts as if its own desires were all that mattered, the stance for which its desires—its very "I"—are everything. Freud recognizes such a stance in the child. The child begins as a desiring machine, someone for whom everything is just the opportunity for enacting its own desires. This is the purely desiring stance, the stance for which its own identity—its own primacy—is absolutely certain, the stance that recognizes no limitation, only itself.[8] Diametrically opposed to the stance of sense-certainty, this immediate self-certainty is the stance that recognizes only the "for" and does not acknowledge any "is"—it is, as Freud might say, the pleasure principle with no reality principle.[9]

This desiring stance, in expressing itself, is making a point. Its actions announce itself; that is, they announce itself as what is real (M167, W/C 120–122). This pure stance of desire announces that the desiring stance is that which determines the nature of things. We see this basic structure in any simple desire. Whenever we act on a desire we reshape the world according to ourselves, and thereby demand that reality acknowledge our primacy, our centrality. Any desire implies the determining power of the self. The stance that does not just *have* a desire but is, in fact, the stance of desire itself—the stance that is committed to the primacy of its desire as such—is the stance that announces itself as the one and only reality.[10] To recognize no limitations to one's initiative is to assert that "there is nothing to oppose me—beyond what is for me there is nothing."

The very nature of desire, however, is that it must determine reality—this is its definition. Its very nature, therefore, is such as to require an other, a field of operations, a receptacle for its determining power. Though desire will not explicitly acknowledge another, it is only as a relation to some other that desire can be (M175, W/C 126). Desire, therefore, constantly faces another that it must deny. This is the very dynamism of desire: it encounters a determination that claims to be other, and desire shows that determination to be false by showing desire's power to overpower it, to determine it (M167, W/C 120–122). Desire faces the challenge of otherness and exists as the perpetual overcoming of the challenge (the necessity of which it fails to recognize in monotonously intoning "me," "me," "me.")

Our analysis of desire shows it to be in an important sense reactive, for it always takes the form of responding to a challenge. Once again (as with sense-certainty) we see an immediacy that rests on mediation, a first that shows itself to be always already second. Desire is determined by the other it negates: it cannot be utterly indifferent to limitation because it is responsive to specific challenges. This immediate recognition of the activity of self-consciousness fails to acknowledge that its activity is inseparable from a passivity, a limitation by which it is determined. While desire gets something important right about self-consciousness—that it is active—it does this only by significantly misrepresenting its nature as consciousness, as something passive in relation to a determining other.

We have seen how the immediate form of our experience admits of being taken up in two ways—as immediately active and immediately passive, as desire and sense respectively—and we have seen how each of these immediacies is self-misrepresentative because each acknowledges only an immediacy that excludes mediation, whereas the immediacy that it *is* is inherently mediated because it is an immediate *negativity* (a "simple difference," in the language of Chapter III, "Force and Understanding").[11] I want now to consider how experience learns of its error, and how it is impelled to develop a better account of its own character of negativity, which, we will see, amounts to recognizing its own character as determinate. I will begin by returning to the story of desire and its education, and use the results of this study to return to the story of sense and its education. This education of the purely desiring self-consciousness is what Hegel analyzes under to title of the "life and death struggle."[12]

2. Desire and Determinacy

The thesis of the stance of desire is that it is the absolute determining ground of experience. This claim is contradicted in every action, because the challenge to which the action responds shows itself, *qua* recognized challenge, to be determining experience, but, to the extent that the action is precisely the overcoming of the challenge, the very nature of desire is to conceal its own dependence on that which it overcomes.[13] Desire, then, contradicts itself, but need not recognize this—indeed, is driven by the refusal to recognize this. Desire meets its insurmountable limit, though, when it is challenged by another desire like itself, that is, not just some particular desire but another stance that announces itself as desire as such, the one and only reality.[14]

In coming upon another stance of absolute desire, absolute desire encounters an untouchable, an undeterminable reality. Why? Because the other desire, like it itself, does not acknowledge the determining power of any outside, and consequently recognizes any effort by the first desire to overpower it as simply a challenge for it itself to overcome. When two absolute desires meet, they cannot meet—neither can overcome the other, for the logic of each is such as to undermine the logic of the other: each claims to be the one who determines, and each therefore meets in the other the impossibility of effecting this stance of agency.

The stance of desire is committed to determining the situation. Any other such stance of desire is thus a challenge to which, according to the demands of its own logic, it must respond. Desire, therefore, must try to determine the other, must oppose every effort of the other to determine, must oppose the other absolutely. In facing another desire, then, desire must desire the obliteration of that desire. Desire, therefore, seeks the death of the other desire (M187, W/C 130–131).

Yet the death of the other cannot count as a sufficient fulfillment of the stance of desire. To kill the other is to eliminate its presence, but it is not the presence of the other desire that challenges desire. It is precisely the absence of the other that is the challenge. Inasmuch as desire is the refusal to recognize the ultimacy of any presence, and is instead the demand that desire, beyond that presence, determines the significance of that presence, there is no presence that can be identified with desire. To kill the other is to eliminate a certain presence, but that presence was never the threat—the threat was *precisely* that nothing the one desire does to any presence has any determining significance for the other desire. The challenge does not come from presence, so the obliteration of presence cannot count as an answer to the challenge.

What then is the challenge? The challenge is precisely the other desire's definitive *power of determining*, the other's initiative, the other's "I." That which must become determined by the victorious desire is the other's *desire*. It is the other's *agency* that must accept the determination of the first desire: it is *as desire* that the other desire must be determined. Success, then, is not found in the death of the other. Success is found in having the other desire *determine itself to be determined by the first desire*, for it is as desire, that is, as self-determining, that the other must accept the determination of the first desire. Desire, then, does not desire the death of the other: it desires the desire of the other (see M175, W/C 126).

But here we see that the very conditions of desire's success are the conditions of its failure. In desiring the other's desire, desire has in fact announced that it is the other's desire that matters; that is, it has determined itself to be determined by the other's desire. It is at this point that desire has admitted that it is dependent on its other; that is, it is passive. In other words, desire—self-consciousness—must itself be constrained by the demands that characterize consciousness. Let us compare this with the situation of sense.

The education of desire was effected through the determinateness—the determinate challenge—within its experience, to which it was responsive. Desire depended on the specific determinacy to which it responded, but this determinacy itself could not force desire to acknowledge it until this determinacy took the form of desire itself. The education of sense similarly is effected through the role of determinacy within experience (and it again will lead us to desire).

Sense-certainly begins by recognizing "there is," but *what* is there? Sense-certainty says nothing specific: it acknowledges only being as such, only simple, empty, indeterminate immediacy. And yet our experience does not just take the form of such an indifferent, unchanging "it is": on the contrary, it takes ever-changing forms. What appears, in other words, is always something or other. Experience is multiple: experiences. One moment—one "now"—is differentiated from another, and so, even though the most fundamental truth we know of any object of our experience remains that "it is," it is equally true that "it" is always specific, always one thing and not another.[15] We are unable to even notice "is" unless "is" is specific; that is, noticing is differentiating. We can see this if we remember the project of sense-certainty.

The very character of the "is" by which consciousness as sense-certainty is so impressed is its determining character: being must give the sense—the direction—to experience. *It* must be the criterion for *deciding* what is real and what is not. In direct opposition to the stance of absolute desire, the stance of absolute sense turns to the determining character of being to oppose opinion, that is, to oppose the subjective views that might be put forward as claims about what is. In other words, one claim is not as good any other: this is the whole point behind sense. Yet what sense-certainty says of being—"it is"—gives no ground for discrimination. The very project of sense-certainty—namely, to be conscious, that is, to be determined by being—requires that it be able to say *what* is, but it is not able to do so. Sense-certainty's own stance, in other words, is inadequate to itself because it wants to acknowledge, but cannot acknowledge, the determinacy in experience (whereas desire did not want to acknowledge but could not not acknowledge this determinacy). In saying "is there now," sense-certainty has the goal of holding onto the richness of the determinate experience, but with only this level of articulation what it can in fact acknowledge cannot differentiate between night and day; that is, it says the same thing—"is there now"—in the face of completely changed sensuous determinacies.[16]

But consciousness is conscious of determinateness. And, as we have just seen, what it is to be conscious of determinateness is to conscious of "this, not that." But to recognize "this, not that" means that what is must be multiple— for there must be difference for there to be this and that—and these different thises and thats—the different beings—must be different individuals while sharing features that allow them to be compared and differentiated. Being, in other words, must be in the form of determinate beings that are individual things the properties of which are their points of contact with other things and are that by which the things both oppose each other and participate in a shared metaphysical space (M111–112, W/C 79–80). Being itself, in other words, must be a unity through difference—that is, through different beings—and the different beings must themselves be unities through difference—that is, one thing through many properties, through many interactions with other things. (These are the lessons of understanding and perception, respectively.) Thus the very nature of consciousness—namely, the project to be determined by the object—requires that consciousness will have to learn thus to recognize determinacy, the very nature of which is to exist only as unity through difference (along multiple axes). This demand to recognize the determinateness within experience also brings consciousness to the issues of activity, desire, and self-consciousness.

First, we have seen already in the inadequacy of sense-certainty that the need to recognize determinacy is a need for consciousness to change *its stance*; that is, the difference between the inadequate and adequate forms of consciousness is an issue of what consciousness *does*. Consciousness, in other words, is active, and this activity—as is implied by the notion of activity in consciousness—is desire. We have seen this from the start insofar as we had to describe consciousness in terms of its project, in terms of what it wants to accomplish. Indeed, the education of consciousness is fueled by the inadequacy of consciousness's actual acts of knowing for fulfilling its desire to know.

Second, we can see more determinately what the acts of consciousness must be in order to recognize determinateness. If such a recognition is a recognition of unity through difference, then consciousness both must hold together differences—what is usually called an act of imagination—and must recognize mediating structures—what is usually called an act of understanding. Recognizing determinateness means holding together differences, and holding them together "as": what Kant calls the synthesis of reproduction in imagination and the synthesis of recognition in a concept.[17] To be passive, in other words, requires very specific and very developed activity.

Third and finally, since we here see that the very nature of the experience is shaped by the activity of the subject, it follows that to recognize—be passive to—the determinacy of the situation will be to recognize it *as* determined by the activity of the subject; that is, the object will have to be recognized as an expression of the desire of the subject.

In sum, then, the immediate—and compelling—recognition of ourselves as passive in sense requires us to develop our cognition to the point of the comprehensive understanding of determinateness, which means being active and acknowledging ourselves as active, that is, acknowledging desire. Similarly, the immediate—and compelling—recognition of ourselves as active in desire requires us to develop our activity to the point of being passive to the determining power of the other, which means learning how to understand the demands that being makes upon us. Each side of the antinomy of consciousness, then—the side of consciousness and the side of self-consciousness—has a immanently driven path of self-development and self-education through which it must come to recognize its identity with the other side of the antinomy. Having now carried these two stories through to their shared conclusion, I want to return to the notion of death, which made its appearance in the education of desire, and consider its place in this story of the sense within experience. We will see the role death plays in making this education possible.

3. Embodiment and Responsibility

Let us consider just what this identification of consciousness and self-consciousness means for how we must construe our own reality. If self-consciousness is consciousness and consciousness is self-consciousness—indeed, if I am negativity, a negative self-relation—then I am my situation in the mode of not-being it (to draw on Sartre's language in *Being and Nothingness*).[18] My consciousness, my selfhood, is not something over and above my situation in the sense of being another determinate being. I am this perspective, the very nature of which is to open out onto other perspectives. I am this unique point of view, this unique sensitivity to others. This means I am a unique bodily reality. We considered the struggle to the death from the side of the winner, and why the victory is a defeat. I want now to think briefly about the same struggle from the side of the loser in order to focus on the necessity of embodiment.

The loser is not around anymore to continue to make its challenge to the first desire. The loser cannot learn a lesson from the struggle to the death, for there is no consciousness left in the annihilation of the desire. Although the loser does not learn anything, this loss demonstrates something to us who are able to look on, and it is another version of the lesson learned by the desire that acknowledges its dependence on another desire. What the loss demonstrates is that in the absence of a relation to another—in the absence of being a living perspective—desire cannot be. Desire must be a determinate being locatable in relation to other determinate beings. I must be a thing in the world in order to communicate with other things in the world, and, while I may exist as an absence, a negativity, this, as we have seen, in inseparable from that from which it is an absence, a negation. There are thus two lessons to be learned from the struggle to the death, two ways in which consciousness as active must recognize its passivity. First, desire needs another desire. Second, desire must be a body in relation to other bodies. It is the moment of death—and its failure as a strategy both for the winner and for the loser—that reveals the dependence of desire on a living body and on another desire. In sum, self-consciousness must exist as a desiring body in relation to other desiring bodies. It is the desiring body, the body *qua* sensitive, that can sense. And it is this same body that can die. The body is this double vulnerability, this double openness.

But it is not just because we are bodies that can die and sense that we are propelled on this path of education. Only certain bodies can advance along this path of education. These are bodies that do not just die, but bodies for whom their own death can be an issue; that is, the vulnerability that allows them to be conscious is itself something of which they can become conscious. The key to the education of desire is that it pass through the struggle to the death: that it take its desire as absolute and that it learn of the failure of this, its project. We saw above that the ability for sense to advance to the adequate recognition of determinacy required specific synthetic abilities, namely, the ability to hold together and interpret a multiplicity as a unity. Similarly, for desire to become educated through the recognition of the failure of its immediate project in the struggle to the death, specific recognitive capacities are required, namely, this desire must be such as (1) to be able to recognize another absolute desire and (2) to be able to learn through its efforts to kill this other that death is something to which it is necessarily subject and to which it must answer, while also recognizing that, *qua* self-conscious negativity, it is not defined by this death but by its relationship to it. Only a being that can adopt such a posture can learn, can rise to the stance of objectivity, for the pursuit of objectivity is precisely the stance of a desire that acknowledges that it will be fulfilled only when it reaches the position that does not respond just to its idiosyncratic desires, that is its desire in its immediacy, but to its desires as fully mediated by the legitimate desires of others: objectivity is the pursuit of what is universal and necessary for self-conscious desire. In other words, the pursuit of objectivity—the very project of consciousness, of sense—is the desire to have the fulfillment of one's own desire be the fulfillment of the desire of the other, which means to pursue objectivity is to have learned the lesson of the struggle to the death.

It is only a being that is capable of taking its own death as an issue that can develop to the stance of objectivity and understanding, of comprehension. Such a capacity does not introduce merely the possibility of such a development, however: it also introduces the necessity. To be a being capable of taking one's own death as an issue is to be a being already characterized by taking stances—setting up commitments—and being subject to the values implied by those commitments, and it is this character of being open to criticism by our own standards that sets us on a path of dialectical development. Our being in relation to our own death automatically opens us onto the path of self-transcendence and self-critique, a path completed only in what Heidegger calls "authentic resoluteness" and Hegel calls "absolute knowing."[19]

We are immanently propelled toward the ideal of objectivity, which is equally the ideal of mutual recognition or sharedness of desire.[20] These cognitive and moral pursuits coalesce in the stance of conscience as universal forgiveness—*tout comprehendre, c'est tout pardonner*—conscience being the stance of choosing in the light of our mortality, and universal forgiveness being the stance of adopting that educated openness to the immanent dialectic of all determinacy that is phenomenology (as we shall see explicitly in later chapters).[21] This is the stance of absolute knowing: what Hegel calls "pure self-recognition in absolute otherness" (M26, W/C 19–21), the making of ourselves passive—open—by developing the sufficient level of activity to recognize all determinations as a reflection of our own desire. It is because of the place of death and desire in Hegel's epistemology that consciousness can complete its inherent drive to objectivity and mutual recognition only in absolute knowing.

Conclusion

The first two sections of Hegel's *Phenomenology of Spirit* are structured like a Kantian antinomy: specifically the third antinomy. The chapters on consciousness build from our immediate certainty of our own passivity through the education of sense to the point of recognizing that this passivity is a kind of activity. The chapter on self-consciousness builds from our immediate certainty of our own activity through the education of desire to the point of recognizing that this activity is a kind of passivity. *Contra* Kant, then, Hegel shows how each side of the third antinomy points to the same solution to the antinomy, that is, to a synthesis. What I have tried to show in this chapter is how this solution is necessitated by the nature of determination and negativity, and how it is our capacity of being able to take up a stance on our own death that is what allows us to undergo this dialectical education and ultimately to solve the antinomy and complete our education as dialectical phenomenologists. In leaving us thus responsible to be always open to what is, our relationship to our own death, the very foundation of meaning, is equally the abyss, for it launches us on a pursuit of objectivity that is fulfilled only in that absolute ignorance which must perpetually wait upon its situation to show itself. The absolute knowing that is the fulfillment of our being in relation to our own death thus will not be a secure barrier against experience (as is often supposed) but will be the stance of ultimate vulnerability in which we are thrown absolutely into the happening of meaning from which there is, for us, no exit.

five
Reading and the Body

Language is clearly one of the most important themes in twentieth-century philosophy. Within the tradition that has its roots in Heidegger, it is a commonplace to suggest that language is a repressed theme in Western philosophy, and that explicit reflection upon language will provide one with a tool to dismember the edifice of Western metaphysics. Something similar is said on behalf of the body, and the emancipation of language and the body is a great theme of recent philosophy. Hegel's philosophy in particular is treated simultaneously as the culmination of the tradition of Western metaphysics and as a closed system in which language and the body are especially excluded; these phenomena, as the limits of the system, are equally seen to mark its collapse.

Like most commonplaces, these commonplace claims about Hegel are inadequate characterizations of the real situation; indeed, in this case they seem to me to propose the very opposite of the truth. For Hegel, language and embodiment are paired themes, and they are absolutely central to his philosophical project. My goal here is to lay the ground from within the context of the *Phenomenology of Spirit* for developing a Hegelian approach to the study of language and the body.

There have been attempts to study Hegel's views on both language and the body, but these treatments tend to be narrow studies that focus only on texts in which Hegel makes explicit mention of either language or the body.[1] My interest, however, is not simply with what Hegel says, but with what his argument requires him to say, and so I will derive a Hegelian orientation to language and the body from considering what is implied in some central moves in the *Phenomenology of Spirit*. In particular, I will consider the emergence of the relation of master and slave and Hegel's analysis of Sophocles' *Antigone*.

I focus on the transformation of a situation into one of mastery and servitude because the body is an essential logical player in such a change, and, more particularly, the transformation is itself *a transformation within the nature of the body itself*; the body here must change from being an unconscious system of life-support to being the freely chosen system of self-expression, that is, language. The relationship of master and slave is also privileged because it marks the beginning of *social* existence, the beginning of the institutional life that is the natural environment of self-conscious selves, so in seeing the place of language and the body in this scenario, we see its place at the heart of institutionalized self-conscious life in general.

It is this last theme that is picked up in Hegel's study of *Antigone*. Hegel uses *Antigone* to analyze the natural form our relation to our social institutions takes, namely, unconscious dependence on automatic systems of mutual recognition that are equally systems of interpretation. These processes of automatic interpretation take on the role of body for self-conscious social agents by being simultaneously the unconscious systems of life-support *and* the gestures that communicate mutual recognition. The self-conscious self proper is the "we," the social system enacted through interdependent "I"s, and social institutions thus provide the proper embodiment of self-consciousness, and this body is necessarily life-supporting *by being* communicative.

Self-consciousness thus properly exists insofar as it is embodied in social institutions that it is constantly in the process of reading. It is the full-fledged working out of this primacy of the embodiment of self-consciousness, and of this primacy of the textuality of the body, that is achieved in dialectic. It is in the dialectical method of absolute knowing that the essential features of self-conscious life that we observe in mastery and servitude and in the social life portrayed in *Antigone* come to completion, and here we will find the proper form of the Hegelian philosophy of language and embodiment.

Section 1 gives an analysis of the transition into "master and slave" that reveals the basic operations involved in communication. Section 2 gives an analysis of *Antigone* that reveals (1) what counts as the human self and the human body and (2) what is involved in the notion of duty. Section 3 considers dialectics and concludes that one can ultimately read only one's own body, and in so doing try to determine who one really is according to what is expressed in and through that body; absolute reading will be the reading that discovers its self to be this very act of self-reading, which means it will be a reading that sees the necessity for doing what it is doing inscribed in its text. In sum, for Hegel: (1) all meaningful experience is essentially reading; (2) all one can read is one's own bodily situation; and (3) *self-consciousness is essentially reading one's body, and it is the recognition of this that completes the development of self-consciousness.*

1. Communication and Embodiment in the Instituting of Slavery

The relation of master and slave is the first form of the collective institutionalizing of patterns of recognition; even though it is an inadequate form, it introduces this institutionalization, the more adequate forms of which provide the foundation for the full development of self-consciousness. For this reason, if we see what goes into the instituting here, we can see what is at the foundation of all developed self-conscious life.

Hegel sees the relation of master and slave as emerging out of a fight to the death of two individuals.[2] Until the advent of a second free self, an individual can function as the center of her world: she is a center who, by utilizing that world, shows that the disposition of the world depends on her will, and that her will is not molded by the things of the world. This feeling of independence is the primitive phenomenon of self-consciousness, but it must be transformed if self-consciousness is to develop. In particular, Hegel argues that the self must come to acknowledge its dependence upon other selves, which means setting up mutually acceptable patterns of behavior that grant due recognition to each other's status as equally self-conscious selves. The relation of master and slave is a first move in this direction, for it introduces institutionalized patterns of behavior; its inadequacy lies in its failure to institutionalize equality into the code of behavior. The impetus to set up any such system of institutions comes from the challenge posed to the self's feeling of independence by the appearance of a second self who equally feels her independence, and acts accordingly.

With the arrival of a second self who had so far acted from that same logic of felt independence that animates the first self, an obstacle is placed in the way of either one of them carrying out the acts that will confirm this sense of centrality, since in the other each faces a will that does not bend to her own, and rather tries to force her own will to bend. Hegel argues that the natural outcome here is for the two selves to enter into a fight to the death, each in order to win the recognition from the other that she is the real center of the world, and to show off that, as independent center, she can risk her life, since, insofar as she is independent, life is not something upon which she depends.

A situation of mastery and servitude comes about when one of the fighters chooses to recognize the other as the center, and simultaneously acknowledges her dependence on her life, and when the other fighter chooses to recognize this recognition and accepts the first one's self-subordination. The fighter who accepts enslavement confirms for the other that that other is indeed the center of reality; the fighter who assumes mastery can now be satisfied that the other was not a real threat, for that other really was a dependent entity, dependent first on her life and now on the will of the master who allows the slave to live. In mastery and servitude these fixed roles—these identities—are mutually recognized by the participant selves, and the habits they develop of acting in accordance with these roles are the social institutions on the basis of which their subsequent communal life is lived.[3]

In order to analyze some of the logical elements required to effect this change in relationship from mutually independent fighters to institutionally related members of a society, we can note first how this new relationship could fail to come about. To the extent that these individuals enter the fight bent on going to the death, the failure of either one to accept the new relationship will make the transition impossible. No matter how much the first self wishes to accept the second self's surrender, if the second is not willing to give up resistance the fight will not stop until one of them dies. Likewise, no matter how much the first self wants to surrender, if the second does not accept the offer they fight until death. The only way, then, for a relationship of master and slave to emerge is for both to bend their wills from the original course of destroying the other and for both to choose to accept a situation of unequal recognition. Now we can see that language and the body are essentially involved for this bending of the wills to be effective.

First, it is not enough, faced with such a situation, for the first alone to will her choice; her choice must also be recognized (chosen) by the second. It is essential that *each* be aware of *both* choices in order for this transition to take place. The choice of each "I" must therefore be a choice of a "we," and this mutual choice is what becomes habitual in social institutions.[4] But it is essential to thus establishing a "communal" consciousness of what the "we" chooses that the choices of each "I" be communicated through an expressing of their wills (and of their mutual recognitions), and through an understanding of these expressions. Language is essential to the formation of the institutional situation that is the foundation for the development of self-consciousness.[5]

Let us consider the slave-to-be. For her choice to be effective, she must express her decision to her opponent. The only means at her disposal are, of course, those over which her will has control, and this means her immediate living body and whatever implements this body can utilize. Up to this point this self lived through its body: her natural access to the world was taken for granted; that is, she overlooked the mediated-relation-to-the-world embodied in her "nature" in favor of the immediate relation to the object of desire made possible by the body's mediation. Now, however, she must change her body from an unconscious-means-for-satisfaction-of-the-will to a self-conscious-means-for-expression-of-the-will. It is only the *aisthetikos*, the intuitable, dimension of its life that is accessible to the other, so the self must now turn the essence of its body into gesture.

On the other side, the master-to-be can become master only through a recognition of the acquiescence of the slave. This requires, then, an understanding of the other's will, and the only access she has to this other is the sensible dimension of the other's existence, which means she must be able to recognize the body of the other *as* gesturing, and she must understand what the gesture expresses. Let us consider the acts of the master.

To be a master means to be an interpreter, which means asking and answering two fundamental questions: "Is there a gesture present?" and "What does the gesture indicate?" Answering the first question involves recognizing the other's body *as* a gesture, which means positing a unit, that is, determining that a certain extent of the other's body is to be treated as a single expressive totality.[6] Answering the second question involves seeing this whole totality as expressing a single meaning, which means seeing the total extent as embodying a unified intent. Interpretation, then, involves totalization and unification, that is, the positing of a determinate extent as a signifier, and the positing of a determinate intent as a signified. Reading thus demands that one assume that there is something to be read, and that this expression is the presentation of a unified meaning.[7]

The criterion for truth in this reading is success, for neither an unrecognized expression nor a misread body will stop the struggle to the death. Both expressing and interpreting—writing and reading—are open-ended projects in which one can never be assured that one has communicated oneself or understood the other except to the extent that one's projection of consequences is borne out by the behavior one encounters. Let us consider, finally, the issue of self-consciousness.

We can imagine a situation in which the slave-to-be is not gesturing, but the master-to-be either guesses from her actions that the slave-to-be would surrender or just offers surrender to the slave as a possibility, supposing that the slave-to-be might be prepared to surrender if asked. Here the slave must still communicate her acceptance of her slavery when asked; that is, the master-to-be may *ask* in the absence of any prompting gesture, but the possibility of adopting a new attitude of lordship in relation to the slave still requires that *the actions of the slave confirm this possibility*, which means that, *in the context of asking whether the slave accepts slavery*, actions are expressive and decisive *whether or not* the slave self-consciously intends to be gesturing. In this situation the slave's attitude *expresses itself* through its *aisthetikos* dimension of action.[8] More will be said about truth in interpretation in the last section, but for now let me recapitulate what we have so far found to take place in the communication within a "we."

In the case of the institution of the codes of behavior that found a society, to write is to use the accessible dimension of what was the lived body as a public expression; reading likewise means treating the accessible dimension of what was the lived body as an expressive gesture. We have seen this transformation from body-as-life-support to body-as-expression in the context of an individual agent struggling to convey significance to an intensely alien other, but the same basic logical relations remain in more sophisticated contexts. Writing and reading still involve using something sensible to convey something other than its own immediate sensibility, and the sensible vehicle will of necessity be a functioning feature of the world that normally supports one's existence, and over which one has control, even if a complex technology dramatically extends the range of what counts as one's body and one's sphere of bodily influence, as we shall see in Section 2.

I define "text" as that which, when experienced, must be experienced as calling out to be read: to experience it as text is to feel compelled to ask the question "what does this mean?" Our account so far allows us to say that text is what-used-to-be-body, and reading is projecting a single message into a posited totality of text. Our account of which behavior does and does not bring about a change in the relation of struggling egos has shown that a true reading is one that succeeds in integrating the totality of the text. To fully understand this last notion we need to get a better understanding of the lived body that can become text, for the institutionalization of social relations and the development of technology have implications for what counts as the body and its sphere of influence; in *Civilization and Its Discontents*, Freud likens the technological advances that come with social development to the emergence of a great prosthesis for the otherwise puny human body, and this image is not inappropriate.[9] This change in the conception of the body has implications for this logic of reading, and for determining what ultimately counts as an adequate reading. For this study of body and language in the context of social development, I turn to Hegel's analysis of *Antigone*, where we will also be forced to reconsider who is the reading subject.

2. Who Is Antigone?

In the emergence of the relation of master and slave, a social system takes the place of the individual ego in two important ways. First, it is the *institutions* that now define who the participant selves are; precisely what the selves collectively decide to recognize in acknowledging their commitment to the relation of mastery and servitude is that something other than their own immediate whims decides their identity. Second, as both selves become habituated to the relationship and their social system comes to function automatically without the continual need to reassert the order and to refight the struggle, both selves find their choices being made for them: it is not the immediate reflective decisions of the participant selves that initiate their behavior; it is rather the social order itself that makes demands on the action of the selves, and their habitual commitment to the social order is thus a subjecting of themselves to the decisive power of the social code—the law—to dictate their choices. Hegel argues that this unconscious commitment to the power of a social code for making one's ownmost decisions is necessarily involved in participation in society, and he analyzes the characteristic form this relationship takes—and the characteristic problems that attach to it—in his interpretation of Sophocles' *Antigone*.

Hegel sees Sophocles' *Antigone* as playing out the dynamics of the relationship in a traditional society between a supposedly divine law that is rooted in the patriarchal institution of the family, and the explicitly human law rooted in the institution of public, communal decision making that is the *polis*.[10] The central conflict is between Antigone and the ruler Creon, where Antigone's sense of duty to uphold her commitment to the divine law passed on through ritualistic family tradition drives her to break Creon's edict not to bury her dead brother. The necessity of habitual commitment to social institutions that we have seen to characterize self-conscious existence has implications for what we must recognize as the real nature of the human self and the human body, and through looking at Hegel's analysis of Antigone's sense of duty in her commitment to the divine law we can see more clearly what is the real self and what the real body of self-conscious life.

With respect to what counts as the human self, we must observe that when Creon and Antigone act, they act on the authority of law; that is, they both act as representatives of or agents for a greater subject: Antigone acts for what she sees as divine will, and what Hegel sees as the foundations of patriarchal association, while Creon acts for human law and the institution of the *polis*, that is, in and through Creon, the *polis* acts, and in and through Antigone, the will, so to speak, of the clan is carried out.[11] If one wants to understand the logic of Antigone's action, it will not do to ask her to report on her own motivations; rather, one must analyze the needs of the institution of the family, and even Antigone would say, "You must ask the gods": certainly her individual psychological history helps to explain how she got into the situation in which she acted as she did, but this will not account for all the mediation or significance implicit in her action. Only when her actions are "read" as actions on behalf of the family do they express a unified intent; to understand the reason for the action, we need to know why "the gods" demand this of her. We also need to know how she has been institutionally educated to understand how she is able to be immediately attuned to the gods' decrees, and in both of these investigations we are required to look beyond her immediate self. The "self" that really acts through Antigone, in other words, is more than her immediate personality. This "self" is that law that is the animating logic of the social relationships that characterize life in the clan.[12]

What is crucial in Antigone's actions representing the *law* is that *she acts the way she does because she feels herself compelled to so act*. Likewise, Creon opposes her out of duty, for he sees it as necessary that law-breakers be opposed. *For* both of them, their actions are law-governed; that is, their acts appear to the agents as necessary: the acts are not "chosen" by the agents; rather, it is as if the laws have chosen the agents, or, at least, they have chosen the agents' actions for them.

Antigone is faced with a situation—or rather, she is involved in a situation, and she can face it rather than live it; that is, she can make it an object that she notices rather than an environment within which she functions virtually instinctively, an environment within which there is an immediate relating of desire to its object by means of an unconscious system of mediation that operates automatically. This transformation of her lived situation into an explicit object comes about when she encounters an obstacle to her continued "automatic" living. Once her "facticity" has stopped being her lived world and becomes an object of reflection, she is called upon to react to it. Here again we see reading as interpretation. Antigone must "make" the object out of the lived world, and this involves deciding what is in the world, and what it counts as. She reads this situation as an offending of the divine law; she reads a hubristic individual violating the rights of her brother, and it is the divine law that animates her that *compels* her to read it this way. She alone, that is, she as an idiosyncratic ego, is not capable of making this decision (*Ur-teil*) about what her object is: the decision is rather made through her by the law that provides her "real self." And necessity does not just characterize how she responds once she has a text; rather, the initial act of positing a text is itself necessary. The unburied corpse presents for Antigone something she must recognize as an obstacle, for it is not something with which the logic of her life will allow her to coexist; in facing such an unassimilable obstacle, she has to ask, "What does this mean?" since the logic of the divine law dictates to her both how she must recognize the "this" and how she must characterize it. Having thus built in the differentiations and evaluations in the constitution of her text, the divine law now dictates to her the further reading of this text: the law requires her to bury Polyneices and resist Creon.[13] The same can be said *mutatis mutandis* for Creon. This account of duty and selfhood has implications for the human body.

We have really been asking who Antigone is, and we have found her real self—her real identity—to be defined by institutionalized patterns of mutual recognition within a society; that is, who she is is not defined by her immediate ego. Along with discovering the "greater" self that represents the law, we here learn that that body upon which this self depends is greater than Antigone's immediate shape would suggest. Body is that upon which the self's actions depend; it is the developed system of necessary preconditions that makes the fulfilling of one's desires or will possible. In order to carry out her deeds, that is, in order to enact the will of the self she really is—namely, the self as representative agent of a social, institutional system—a much more elaborate system of life must be in place for Antigone than the one considered at the level of the desiring egos struggling to the death, and this body is all the "material conditions" of social life. Antigone's very identity is *gebildet*—developed—and who she is rests on the social, institutional support that both provided her education—her *Bildung*—and now dictates to her the parameters of meaningful existence. These very institutions that form the substance of her identity as a self are equally what play the role of her substantial embodiment. The social institutions of life support, education, and so on are the automatically functioning systems of mediation that facilitate the relating of the will—here, the divine law—to its objects. In their absence, Antigone's real self cannot exist. So the institutions that maintain the existence of the natural and social identities, both of the single agents and of the total community, are the inconspicuously functioning system of material mediation that embodies the cultivated identity of social agents, and, as happened in the transition into a relation of mastery and servitude, this body of the socially constituted self is a self-expression and it can have its status change into an object that must be interpreted. Let me draw a few conclusions from these observations about the human self, the human body, and duty.

Through Antigone, Greek society reads itself. The self that reads through Antigone is, more particularly, divine law; the expression it reads is that material situation or social substance that used to be its own lived body; the need to read its own body and the way it reads are both dictated by its own internal logic. In sum, because Antigone acts from a duty that is socially instituted, her act enacts the self-cognition of Greek society. Of course, the same could be said of Creon's act: indeed, Antigone and Creon fight precisely because they are each animated by a one-sided logic, and their logics are mutually exclusive. In this case, both readings are equally justified, since each is legitimately rooted in the necessary institutions of their social existence. This is Hegel's point: both do read justly, and the contradiction of their readings demonstrates the contradictions at the heart of this kind of traditional society.[14] By going on now to consider what Hegel's reading of this society is, and how it differs from each of these readings, this account can be concluded in a theory of absolute or dialectical reading.

3. Absolute Reading

Let us consider *Antigone* again. It is perfectly understandable why Antigone reads the way she does, as it is equally intelligible what animates Creon. We can, further, acknowledge the necessity of their readings in the sense that we see how it is that, given their situations, there were no other real options open to them. Nonetheless, while each legitimately or truly represents the Greek self-interpretation (or, rather, each represents *a* Greek self-interpretation, and the two together in their interrelation represent *the* Greek self-contradictory self-interpretation), neither can be said to provide a philosophically adequate reading, and this is precisely what is shown by the opposition to each of an equally legitimate other—indeed, an opposition in which each recognizes the legitimacy of the opponent's position.[15] Let us recall what is being read.

Each is trying to see how a certain obstacle to her or his automatic reading can be integrated into her or his system of reading—Antigone reads that expressed by the presence of the unburied corpse in her world, and Creon reads that expressed by the presence of this rebellious woman in his kingdom. Each is faced with something that interrupts the familiar smooth functioning of a world in which the will can immediately relate to its object—each faces a disruption in the lived body; that is, the material system of support refuses to carry out the intent of the reading ("real") subject. Contradictions in the body (the text-to-be) force the reader to ask, "What does this mean," that is, they force the reader to turn her lived body into an explicit text.[16]

That animating logic (that is, the law) that forces each reader to interpret also determines and dictates how that reader must interpret; that is, this logic dictates what meaning is possible—how it is possible to fit the parts of the extent of the text together into a unified meaning. Here we can see the logical content of the second act of interpretation (unification): to find the signified in the signifier demands that one ask how it is possible to see the totality of the extent as unified in making a single expression, which demands that one ask for the rationality or intelligibility that can make the textual contradictions explicable: it must aim to see how each and all the components are necessary and relevant.

But (1) different logics will not all be capable of recognizing all the elements, and (2) different logics will also have differential capabilities for recognizing what can be rationally connected. Antigone and Creon are both animated by one-sided logics that do not allow them to recognize or respect the full integrity of the text in all its potential articulations. Neither has a sufficiently developed sense of rationality to really know rationality when she or he sees it; neither has read Hegel's *Logic*.

The basic demand of Hegelian reading is that the reading must be comprehensive, which means that the extent to which it excludes is the extent to which it fails. It cannot, therefore, begin by selectively rejecting certain phenomena as not part of the rationally unified text. The absolute reading will have to recognize the *integrity* of its text *in and through those disruptions that precipitated the reading*; this reading will be obliged to read with a rationality that reconciles contradictions.[17] There are two important implications to the comprehensiveness of this reading.

Note first that this reading that aims to reconcile everything is fundamentally at odds with the readings of both Creon and Antigone—each of whom has an a priori commitment to defend the institutional system whose automatic reading was disrupted—since the Hegelian reading demands the object be absolutely or unconditionally forgiven, that is, seen as good on its own terms.

Note second that this principle of comprehensiveness demands that the reading not exclude itself. The Hegelian reader must see herself—and herself *qua* act of comprehensive reading—as an essential element in the constitution of the text, and, as such, her presence must be accounted for in the reconciliation. This is, then, the third step in what I will formulate as the general conclusion of the *Logic*: the only approach to a text that can do justice to its multiplicity is the dialectical approach (1) that begins with the question "how is the totality I [must] face rational," (2) that comes armed with an ability to recognize rationality, developed by having worked through all the one-sided understandings of rationality and having been driven to the Hegelian dialectical reason according to which the thing (*Sache*) must be allowed to educate the reader into its own immanent rationality, and (3) that enters into dialogue with its object *precisely in order to see the ways in which its pre-reflective approach to the object has already been constitutive of the extent of and differentiations within the object,* that is, in order to see how its body is its expression.

We must not, however, make the mistake of identifying the reader with the idiosyncratic ego. The self-justifying reading is one that, like Antigone's reading of her situation, is animated by that ability to recognize reason that the reader has been compelled to develop or adopt, but the absolute reading must show that the source of its duty to adopt dialectical reason is pure reason itself. The point of the *Logic* is to reason about the adequate conception of reason in order to demonstrate this conclusion. With respect to our concerns for reading, this adequate conception of reason is that which comprehends itself in comprehending its text and which demonstrates the rationality of its own emergence in the same act in which it demonstrates the rationality of the rest of its textual composition. The self-justifying reading concludes when it can show how its act of questioning wrote its text, but, equally, how the necessity or duty for it to so write was already (potentially) inscribed in its text; it shows how its act of reading retroactively actualizes the potentiality of the text to have been demanding this reading.[18] The reader, in sum, must see how she wrote the text, but (1) the "she" who wrote the text was not her merely idiosyncratic willing ego, and (2) the text she "unwillingly" wrote prescribed the necessity for this act. It is the *real* self (as we defined this in Section 2, namely the self as already engaged in a "we" that provides its definitive identity) who reads, and this self turns out to be that which was always being expressed in and as the text-body; the absolute reader will be the one for whom the ability and the compulsion to recognize dialectical relations is constitutive of her real self, and her act—this real self's act—of self-reading will reveal her as such.

My reading, therefore, is absolute when it meets the following conditions: when the totality of being that I try to comprehend is that which I, as a self involved in the larger human self, am obliged by my situation to recognize; when the method of searching for its rationality is that which my intersubjectively and historically educated reason demands; and when the imperative to begin the reading and to carry it through in the way I have done can itself be shown to be inscribed in the text. Absolute reading thus occurs when my social substance reads itself through me, and when this act of self-reading/writing reads/writes an inscribed prescription to have so pre-in-scribed. Absolute knowing is the recognition that I can read only the autobiography I have always already been writing, or again, I can write only the autobiography I have always already been reading.

six
Hermeneutical Pressure: Intersubjectivity and Objectivity

We typically think of ourselves as free. We typically find our identities to be obvious, and likewise the identities of the things within the world. This straightforward recognition of things seems equally straightforwardly to impose upon us the ideal of objectivity in knowledge: like the identities of the things themselves, this ideal seems fixed in the very nature of things. Hegel's argument, however, is that all these identities—the sense we have of ourselves and of our world—and their attendant ideal of objectivity are products of fundamental acts of interpretation that emerge in response to the demands of intersubjectivity and that realize themselves as traditions of interpretation that conceal their own reality. By considering the figure of the slave from Hegel's *Phenomenology of Spirit* we can find a route into studying these founding acts of interpretation, and by considering Hegel's account of the inadequacy of self-conscious reason to account for the experience of duty we can find a route into studying the mechanism of tradition according to which tradition conceals itself by making other identities obvious. This will allow us to understand the dialectic of spirit as the phenomenon of freedom inasmuch as spirit will be the living enactment of the intersubjective interrogation of the tradition that is its own substance. This, equally, will allow us to see why our existence as single self-conscious agents must ultimately take the form of "unhappy consciousness." Throughout, my goal will be to show how Hegel's position in the *Phenomenology of Spirit* is responsive to the themes of Kant's Critical philosophy, and how Hegel's transformation of these themes—specifically the themes of objectivity, self-consciousness, and freedom—brings us, in Hegel's concept of "spirit," to a conception of human existence comparable to Heidegger's conception of the occurrence of being-there, the *Ereignis* of *Dasein*.

1. Objectivity: Hermeneutical Pressure, Slavery, and the Syntheses of Consciousness

There are ways in which most of us face the same situation as the slave. Like the slave, we operate in a world in which we have already made concessions and we face constraints. Like the slave, we inhabit a world in which we must labor and die. Like the slave, we must struggle to make sense of our environment, we must struggle to shape our environment, and we must struggle to identify ourselves through our engagement with our environment. There are other ways in which we are not like the slave. Unlike the slave, we operate in a world in which we have already been granted public status as free and equal to others. From the slave's situation, we can learn a great deal about the nature of the hermeneutical character of human existence, both because of the hermeneutical dimensions definitive of the slave's existence and because of what the slave is defined as lacking, namely, freedom.[1] Let us consider what it is to be a slave.

The slave must take orders from the master. The slave can die or be tortured, and it is in recognition of this that the slave accepts being ruled by another who threatens. The slave can die or be tortured because the slave has a natural existence—the slave is a body—that is vulnerable to bodily assaults from another.[2] The slave is a slave through fear of death at the hands and by the will of another. The slave is a slave by virtue of living a life that values staying alive over being unfettered.[3]

Hegel's analysis of this situation of slavery identifies two definitive structures of the slave's experience: *Furcht* and *Dienst*, fear and service (M194–196, W/C 134–136). The experience of the slave is characterized, on the one hand, by the universal presence of fear for its life, and, on the other hand, by the need to serve at the behest of another (the one feared). Both of these structures of its experience are structures of necessity.

The experience of fear follows from the definition of the master. The master is defined by the slave as the one who constitutes the essence of the situation. The master is the one who is entitled to dictate the form things take. The master, because she controls the slave self as such, that is, as a self, controls the totality of what the slave encounters. Therefore, the master's identity—the master's identity as ruler—is reflected to the slave through everything that the slave encounters. Everything, in other words, is the master's own, and its disposition is the master's alone. This is true for the disposition of the slave's own body as much as it is for the master's house, fields, and so on. There is, therefore, nothing the slave can do on her own initiative. There is, therefore, nothing the slave can do. Every determination that the slave encounters embodies the threat that the master constitutes for the slave; everything is worth more than the slave and has the power to condemn the slave on behalf of the master. The slave's fear for her life is therefore a universal fear, a fear that is afraid of the presence of the master that constitutes the essence of every determination encountered by the slave. Any act by the slave is thus necessarily a transgression of the limits of the slave's proper position, a transgression into the proper domain of the master, for in any action the slave takes it upon herself to determine the disposition of something in the world. In any action the slave takes initiative and therefore violates the definition of slave. The universal fear that is constitutive of the slave's identity thus takes the form of the imperative not to act. Being a slave means experiencing the necessity not to act. This is the universal element of its experience.

At the same time, however, the slave is not allowed not to act. To be a slave means precisely to be in the service of the master; that is, the slave must take orders and act on them. Exactly opposed to the slave, the master is the self for whom her desire is defined as automatically constitutive of reality. The master experiences reality as utterly unresisting. The master faces no need to accommodate anything. The master merely specifies her desire and the slave is required to effect the desired situation. Being a slave, then, means always being called upon by the master who defines the slave's situation to engage in particular, determinate tasks. Consequently, the slave's situation is also constituted by a second necessity that contradicts the first. Just as there is a universal necessity not to act, there are also particular necessities to act. These two contradictory dimensions of necessity are both utterly compelling and utterly definitive.

Within the world of the slave, there is a constitutive necessity not to act. There is also a constitutive necessity to act in various particular ways. There is a third necessity as well, and that is the necessity that these other two necessities "apply," as it were, to the self-same self: the slave cannot escape the bearing of these necessities upon herself as the center of initiative within her reality. The slave cannot escape the necessity that she *be* the one who is singularly responsible for negotiating this situation: it is her situation, and it is she who is the subject of these necessities, that is, both the one who is subjected to them (passive) and the one who has to deal with them (active). For the slave, the twin necessities of fear and service are both utterly compelling and utterly definitive, while being mutually contradictory. Being a slave means successfully negotiating this situation that is by definition impossible. Being a slave means experiencing these contradictory necessities as not a matter of abstract logic: the third necessity is the necessity that this contradiction be a compelling, lived problem and a lived demand for a solution. The slave as singular must contain this contradiction—her singularity *is* the demand to find a way to reconcile this contradiction.[4]

Whereas the master has no need to respect anything—the master can be as arbitrary and self-contradictory as she wants without violating her identity[5]—the slave must give up such prerogatives and develop an attitude of respect. Specifically, what the slave must not do is violate the identity of the master's world; what the slave must do, then, is *learn* how to act in such a way as to respect that identity. While in principle the existence of the master demands the necessity not to act, it is also true that the master is a determinate individual with determinate desires. Consequently, the slave can maintain her situation if she can find the ways to act that accord with the determinate nature of the master's desires, such that the master says, "you did what I wanted." In order to be a slave, that is, to maintain this situation that is inherently self-contradictory, then, the slave has to learn how to *interpret* the master's desires successfully. The slave must learn to interpret the situation according to the value of letting the situation itself dictate the terms under which it will tolerate approach. It is with the slave, therefore, that the issue of objectivity arises. The slave must learn how to respond successfully to the demands of the master—her ultimate object—by way of learning how to respond successfully to the demands of the determinate features of her situation—her proximate objects. What the slave has to learn is how to make her own actions not be actions that violate the parameters of her object—proximate or ultimate—but actions that that object will support.[6] The slave must learn to work with the things of the world in order to produce results that will satisfy the master. In place of the opposition on the basis of which the relation of master and slave is *established*, then, the relation of master and slave can be *realized* only through cooperation.

The ideal of objectivity arises, then, in the context of intersubjectivity, and it arises in response to the need to reconcile the contradiction that is definitive of self-identity. The ideal of objectivity is equally inseparable from the project of interpretation. Objectivity *is* interpreting the situation in a way that recognizes the weight of the demands of the other that (who) is the object. The issue of objectivity arises within this context in which something is at stake with respect to which it is possible to be right or wrong and within the context where the one who can be right or wrong is a being capable of interpretation. What is at stake for the slave is her very identity, her very existence, and it is only because she is an interpreting being that it is possible for her to be right in this context. The task of the slave involves interpretation at various levels: the slave must receive the orders, the slave must recognize them as orders, the slave must establish a plan to carry out these orders, the slave must enact the plan, the slave must present a satisfying result to the master. Let us attend a little more closely to the dimensions of the hermeneutical pressure that is constitutive of the slave's existence.

The primary task of the slave is to satisfy the desires of the master. To be a slave therefore requires that the slave be able to recognize a master and to recognize commands. Slavery is an intersubjective phenomenon: to be a slave is meaningful—is possible—only in a context of interaction of at least two self-consciousnesses, namely, the master and the slave. This "interaction" implies communication, for it is *qua* self-consciousnesses that they must interact. To be a slave, then, presupposes sending and receiving messages, which necessarily involves the essential use of the medium of contact: sense, intuition. To be a slave presupposes finding the medium of sense *meaningful*.[7] The slave must be responsive to what she intuits—the sensible realm within which the master must make an appearance.

This responsiveness means acknowledging what she intuits as calling for her to act upon it, to take it up: it requires interpreting what she intuits precisely as "to-be-interpreted." If this were not so—if the slave did not see what she intuits as calling to her to make sense of it—the slave could never recognize an order, for whatever sensible medium was chosen for expression (speaking, writing, pushing, etc.) the slave would receive it as a dead end:[8] she would be affected but nothing would follow from it. In order for there to be significance within the slave's experience, immediate appearances must be charged with significance—they must be recognized, interpreted, as significant, which means they must be interpreted as contextualized by other possible sensings to which they point: the slave must, for example, recognize that the pain in her arm is related to the sounds earlier heard if she is to be able to recognize a situation as "being hit for not obeying an order."[9] What would keep one from being a slave, then, would be to fail to take up one's intuitions *as* (1) in principle significant, as needing to be made sense of, and (2) already contextualized by a past and a future, that is, as open to meaningful combination with other intuitions. Only a being who can thus apprehend its intuitions as potentially significant and who can imagine other sensory situations upon which those intuitions could have some bearing (or that could have some bearing on them) could ever recognize an order, and it is only *as* enacting these interpretations that the experience of the slave is possible. Further, to recognize the potentially significant sensing that is thus noticed and collected *as* actually significant will require identifying the significance, the single identity, that pervades this whole: to recognize a master requires an ability to deal with terms that unify multiplicities or, as Kant says, representations that unite other representations: concepts. The slave must be able to recognize—understand—that the total extent of the imaginatively connected sensory whole expresses a single intent. In other words, the dimensions of interpretation that are necessary to existing as a slave are the same three basic syntheses of apprehension, reproduction, and recognition that Kant identified as the conditions of objectivity.[10]

The condition of the slave is one in which the demands of understanding and the pursuit of objectivity in knowledge (the form of which has been demonstrated by Kant) are not abstract or "academic" demands. They are the demands that emerge from the lived necessity to negotiate the impossible situation that defines the slave's existence. For the slave, objectivity is a "pragmatic" value, a response to "hermeneutical pressure." To be able to recognize an object—to be able to achieve objectivity in knowledge—is a necessary condition for being a slave, and we have now seen the most basic interpretive conditions that are inescapably necessary for recognizing objects. Hegel's dialectic of consciousness (in the first three chapters of the *Phenomenology of Spirit*) studies the emergence of the recognition of these interpretive syntheses within experience.[11] Hegel's phenomenology of consciousness shows these synthetic structures as developing one out of the other; Hegel shows that the very act of sensing ("Sense-Certainty") presupposes the contextualizing of experience into unities-through-difference ("Perception"), and that the recognition of such unities further presupposes that there is a general field within which these unities themselves are comprehended ("Understanding"). What is interesting in Hegel's account (and how it differs from Kant's) is that Hegel argues that it is desire that supplies the ground for the unification of the field of experience.[12]

Like Kant, Hegel will go on to show that there are issues of universality, necessity, and reason that must come to operate within the sphere of understanding, and that there are "impersonal" criteria that must be met in order to claim scientific, or "objective," knowledge. Hegel's argument, however, shows how these "impersonal" ("unbiased") criteria themselves emerge out of the dynamic of desire ("bias") and interpersonal relations.[13] Kant finds the foundation of all the structures of understanding in the transcendental unity of apperception, that is, in the need to be able to be a coherent self throughout one's experience, which means to recognize oneself throughout all one's experiences. It is this transcendental unity of apperception or self-consciousness that in Hegel begins as the attempt to realize one's desires in the context of dealing with desiring others.

Our employment of the slave to study objectivity is not arbitrary, because the situation of slavery is, according to Hegel, one of the essential situations that comes into being within the natural development of self-consciousness. The slave's attitude toward objectivity is an attempt to cope with the same pressures that are constitutive of all self-consciousness, which is, according to Hegel, an intersubjective affair in which our individual desires are challenged by the desires of others. By now considering self-consciousness on its own terms, and addressing the themes of desire and intersubjectivity, we can understand both why the situation of slavery emerges and why it is inadequate as an ultimate stance of self-consciousness. Having seen some ways in which we are like the slave, we can now consider ways in which we differ from the slave.

2. Self-Consciousness: The Tension within Intersubjectivity as the Context of Objectivity

In considering the notion of objectivity, we are considering the demand that an other makes upon us to measure up to its identity. In the context of the slave's dealings this has meant that the slave has to learn how to act upon the things of the world in a way that they will accommodate. This demand is contextualized by the more fundamental demand that the slave learn how to satisfy the desire of the master. These two demands are of the same general type, but they are significantly different species of the need to live up to the demands of the object. What makes the master a distinctive object is that the master's identity is not contained simply within the natural body with which she was born. The master's identity, on the contrary, is reflected through all the determinations of the slave's world (including even the slave's own natural body). The master, in other words, is not just one of the objects within the world, but is, for the slave, the defining essence of the world as a whole and all the things in it. It is the master's *desire* that defines the nature of the world.[14] (This, recall, was the ground of the universal fear.) Let us consider this notion of desire.

The reason the master is a distinctive object is that the master, like the slave, is a self-consciousness; that is, the master is that kind of being that can recognize its own desires and engage in the explicit project of shaping the world to accommodate its desires. Such agents—both the one who becomes master and the one who becomes slave—are, *qua* desiring, engaged in specifying what they take to be the significance of things in the world and of themselves. That demand for objectivity that characterizes slavery emerges only because of the constraints on the slave's desire (which emanate from the specifications of the master's desire to which the slave has made itself subject by bowing to the master's threat of force). The immediately desiring self-consciousness by itself, however, is not so constrained.

Desire begins precisely by refusing "objectivity" and by specifying itself as that which determines the nature, the significance, of things: desire is purely "subjective." Unlike what is the case for other things, for such desiring beings their own being is an issue, and they mark themselves as the defining powers within the world: *for themselves* they are other to all other things; that is, being other is not a passively received designation flowing to them from things outside them, but is precisely the self-definition they enact.

In facing another self-conscious being *as such*, then, one faces that being *as* a being that defines itself, and as a being that must *grant* one one's significance: one cannot be "objective" in one's view of this other unless one recognizes it as that which determines the significance of things, and that entails that it is that which determines the significance of oneself. Unlike other things, then, another self-consciousness puts up the most extreme demand of objectivity, for it does not immediately assent to the sense of its significance that one's desire immediately projects, and determining the identity of that other must therefore go by route of that being's own self-consciousness. It is for this reason that self-consciousnesses, simply in recognizing the existence of other self-consciousnesses, inescapably involve themselves in the demand for objectivity, which derives from the struggle to reconcile the opposed necessities that each (*qua* desiring self-consciousness) be the determining source of reality, and which ultimately amounts to the demand to establish a mutuality of recognition between oneself and that other. It is out of the slave's effort to deal with this kind of object that the relation of master and slave emerges.[15]

It is this tension of two would-be centers of meaning running into conflict with each other's desires that initially produces the situation of master and slave. Each begins as a desiring self, which means it begins as the immediate sense of its own importance in that it automatically construes whatever it encounters as "for it."[16] In encountering the other desiring self, though, each encounters another that resists this definition by the first self as "for it" and insists, on the contrary, that the first is "for it" instead. Given that this desire is constitutive of who each is, the interpretation of the other as "for it" is felt as a demand. This hermeneutical pressure leads each to attempt to force its view on the other, but in each case the other is in principle unable to succumb to this force inasmuch as this same hermeneutical pressure is constitutive of its very self.[17] The relation of master and slave is an attempt at a compromise: one agrees to give to the other the privilege of being the one for whom things are defined in exchange for leaving the forceful contest of wills. As I noted at the beginning, the slave is the one who gives up trying to prove that she is the real "for itself" in exchange for not being hurt or killed.

The nature of the intersubjective context that gives rise to this institution of slavery allows us, however, to recognize an incoherence built into this compromise. The deal that the master and slave strike is that both will recognize the master as the only one whose desires matter, as the only one who can choose what is the significance of things. This, indeed, is how the master seems to win the struggle of the opposed wills. The victory is merely apparent, though, for the deal is inherently self-contradictory. The deal, by its very nature as "deal," has already implied that the slave has choosing, desiring—interpretive—authority: in order to become the slave, the slave had to recognize the master as master; that is, the slave must be in a position to determine significance if the two of them are to agree to their mutual definitions. It is her status as a hermeneutical agent that has allowed the slave to become a slave, and this is equally the very status that the designation as "slave" officially refuses to the slave. The master, *not the slave*, is supposed to be the one who interprets things; yet it is precisely the slave's interpretings that realize the relationship. The form of the relationship (mutuality, equality) contradicts its content (non-mutuality, inequality), and this is displayed in its realization, as we have noted in the first section.[18]

Indeed, our whole study of the hermeneutical pressures of the slave has been done in the context of considering that section in which Hegel is describing those aspects of the slave's situation that show why the slave cannot truly be a slave; all these definitive hermeneutical pressures are precisely the marks of a free being. Hegel's point in the sections in which he discusses fear and service is that through the slave's own successful actions the slave is building in her products a mirror for—a reflection of—herself as free, that is, as an educated, powerful, desiring agent who has learned how to be objective, and cooperative. The things of the world that respond to the slave's efforts show that they endorse the truth of the slave's hermeneutics, and they thereby say something at odds with what the master—who is supposedly their truth—says. In her products, then, the slave faces objects that announce the falsity of the claim to which the master and the slave have agreed. In trying to be objective, then, the slave would ultimately be forced to confront the inadequacy of her own hermeneutical program of self-interpretation as slave and the interpretation of the master as master. In other words, consistently to carry out the project of objectivity launched—*constitutively* launched—by the project of slavery is to become self-critical, and to interpret the very situation of slavery as self-contradictory in the way we have just identified.

Let us summarize what we have learned from the situation of the slave. The need to do service for the master gives rise to the specific need to recognize the things of the world to which the Kantian analysis of objectivity applies. The fear of the master herself is what gives us the other as such as the ground for the demand for objectivity; that is, the specific hermeneutical pressures placed upon the slave by the determinate identities of her world are themselves contingent upon the more basic hermeneutical pressure of recognizing the master. Even this pressure to be objective, though, we have seen to be yet more fundamentally rooted in the very nature of the initiative of the slave-self; that is, it is only because her experience is inescapably her own and because she subjects herself to the hermeneutical pressure to be a slave that the whole system of pressures has a compelling power. The pressures, then, derive from the others, which in turn are subordinate to the pressure from the Other, which in turn is subordinate to the pressure from the self.[19] It is because this self is an embodied, intersubjective, hermeneutical power that the demand for objectivity takes this form: it is because to be a self-consciousness is to be a center who recognizes other centers and is thereby vulnerable to their communication that there is an ideal of objectivity, and this character of self-consciousness also shows us the form objectivity must ultimately take.

Since to be a self-conscious agent is to be a center of desire involved with other self-conscious centers of desire, we cannot ever succeed in being ourselves by ourselves, since our identity is in the hands of these other centers. It is only through shared commitments to a project of mutual recognition that this tension of being a de-centered center can be successfully navigated. We have also seen, though, that not every form of shared commitment will work, for a shared commitment to unequal status will contradict itself because of its own inherent ideal of objectivity. The hermeneutical situation of the slave, therefore, reveals to us that the only way we can be objective, which means the only way we can live up to the necessarily compelling demands of intersubjective life, is by mutually establishing systems of equal recognition, which means establishing systems of freedom. The intersubjective nature of self-consciousness entails the need to institute relations amongst ourselves in which all the participants are recognized as equal participants. This realm of equal recognition is what Hegel studies in the chapter of the *Phenomenology of Spirit* entitled "Spirit," and he there studies collective commitments to a shared sense of duty as the primary phenomenon of equality of recognition. Let us consider this phenomenon of a collective commitment to duty as a hermeneutical attitude of self-consciousness.

3. Freedom: Duty, Tradition, and Autobiography

We have so far considered the slave as reading. Let us begin now by considering the slave as writing.[20] We saw the slave's hermeneutics to be a hermeneutics of obedience, which amounted to learning as reconciliation of opposite necessities. This is a learning, however, that manifests itself as action, as the action of producing adequate responses to the orders of the master. The slave has to read the master's desire and, as it were, write back an answer. This writing, though, expresses more than just what the master wants to read. It also expresses the education of the slave. In being able to produce results by coop-eration with the master's world—cooperation with nature, and so on—the slave's actions evince a level of development, a level of power—indeed, pre-cisely a level of power to fulfill desires—that is lacking in the master. In the products of her own labor, the slave is constructing a mirror, writing an auto-biography, of herself as an educated being. The publicly existing—objective—products of the slave's actions thus stand as a monument to who the slave is: in recognizing her own products, the slave effects an implicit self-portrayal that is at odds with the official portrayal of herself that both she and the master endorse in their roles as master and slave. To the hermeneutical enterprises we discerned in our study of the slave's action we can now add the performatively self-exegetical act of interpretation that is the implicit inscription of auto-biography in the products that are the response to the hermeneutical pres-sures. Being objective and being self-expressive are thus inseparable activities of intersubjective life. We have studied these issues in relation to a particu-lar (unequal) approach to intersubjectivity; I want now to look further at the autobiography inscribed in the mutually endorsed commitments to self-definition that characterize our being free with each other. We must first consider the nature of freedom.

We typically think of ourselves as free, and by this freedom we understand the ability to choose for ourselves our values.[21] We portray ourselves as agents who have our options before us, confronting us as objects of deliberation, as agents who have the power to pick our values rationally, and as agents who know what choices we have made. At the end of his study of reason, Hegel challenges this essentially stoic conception of ourselves as self-conscious, rational, choosing selves who are responsible for selecting our own values and thereby enacting and demonstrating our freedom. In this section, Hegel considers the experience of duty as the fundamental phenomenon of rational freedom.[22] His claim in this section, following Kant, is that to experience duty presupposes that we are free beings, that we do have an experience of duty, and that the key to this experience is that we find ourselves compelled.[23] Hegel's challenge to the stoic conception of the choosing self comes by way of a phenomenological description of the experience of duty to an ethical imperative. To recognize a duty *as* a duty is to recognize it *as* necessary, which means to find it compelling. The stoic portrayal of choice—like Kant's own analysis— would require that the choosing self have its values present to it as objects upon which to pass judgment. Hegel's claim, on the contrary, is that the necessity in the experience of duty is not something recognized about the law as an object upon which we pass an interpretive judgment; rather, it is immediately felt as that which is obviously and immediately true, for to experience it otherwise is to experience it as subordinate to our own judgment, rather than as that which has power over ourselves. The experience of duty to an ethical law is not a discursive reflection but is an immediate intuition.

Like a neurotic compulsion, the experience of duty means finding the obviousness of a certain recognition inscribed in one's very being, in one's very body.[24] Antigone—Hegel's example—cannot live with herself when confronted with the unburied body of her brother. The necessity to bury the dead is as immediately obvious to her as the daylight, and it is disgusting and crippling to her to leave his corpse exposed. This, Hegel claims (contra the stoic), is the way in which we experience our own most basic values (M437, W/C 286–287).[25] Our values do not confront us as alien objects about which we make a deliberate choice, but appear as the very stuff of our reality, the very fabric of our identity. In this way, the lived experience of the ethical agent acts as an effective critique of the stoic conception of human freedom.

Contra the simple ethical agent, though, Hegel argues that these values are not, in fact, fixed in the nature of things, but instead, as the stoic rightly insists, they are rooted in our power of choice and interpretation. Rather than being divine commands, these values are the commitments made by the members of a human community. They are commitments to a mutual sense of self-identity, commitments whose institutionalization allows the members to function together cooperatively. These values, like the shared view of the master and the slave that they are a master and a slave, are the instituted self-interpretation— the self-inscription—of the community in which the identity of the whole and the relative roles of the various members are determined. It is precisely these values that establish the equality of recognition between the members of the community, for insofar as each identifies itself with these values, each has accepted the same principles of desire, and thus each, in endorsing its own desire, endorses the desire of the others: in such ethical—traditional—action, acting on behalf of "me" is always acting on behalf of "us."[26]

In acting out of duty, then, we think of ourselves as simply interpreting—simply reading off—the imperatives that constitute the essence of reality. We can illustrate this by drawing on Hegel's own example of traditionally established sex roles. The man who recognizes himself as heterosexual and who cannot control the fact that he finds desirable the woman walking down the street says "she is attractive," and he portrays himself as simply responding to the compelling demand uttered by the very being of the woman: he portrays himself as being natural and right and having feelings that are natural and right, and in this he receives the support and recognition of others.[27] In fact, however, our efforts to be thus ethical—and the ethical character of this choice is clear in the righteousness of the stand opponents take to homosexuality—and to respond to the nature of reality are more fundamentally a tacit self-portraiture than a response to "nature": they really are our display of the prejudices of mutual self-definition that animate our hermeneutical practices. We act out of a lived commitment to the intersubjective ideal of objectivity—being true to the nature of things—but our actions reveal the interpretive practices that we use to direct our initiative, just as the slave's actions in reading the master's desire—in being objective—reveal her initiative as a hermeneutical agent.

These dutiful actions are the actions in which we carry out the traditional practices of our culture. Our culture exists as a space in which we can recognize and be recognized by others because it has at its core a code for recognition, an instituted vision of "who we are." It is by perpetuating in our actions this communal tradition of self-interpretation—what Hegel calls "spirit"—that we are able to navigate our intersubjective life.[28] These very traditions, then, are themselves products of human initiative; the very way they appear to us, though, is as non-human—as divine, or as natural. Our traditional behavior, *qua* traditional, portrays us as subject to the gods or nature in precisely those contexts in which we are most human. It portrays us as necessarily compelled, when in fact we are historically, contingently committed. Like the slave's actions that realize her identity as a slave, our traditional practices explicitly portray us in a way that is at odds with who we have to be to perform these practices.

One thing we learned initially from our study of the situation of the slave and now from our study of tradition is that we can be wrong about who we are. We can operate from a constitutive sense of ourselves that the enacting of our experience shows to be inadequate. In particular, we have seen that any situation in which we define ourselves as not the hermeneutical agents that we are will have to be at odds with the very requirements of setting up such a situation.

We have seen the need to recognize the self as free. Now our first explicit sense of ourselves as free beings—the sense the stoic exclaims—is that "aha, I am free, I can choose for myself." This first sense portrays us as immediately in charge of our own value systems, that is, immediately able both to control them and, more fundamentally, to recognize them. This initial way in which our explicit self-recognition as free selves happens, while acknowledging something misrecognized by the slave, is on other grounds still inadequate to living up to the hermeneutical pressures of the situation of self-consciousness. What we have seen is that our freedom is initially lived in the form of our feeling compelled by traditional roles. Even though the experience of these duties is the experience of freedom—these experiences of duty are what allow us to be with others in mutually recognizable roles that are not specifically roles of subordination and domination—this experience of freedom, or "spirit," is not at all what we usually think of as the experience of freedom, namely, stoicism. Like the stoic, we typically think of ourselves as individual, rational agents who can explicitly choose our paths. In fact, the phenomenology of *Sittlichkeit*, of commitment to traditional, ethical duties, shows that our ownmost choices—the choices through which our familiarly recognizable self-identity becomes shaped—are not immediately our own. Our original choices are communal rather than singular, they are hidden rather than manifest, and they are compelling to our will rather than subordinate to it. We need, then, to conceptualize the nature of our free, self-conscious selfhood in such a way that we define ourselves neither as slaves nor as stoics. Let us turn, finally, to the vision of the free human agent that is implied in Hegel's argument that spirit—these traditional forms of communal self-recognition—is the fundamental phenomenon of free self-consciousness.

4. The Freedom of Self-Consciousness: The Self-Interrogating Spirit of Dialectic

From our analysis of the slave, we have seen why an adequate self-interpretation cannot portray us as slaves, namely, because we have a hermeneutical initiative; that is, we are free. On the other hand, we cannot portray ourselves as free in the immediate way assumed by the stoic. The stoic portrays herself as immediately capable of determining her own values. What we have seen, however, is that the very nature of duties—the very nature of the values to which we are committed—is that they are not immediately under our control. Our ability to recognize ourselves as immediately free, choosing agents is something that is made possible *by* these original valuings; it is not the source of these valuings. Contra the attitude of the stoic rationalist, for whom our own identity seems as obvious as our immediate freedom, as self-conscious beings our attitude toward ourselves must be the question, "what is the adequate way to interpret ourselves?"

What we have seen is that the interpretive reading of the object that operates *within* the presupposed parameters of our intersubjective life is itself a self-inscription that is not itself the object being read. The adequate self-interpretation will come when we bring to bear our demand for interpretive objectivity upon this very self-inscription. We must find out *through our writing* who we are: we must read ourselves through our self-expression. In other words, we must question our traditions, and read our identities within these traditions. It is by interrogating our traditions that we find out who we have been as hermeneutical agents.

What is the nature of this interrogation of the tradition, though? Do we know how to question? Can our questioning of the tradition be an opposition, in which and by which we simply announce ourselves as free of the tradition? Do we know which questions to ask? If we cannot simply be stoics and say that we are free selves who choose our own values, can we simply be skeptics who claim to be free of any compulsion to the point of not even acknowledging that we are selves, not acknowledging that we are the selves inscribed by the tradition?[29] Can questioning be the simple denial of the categories of traditional self-interpretation? Once we recognize that our traditional sense of ourselves as stoic selves is misrepresentative of the founding hermeneutical situation, the pressures of which give rise to our apparent stoic identity, are we thereby empowered to shrug off this false consciousness?

As does the stoic, the skeptic too easily entitles herself to be separate from the hermeneutical compulsions of intersubjective life. We cannot immediately step out of the identities we find ourselves living any more than we immediately stepped into them through our own choices. We are no more in immediate control of leaving them than we were in immediate control of making them. Consequently, our questioning of the tradition cannot be an easy skepticism. We cannot assume about ourselves that we know how to question ourselves, that our questioning will be our entertaining certain criteria as objects of deliberate evaluation, any more than we can treat ourselves as knowing our own commitments and as choosing our ownmost values through deliberate reflection. Like our founding values, our questioning must itself be something we find ourselves "given" by the hermeneutic tradition of which we are the self-expression.

Interrogating the tradition, then, must mean questioning the tradition according to the questions to which it itself gives rise. It is by initially giving rise to us as interpretive agents inspired by an ideal of objectivity that the hermeneutical situation itself can become an object of interrogation. We have seen this project emerge in the slave for whom the ideal of objectivity, by its own natural propulsion, should lead to a recognition of the inadequacy of the form in which the hermeneutical situation is being realized. Our analyses have introduced us to such recognitions by identifying disparities within the practice of the slave, and within the very concept of tradition, between the self-identity announced and the self-identity performed. It is for such disparities that we will question our traditions. Our questions cannot be simply external challenges (as come from the stoic or the skeptic who too easily thinks she is freely outside the tradition). On the contrary, our questioning of the tradition must be a challenge by way of a self-critique: we must first *find out* who we are and *what we are doing* before we can claim to be engaged in this interrogation; otherwise, our "questioning" will in truth effect a more fundamental endorsement of that tradition, for the self-proclaimed "questioning" will be at odds with the untouched dynamism of traditional identity that is tacitly reperformed by the "questioner": the "who" of the questioner cannot be so readily assimilated to our familiar selves. In other words, it is our very sense of ourselves that we will have to change if we are to question the tradition, for the sense of ourselves with which we are comfortable is precisely the presence of the tradition in us. It cannot, therefore, be from the secure position of this identity that the critique is launched, for the endorsement of this subject-position—by either its too simple acceptance or its too simple rejection—is precisely the endorsement of the tradition.

Our freedom, then, will be found in the self-critique engaged in by the founding hermeneutical power itself. Our freedom will be enacted as the turning upon itself of the hermeneutical response to the pressure for objectivity. Our freedom is something we will always find occurring in us and as us, but we cannot properly call our single selves the agents of this *Ereignis*, if we mean those familiarly recognizable selves of daily life. Such selves are the products of the hermeneutical power, not its source. What we are is the privileged location for the occurring of this self-interpretation, the space of dialectic. After the fact, we cannot fail to say that it is we who do this—we cannot fail to identify with this hermeneutical power—for its dynamism gives itself as our self-recognition. This inescapable self-recognition, however, is always a retrospective realization that "that's who I was": what the stoic and skeptic fail to adequately recognize is that we must always wait to be shown to ourselves by ourselves, which is the stance of the "unhappy consciousness," the consciousness that knows itself to be divided from its own dynamic source, and that finds itself there, in a world, with others.[30] And because this hermeneutical pressure and response is always intersubjective, it is always as a "we" that the hermeneutical power that is our identity realizes itself in its dialectical process of self-interpretation through self-expression. This is what Hegel means by "spirit": spirit is hermeneutics as this intersubjective interrogation of the tradition by itself.

seven

The "Freedom of Self-Consciousness" and Early Modern Epistemology

Denn die vernünftige Intelligenz gehört nicht dem einzelnen Subjekt als solchem wie die Begierde an, sondern dem Einzelnen als zugleich in sich Allgemeinen.[1]

"The Freedom of Self-Consciousness" is the title of the concluding section of Chapter IV, "Self-Consciousness," in Hegel's *Phenomenology of Spirit*. This section has been variously interpreted in the last few decades. In Alexandre Kojève's influential *Introduction à la Lecture de Hegel*, the three forms of this freedom of self-consciousness—namely, stoicism, skepticism, and the unhappy consciousness (*das unglückliche Bewußtsein*)—are understood as "slave ideologies," that is, they are various unsuccessful strategies by which the slave defers an act of rebellion by instituting some form of intellectual escape from slavery.[2] H. S. Harris, on the other hand, sees this as history's first entry point in the *Phenomenology*; this line is followed by many interpreters who stress the references to Hellenistic philosophy in "Stoicism" and "Scepticism," or who argue about how well "The Unhappy Consciousness" portrays medieval Christendom.[3] My own approach accords more with work by John Burbidge and others who stress the transportability of the *arguments* of these sections.[4] In particular, my analysis would focus on how the forms of the freedom of self-consciousness provide universal and necessary stages in the development of the completed form of self-consciousness that is achieved in the third stage of unhappy consciousness.[5] My purpose here, however, is not to consider the position of this section in terms of the intrinsic demands of the argument of the *Phenomenology*. Rather, I want to take advantage of the transportability of these forms of self-consciousness to develop an account of how Hegel should be understood as responding to traditional problems in seventeenth- and eighteenth-century epistemology. In particular, I want to bring out how the forms of the "Freedom of Self-Consciousness" work out epistemologies of rationalism, empiricism, and transcendental idealism, and systematize these positions in a way that shows us why their characteristic problems emerge and how the problems should be handled. It is in this sense that my ultimate goal is to show how and why the "unhappy consciousness" is the key to Hegel's epistemology.[6]

This chapter will be a consideration of this primacy of unhappy consciousness from the point of view of epistemology, with a special focus on Cartesian epistemology.[7] I will ultimately show how it is that this epistemology of unhappy consciousness of which Descartes is such a powerful exponent is equally the basis for Hegelian epistemology; the basis, but not the completed form, for in Hegel this epistemology transforms itself in a way that simultaneously perfects and destroys the Cartesianism from which it arises. Essentially, the Cartesian form of the argument will produce a distinction between transcendental and empirical selfhood and a dualism of mind and body. The full development of this argument, however, will lead to a conception of reason as self-determining, which would in turn lead us to reject the mind-body dualism of Descartes and to replace it with a dialectical phenomenology of reason as self-embodying. Let me begin this journey by explaining what is behind my reference to "an epistemology of unhappy consciousness."

1. Stoicism, Skepticism, and Empiricism

One of the most distinctive features of the so-called Scientific Revolution is the assertion that knowledge is something that one can attain on one's own, by one's own efforts. Any one of us, evidently, can be a scientist, for the essential tools that are employed in the search for knowledge are our reason and our senses: we need to be able to observe what goes on and to be able to appreciate how what happens happens according to a rational order. This focus on the independence of the mind in the pursuit of scientific knowledge that we associate with such names as Bacon and Descartes is equally the focus in "Stoicism" and "Scepticism" in Hegel's *Phenomenology*.

The stoic is the agent who recognizes her own self-containedness. The stoic recognizes that her choices reflect herself and herself alone, in that there is no external force capable of compelling her will to move.[8] Thus any choice she makes is clearly her choice, her responsibility. This means, then, that whatever she accepts as truth is something for which she is accountable: what she accepts is what she chooses to accept, and thus, just as nothing external can force her will, it is equally the case that no external authority can be invoked to justify her adherence to her beliefs. In particular, whatever she chooses to accept about reality is precisely that: it is precisely how *she* has *chosen* to interpret what confronts her, whether what confronts her is scientific data, simple observations, or authoritative opinions.[9]

This, then, is the double-sided emergence of the scientific initiative: it is both the *liberation* of self-consciousness from reliance upon authority and the *responsibility* of self-consciousness not to rely upon authority. The freedom of self-consciousness is thus just as much a discovery of new power as it is an acceptance of a new limit. Indeed, it is the shifting emphasis on these two sides of this freedom that marks the development through the three forms in Hegel's "Freedom of Self-Consciousness." Hegel's category of "Stoicism" primarily marks the primitive recognition of this freedom, and the recognition takes the form of differentiating the sphere of one's choice from the sphere of those things over which one has no control: I cannot, for example, control what goes on in your sphere of choice, or in the sphere of natural causality; in other words, the "insides" of the things I encounter are outside the sphere of my choice, but, equally, this demarcates the sphere of my choice as something independent of the choice of others or of natural causality.[10] Stoicism thus involves an inherently atomistic anthropology, and it is not hard to see how the posited alienation from nature will equally make epistemological skepticism its real outcome.

The best the stoic can offer as a scientific method is careful observation and rational judgment on that observation. This (empiricism, basically) is no small offer to be sure, but in such an immediate and indeterminate form this epistemology can do little to answer serious challenges.[11] The stoic wants to be responsible in taking account of why she believes what she does, but really to give a fully rational account of her observations will involve acknowledging that these observations are precisely limited to being *her* observations, and there is no ground by which she can justify generalizing the particularities of her experience to universal claims about existence in general. What would be required to do so would be to be able to claim that her experience is representative (of experience as such), but this is precisely what she cannot do, since her initial premise was her alienation from the essence of nature and the essence of other selves, so, in the absence of some claim of an immediate identity between her thought and reality, there is no justification for assuming either that others see things the same way or that nature always shows a typical face. And the claim about an immediate identity of her thought and truth is absent, since (1) an alienation is initially posited, and (2) even if the claim *happened* to be true, there would again be no way for the stoic to know this or, even if she had some such intimation, to prove this.[12] Thus really to take responsibility for her judgments on her observations, the stoic scientist must admit that she has no science; indeed, the stoic must ultimately conclude that science is in principle impossible—the stoic must ultimately become a skeptic.

The experience of the power of singular self-consciousness thus turns into the experience of the limit.

Stoicism begins in an attempt to differentiate that specific kind of reality that one has as a self-conscious self from the reality of whatever is not self-conscious, but this attempt itself concludes in the impossibility of making this differentiation, for there is nothing to which one has access from which to make this differentiation. Skepticism is the recognition that all one encounters has ultimately the same status of being products of one's own powers of choice and judgment: all being is essentially the same, for all that exists is my experiences.[13] Hegel's description of the skeptic self as a "medley of sensuous and intellectual representations" perfectly matches Hume's characterization of the self as a "bundle of perceptions," for precisely this reason: all there is is experiences—"idea and impressions"—and there is no possibility of situating them in a scheme that differentiates the two poles of self and other, for these two are themselves at best constructions *within* experience, and not self-subsistent items to which experience could ever have or justify access.[14] There is thus only one accessible reality, and this reality does not permit scientific claims about anything beyond itself.

This conception of the essentially stoic self underlies the epistemological debates of early modern philosophy, and the problem of skepticism is its real driving issue. This stoical self with a skeptical epistemology is visible in Locke's empiricism, with its emphasis on recognizing the limits of human knowledge, in Hume's focus on the problems surrounding induction, analogy, and necessary connection, in Descartes's response to skeptical arguments with a self-certain ego that passes judgment on sensation, or in Kant's "Copernican Revolution" that limits knowledge to things as they appear rather than to things as they are in themselves. Clearly, then, Hegel's treatment of this dialectic will be pivotal for understanding his relationship to early modern epistemology. Let us look further at Hegel's treatment of skepticism.

Every shape of spirit studied in Hegel's *Phenomenology* plays a double role: it simultaneously (1) marks out a real phenomenon of, and permanent possibility for, human existence and (2) enacts the self-destruction of an inadequate candidate for the status of the absolute nature of spirit. In relation to skepticism, this means that (a) there really are essential experiences of being divided from others and of having no ground for making decisions, but (b) this is not an adequate characterization for the whole reality of human life. A schizophrenic, for example, may live out the exact life of the skeptical self, finding a constant contradiction in every possible decision or action, being unable to stabilize the flux of experience, and to have an integrated experience of selfhood.[15] Further, the general demand that one establish that one's perceptions are representative before going on to make universal and necessary claims about the real nature of things is an absolutely legitimate demand, and has problems attached to it that makes a skeptical response to many claims entirely justified. In these senses, skepticism is not to be overcome, in Hegel or anywhere. *As a characterization of the fundamental nature of self-conscious selfhood as such,* or *of knowing as such,* however, it is inadequate, and this is the direction Hegel's critique takes.

The skeptic self is, on the one hand, not a determinate being apart from the appearances, but is just the assemblage of these appearances, and this is the claim that the skeptic puts forth as an adequate characterization of the nature of self-conscious selfhood. Yet it is just as true, on the other hand, that the skeptic self *is* a single self that opposes itself to ("negates") this flux and multiplicity inasmuch as the skeptic is the single point of view (what Hegel would call the simple power of "negativity") for which there is experienced difference, and which recognizes the insubstantiality of these determinations of appearance.[16] Even though the immediate "show" of consciousness is already a product of self-conscious negativity, that is, of perspectival judgment, and even if self-conscious negativity or intentionality must be recognized as the very substance of appearance, one can logically differentiate, as distinguishable moments within the negativity that is self-consciousness, (#1) that negation that is the implicit *pre*-judging that has already operated in providing for the self a world of appearance from (#2) that negativity that is the explicit judgment that is called upon to assent to or dissent from these appearances.[17]

The actuality of the skeptic self is precisely the unreconciled relation of these two aspects of selfhood, each of which depends on the other: "it pronounces an absolute vanishing, but the pronouncement *is,* and this consciousness is the vanishing of what is pronounced."[18] Arguing on the one hand that the self is just the flux of appearances presupposes the stasis of the self as the unified power of recognizing that posits the appearances as merely appearance; to argue on the other hand that this self-identity is the true determination of skeptical self-consciousness, one must presuppose the presences of those immediate appearings that constitute the consciousness of which this unified self is the agency and orientation, and upon which it thus depends as upon its "materiality." Skeptical self-consciousness is in bad faith: it claims both that the self is the static, unitary, self-consistent power of negation (intentionality) that (to use Kantian language) supplies the (negating) form of consciousness, and that the self is a flux of multiple, non-self-subsistent determinations that supply the (negated) matter of consciousness, without admitting that it is saying two different things; indeed, to maintain either claim alone requires maintaining the other in its place: "its deeds and its words always belie one another and equally it has itself the doubly contradictory consciousness of unchangeableness and sameness, and of utter contingency and non-identity with itself."[19]

In epistemological terms, this means that it is not possible simply to deny any ground for knowledge within the sphere of self-conscious selfhood. While it is true that "the self" is not another datum alongside a set of units of information given without intrinsic connection, it is not true that there is no reality to selfhood as a phenomenon in its own right. Equally, while it is true that there is no access to some other object of knowledge *outside* the sphere of self-conscious experience, it does not thereby follow that knowledge of truth is impossible. What the phenomenology of the skeptic self reveals is that there is a complexity and an intrinsic dynamism *within* self-consciousness that is itself sufficient to play all the roles in knowledge: experience may well be only the self's experience of itself, but this "self" *is not in immediate and full self-communion*, and, indeed, experience is precisely this self's experience of itself as *opaque* to itself. Thus the self may itself be the truth or the reality of the objects of experience, but truth, reality, and objectivity are no less true, real, and objective on that account.[20] The discovery of the two correlative aspects within self-conscious selfhood—the moment of overarching negation and the determinate moments as negated—reveals that there is as much difference and lack of self-identity within self-consciousness as there is identity, and the dynamic of selfhood will simultaneously be the pursuit of self-consciousness and the pursuit of knowledge as such, and it will take the form of the transformation of the immediate identity (and, equally, the immediate difference) of these two sides into a fully developed systematic relation. It is the "unhappy consciousness" that provides the basic character for this completion of self-consciousness and of knowledge.

2. Unhappy Consciousness and Scientific Rationalism

What primarily characterizes unhappy consciousness, especially in relation to questions of epistemology, is that the unhappy consciousness *finds itself compelled* to be the being that it is: unhappy consciousness is the experience of necessity *within* the sphere of its own self-conscious selfhood.[21] A stoic epistemology posits the independence of its own rational powers, but posits this independence as an isolation from the world that will ultimately be the intended object of its knowledge. The skeptic epistemology emerges from the recognition that this stoic positing of self-independence as self-isolation in fact precludes any coming to identity with the intended object of knowledge, and skepticism posits instead the ultimacy that the self only deal with itself. The unhappy consciousness accepts the skeptic claim that there is only the independent world of the self, but acknowledges, further, that this is not an immediately harmonious world and that the alienation that the stoic posited between the knowing subject and the world that is its would-be object is in reality the opacity of the self to itself. The unbridgeable gap of subject and object posited in skepticism is overcome in the recognition that the self is indeed after itself in cognition, and the meaninglessness of the empty self-identity or of the equally empty absolute differentiation that characterizes the stoic/skeptic epistemology is overcome in the recognition that complete self-identity within experience is not immediately present. Unhappy consciousness recognizes a play of identity and difference within self-identity, and this is the foundation of systematic knowledge.

In the *Phenomenology,* Hegel draws his illustrations of the phenomena of unhappy consciousness from the world of religious devotion, for it is here that there is manifest a self-conscious self that distinguishes *within itself* an apparent self and a real self, and recognizes that real self as what guides the self it apparently is. We need not consider these religious images, however, to understand the basic logical relations of this form of self-consciousness, especially as regards their relevance to epistemology.

Unhappy consciousness is logically subsequent to stoicism and skepticism, because it involves the recognition that "I am myself the substance of my whole experience" or something similar, but within this recognition that the self encounters only itself the agent can identify those aspects of experience wherein it finds that what it itself does is something it *has* to do: the unhappy consciousness is the self that finds compulsion *within* itself; that is, *who it really is* forces it to act in ways that are not under its own *immediate* control. Unhappy consciousness is thus the self that finds itself subject to an intrinsic necessity.

There are three essential forms of this unhappy consciousness.[22] In the first form, the apparent self posits a real self that makes its decisions for it, and this real self is conceived of as entirely alien to the apparent self: the dualism of inner and outer that characterized the stoic metaphysics is here reintroduced *within* the sphere of self-conscious selfhood; here, however, both of the sides of this duality are the self, and the apparent self thus puts itself in the moment of the outside, with the impenetrable other moment posited as its real inner self. The first form of unhappy consciousness recognizes itself as essentially the moment of negated consciousness *for* the real negating self, which is the source of necessity that directs the life of the apparent consciousness but that does not in turn suffer any influence from the apparent self. The second form of unhappy consciousness still posits this mutual alienation, but posits a third term mediating between the two extremes. In terms of the religious images of Hegel's presentation, this is Christ the god-man who mediates humanity to the godhead; in terms of our epistemological story, we would see such a mediating term in sense data taken as that which we can perceive truly and which can lead us to the truth of our object, though it is itself not directly perceivable. The second form of unhappy consciousness is the approach to a dynamic of real and apparent selfhood that posits some similar intermediate in the process of the apparent self trying to come to terms with its real identity. This is again a self that wants to identify with its own real, governing selfhood, but that posits an impenetrability there, and looks instead to substitute means, rather as someone claiming to be a Hegelian might, when challenged, refuse to turn to direct explication of Hegel's text to justify her claims, and turn instead to commentators. What matters for our account, however, is not these two preliminary forms that repeat errors characteristic of stoicism and skepticism within this new context, but the third, completed form of unhappy consciousness.

In the third form of unhappy consciousness, the alienation of the real and the apparent self is not the first premise: for the first form, the two are taken as simply separate; for the second form, the absolute isolation that is the implication of this simple separation is recognized, and to overcome the isolation the real and the apparent self are taken to be related indirectly through their respective relations to a common third term. For the third form of unhappy consciousness, the apparent and the real self are taken to be *already* in relation *in themselves*, and the two terms do not thus stand in a dualistic relationship. It is here that we see the proper appreciation of the two moments of negating and negated selfhood that we first discovered in the skeptic epistemology that failed to recognize their difference. Here, the apparent self *is* capable of identification, indeed, already is identified in principle, with its real self, and the actualizing of this identification is precisely the overcoming of the opacity within its experience. The apparent self comes to identify with its real self when it explicitly responds to its experience *as it finds itself compelled to respond*, for here, in allowing itself to be directed by its own intrinsic necessity, its own experience of necessity, it is acting as the representative—as the real appearing—of the real self. From the point of view of our epistemological concerns, the unhappy consciousness is that agent who distinguishes within her experience a set of decisions and choices that are arbitrary and idiosyncratic, and that set of decisions to which she is driven by her very nature—by the very demands of self-consciousness as such. The unhappy consciousness knows it is in truth when it can show that it is acting the way it is compelled to act by its nature as self-consciousness, which means when it can show how its judgments are judgments that are demanded universally and necessarily of self-conscious agents. The stoic found freedom in an ability to assent. The unhappy consciousness finds truth in its ability to have its assent compelled. Truth is found in the universal and necessary judgment, for when she makes this judgment the apparent self acts as the legitimate representative of the real self, which means her judgment is one that she legitimately passes on behalf of any who share in the nature of self-consciousness.

Articulated in this way, unhappy consciousness is clearly the category in which Descartes's rationalism is to be placed. Descartes argues that it is only knowledge derivable on the basis of self-consciousness as rational self-cognition that can count as access to truth, for it is here that any agent *qua* self-consciousness is compelled to assent. Notice that this is like the stoic position in that it is the single agent herself whose own singular selfhood compels the assent, but because it is a compulsion that derives from the very nature of self-consciousness as such, it is a compulsion that will equally affect every self-conscious agent singularly.[23] The fact that it derives from the nature of self-consciousness as such implies its universality; the fact that it is *not* an external authority of the sort the stoic self can ignore but compels each agent *singularly* and *intrinsically* implies its inescapable necessity. Just by understanding Descartes's arguments, then, one is compelled to assent to them.

It is important to see that Descartes is not simply a stoic. It might have seemed initially that stoicism, skepticism, and unhappy consciousness would neatly parallel the trio rationalism, empiricism, and idealism, but in fact the rationalism of Descartes and his successors is far more sophisticated than the logic of stoic assent, and is itself already closer to the Kantian and Fichtean arguments normally titled "idealistic." The key to stoicism, remember, was simply the discovery of the self-containedness of the immediate, singular ego; this conception really gives foundation only to a naive empiricism. For Descartes, however, *that ego is not* the one who apprehends truth: it is only that ego *after having gone through the purificatory trials of skepticism* in Meditation 1, and *after having discovered a sphere of compulsion within its experience* in Meditation 2, that is in a position to know. The Cartesian ego must essentially distinguish what in Kantian language we call a transcendental and an empirical ego, where this transcendental ego is the universal and necessary demands upon experience that impinge on each self-conscious agent singularly by virtue of that agent's nature as a self-conscious self. Truth for Descartes, then, does not come simply through the immediate efforts of the immediate ego, but emerges through the mediating process of the empirical ego coming to identify with the transcendental ego. Let us consider what this means in relation to Descartes's actual argument.

The second meditation in Descartes's *Meditations on First Philosophy* contains the argument that is the foundation for Descartes's response to the universal skepticism developed in the first meditation and, consequently, the foundation for his epistemology. Essentially, the argument is that any attempt to deny one's own existence is self-refuting, for it enters into an *immediate self-contradiction* by announcing a conclusion that is at odds with the very enacting of the announcement. To say "I do not exist" is simultaneously to posit and enact an "I"—a subject, as agent of awareness for which this putative nonexistence is the object, the observation—at the same moment as *this very "I," this very denying agent,* is posited as not existing. The statement is the performance of its own falsehood.[24]

The basic argument is easy enough to follow, but its significance is by no means obvious; I will here develop the implications of this argument, and maintain that the actual logic of the argument is, in fact, very close indeed to what Descartes says it is. From this argument that " 'I think' is true every time I utter it" will be derived the notions of self-refutation, of experienced necessity, of universality and necessity in (self-)consciousness, of the distinction between mind and body, of transcendental and empirical selfhood, of the insufficiency of finite selfhood to account for its own infinite ideas, and of the impossibility of global skepticism. We must begin in this endeavor to explicate the *cogito* argument by asking, "*Who* is the self whose existence has been thus proved?"

The question "who?" is itself asked by Descartes, and his answer is that it is "I" *as* a thinker—as *res cogitans*—that cannot doubt its own existence. The first meditation has established that much of the way things immediately appear to me is dubitable, and this is as much true of the identity of things in the world as it is of my own identity. When it is established that, *qua* the agent doing the doubting, my existence cannot be doubted, the "I" whose existence is proved is not the "I" that I normally identify as me—I am not, for example, a "rational animal," or anything else that has been posited by an imperfect philosophy— rather, the "I" whose existence is proven is precisely the agent defined by the necessary conditions for the possibility of doubt. We will go on to specify these conditions, but let us first note what we have already established, just at a formal level.

We have established a distinction within selfhood between those aspects of selfhood that are necessary and those that are not; as indicated above, the argument of the second meditation works for *each* and *any* reader, which means that (1) it is "personal," that is, it speaks to each of us in our uniqueness as "this self," as "I," but (2) it does not attach to any of the idiosyncrasies of the self, but only to those features that are universally present in self-conscious selfhood as such. Indeed, feature (1) is just an instance of feature (2); that is, being individualized is a universal and necessary feature of self-conscious selfhood. The distinction above between the self as it immediately appears to itself and the self whose existence cannot be doubted has become the distinction within the self between the "I" as idiosyncratic and the "I" as universal and necessary, that is, between the empirical ego and the transcendental ego. Let us turn to a further characterization of the self whose existence cannot be doubted.

Let us first consider what is the criterion that gives us truth in this *ego, cogito* argument. It is the experience of necessity, or rather, it is the threat of immediate self-contradiction, that is to say, the experience of the "necessarily not." This same criterion for argumentative certainty is invoked at another crucial juncture, this time in the third meditation. It had seemed that the truths of mathematics could be doubted, but in the third meditation we discover that this is not so: it can seem so only for so long as one does not actually *think* about what one is saying. While it seems to be a logically entertainable idea that an all-powerful god could deceive us even about these things, the content of this idea undermines this formal possibility:

> Yet every time I turn my attention to those very things that I think I perceive with such great clarity, I am so entirely persuaded by these things that I spontaneously burst out with these words: "let him who can deceive me; as long as I think that I am something, he will never bring it about that I am nothing, or one day make it true that I never existed, because it is true now that I am; nor will he ever bring it about that two plus three yield more or less than five, or that similar matters, *in which I can recognize an obvious contradiction*, exist."[25]

In an arithmetical puzzle, for example, to think the quantity "2" and simulta-neously to think another quantity "2" is no different than to think the quantity "4," and the operation of summation does not add any new material to the added quantities: addition is just the act of synthesis in and by which the two thoughts of quantity are held together in and as a single thought. So to think "$2 + 2 = 5$" is to think "$4 = 5$," which is to think "$4 = \text{not-}4$" that is, to simultaneously affirm and deny the identity of the thought of 4. Immediately apparent contradiction, then, is the criterion of truth because it is that which the ego cannot resist: its very existence *as this ego* has implications; that is, its very identity prescribes assent to, and dissent from, certain claims. The key to this Cartesian epistemology, then, is the notion of self-determining self-integrity that exists as an act of resistance to self-contradiction. Now let us consider this self-identical act of self-affirmation, to see how the autonomy of this self that is structured by universal and necessary truths is equally a self that must not be defined by any bodily involvement.

The very nature of the ego is that it is *in its being experienced as me* that this "I" has its identity.[26] This is the ego whose existence is proven, for (recall our discussion of the criterion above) the proof comes precisely in the immediate self-contradiction that would be *experienced* by positing this self's non-existence; therefore, whatever extraneous conditions might characterize the existence of the ego do not affect this argument.[27] This is simply an *autonomous* derivation from the very concept of being self-consciousness, and it is in no way dependent upon body unless one can show that body is already necessarily involved *in its very concept* (which would be the Hegelian tack).[28] But Descartes's argument has aimed to show that body is *not* involved in the concept of self-consciousness, for he can doubt body without doubting self-consciousness, so, if body is thus external to the concept, it is external to the existence. From here, of course, comes the celebrated dualism of mind and body, and its attendant problem, namely, that if mind and body are utterly independent substances, they can have no communication, yet it seems they do communicate. For now, however, that problem need not concern us; we need only see that it follows quite naturally from the argument about self-consciousness that *self-consciousness must be autonomous, which means its external conditions cannot affect it.*

We have, then, a clear picture of the subject of knowledge, namely, the self-conscious, autonomous ego, driven only by a self-determining necessity that resists immediate self-contradiction. This ego is further specified through Descartes's argument.

The wax argument in the second meditation essentially continues the story of the self-determining nature of self-consciousness, arguing that the form our experience takes is given by intellect. Descartes describes this feature as the claim that "the human mind is more known than body," and the argument about the wax serves to establish that "clear and distinct ideas," that is, structures of significance that are constitutive of self-conscious experience, function as the innate grounds of meaning.[29] The argument works essentially as follows. A given piece of wax continues to be recognized by me as one and the same piece of wax despite the transformation of each and every one of its sensible features; indeed, I would recognize the self-same wax through more changes than I can imagine. Consequently, it can be neither sensation nor imagination that is the foundation of the recognized identity of the wax; rather, it must be the mind that approaches its sensation with the predisposition to recognize substantial unities "stretched out" through spatial and temporal continuities, which latter are themselves features, then, of what must be an innate idea of body. A substantial unity, in other words, is not something that is *seen*, but something that is *understood*. Such an idea of a spatially and temporally continuous substance—a "body"—is a logically clear idea and a logically distinct idea. It is the foundation of one's determinate experience, while not being itself a content derived from that experience; that is, it is innate, rather than adventitious or factitious. Innate ideas, then, are not products of my imagination, but neither are they received from without; thus they are internal, but I am subject to them, rather than vice versa.

Since I thus find them as constitutive of my experience, they are the grounds of truth in experience. These ideas are really of two types. The first type is the type we have already seen in the demonstration of the existence of the thinking self, and in the demonstration of mathematical truths, namely, those ideas the denial of which is an immediate self-contradiction; we will see another such idea in a moment when we consider the idea of God. A second type, like the idea of body, does not so immediately reveal a contradiction when it is denied, but still guarantees truth. Descartes articulates this guarantee in terms of the concept of a God: God is all-good, so he cannot be a deceiver, and therefore he cannot have put us in a position of being forced to believe something if it is not true, so, if our innate ideas compel us to think a certain way, that must be truth. We do not need this language of God to see the strength of the argument, which is entirely contained in the last line. By being ideas *to which I am subject*, they function as necessarily true *for me; that is, I must* take them as true of reality, for I have no faculty for challenging them. Here, it is not the *content* of the idea the denial of which leads to immediate self-contradiction; rather, it is the very form of an innate idea that makes it a literally meaningless proposal for any one of us to claim that we doubt the idea. And notice, finally, what this consideration of the innate ideas that structure our experience says about the self: since I am subject to these ideas, they are unaccountable for by me, that is "I" am really on the side of empirical ego, always finding that the transcendental ego does me the courtesy of allowing me to make use of it, and to identify with it (that is, I say "I understand that," and so on). Thus the "I" exists and functions in the realm of necessity when I live by reason, which I *qua* finite cannot account for, and which "I" am only identical with precisely in being indiscernible from any other "I," that is, it is my *universal* self, rather than my idiosyncrasies, that puts me into the realm of truth.

But here we have just seen the force of Descartes's argument for the existence of God in the third meditation: the determinacy of the ideas we find in our minds (their objective reality) is not accountable in terms of the substance of our finite consciousness, which is the medium of their appearance (their formal reality). We find ourselves subject to a reality greater than ourselves, which is both the source of our own experience and universally the source of the experience of every self.[30] I want now to consider how this Cartesian conception of selfhood lays the foundation for a *scientific* epistemology.

The key to differentiating scientific rationalism from simple stoicism is that the latter is built on an essential *withdrawal* and *isolation* from "the nature of things," whereas the scientific epistemology is geared toward a *reconciliation* with all reality and is premised on the fundamental identity of the real and the apparent self into which context the argument has been transformed. Science is the attempt to find out why experience *had to* happen the way it did: the scientist has to see how she has already been compelled, why what appeared to happen had to appear to happen. This comprehension must utilize the scientist's own *necessary* method—that is, reason—to see why the world is what it is by necessity, that is, why it is rational. Scientific rationalism is thus the recognition by the apparent ego of the need to identify with its real self by answering the demand to identify its real self—the necessity of self-consciousness in and for itself—with all reality as reason. Thus whereas the stoic finds herself by *differentiating* herself from all reality, the rationalist finds herself only *in and through identifying* her real self with reality *qua* rational. It is in the identification with the rationality of her *world*, then, that the apparent ego is here able to identify with her real self.

It is the recognition of one's real self in the recognition of the (rational) reality of the other that is thus especially characteristic of an epistemology of unhappy consciousness, and it is because it takes this form that scientific rationalism, or transcendental epistemology in general, must be understood as primarily an actualization of self-consciousness as the third form of unhappy consciousness.[31] Chapter V of Hegel's *Phenomenology of Spirit*, "Reason," goes on to show that the particular form of this identification of self and world that characterizes such immediate scientific rationalism is inadequate because too abstract, and it is the progressive improvement of this project that is gradually achieved first in the phenomena of "Spirit," in which the apparent ego identifies with its real self through enacting a mutual, social recognition in social institutions, and then further in religious communion, and ultimately in the completely self-conscious standpoint of philosophical science called "absolute knowing." Having now found in the logic of unhappy consciousness the key that simultaneously allows us to see the strength of the achievement of early modern rationalism and idealism and allows us to see the need to go beyond its actual achievements, we can look explicitly at how the Hegelian epistemology proper completes this project in dialectical phenomenology even as it undermines the most cherished belief of this rationalism, the dualism of mind and body.

3. Dialectical Method, Phenomenology, and the Problem of Induction

These transformations that institute an epistemology of unhappy consciousness leave us with the conclusion that in knowing the reality of the other I know the reality of myself, and that, indeed, it is *as thus recognized as the reality of the self* that the reality of the object is found. I have called Descartes's epistemology an epistemology of unhappy consciousness, but, while his transcendental argument *operates* according to such a logic, it is not clear that Descartes himself *realizes* this; that is, it is not clear that his philosophy *posits itself* as a philosophy of unhappy consciousness. Before going on to see how such an epistemology flowers in Hegel, then, I want first to consider briefly how this epistemology of unhappy consciousness comes to recognize itself as such in the German idealism of Kant and Fichte that effects the transition from Descartes's early modern rationalism to Hegel's absolute idealism.

In Kant, the identity of our selfhood—the transcendental structures of consciousness—with the form of objects is posited, that is, in knowing the forms of objectivity we are equally knowing the truth about subjectivity, but Kant still operates with a dualism of things-as-they-appear and things-as-they-are. For Kant there remains a permanent need to make this distinction, and that from which things-as-they-appear are distinguished remains an otherness that it is necessary to posit, and to posit as necessarily inaccessible (two claims that it seems impossible to mutually endorse inasmuch as the simple positing of this otherness already amounts to a kind of access to its determinateness).[32] Here, then, a *necessary* feature of that which exists for the subject is posited as *not* a product of subjective synthesis, and there is thus an incomplete carrying out of the project of finding out the identity of the self through the other (indeed, through the necessary form in which the other appears).

It is with Fichte that the decisive entry in the real self-conscious epistemology of unhappy consciousness is made, for Fichte systematically argues that the very form of objectivity is itself a function of selfhood. There is, in other words, no absolutely existing other from which to distinguish self-conscious selfhood, for the very category of otherness is itself to be identified as a player *within* the dynamic of self-conscious selfhood. (Here we are clearly seeing replayed the moves from stoicism to skepticism to unhappy consciousness *within* epistemologies of unhappy consciousness.)[33] Here, then, we have an epistemology of unhappy consciousness recognizing itself as such.

Fichte gives us one thing more, which also helps us in our attempt to characterize the ultimate form of this epistemology. The recognition that otherness is itself a stage in the self-positing of the transcendental ego is representative of the whole move by Fichte to unite Kant's transcendental unity of apperception with Kant's categorical imperative, and to see here in the "Category" a *dynamic* principle from which all the more determinate forms of transcendental subjectivity are generated. We are not left, that is, with a transcendental ego *and* twelve categories, but have instead one self-same process of self-determination or self-differentiation. Thus, if we want to know finally who is the real self, we will find that self by seeing the *totality* of the determinate categories *as* the unified expression or self-development of a single animating principle. With this, our story of Hegel's relation to seventeenth- and eighteenth-century epistemology is nearly complete.

The epistemology of unhappy consciousness, as it is developed in Fichte and Hegel, tells us that in looking at what appears, we see its reality when we see it as the integrated totality of determinateness of a self-determining system, and the "self" of this self-determining is equally our real self. Subjectivity as such—rationality, mind, self-consciousness, or however we want to term it—thus is that which realizes itself as the totality of appearance. The real self, mind as such, is, ultimately, nothing other than the totality of determinations of that which appears taken in their unity. But this means that all determinations that could count as "body" are not to be dualistically separated from mind as one substance is separated from another, but must be seen as separated only as object is separated from subject in a process of self-othering self-consciousness. No doubt the detailed response to the dualism of mind and body that is typically associated with Descartes needs to be addressed on its own terms, and needs to show its self-refutation in the context of a detailed phenomenological observation, but we can see here why *in principle* the very dualism that allows Descartes to launch his transcendental epistemology of unhappy consciousness is precisely what falls in the culmination of that project. Various other versions of this dualism still exist in Kant and Fichte, and the detailed phenomenology of the self-development and self-refutation of mind-body dualism would indeed have to develop through these shapes. In Kant, an analogous dualism appears between sensibility and understanding, and, more importantly, between things-as-they-appear and things-as-they-are-in-themselves. In Fichte, it is posited that there *should not be* such a dualism—that is, alienness as such *must* be a product of subjectivity—but an ultimate dualism between the self and the other remains in Fichte, in the portrayal of the other as *Anstoss*, as the ultimately underivable "check" about which we know *that* it ushers from our "true self" but never *how* it can do so.[34] It is because some such dualism is at the core of all the pre-Hegelian idealisms that Hegel's epistemology of unhappy consciousness, while completing the epistemological project of early modern philosophy, simultaneously is its radical rejection, and its transformation into something quite new. Having now seen where Hegel stands with respect to early modern epistemology in the forms of simple empiricism, Cartesian scientific rationalism, and Critical idealism, I want to end this chapter with a brief articulation of what this new stance is that comes with the Hegelian completion of unhappy consciousness.

The logical core to the epistemology of unhappy consciousness is the recognition by the empirical ego that it must wait upon the transcendental ego to effect the synthesis within experience that will produce knowledge. Once this happens, the empirical ego certainly legitimately says "*I* know," indicating that it is really *itself* who synthesizes, but the enacting of this synthesis is something that happens "behind its back," that is, it is not immediately in control of the motor of its own self-consciousness. In our discussion of Kant and Fichte, we have seen that the form that scientific observation must take, given this epistemology, is to recognize appearances *as* the appearances of a self-developing system. These two sides of our story neatly coincide.

To *see* the other *as* engaged in a process of self-development means to approach it in the form of asking it how it is a self-determining process. This means (1) to look for how it is what it is by being the expression of a single drive, and (2) to see how this drive precipitates changes in itself through its very enactment. We must ask of the other, "how are you a self-mover, a self-developer?" To see the object of our experience in this fashion will require us not to bring external criticisms to bear upon it, not to start with some positing of the metaphysical ultimacy of this or that kind of relation of subjects and objects, and so on: it is *what is appearing to us* that is our object, and it must be our object *precisely as such*, and our task is precisely to describe *how it appears*. The epistemology of unhappy consciousness thus prescribes a phenomenological method.

Equally, our wait for synthesis is no different from our looking to the object's own movement: (1) the need to wait means our idiosyncratic "empirical" egos *cannot* perform the synthesis on their own, and (2) the goal of watching the other's self-movement means our empirical egos *must not* perform the synthesis. The two themes thus dovetail perfectly. What we *can* and *must* do is look and ask; we must approach the object precisely as those waiting for an answer, where the precise question is "how are you a self-determining unity?" (And, as those of us who have gone through this process in the *Phenomenology of Spirit* know, it is this fundamental activity of looking for unity that will ultimately be the name of the real self that is the self-developing source of the whole systematic story of appearance, which means our very existence as such questioners is precisely the immediate form in which the transcendental ego appears.[35]) We are, then, just open projects in search of completion, and we must wait upon the object to answer our needs. But whereas in Fichte's system we are *necessarily* left with an infinitely unfulfilled *Sollen*, Hegel's method will not allow such a specification in advance, for precisely what its openness demands is an openness to finding closure, and, indeed, this is where the dialectical phenomenology ends, although this can be presented only as an undefended abstract statement until the actual phenomenological viewing finds the object demanding of it that it complete the investigative activity.[36]

In this openness, then, we see that the dialectical phenomenology that enacts an epistemology of unhappy consciousness ultimately returns us to a kind of empiricism. Empiricism is indeed right in its first principle of the necessary singularization of self-conscious egos, and the need to develop all knowledge from this point of view; indeed, this is precisely the source of Hegel's demand for a "ladder to the absolute" in the Preface to the *Phenomenology of Spirit*. The dialectic of the "Freedom of Self-Consciousness," however, shows us—and this is played out in the history of early modern epistemology—that this empiricism needs to become science. This science, in turn, needs to become dialectical phenomenology, that is, science in Hegel's sense. This, finally, is a return to empiricism, but empiricism as *aufgehoben* by way of its own dialectic.

This *aufgehoben* empiricism is no longer a *passive* empiricism in the manner of Locke, but is an *active* empiricism in the manner of Aristotle:[37] it is still essentially open, and waiting for the other to give it determinateness, but it is active in its search for this other, which means asking of things, "how are you a self-unity?" In this new context, the empiricist "problem of induction" the core of skepticism—is equally *aufgehoben*, now appearing precisely as the phenomenological observation that must wait upon the intrinsic dialectic of the object to enact the synthesis that organizes experience.[38] That is why Hegel's Introduction to the *Phenomenology of Spirit* portrays phenomenology as the new skepticism, as a *concrete*, rather than an *abstract*, skepticism, which is not burdened by the bad dualistic metaphysics of the alien other, because it has *returned* to skepticism *within the context of unhappy consciousness*, and can now see negation—the characteristic of self-consciousness—as intrinsic to the very being of the object.

PART 3. THE ABSOLUTE

Reason

eight
Reason and Dualism

Hegel's philosophy in general will not tolerate any unreconciled dualism, and how this commitment works itself out in relation to the philosophy of mind is the particular theme addressed here. The dualism of self-as-mind and body that is often associated with the name of Descartes has, at least since Plato's *Phaedo*, always been the strongest opponent of the non-dualistic view; the key to the Cartesian argument is that self-consciousness is constituted by a direct identification with universal and necessary rational truths that are not dependent on any bodily conditions, and thus the self *qua* rational is independent of the body. The crucial logical feature of this dualism, then, is the conception of an *immediate communion* of an independent, autonomous self with itself. This dualistic conception of the rational self and the body is present as the animating spirit throughout Chapter V, "Reason," where the forms that rational self-identity takes, the forms its embodiment takes, and the kinds of dualistic relations encountered are manifold.[1]

An a priori refutation of such dualism is not hard to articulate. If mind and body are truly independent, then there can be no state of either that is dependent upon the other; that is, there can in principle be no relation between the two independent realms. This means there can be no knowledge of body, for this would amount to a state of mind dependent upon body. Thus even the articulation of the dualism becomes impossible, since it is not possible to articulate that from which mind is being differentiated.[2] Mind-body dualism is thus a meaningless name. This explains why, if the possibility of a relationship is presupposed, the attempts to account for such a relation are doomed to failure. To account for the means by which the body affects the mind will involve positing a bodily means; that is, since the body exerts a bodily causality, what body affects will always be body; thus the question of how the relation is effected will always involve positing a body as the mediating moment between body and mind, which will still leave unanswered the question in principle of how a body (now the mediating body) can affect mind. Similarly, to account for how mind affects body will involve the same positing of new moments of the mental as mediating moments, forever leaving unanswered the question in principle of how the mental stimulus can ever affect the body. Hegel is certainly familiar with these arguments[3]—indeed the problem of mediating a dualistic relation is a pivotal theme in all his thought—but such refutation in principle is not his goal in Chapter V, "Reason"; rather, Hegel's treatment of reason lays out how such a dualistic reason *comes to refute itself through its own immanent dynamic.*

Hegel's account of reason is long and complex, and I will not analyze it in detail; rather, I will trace out the general logical movement that is relevant to the notion of embodiment that is operative in Hegel's analyses. This approach has the particular advantage that it will make clear how this difficult chapter works as a whole to tell a single coherent story. This development of the argumentative unity of this chapter in the *Phenomenology* in relation to the issue of the rational self and its embodiment will be concerned mostly with the problems of identity and difference, and of empirical and transcendental selfhood. I will be focusing on reason as a way in which an identification is posited by the singular empirical self and the universal rational self.

What will become clear through the analysis is that *on its own terms* reason is inadequate, for its constitutive commitment to different forms of dualism will in each case preclude it from fulfilling the project of universal identification to which it also has a constitutive commitment. In studying Chapter V, Section A, "Observing Reason," we will see how reason's conception of selfhood implies a dualism of reason and nature, of inner and outer, of identity and difference, and how observation animated by such a commitment to dualism is ultimately sterile, and unable to live up to its own constitutive principle, namely, the "scientific imperative." In Section B, the same reason, now "practical," will be unable to live up to its constitutive objective of winning the intersubjective world over to rationality, because it is again plagued by a dualism, but in this case the dualism is between reason and social institutions, rather than reason and nature. In Section C, "self-determining" reason is unable to recognize that the process of expressing or acting on an intention can reflect back on that intention, and this dualism of intention and actualization will keep the rational individual from fulfilling its project of being in accord with the universal. Overall, then, reason's commitment to the immediacy of the self-communion of the rational self excludes *nature, institutions,* and *expression* from having a constitutive role in rational self-identity, and in each case this commitment to the exclusion of mediation will lead to the failure of reason to fulfill its own definitive project. Before we study these various forms of reason in detail, however, a short account of reason in general will be helpful.

1. Reason in General

Hegel begins his account of reason by identifying it as a form of consciousness that is the product of a history of development and that, as such, bears the mark of this history in itself, but that does not itself recognize that it is such a product: reason believes itself to have entered onto the scene full-blown and immediately.[4] What in general characterizes the stance of reason is its desire to reduce all experience to a rational unity, and it believes that in so doing it is performing a natural task that can and should be performed by all agents facing the same situation. Reason will take any opponent and show how its position is not rationally supportable, or show how the rational evaluation of the evidence points to a different point of view, and so on. The behavior of reason is indeed reasonable; what we must first see, however, is how reason's rational behavior of responding to every challenge with an appeal to canons of rationality is a product of its own history of development, and especially how it is a form of unhappy consciousness. There are, I contend, three essential lessons that the self-conscious self had to learn in order to be a rational self. The achievement of rationality is founded on the recognition of *challenge, respect,* and *authority.*

The entire dynamic of desire that is developed in the opening section of Chapter IV, "Self-Consciousness," is animated by the self's attempt to eliminate the possibility of *challenge;* for the simple desiring self, every determination of being amounts to a challenge to the centrality and independence of the self, and the dynamic of desire is the perpetual attempt to overcome this challenge through consumption. The advance to subsequent shapes of self-consciousness is made through the tolerance of such challenges, that is, through the recognition that they are essential and constitutive to the nature of self-consciousness, and, therefore, inescapable.

The subsequent dynamic of "lordship and bondage" in the same chapter culminates in the analysis of the new and more sophisticated form of self-conscious selfhood that is developed through the institution of slavery. What especially defines this new slave-self as more sophisticated than the simply desiring self is its *respect* for what it faces; the slave learns that, and how, she must respond to her other on terms that *it* sets, and that she is not simply independent, and free to act according to desire.

Finally, the dynamic of "the freedom of self-consciousness," which culminates in the phenomenon of the unhappy consciousness, reveals a self-conscious selfhood that becomes progressively more sophisticated as it finds itself progressively more compelled to recognize itself as *already subject* to an *authority* the necessity of which is *intrinsic* to the very nature of the self. It is such a self that respects the integrity of the challenges of otherness according to the demands of an intrinsic authority who acts out the drama of Chapter V, "Reason."

What reason amounts to is a commitment to "the category," which is the name for the immediate identification of the empirical ego with transcendental ego, or what we can call the apparent self and the real self; what reason knows according to this identification is that it can and must find the unifying ground of things, and that this ground is identical with *its own* self, and equally the ground of *universal* agreement, for precisely what it has immediate access to are the canons of *necessary assent*. Reason knows that things must *be* in whatever way they *must appear* to the rational self. Reason's imperative is (1) to notice what appears (which marks the continuing status of, or, in Hegel's terms, is the *Aufhebung* of, the moment of challenge),[5] (2) to see what appears in its proper (scientific) perspective (which is the *Aufhebung* of the moment of respect), and (3) to perform these operations in a form that is universally defensible to all other rational selves (which is the *Aufhebung* of the moment of authority). Reason's imperative is to see how it is that what appears appears as a logical unity.

The germ of the method that governs reason's operations is the positing of the primacy of identity in its pursuit of unity, but it is a positing of identity that excludes difference, and this ultimately leads to a sense of identity modeled on the identity of inert substance rather than on the identity of subjectivity.[6] Simple identity can be found in experience, and this lends the method necessity, and, insofar as every empirical ego can identify with the transcendental ego by positing identity, the arguments of reason do have universality. Thus reason *is* authoritative. Hegel's argument does not dispute this absoluteness of reason's claims, but shows, rather, that their abstractness (and essential substantiality or positivism) cannot pay adequate respect to the challenge of otherness.[7] This is what reason learns through its own dynamic throughout the drama of Chapter V, "Reason." The three sections of Chapter V follow reason in its attempt to find or produce the rationality of its object through three different "methods," first through the (supposedly) passive observation of what it takes to be substantial "things," second through the active transformation of social relations, and finally through the rational transfiguration of its own self. We can now turn to a brief consideration of each of these three stages.[8]

2. Reason and Observation

In Chapter V, Section A, "Observing Reason," we watch the drama of scientific reason; reason here wants a rational account of why things are the way they are, that is, why they have the identity they have, and, to find this identifiability of things, it looks. There are two crucial points to note here: first, the *passive* stance adopted by reason; second, the *external* nature of reason's reflection. Understanding these points will allow us to see that "Observing Reason" essentially provides a *reductio* argument against the possibility of reason finding itself reflected in simple *being*, or static, substantial externality, and this precipitates the move to Chapter V, Section B, "The Actualization of Rational Self-Consciousness through Itself," and the attempt to find reason reflected in *action*.

Although the various stances through which observing reason passes represent quite different degrees of philosophical sophistication *at some levels*, what unites them *as* observing reason is their ultimate adherence to an ethos of "passive empiricism." Within the treatment of "the observation of nature," the opening section on simple description[9] is very much a simple Lockean-style empiricism, while the closing sections on the observation of organic nature[10] are clearly derived from the Schellingian school, yet what both share at decisive points is the commitment to the discovery of a simple, observable being that will determine the identity or intelligibility of that being studied: the initial approach tries to establish identity through a simple enumeration of observable features,[11] while the culminating form seeks the essence of the embodiment of life in e-numerating differences in "specific gravity," here taken as an observable property that accounts for all other bodily properties.[12] In each case, reason wants to *find* something that will *tell* it (reason) what the object of its study is, and why it is thus. Reason thus takes itself to be passive, that is, just receiving what is already "there," and what it takes itself to be receiving is a given, simple, immediate being: "data." This is equally true of the approach taken to the observation of self-consciousness, which, in its generation of logical and psychological laws, again seeks a static, measurable content that will account for the rational identity of the subject of its observation;[13] and it is what is indeed most definitive of the operations of physiognomy and phrenology, the analysis of which concludes this section on observation.[14] Reason, Hegel argues, is, however, not passive, for reason is really "putting nature on the rack" and forcing nature to answer reason's question, namely, the question of what is the rationality of the identity of the observed.[15] We can see this better if we go on to the second crucial feature of observing reason, namely, the *externality* of its reflection.

The externality of reflection is really implied in the passive stance just identified, for reason's observation *defines itself* by its relation to a "given," that is, to something that is not its own product, or, again, something to the inside of which it has (or has had) no access. The observational stance thus begins by positing the self-containedness of its object, and posits itself as a parasitic voyeur whose own activity is *indifferent to* and *outside of* its object.[16] What observing reason will produce, then, will forever be only something superimposed on its data: having defined itself and its object as indifferent, self-contained beings, all it will ever encounter is its own formalization of the observability—the outside—of its object. There is more to say about the epistemological problems this externality engenders, but first we must note the essential dualism of inner and outer, or of identity and difference, which it implies.

By virtue of the phenomenological investigation in the first four chapters of the *Phenomenology of Spirit*, Hegel is able to claim that the essential thesis of reason—its scientific imperative—is to find itself to be identical to all reality.[17] This remains *for reason*, however, a merely lived imperative; that is, this is not a demand it self-consciously posits, and reason is thus properly only the "instinct" of reason, *Vernunftinstinkt*.[18] What we in fact see in our observation of observing reason is that the method of observation that it adopts—namely, external reflection—is *necessarily* at odds with its implicit objective, for precisely what this method *presupposes* is that reason *cannot* identify with its object, for the given is, again, outside of and indifferent to reason; that is, it is *defined* as excluding reason.[19] Reason is thus *essentially* dualistic in its presuppositions, for it operates on the basis of (1) an ontological, that is to say essential and necessary, distinction between itself and its object, (2) the concomitant distinction between the given outer and the hidden inner, and (3) the equally essential distinction between the identity it will discover/produce through its investigations and the differences that it will pass over to get to this identity. The first two of these dualisms are just reformulations of the dualism of observer and observed already explicated in relation to the practice of external reflection, but the last dualism, the dualism of identity and difference, can be better seen if we proceed to consider the epistemological problems that necessarily plague observing reason, and to do this we must first see how the phenomenology of observing reason is structured.

In the successive subsections of the "Observation of Nature" (and, indeed, in the observation of self-consciousness and of its immediate actuality but there in a less detailed fashion), the object under investigation becomes progressively more sophisticated, moving from inert inorganics to chemicals to organisms, and *up to a certain point* so does the method of observation.[20] I have already argued that the method throughout remains one of passive empiricism, but there are refinements to this method in the three main subsections of the "Observation of Nature": the method changes from simple description to a search for laws to a teleology.[21] What is interesting here is that, up to a point, the methods are suitable to their respective subject matters. Because absolutely inert inorganic matter would have no constitutive moment of being-for-self, all one could ever really do is describe it, that is, describe the forming that it happens to arbitrarily undergo, and because chemicals have a constitutive tension between their being-at-rest and their being-in-relation, all one can ever do is know them in relation to a law of their transformations.[22] Finally, because the organism is an individual, that is, a totality that is reflected-into-itself, it is proper to understand it as goal-directed.[23] Thus Hegel's phenomenological description of observing reason does not merely amount to criticism, but equally shows the positive developments within observing reason from the point of view of the Hegelian project of philosophy of nature, and it is crucial to the reading of this section to recognize that this is going on.[24] Where then is the problem in observation? The problem is that the development here is only visible from the point of view of Hegel's philosophy of nature, and the *Vernunftinstinkt* that makes this development does not itself know what it is doing.

Although in its practice it moves from description to chemical laws and organic teleology, in its philosophy observing reason remains animated by the project of description. The crucial move from description to law is the move from perception to understanding; that is, it is the move whereby one recognizes that only through *understanding* it can one recognize the unity of the process, and that it is only on the basis of this understanding that the relata can be identified and known;[25] observing reason, however, still thinks its knowledge is coming through its *observation* and thus posits the relata as primitive and the law as derivative.[26] Likewise, the crucial move from law to teleology is the move whereby one recognizes a *reflective totality*; that is, one recognizes a unity that *maintains itself in and through* the distinct operations of *the differences thus united*; or, again, it is the recognition of a totality that operates *as a* unity, where the *goal* of that activity is simply *itself*. Observation, however, posits the goal that accounts for the unity outside of the differentiated totality that does the acting, for, *qua* observation, it only posits immediate and not reflected determinations.[27] In other words, in both the case of the relata of the law and the case of the organs of the organism, these determinations are only recognized (understood) *as* relata or *as* organs by seeing that their very being is determined intrinsically by the relation to the whole (the legal *relation* or the organism) and to the others that make up the whole, but this recognition requires positing an *unobservable* determining ground; that is, it means seeing the observable in terms of the understood ground, rather than deriving the law on the basis of the observable.[28] Thus, to the extent that reason remains governed by the ethos of observation, it can never even appreciate the progress it actually makes in these successive developments of its science. We can now say something about the epistemological problems its science is left with as a result of its inability to move beyond a doctrine of external relations to one of internal relations.

Reason wants a rational account for why things are the way they are, that is, why they have the identity they have, but, *qua* observation, it takes this account to be the discovery of some "thing," rather than the assembling of the elements of its observation into a coherent story in which they are the participant members; the story reason really needs to tell is the story of how the observed is really the necessary expression of rationality as rationality; that is, it needs to develop the forms of the given from out of the very concept of reason (which is what the Hegelian philosophy of nature achieves). To do this, however, would require positing the objects of its experience as intrinsically mediated; observation, however, takes what it finds to be immediate existences, and, even when, in teleology, it posits a determining goal, or when it posits an inner for the observed outer, the goal and the inner remain external to the observed being, and the observed being is still treated as a self-contained immediate existent (and, indeed, so is the posited goal or inner). By thus, again, setting up a dualism, here excluding the mediating being from that which it mediates (which is just the dualism of inner and outer referred to above), reason precludes the possibility of its ever giving an account of the given as rational, for it takes what it immediately finds to be *intrinsically* immediate, and, *ipso facto*, not intrinsically mediated by reason. This leaves observing reason with only three options for the form its science can take, all of which are inadequate to reason's project.

Since the given is always a self-enclosed immediate being, no relation between it and any other being could be *constitutive* of the being of it or its other; thus, any "law" "discovered" by observing reason will ultimately end up as either (1) an empty tautology, because it simply defines conditions that apply irrespective of the determinate conditions of its supposed relata, since these determinate conditions, as self-enclosed, cannot enter into the terms of the legal mediation, or (2) the simple description with which observing reason began, which simply enumerates features without being able to advance any explanatory ground; it can, that is to say, only articulate either the simple condition of empty self-identity, or else provide an uninterpreted list of simple differences. These are the two ways its pursuit can end; there is a further possible route, although this takes the form of a bad infinite, that is, a pursuit that can never end.

The above two results are results that can be had when the goal of explanation is given up; as long as observing reason tries to explain, however, it will face a never-ending task. The limitation of its method, *viz.*, its methodological inability to recognize anything other than immediate beings, means that any time observing reason posits an explanation, it must posit an immediate being. If, for example, it wants to explain the outer, it must posit an inner, where each, outer and inner, is posited as an immediate being; here, of course, nothing is explained, for the relation between the two beings remains a mystery. If, then, it tries to explain the relation between these two beings, all it can posit as an explanation is another immediate being. This solution will face the same problem, and thus the process will have to be repeated *ad infinitum*, and no explanation will ever result. Observing reason is thus faced with three options: empty tautology, empty description, of the empty, infinite multiplication of middle terms.[29]

The problem observing reason faces really can be expressed by the dualism of identity and difference mentioned above. It seeks the identity of things, but it needs to recognize that identity is a reflected determination; that is, it is mediated, rather than simply immediate, and its mediation is a self-mediation. In the organism, "the organism" is not some further "part" above and beyond the organs, but is simply the unified totality of the functioning organs themselves. The identity *it* (the organism) has is an identity *they* (the organs) share and constitute; that is, it is an identity only in and through the reciprocal determination of differences. The logic of identity is thus a logic of reflection, and cannot be captured in a simple logic of immediate beings.[30] As the objects of observing reason grew more sophisticated, it was precisely their internalization of difference that constituted this sophistication. What this means is that the very ability of observing reason to *recognize* these observables *as* units *presupposes* that reason's cognition is *implicitly* animated by a logic more sophisticated than that which it explicitly adopts in its scientific practice. What we, the phenomenological observers, recognize is that it is only reason's own sophistication in the posing of perceptual questions that allows it to recognize the more sophisticated objects of its experience, and we who have studied the first four chapters of the book know the drama through which this cognitive capacity developed; we thus know that the answer reason seeks to its question of the determining ground of the identity of the objects of its experience will only be found through the *self*-investigation by which it comes to perform the very phenomenological observation that has been underway in the *Phenomenology of Spirit* for four chapters. When observing reason turns to itself, however, its observational limitations will only allow it to find its own inadequate method,[31] for it still needs to develop from out of its own self the recognition of an identity in and through difference, and precisely where it will first be driven to find this is in its own attempts to be *responsible* to its own identity; this will be the culmination of Chapter V, "Reason," but before we get to that point we must first consider that form of reason that recognizes that the rationality of its world is a product of its own activity. This will be a form of reason that has advanced beyond the attempt to find reason—identity—embodied in an immediate being, and has turned to a *dynamic* embodiment of reason. This is clearly an advance, insofar as we saw in our consideration of the concept of the organism as a reflective totality that it was only in the unified activity of self-maintenance that the infinite self had its selfhood, but this approach will remain limited to the extent that the activity in which reason finds itself reflected will still be construed as not intrinsic to its own nature, that is, not intrinsic to *being* rational, but only intrinsic to making its *object* rational.

3. Reason and Action

Whereas observing reason took itself to be passively observing data, we recognized from the start that it was in fact engaged in a process of actively transforming its cognitive environment from contingent perception to rational comprehension; reason, we said, was the certainty of its identity with all reality, but the reality with which it is identical is only a reality won over by reason. The truth of reason's behavior, then, is that it transforms what is rationaliz*able* into what is actually rational, which means that reason is fundamentally to be found in an act of *making rational*—a dynamic activity—and not in an inert immediate being. Given, then, what we know about reason's own character, we can see that the very project of observation was doomed from the start since (1) reason misconstrued the nature of its own activity and the relation of this activity to its object, and (2) the object in which it hoped to find itself reflected could never provide such a reflection. The dialectic of Chapter V, Section A has made these points clear, and Section B, "The Actualization of Rational Self-Consciousness Through Itself," gives a phenomenology of the next more sophisticated kind of rational activity, an activity that addresses these very problems that we identified with observing reason. We will see here again, however, that this self-actualizing reason, while making an advance over observing reason, will still be plagued by the same basic dualism of immediacy and reflection, identity and difference.

The forms of self-actualizing reason are all forms of social revolution, that is, activities that seek to advance the social order from its existing irrational form into the rational form that is its destiny. The advance over observing reason is clear,[32] in that reason does not now pretend to be passive, but actively seeks to transform, and it finds reason embodied, not in inert immediate being, but in what is achieved in its action.[33]

Reason, we said, begins with the *imperative* to identify; that is, reason is always characterized by the obligation to make rational. In Chapter V, Section A, the practice of observing reason operated on the presupposition that this was not the case. Here in Section B, however, this imperative to transform is now operative; that is, it is the presupposition of the practice of self-actualizing reason that it must make its object rational; this imperative remains, however, inexplicit or unthematic. (This notion of reason as imperative will only become explicit to reason in Section C, "Individuality Which to Itself Is Real in and for Itself.") What this means, then, is that the self-conscious agent we here consider must be working to make the world rational. This is essential to its status as reason: the revolutionary practices must not be based on *merely* idiosyncratic desires, but must be rooted in the *assurance*—if not the express assertion—that it is *qua* rational (that is, universal and necessary) self that one has the right, or, rather, the duty, to change society.

In order to transform its object, then, the rational self-consciousness must posit that object as *destined* to be rational, and, recognizing itself as the carrier of the destined rationality, it must posit rational self-consciousness itself as the very goal; thus the object to be transformed into rational form will be the object as self-conscious, that is, society.[34] We can now consider briefly the three forms of social revolution that Hegel describes; we will be considering them in relation to the themes of self-identity and difference.

"Pleasure and Necessity" is the first drama of self-actualizing reason;[35] Hegel draws his images here from Goethe's *Faust*, but we might just as easily imagine characters from Ayn Rand's *Atlas Shrugged*. Here, the would-be agent of the world's destiny sees the vindication of the world in its providing fulfillment for her personally.[36] In "Pleasure and Necessity," the rational self-consciousness actualizes herself through love; that is, she finds the world to have achieved its destiny in providing her with another singular self-consciousness in which she is reflected. This is not simply the desire of Chapter IV, "Self-Consciousness," which consumes its object, for (1) she preserves the immediate being of her other, and enjoys only the conversion of the other's self-consciousness,[37] and (2) even though she wants to see herself as a singular agent reflected, she maintains that it is *because she is a rational agent* that it is right for her to be thus reflected; that is, the agent of destiny sees this love as the goal of reality *only because this agent sees herself as the fulfilled shape of human individuality.*[38] In holding out her love as an ideal for the world, the agent of destiny realizes that the great mass of society opposes her,[39] but she has no concern for society, for rationality is to be found in singular self-conscious selfhood.

This elevation of herself beyond the limits of society proves impossible, however, for the very fulfillment of this elevation—the consummation of love—is the institution of a society; that is, love means entering into a commitment to an other, and finding oneself to be dependent on the reflection of that other. Thus the consummation of the celebration of individual excellence is only achieved in the *overcoming* of singularity, and the instituting of an inter-subjective universal.[40] Through love, the agent of destiny had tried to celebrate the rational excellence she already carried, but the fulfillment of this goal reveals the singular self to be only a moment in the true self-actualized rational self-consciousness. This contradiction between the intended goal and its actual fulfillment is felt by the agent of destiny as the simple shock—the "riddle," "*Rätsel*"—of finding the unity of love to be replaced by the pain that accompanies the death of the other. We can see that this is the necessary outcome of the pursuit of reason that institutes a society, but, to the agent who still holds her rational self to exist entire on its own in independence of the relation, this is unintelligible.[41]

What is crucial to our account here is that that which is explicitly the goal of self-actualizing reason is a self-identity that takes the form of a unity *reflected in itself*; it is an identity that is constituted only in and through the maintenance of differentiated units. Hegel notes this explicitly:

> The *object*, then, that is, for self-consciousness as it takes its pleasure, its essence, is the expansion of those simple essentialities of pure unity, of pure difference, and their relation.[42]

Hegel here articulates the point that we made in relation to observing reason:

> Unity, difference, and relation are categories each of which is nothing in and for itself, but only in relation to its opposite, and they cannot therefore be separated from one another.[43]

We can see that this notion that identity is not external to difference now characterizes the explicit goal of self-actualizing reason, but the extent to which the agent of destiny still feels the pain of the other's death to be a product of an alien necessity, and not a product of its own action, is the extent to which she has not made this realization herself.

The remaining two forms of self-actualizing reason are further developments of this same basic tension. In "The Law of the Heart and the Frenzy of Self-Conceit," the agent of destiny explicitly posits the identity of her goal with the harmony of the social whole, insisting that we love one another, explicitly denouncing the goal of the fulfillment of a singular will in opposition to the will of others; "The Law of the Heart" is thus the specific negation of that agent we studied in "Pleasure and Necessity."[44] The basic dynamic here is that the agent of destiny takes herself to be immediately an agent of universal love, but, in trying to actualize the rational self-consciousness of all in universal love, she meets with opposition, and ends up opposing her private vision to that of the whole, thus violating the initial project of universal love, and, again, positing the self-identity of the singular agent in abstraction from the social whole to which it belongs as a committed member.[45]

Finally, in "Virtue and the Way of the World," the agent of destiny has realized that she cannot really be the "agent" of destiny, for, as we have seen, the very function of the so-called agent is to be superseded, and to become only a moment in the self-actualized rational self-consciousness.[46] The project of virtue, in other words, is the project of self-effacement, that is, of the sacrifice of one's identity to the larger whole. We can see already, however, that this project still makes the same essential logical error as the two preceding shapes, but that this project makes the error in reverse. Virtue still posits an identity that exists independently of difference, but this time it is not the singular self that is indifferent to other singulars and to the whole, but it is the universal that is indifferent to the singulars.

The notion of an identity that is reflected into itself is the notion of a systematic unity in which differences are integrated into an overarching unity, but in which the differences are still maintained as differences. To truly understand the social self-actualization of rational self-consciousness as such an identity would mean to recognize the essentiality of *both* the overarching totality *and* the participant members. We can articulate this in terms of the issues in "Virtue and the Way of the World."

What the knight of virtue recognizes is that she has certain capacities for enacting the true and the good—her rationality, or her identity as a member of the *universal* self—and that it is *these powers* rather than her singular self-conscious selfhood that represent the rational self-consciousness that is to actualize itself.[47] The goal of the knight of virtue is to have these powers achieve their rightful place as the order of social reality, and to have the rule of singular wills disappear.[48] We can see, however, that the very goal of the rule of these powers is fulfilled in, and only in, the situation in which these powers are put to use for the necessarily individuated objectives that singular agents pursue.[49] The goal of the knight of virtue can thus only be fulfilled in *action,* and in the action of agents who, while acting as members of a community, equally act on their own goals.[50] Thus it is the "way of the world" itself, that is, the actions of individuals who "pervert" the powers in "misusing" them for their own ends, which really fulfills the program of virtue.[51]

In each of these three dramas, then, we have seen the goal of self-actualizing reason to be rooted in an essential equivocation regarding the identity of this "self," and it amounts to a vacillation between rigidly identifying the self with the singular unit that participates in a larger system, and rigidly identifying the systematic identity as the only self; we have seen, however, that the only self-identity that will adequately fulfill the demands of the logic of self-reflectedness is the notion of the self that, in the fulfillment of its individuated pursuits, equally realizes the objectives of the systematic identity in which it is implicated. With this notion of individual self-identity as simultaneously singular and universal, we have the basic concept of the "real individual" of Chapter V, Section C, and it is to the dialectic of this individual that we now turn.

4. Reason and Responsibility

The real individual of Chapter V, Section C, "Individuality Which to Itself Is Real in and for Itself,"[52] is the agent who takes the enacting of her intrinsic intentions to be the actualizing of the universal good. As is Section A, "Observing Reason," Hegel's analysis here is essentially a *reductio* argument, and it divides into three sections: first, we study the most immediate form in which the real individual identifies her action with the fulfilling of the universal, and vacillates between identifying her real individuality with her private and with her public self; second, we see this vacillation decided in favor of the public self, but here taken in the abstract sense of the formal structures of selfhood that universally and necessarily are constitutive of all real individuals; finally, we see the emptiness of this identity with the universal, for, as we have seen in previous analyses, the identity is formal, and abstracted from all self-differentiation, and consequently is restricted to the same emptiness of tautology to which observing reason was reduced.

In "The Spiritual Animal Kingdom and Deceit, or *die Sache selbst*,"[53] we study the individual who most directly recognizes the identity of the singular use of one's "gifts" with the pursuit of the universal good. Here, each individual is conceived of as constituted by an original determinate nature that is intrinsically good, and doing the good amounts simply to the exhibition of this intrinsic nature.[54] Because of the identity of the singular with the universal, "just being itself," or "doing its own thing" means working for the good, so in all its actions, the actions are already vindicated as enactments or fulfillments of *die Sache selbst*. Since there is no opposition between what one is and what one should be, no action is criticizable, and, further, no essential distinctions can be made within the individual that would allow one to use one of the distinguished moments to criticize another, for if this were the case, then the singular would not be *directly* harmonious with the universal, but would only be *mediately identifiable*.[55] It is this immediacy which will be a problem, for it does not allow that the enacting of a project, or expressing of an intention, can be in any way constitutive of that project or intention. The real individual *exhibits* her nature, but this exhibition does not reflect back on what is thus shown forth, but is simply a spontaneous but superfluous overflow.

This problem appears in the dynamic of the real individual in that the inessentiality of the distinction between intention and its expression in action implies that she knows or possesses herself immediately, without the action being cognitively revelatory; thus what she takes to be her intention and motive is, *ex hypothesi*, her intention and motive.[56] What this immediate transparency of the self to itself does, however, is introduce the ground for a distinction between (1) this self-transparency and (2) the immediate identification between the singular and the universal on which this self-transparency is premised.

Through action, a public work is produced, and in this public realm individuals have an impact on each other. On the one hand, the very concept of real individuality is the concept of the responsibility of the singular to the universal, and the claim that *what one's acts are* are ways of being publicly responsible; yet the equally essential implication that private intention is primary introduces the distinction within the works of the singular between what the public impact is that the works have, and what the individual meant the impact to be, and the concept of the immediately real individual commits the singular self both to the distinction between the two, and to their equiprimordiality. The "deceit" of the title refers to the form the action of the singular takes as it vacillates between identifying with the public and the private interest, that is with *die Sache selbst* and with *seine Sache*.[57] The point of this phenomenology of the spiritual animals is that this vacillation is *necessary* given the way the selfhood is defined, for the immediacy of the identification of singular and universal leads to the immediacy of the identification of the singular with itself, and thus precludes that the action of exhibition be constitutive, thereby setting up an opposition between what the self is for others and what the self is for itself, while the premise of the immediate identification of the singular and the universal was the identity of being-for-self and being-for-another.[58] It is this dualism of self and activity which will animate the two subsequent analyses as well.

In "Reason as Lawgiver," a qualification is introduced into the identification of the singular self as a real individual: it is only *qua* universal that the self is a real individual.[59] This means that it is when the self is *not* acting on *merely* private intention, but acts, rather, according to that law that is objective to all that she is a real individual. For the spiritual animal, it was a private intention that provided the object for her self-consciousness, and set the objective for action; living under reason as a lawgiver means having rational law as the *necessary* object of one's self-consciousness for it is the object characteristic of all self-consciousness *qua* self-consciousness.[60] Thus, both here and in the next moment, "Reason as Testing Laws," we have "the category" as "the categorical imperative"; in this first moment the category is thought of as generative of determinate laws, while in the next moment it is thought of as a criterion for the evaluation of would-be laws.

The category is generative of laws if it can specify a value—a determinate code of action—to which all self-consciousness is committed to conform simply by virtue of being self-conscious.[61] Here, then, the empirical ego has made itself *subject to* the *transformative* power of the transcendental ego, and has as its objective its self-transformation into a fully rational shape. Two examples are developed to show that what initially seems to fulfill this role of being a prescriptive aspect of the real self is really not a determinate law at all, but is simply vacuous. The first example is "tell the truth."[62] This statement is *meant* to identify a determinate course of action, and to put it forward as an objective that each self-consciousness must make its own singular objective. But because the initial imperative only makes sense as an imperative to singular self-consciousness if it is interpreted in relation to the actual situation of this self-consciousness, the imperative must be re-articulated in light of this interpretive context as "one should tell the truth as far as one knows it." At this point, however, the unconditioned absoluteness of the imperative is lost, and the command is open to all the mediating interpretation that the contingencies of the singular situation puts forward, and the universal objective has been reduced to conditioning by private concerns; the only "ought" that can now be expressed is that "one ought to know (what, in general, the truth is which is to be told)," but this no longer has the pretence of dictating any determinate course of action, and the content that the supposedly self-determining universal law gave itself turns out to be no content at all. The second example, "love thy neighbour as thyself," again can be put forward as a universal law of self-consciousness, perhaps on the ground that to be self-consciousness is to be committed to the value of self-consciousness, which means being committed to others as to oneself.[63] Here again, however, the mediation implicit in the content of "love," just like the mediation in the concept of "telling the truth," above, results in this command not being immediately intelligible, but, rather, being intelligible only in relation to the determinate and contingent features of singular situations, yet again revealing that the action immediately dictated by the imperative is not a determinate content, but only an empty concept in need of mediating interpretation. What these examples illustrate is that the conception of a universal law making commands that can be laid overtop of experience, and that are not themselves already that upon which experience is based, can only produce empty commands that need to be interpreted by the intrinsically differentiated actuality, rather than producing commands that can lead our interpretation of that actuality.[64] Like the reason of observation that was laid overtop of phenomena, this law-giving reason likewise ends by producing empty concepts whose only claim to rationality is their conceptual self-identity; that is, the law is just tautology.[65] We must note two things here, then.

First, reason was pushed by the failure of the spiritual animals to recognize the necessity of the universal as *a self-legislator; that is,* insofar as the category—the transcendental ego—specifies determinate laws, *it is a unity that maintains its unity precisely in its self-differentiation.*[66] We have also seen, and this is the second point to note, that reason as here conceived proves sterile. In sum, then, reason has, by its own steam, been driven to the need to posit an identity that is self-differentiating, but its own actuality is inadequate to live up to its posited ideal. Reason's attempt to legislate is thus simultaneously a conceptual advance and an empirical failure.

The final attempt to salvage immediately self-identical reason as the ground of the universality of real individuals is the endeavor to use this simple standard of self-identity as a regulative principle to which laws are forced to conform, rather than as a legislative principle by which laws are generated.[67] Because the only principle of reason is tautology, or formal identity, however, law-testing reason cannot differentiate laws on the basis of their content, but, indeed, this is what it would have to be able to test if it were to be useful.[68] Using the examples of a law for private property and a law against private property, Hegel shows that reasons can be given for advocating both laws, and that law-testing reason will have to recognize that both are admissible laws, since both are intelligible, that is, self-identical.[69] Thus reason is not capable of testing laws.

Hegel concludes this section by arguing that it is precisely the notion of reason as something superimposed, that is, a self-identical law that is not the intrinsic life of the differences, which is the source of the failure here.[70] The demands that reason feels here when it posits the need for objectivity and universality are entirely justified, but its whole stance as separate from actuality precludes it from recognizing that the only phenomenon that *would* satisfy its demands would be the law to which self-conscious actuality is *already* committed, that is, that law that really does characterize its very being as self-consciousness and that thus does not need to be superimposed on experience.[71]

Throughout Section C, then, we have seen how the immediate conception of reason fails at every turn to produce what it must produce, namely, a ground for identifying the singular self with the universal. In each case (spiritual animals, legislating, and regulating), the immediacy of the universal, and the immediacy of its intended identification with actuality, precluded any capacity for a penetration into the intrinsically self-mediated realm of activity and actuality, and in each case we have seen that actuality provided the real ground upon which the universal was a parasite, where the precise opposite was what reason posited.

Conclusion

Descartes' *Meditations on First Philosophy* offer a strong argument for the ontological independence of the singular self that is immediately identical with the universal, and this argument for the separability of self-contained self-consciousness from living embodiment has always remained the most compelling ground for an ontological dualism of self and body. In Chapter V, "Reason," we have studied the dynamic of this self that identifies a "transcendental ego" and takes itself to be immediately identical with this universal self. In Section A, "Observing Reason," we saw how this conception of selfhood implied a dualism of reason and nature, of inner and outer, of identity and difference, and we saw that observation animated by such a commitment to dualism was ultimately sterile, and unable to live up to its own animating principle: the "scientific imperative." In observing reason, then, there is a contradiction between its concept and its actuality.

In Section B, the same reason, now considered as animating social practice, found itself unable to live up to its constitutive objective of winning the world over to rationality, but in this case it was plagued by the dualism of reason and social institutions, rather than reason and nature; here, rational self-consciousness *modified its identity* through committing itself to social institutions, but it was unable to recognize this change of identity, for it could not acknowledge that institutions could be constitutive of the actuality of reason.

Finally, in Section C, reason again faced a dualism, this time a dualism of reason and its expression. Here, reason found itself unable to recognize that the process of expressing an intention, that is, the process in and through which an immediate project or imperative comes to give itself actual content, could reflect back on the intention: reason's commitment to the *immediate self-identity* of the universal would not allow it to find the identity of the universal existing only as a self-reflected individual that is a unit only as a *result* of a mediating process of actualization, or self-differentiating self-expression.

Thus the three mediating, intrinsically differentiated elements that have here been excluded from having a constitutive role in the self-identity of the rationally self-conscious self are *nature, institution* and *expression*. We have seen, in each case, that it is the failure of reason to recognize the constitutive role of each of these moments that has led to its failure to fulfill its project; that is, we have seen that the real imperative facing the rational self-consciousness is to find its identity only in and through these moments. What we have learned by the failure of reason is that we must not operate on the dualism of identity and difference that is the genus of all the dualisms we have encountered; we have learned that self-identity must be reflective and self-differentiating, and that therefore selfhood *must be embodied*; and we have seen that this embodiment is precisely characterized by these three moments of *nature, institution,* and *expression.*

Spirit

nine
Spirit and Skepticism

It is common to notice that, whereas the earlier sections of the *Phenome-nology of Spirit* advance from certainty to truth, the argument of the "Spirit" chapter advances from truth to certainty, from "The True Spirit" to "Spirit That Is Certain of Itself." My interest in this chapter is in understanding why it is that the dialectic of the concept of spirit takes this form of moving us away from an established ground to a situation of subjective ungroundedness. I will try to make sense of this first by turning to the dialectic of skepticism to see how truth—the answer to skepticism—is established in and by phenomenological method, and then watch the dialectic of this truth—the truth that is spirit—to see a reemergence of a skeptical dialectic. *This* dialectic of skepticism will ultimately coalesce with the dialectic of spirit in a spirit that is certain *only* of itself, a skeptical spirit, or a spiritual skeptic. Here we will see how the problems of ethics and epistemology are ultimately the problem that is phenomenological method itself.

1. Skepticism and Ethics

The dialectic of skepticism contains *in nuce* the whole form of the dialectical phenomenology that is the project of Hegel's *Phenomenology of Spirit*.[1] We could come to this conclusion on external grounds, simply by looking to the "Introduction," in which Hegel's phenomenological method is explicitly developed from a reflection on skeptical concerns.[2] I want, however, to establish this claim through a more internal consideration of the dialectic of skepticism as it is described in the section entitled "The Freedom of Self-Consciousness."

The skeptical stance of which Hegel offers a phenomenological description is the stance of self-interpretation that can find no reliable criterion for self-interpretation. To understand this position, the ancient skeptics are better models to turn to than Hume, who is more likely to be the figure we moderns more immediately associate with skepticism. Though Hume is "skeptical" in the sense that he concludes that we can have no knowledge of the form of the world, he remains dogmatic inasmuch as—on the standard interpretation, at least—he identifies a single source of reliable knowledge; that is, he confidently asserts that our experience is made up of ideas and impressions that he interprets as having their origin in sensation, and he advances this claim polemically against the claims of reason. For the ancient skeptics, on the contrary, sensation is no more reliable than anything else.[3] Let us consider, for example, the "ten modes" of Aenesidemus.

What Aenesidemus offers is a method for challenging any claim. He offers ten techniques for establishing a counter-claim to any truth claim that one might put forward. Through the counter-claim, one establishes a kind of antinomy—on the one hand this seems true, but on the other hand that seems true. Once the antinomy is established, it cannot be resolved, for the adjudication of the claims needs a criterion to turn to, but to select one criterion over another begs the question of the antinomy, since it is precisely the criterion for truth-claims that has been challenged in the antinomy. Thus, to a claim of reason one opposes a claim of sense or vice versa, and this opposition of criteria cannot be resolved by either rational argument or appeal to experience, inasmuch as either mode of resolution would presuppose what needs to be proved.[4] Unlike the Humean skeptic, who knows that we cannot know the external world, the ancient skeptic cannot decide whether we can know it or not and must settle, rather, for the unresolvability of the epistemological, metaphysical, and moral conflicts with which we are confronted. In this respect, the antinomies of Kant's dialectic are better exempla of ancient skepticism than is Hume's empiricism, inasmuch as they attest to the unresolvability of the *equally compelling* claims of rationalism and empiricism with respect to all the major themes of our existence. For the skeptic as Hegel understands it, then, our experience is "a medley of sensuous and intellectual presentations," which cannot be hierarchically ordered according to a principle: they are qualitatively indistinguishable experiences, differing only as different "quantitative magnitudes" of the self-same genus of, perhaps, "subjective experience."[5]

Now, for an ancient stoic (the rival of the ancient skeptic), these different magnitudes would be taken to be so many *objects* of experience to which I can assent or from which I can dissent; that is, the self would be experienced as that which can withdraw from this medley and determine for itself its own stand. The skeptic is more consistent than the stoic, however, and recognizes (as does Hume) that the self is nothing over and above these experiences. The "self" just is this "absolute dialectical unrest": "it is just in this process that this consciousness, instead of being self-identical, is in fact nothing but a purely casual, confused medley, the dizziness of a perpetually self-engendered disorder."[6] The skeptic cannot stand aloof from these experiences and judge them as objects, for the skeptic is just the experience that these conflicting claims are its very reality, its very capacity for judgment or "negativity."

In this last point, however—that is, in the inability to stand aloof from these conflicting claims—we have the seed for the dialectical transformation of skepticism into a new mode of self-consciousness. The stoic announces its freedom as a kind of arbitrariness of judgment, the power of "free will" to assert itself according to its own self-controlled sense. The skeptic, however, reveals that self-conscious selfhood is not a sphere of arbitrary and immediate self-control but is, rather, the experience of various claims as *immediate compulsions within its own judgment* rather than objects for judgment. For the skeptic, experience shows it what it is *already* committed to, what judgments it has already made. The skeptic self-consciousness finds itself *already committed*, and not free to decide what it believes—and its commitments conflict.

This skeptical self-recognition holds the key to its own self-overcoming, however, because it opens the door to the study of the experience of commitment—the experience of necessity *within* self-consciousness. Because the skeptic has abrogated the authority to decide between its commitments, the skeptic cannot decide for itself or in advance whether it really is true that its commitments conflict unresolvably—for this information, it must turn to the description of its own experience in order to let its experience reveal to it what are its commitments. The skeptic cannot legitimately object, in other words, to the discovery that he or she is overpoweringly compelled in one direction or another, or to the discovery that its commitments do not conflict. It is to phenomenology—the description of the commitments of consciousness as they are actually lived—that the skeptic must turn for the answer to this question, and to object to the discoveries is simply to fall back into the stoic stance of the presumption of self-control, that is, the stance that the skeptic self-consciousness has already shown to be bankrupt. Hegel describes this dialectical advance from immediate skepticism to phenomenology as beginning with the recognition that the experience of the conflict of compulsions must itself be the experience *of* a single self-consciousness; that is, there must be, so to speak, a unified space of experience *as* the experience of the *conflict* itself.[7] It must be the case, in other words, that "I" experience this conflict; or, as Kant might put it, experience, even the experience of conflict, must occur as or within the realm of the transcendental unity of apperception.

Thus the skeptical experience leads naturally into the project of the phenomenological observation of consciousness in which the object of the observation is the *internal* dynamic of the compulsions that constitute the life of experiencing consciousness, which is, of course, Hegel's project of dialectical phenomenology.[8] The simple skeptic is too quick to decide that experience does not make sense: this skepticism is not sufficiently empirical, in that it does not sufficiently found its claims on the description of the actual experience of consciousness. Indeed, we have seen that the skeptical project properly pursued leads us to look for the compulsions that establish for the experiencing consciousness the form of a coherent self-experience, the space of the "I" as the one *for whom* there are conflicts. What Hegel's phenomenology goes on to show (in the last four chapters of the *Phenomenology of Spirit*) is that the conflicts that the conscious self experiences do not, in fact, have the form of simply a "confused medley," but a form that is, rather, intelligible, systematically self-organizing, and therefore open to science. In order to make the connection, now, to the concept of spirit, I want to conclude this first section with a consideration of Hegel's description of *ethical* experience as the lived recognition of the coherence of compulsion, as this is described in the final paragraph of the "Reason" chapter.

In this final paragraph of the "Reason" chapter, Hegel describes the *ethical* experience, which he illustrates through Sophocles' portrayal of Antigone.[9] This paragraph comes at the end of a critique of a Kantian approach to dutiful moral action,[10] and the grounds of Hegel's critique here resemble the arguments just considered in relation to skepticism. According to the Kantian approach that is here under critique, various principles for governing action present themselves to our rational judgment, and the moral stance is the one that determines its mode of action through evaluation of the rationality of the contending principles. This description should remind us of the stoic response to the conflicts within experience; that is, it should remind us of the attitude that presumes its own sufficiency to decide how it will evaluate competing claims that present themselves as so many objects for judgment (with the caveat, now, that the judger is to judge according to the dictates of reason and not according to the arbitrariness of will). Hegel turns to Antigone's experience of ethical duty as an experience that is not *confronted by* a set of options for her own judgment; instead, she experiences immediately the lived compulsion to accept one path and reject others. For Antigone, the laws that command one's action simply *are*: their compelling force as duties does not require any mediation of singular rational judgment but is lived, rather, as the immediate form of intelligibility within experience, the immediate form in which things make sense. This, according to Hegel, is what a phenomenological description of the experience of duty reveals. The experience of the "should" is not to be understood as an imposition upon, or a derivation from, our experience of what is, but is, rather, *already* present in our experience of "is." Within human experience, we do not have to "get to an ought from an is," for there can *be*, for us, only insofar as we find ourselves subject to "should."[11] For Hegel, the ethical dimension is the always already present experience of immediately compelling "shoulds" in the organizing, form-giving position within our consciousness of what is.

What Antigone shows us is that the immediate experience of duty is one of finding one's experience *already* organized into a coherent form such that, unlike the skeptic, one lives with presentations that are not mere quantitative variations on a single experiential quality but that present, rather, an organized, qualitative hierarchy of compulsions. What Antigone's experience shows, in other words, is that skepticism does not present a neutral phenomenological description of experience but is, rather, a specific stance of experience that is itself based on an endorsement of a particular mode of selecting and interpreting experience according to principles of judgment and self-description that are not, ultimately, coherent. The principles of skepticism in fact imply the need for an endorsement of phenomenological description, and phenomenological description reveals that we find ourselves committed to lived systems of interpretation that are experienced as immediate duties to interpret in specific ways. It is this experience of ourselves as participating in a world already organized by such duties—a world in which we are subject to the governance by laws of human action that are not themselves the product of human rational judgment—that Hegel studies under the name of spirit.[12]

2. Spirit and Skepticism

I have just been suggesting that a phenomenology of ethical experience refutes the skeptic's claims about the form of experience, revealing, in place of the "dizziness" of the "confused medley" of perceptions, a comfortable unity and coherence within experience. Contrary to the skeptic's claims, such comfortable coherence is the immediate form of our being-in-the-world. What we will see in our study of spirit, however, is the return of a certain version of the skeptical experience with a phenomenological legitimation that was lacking to it in its formulation as a simple stance of self-consciousness, as a putatively neutral description of the immediate form of experience. *Through* the very dynamism of the compulsions of ethical life itself, as well as the dynamism of the other forms of spiritual life (culture and morality), we will be led to experiences of lived conflict that will, in the end, present something like the experience of "dialectical unrest" and the rejection of absolute knowledge with which skepticism presented us. To make this point, I will discuss the three forms of spirit and consider how each of them gives rise to an experience of skepticism. First, let me return to the ethical experience—Antigone's experience—to see how a phenomenon of skepticism emerges within it.

a. Ethics and Skepticism

The ethical experience is essentially communal. An ethical community is formed by those who recognize that they share a place in reality inasmuch as they share a sense for how actuality makes demands upon them to behave toward each other. Hegel defines spirit as the "I that is We and We that is I," and this shared sense of what is to be done is the initial experience of the "we."[13] In the experience of ethical duty, I experience myself as defined by the requirement that I act in certain ways. My very "I" is formed by its placement within the logic of the laws it endorses. The "we" of ethical life is the community of those who share the sense of how their identities are defined by the laws prescribed to them by reality.

Now, in the ethical community, these laws are taken to be of the order of things, and not rational judgments: "the ethical order exists merely as something *given*."[14] This experience of one's identity as formed through the subjection to an already existent reality immediately formed by "shoulds" has the consequence that one's personal subjective judgment is not essential to defining oneself. Thus, in the realm of ethical life, Hegel writes,

> The single consciousness is only the existent unit insofar as it is aware of the universal consciousness [i.e., the law or custom] in its singularity as its *own* being, since what it does and is, is the universal custom.[15]

In ethical consciousness, one takes oneself to be defined by actuality, and not to be in possession of the power of singular self-definition.

> The single, individual consciousness as it exists immediately in the real ethical order, or in the nation, is a solid unshaken trust . . . and therefore he is not aware of himself as being a pure singularity on its own account.[16]

The ethical community is the individuals who define themselves by their participation in the ethical we, which itself defines itself by the preservation of its laws, and not by the recognition of the singular judgments of individuals.

The ethical life is the life of a community that experiences its identity and the identities of its members as given to it by nature or the gods, that is, by independently existent actuality itself. In an ethical community, the members do not have to make their own identities or wonder about what is to be done, for reality has already accounted for that. The members of the ethical community experience the immediate actual situation as sufficient to dictate action. Hegel refers to this situation in which all questions are given as already answered as the "happy state" of the ethical substance,[17] or "the true spirit."[18] The ethical consciousness trusts in a "pre-established harmony" of actuality to guarantee that the realization of the good is possible, and it trusts in its immediate sense of ethical duty to be the guide to achieving this goodness. It is this trust, this "troth," that is the sense of "truth" in Hegel's "True Spirit." This security, this happiness, turns out, however, to be unsatisfactory as a stance on the demands of self-conscious existence.

In fact, the experience of duty presupposes freedom (as Kant showed in the *Groundwork of the Metaphysics of Morals*). To have a sense of a duty I must perform, I must recognize myself not to be a part of nature—not to be a subject of simple mechanical causality—but to be a being capable of spontaneity, of the inauguration of action.[19] The notion of duty relies on a notion of obligation, where this is understood to be something that must compel the will of a being capable of doing otherwise. The ethical consciousness, however, denies the essentiality of its singular initiative—its singular capacity to inaugurate significance—and treats duties as properties of the natural world to which it is naturally subject, as in the case of a young man who lives from the view that "I am just a son, beholden to the demands of family life." The ethical self experiences its own identity as flowing from the laws, without recognizing that the laws owe their efficacy—their very identity as laws—to the single wills that accept them.

The ethical consciousness is committed to the trust in the harmony of its world, but this harmony, in fact, is not guaranteed. The ethical consciousness presumes that actuality will lead itself forward harmoniously, when in fact reality's march into the future is shaped by the ways in which the spontaneous freedom of the individual members is deployed—actions in accordance with duty, in other words (and this is the realization of the harmony), do not occur naturally.[20]

Furthermore, the ethical consciousness is committed to the view that its ethical consciousness is simply the straightforward perception of the nature of actuality. In fact, however, many different and conflicting "duties" can be thus ethically "perceived" by different agents. Separate agents and separate communities develop this same ethical frame of mind without recognizing the same duties to be the ones that are naturally prescribed. The ethical consciousness, in other words, is not simply the unbiased perception of nature but is developed, rather, through habituation to the particular customs and traditions that have evolved historically within a human community.[21]

Because these customs do not emanate simply from nature, but rather from the historical ways that human communities have come to shape their practices, there is no guarantee that the principles and values behind these laws are coherent, and the trust of the ethical consciousness in the laws is in fact unjustified. The insufficiency of the ethical consciousness comes to its own consciousness in that situation in which the duties to which it considers itself beholden conflict, that is, when they show themselves to be insufficient to determine how to behave in some situation. In such a situation, the ethical agent must improvise, either deciding how to act in an unspecified case or deciding between laws that prescribe different actions. The law is to accept as king the son of the deceased king—but there are twin sons. The law is to obey the king and to bury the dead—but the king orders the dead not to be buried.[22] In such situations, the individual ethical agent must act in a way that is not "mechanically" prescribed by the law, and it is in this situation that the ethical world is experienced by the ethical consciousness to be insufficient to determine the situation and to be in need of supplementation from the initiative of the single agent.

The trust of the happy ethical consciousness in the preestablished harmony of its world is fated to be shattered in the experience of the insufficiency of the ethical order adequately to prescribe action.[23] Here we can see the motivation for the emergence of a skeptical consciousness from within ethical commitment. An ethical community cannot provide an adequate orientation to self-conscious life, because, by presuming there to be a natural, preestablished harmony to existence, it fails to account for the role of human spontaneity in shaping human life. There thus emerges from the ethical world an experience of the insufficiency of the ethical criterion for determining action, an experience of a need for interpretation and action that is not supplied by ethical commitments. The ethical consciousness thus naturally motivates the emergence of a consciousness withdrawn from ethical life, not sufficiently compelled by the putative laws of the world. While skepticism may well be inadequate as a phenomenology of self-consciousness, there is certainly something right about it, in that it identifies a phenomenon analogous to that which we see legitimately emerging within the phenomenology of ethical life.

The insufficiency of ethical life that motivates the emergence of a skeptical attitude is specifically the inability of ethicality to recognize the weight of human singularity in shaping commitments. The skepticism it engenders is, correspondingly, a skepticism that amounts to the experience of singular withdrawal from the compulsions that attach to the customary institutions of established tradition. Let us now consider "Culture," the second form of spirit identified by Hegel, in order to see both how it answers to this ethical skepticism and how it engenders a skepticism of its own.

b. Culture and Skepticism

Once one has recognized the essentiality of one's singularity, this recognition cannot be effaced. The ethical order cannot retain its compelling force once one has experienced the compulsion to experience oneself as withdrawn from the immediacy of duty. In the skeptical experience that emerges from ethicality, one recognizes that one can no longer be part of the ethical "we"— the parameters of the we no longer speak on behalf of oneself, of one's own commitments. This emergence of a new sense of the I—the I as alienated from the ethical order—motivates in its turn, however, the emergence of a new we.

Initially, this skeptical moment simply undermines the we, inasmuch as it is the specific refusal to be defined by the identity the ethical we projects. Perhaps we can imagine something like this in the initial experience of the adolescent who suddenly recognizes him or herself to be immediately freed from the constraints of family identity. Adolescents, however, regularly go on to grow into new identities that are neither simply reinstatements of the ethical community nor simply lives of singular isolation. Similarly, this skeptical moment, while it is the collapse of the ethical we, is not, for that reason, the collapse of the we as such. The we that emerges from ethical skepticism is the we that Hegel's calls by the name "*Bildung,*" or "culture."

The ethical society is defensive against the power of the single will. Culture, on the contrary, is the society that embraces the single will and finds within the experience of singular initiative a motivation toward a communal good. Culture is the society that recognizes in human identity a destiny and a worth that is distinct from what is immediately offered by actuality.

> This equality with everyone [that characterizes the world of Culture] is . . . not that immediate recognition and validity of self-consciousness simply because it *is*; on the contrary, to be valid it must have conformed itself to the universal by the mediating process of alienation.[24]

Culture posits human identity as realizable only through culture—through cultivation.[25] Culture is thus the society that calls upon single individuals to reject actuality as it immediately occurs and to draw it up to a higher good. The skepticism that grew out of ethical life recognized the insufficiency of immediate actuality to account for the values it experiences. Inasmuch as the ethical consciousness operated on the presumption that meaning was given by immediate actuality, this rejection of immediate actuality seemed also to be a rejection of meaning and its replacement by arbitrariness. This was a hasty conclusion, however. Turning away from actuality does not have to entail turning away from meaning, and this is what culture recognizes—it is the skeptical moment turned to a new constructive purpose in recognizing a new possibility for value beyond what is offered by immediate actuality. The we of culture is the we based on this vision of a value beyond actuality, and culture is the social life lived in the hope of realizing this better identity.

To participate in this culture is to experience one's own singularity as drawn toward and judged by a higher identity. Here, we see a new experience of qualitatively ordered compulsions within the single ego that again gives the lie to the skeptical phenomenology of self-consciousness. For the self of culture, however, the compulsion takes a different form from that experienced by the immediate ethical consciousness. The self of culture does not experience immediate actuality as the bearer of the should. The self of culture, rather than harmonizing with nature, experiences immediate actuality as in need of transformation and experiences its own self as compelled by higher powers that demand this transformation: "The self knows itself as actual only as a *transcended* self."[26] Indeed, the self of culture experiences something more like the "should" we associate with Kantian moral philosophy, for it is the experience of a "should" that has its value conferred on it precisely by the commitment offered by the single will. The self of culture experiences the compulsion to be singularly responsible for cultivating meaning.

Culture is characterized by practices of, for example, nobility, good will, criticism, or taste. All of these are practices of conversion: they require, first, the act of conversion within the single will from a natural life to a commitment to a *chosen* criterion for critical judgment of one's own values, and, second, the practice of conversion as a work to be performed in the world in which its natural existence is subjected to cultivation and criticism according to this same standard. In each case, self-conscious identity is fulfilled and the good is realized through the choice of the single individual to accept the responsibility for acting according to a higher identity, and the society of culture is the we that embraces this value: it is a society of universal humanity that admits as its members a universal humanity inasmuch as all self-conscious agents, qua single egos, have the capacity to recognize this value and make this conversion, and this society holds all single egos responsible to make this conversion. This society of conversion—whether the religious society that demands conversion to, for example, Christianity, or the democratic society that demands conversion to universal rationality—differs fundamentally from the ethical community, then, for three related reasons. First, it builds itself within the recognition of the single will rather than in opposition to it. Second, it is a society that specifically posits itself as distinct from nature and as a product of human achievement rather than a preestablished harmony. Finally, this is a society that recognizes humanity as a universal phenomenon, in opposition to the particularity that characterizes the identity of the ethical community and its distinctive traditional commitments.

What I have tried to describe here is the way in which there is a second form of we that corresponds to a second form of experiencing a qualitatively distinct, self-interpretive criterion for one's self-consciousness. I have also tried to show that this responds to the distinctive form of skepticism that emerges within ethical consciousness. What I want to show now is that this form of experience again motivates the emergence of a distinctive form of skepticism.

The human identity projected in culture is an identity alienated from itself. The premise of culture is twofold: it is a critical withdrawal from immediate actuality, and it is an endorsement of the universal features that characterize singular self-consciousness. These two premises are closely related in that they both amount to a denigration of the relevance of the determinate specificities of one's situation in defining one's identity. Indeed, culture sees worth in these particularities only insofar as they are fodder for rejection in favor of what is universally self-same in self-consciousness. The very determinacies that mark the distinctiveness of our situations are denied essentiality in defining our identities.

Skepticism of culture takes the form of the compulsion to embrace particularities, despite the prescription to renounce their essentiality. In fact, we always do retain an ineffaceable commitment to particularities inasmuch as we must always be devoting our resources to specific circumstances as they present themselves to our perspectival situation. Whereas ethics collapses in the experience of singular free choice, culture collapses in the experience of the particularities of desire. Even in one's most virtuous efforts to work for the universal good, one privately chooses where one invests one's efforts, and one benefits oneself; even in serving God, one wins one's own salvation. Indeed, our identities are always invested in a range of particularities, from the determinacies of our bodies and family memberships to our set of friends, interests, perspectives, and histories. To act will always be to act upon, and on the basis of, these determinacies. To be a determinate act, an action must be exclusionary, particular: it must respond to *this* situation, and not that. The skepticism that attaches to culture is the recognition of one's commitment to such particularity, the recognition that an abstracted universality cannot account for the determinacy of one's identity.

This skepticism can be expressed simply as dissatisfaction with the abstract universalizing of the cultural stance. One can simply experience a conflict in the demand to submit the particularities of one's life to the impartiality of reason or the dictates of faith. Indeed, such a conflict is always lurking in the life of culture. Here, the experience of skepticism would be the experience of oneself as unequal to the task of full conversion while being subject to the weight of the universal juggernaut as if it were a bulldozer leveling all particular claims that lie in its path. Skepticism here, then, is not the experience of singular withdrawal from actuality in choice, but the experience of the inability sufficiently to abandon one's determinacy, one's desires. As with the response to ethical skepticism, the response to this cultural skepticism takes two systematic forms—one destructive, one constructive. Let me describe the destructive taking up of this skepticism; the constructive response to this skepticism will be the subject of the next section.

The destructive taking up of this skepticism is a reactionary reversion to ethical sentiments: against the emptiness and anti-naturalism of culture, traditional institutions such as the family can be invoked as binding particularities against, for example, the libertine who shows determinacy *is* only to-be-overcome (the libertine who fulfills culture by showing its emptiness in an attitude that appears the very opposite of the ideal of being "cultivated"). One finds that one can never be sufficiently impartial to live up to the demands of culture but is instead always using one's powers and abilities to pursue one's own particular interest. To take a stance on this recognition of the ineffaceability of particularity within the terms of reference available in the cultural world can amount only to a reversion to the ethical stance that culture has already transcended. (We see this in a politically conservative response to rational democracy, for example, that insists on a reversion to family values or to ancient models of virtue, and so on.) This skepticism is clearly a kind of hypocrisy inasmuch as it must revert to a stance of which it already lives the refutation, and this is the cultural version of the experience of an "antinomic" commitment to two opposed values—here the experience of (1) the obligation to convert and (2) the inability to abandon one's particularity. While this stance is hypocritical—indeed, it is skepticism as hypocritical dogmatism—it nicely demonstrates, though, the experience of the emptiness of culture, and the need to find a way to coordinate the conflicting commitments to particularity and universality within one's life. In turning to morals, or "spirit that is certain of itself," we will see the constructive taking up of this cultural skepticism.

c. Morality and Skepticism

What the ethical and the cultural spirits share is a sense that the universal—the good—is an already existent reality to which we must conform. The ethical spirit sees its duties as already prescribed in nature, while the cultural spirit sees its duty to be inscribed in an already existent beyond. The essence of the moral spirit is that it takes its orientation not from some already established universal good but from the really existing singular self in its particularities; in this realm, the good is to be accomplished, not to be reached.[27] I want to explain more of how I understand the moral spirit by returning to the skeptical concerns that I saw to be motivated by the cultural spirit.

The cultural spirit is always called upon to identify with the universal, but its very self is inescapably constituted by determinate particularities. Consequently, cultural *action* is always forced to find the ways in which the universal can be found in and realized through its particularities; that is, it is the terms set by its particularities to which the universal must speak. The *imperative* of culture, however, is the opposite: culture demands, on the contrary, that particularity answer to the terms set by the universal. The moral stance simply amounts to seeing this problem of culture as a success and not a failure. Rather than experiencing the need to remain particular as a failure while still feeling constrained by the cultural imperative, the moral stance endorses the need to begin as and remain a single, determinate individual, and transforms the skepticism into a critical reevaluation of the conception of the universal good.

In each of the two preceding shapes of spirit, the pattern of the dialectical advance was the experience of a skeptical experience of being driven back from the "we" to the "I," first in its singularity, then in its particularity. The emergence of the new spirit of culture from the I-experience of ethical skepticism was this I finding itself compelled by a new we. So too here, the moral spirit that emerges out of cultural skepticism is again the skeptical I finding itself compelled by a new we. Unlike the we of ethics and culture, however, the we of morality is not an existent identity with which to identify, but a we that needs to be performed through the singular actions of particular selves.

The moral spirit—the moral we—is a we that is not guaranteed, but is real only through the actions of single agents who make it real by establishing a shared identity through cooperative action. The moral stance is the stance that recognizes the need to bring a shared community to birth within the particularities of the relationships of single selves who cannot turn beyond themselves for the means and the actuality of doing so. What has been proved by the dialectic of spirit is the indubitability of one's commitment to one's own singularity and particularity, while the universal, which appeared indubitable in the earlier spirits, has been cast into doubt. The *moral* commitment is a commitment to human singularity and particularity, and to the need to turn to these moments of singularity and particularity as the only possible source for the universality in human life, the need for which we experience as a similarly inevadable compulsion.

> [The moral spirit] is essentially the movement of the self to set aside the abstraction of immediate existence and to become conscious of itself as a universal—and yet to do so neither by the pure alienation and disruption of itself and of actuality, nor by fleeing from it. Rather it is *immediately present* to itself in its substance for this is the intuited pure certainty of itself, and just *this immediacy* which is its own reality, is all reality.[28]

The we of morality is a we experienced as to be realized, and to be realized here and now. Now once again there is an experience of skepticism that attaches to this moral spirit, but, I contend, this skepticism, unlike the earlier forms of skepticism, does not amount to a transformation of the moral stance but is, rather, its own proper form.

The skepticism that attaches to morality is simply the inability to find a guarantee for the propriety of one's actions outside the realm of one's experience. It is, in other words, the experience of the inability of one's situation to compel action. The moral stance turns to its situation and its commitments for motivation, but this motivation can never absolve the individual of the need to have its actions evaluated by the others for whom he or she acts, that is, for the moral stance, the we is experienced as my belonging to a world of others to whom I am accountable, without any guarantee that my actions will satisfactorily recognize them or be recognized by them. Thus the moral stance is inherently skeptical about itself. This skepticism, however, is neither an inhibition to action (the beautiful soul) nor something to be resolved and eliminated (in the guarantees of Kantian moral formalism). It is, rather, the stance of vigilant self-criticism and vulnerability to the need to be recognized according to the perspectives of others (which Hegel calls "conscience").

3. Moral Skepticism as Phenomenology

With the coalescence of the dialectic of skepticism and the dialectic of spirit, our story is complete. What I want to note by way of conclusion is that this dialectical development has led us to the same point to which the internal critique of skepticism in the "Self-Consciousness" chapter led us. The analysis in the "Self-Consciousness" chapter led us to conclude that the truth of skepticism is the phenomenological method. This, in fact, is the same conclusion to which we have been led through our tracing of the role of skepticism within the dialectic of spirit. What I have called "moral skepticism" is just phenomenology.

The skeptical stance of the moral spirit is precisely the enactment of the self-judging character of the particularities of our lived situations. In morality, we look to our own situation of localized, particularized, and singularized intersubjective life to see how the particularities of the situation give rise within themselves to universal principles of self-criticism and self-transformation. Moral action as I have described it is precisely the attempt to enable our situations to enact their own dialectical self-criticism without reference to an external standard. Unlike the ethical or the cultural agents who look to an already existent universality by which to judge situations, the moral agent must watch for the immanent emergence of criteria for judgment within the determinate situation, and his or her observations will be vindicated or vitiated only by the recognition of this intersubjective situation itself. Surely this is just the description of Hegel's own phenomenological method, itself a reanimation of the Socratic practice of philosophy.

ten
The Contradictions of Moral Life: Hegel's Critique of Kant

Our experience is fundamentally intuitive. What this means is that we will always be finding our way in life through experiences that impress themselves upon us compellingly, without the possibility of stepping beyond our own ways of making sense to find some independent ground of justification for our beliefs. The great philosophical positions amount to so many articulations of these compelling intuitions that we use as guides to organize the broader range of our experiences. Each of Hobbes, Hume, Kant, and Hegel has introduced such a compelling insight into our philosophical discourse, and the compelling force of these intuitions has in no case been spent. Hobbes or Hume will not be studied in this chapter, but I mention them because in many ways it is against their empiricist insights that Kant articulates his own most compelling insights. What this chapter will address is the conflict between the Kantian and the Hegelian insights.

The conflict between Kant and Hegel has been frequently and ably studied by many. Most frequently, these studies have focused upon Hegel's accusation that the categorical imperative is empty or upon the different metaphysical bases of Hegel's position that lead him to construe reason in a manner opposed to Kant's.[1] While such approaches are entirely fitting, I shall maintain that the real source of Hegel's critique comes from his commitment to a phenomenological method and that this is where we must turn if we want to understand the way in which Hegel understands his position to result from the immanent self-critique of the Kantian philosophy. This chapter will begin the articulation of this side of the Hegelian critique by following his study of the central Kantian moral insight as he approaches this in his *Phenomenology of Spirit*. My central concern will be to show why Hegel believes Kant to be ultimately duplicitous in answering the question "what is primary?" within moral experience.

According to Hegel, Kant's moral position is ultimately contradictory, and he specifies the central contradiction of the "Moral View of the World" in a paragraph of the *Phenomenology of Spirit*:

> Consciousness starts from the idea that, *for it*, morality and reality do not harmonize; but it is not in earnest about this, for in the deed the presence of this harmony becomes *explicit for it*. But it is not in earnest even about this deed, since the deed is something individual; for it has such a high purpose, the *highest good*. But this again is only a dissemblance of the facts, for such dissemblance would do away with all action and all morality.[2]

This claim is the core of the argument of the section of the *Phenomenology* called "Dissemblance," in which Hegel unravels a "whole nest" of purported contradictions within the Kantian moral philosophy. The technicalities of Hegel's treatment of Kant in this section have already been very helpfully analyzed and soundly rejected by R. Z. Friedman and defended by H. S. Harris.[3] I myself am not going to go through the details of the textual argument, nor pursue how, precisely, the different stages of Hegel's account of the moral worldview correspond to the details of Kant's position. I want, rather, to try to articulate the argumentative core of Hegel's critique. In Hegel's view, there is something simultaneously very important and damningly self-contradictory in the Kantian project of morality, and this basic sense is what I will here articulate. The contradiction can be put simply by saying that, on its own terms, Kantian morality needs immorality; that is, if moral action were successful in bringing nature, inclination, and reality in general into line with reason and duty, morality itself would disappear, for it exists only when it has an immoral, irrational other to oppose. Expressed in this way, however, this argument that success is self-annihilation seems quite formal and unconvincing. The goal of my paper is to explain this argument in such a way as to show that it is not just formal, and not at all empty, but does, rather, go to the very heart of both the value and the problem of Kantian morality. I will begin in section 1 by discussing what I take to be the core insight of Kant's moral philosophy, and then turn in section 2 to an explanation of what I take to be the core of the Hegelian critique, concluding in section 3 with a positive description of where this critique leaves us.

1. Kant

The strength of Kant's position is his focus on the precise character of what makes a moral action moral. Kant's moral philosophy could be called a phenomenology of duty—or at least, it relies on one. We know what it is to experience a duty. Indeed arguments that attempt to show that we can never really act from pure duty inasmuch as we always respond to self-interested motivations at least know what it is they are arguing against: whether it is Hobbes or Nietzsche who is attacking moral philosophy, the critique still admits that there is an experience of duty—it is just that it is a fraud. Kant's technical argument establishes that even to be able to engage in this debate entails that we have the very reason and the very freedom whose nature it is to put us under obligation, so, for Kant, the simple admission that one under-stands what he is talking about is all he needs to prove himself right. I do not here want to pursue this argument, though. I want to attend, rather, to what I have called the "phenomenology" of duty—I want simply to consider what we normally mean by the term "moral."[4]

Morality fundamentally refers to a kind of agency—morality is a charac-teristic of things we do, of the ways we behave. Moral action needs to be distinguished from two other types of action. First, moral action needs to be distinguished from simple natural or instinctive action. If our actions were all natural—all automatic—like the changes that take place in a plant, these actions would not be moral. Indeed, it might not be proper to call them "actions" at all: they would be changes that happen, but they would not really be "done" "by" "me." This is true whether we think of nature on an Aris-totelian model of dynamic substances or whether we think of nature on the model of a machine deterministically governed by causal laws; in either case, the reason that the changes happen does not reside in a decision or a recogni-tion by the thing that undergoes the changes. Basically, there is no choice, no freedom, involved. We might be happy to have a machine that runs into burning buildings and saves children, even a "human" machine who does this, but such a machine would not warrant moral approbation. We cannot be proud or respectful of a machine that just does what it is programmed to do—at best, we could feel that way about the free being who did the programming or the designing. What is morally valuable about the person who risks her life to save someone (assuming we accept this as an example of moral worth) is that she had to find the motivation in herself—it is the expression of her "her-ness" to run into the building. Even without a successful result, we can respect her choice, her will, whereas even with a successful result from the robot, we are only happy with the result, and do not have our esteem for the machine's identity elevated.

Moral action is, then, action that comes from choice, from freedom. But here, too, it must be distinguished from another kind of action. We typically think that our freedom allows us to choose to do whatever we want. This character of choice does very much make our actions "actions," i.e., not just changes that happen but expressions of decision, of will. Such actions, though, also do not automatically qualify as moral. The simple fact that I chose to do something does not make me morally good. What makes the action moral is that my choice was based on the nature of the action—on its inherent value—and not on the nature of my preference, that is, the value of the action evaluated in reference to me. Kant expresses this by saying that for an action to be moral it must be an action that we have chosen because it is good in itself. According to Kant, to choose an action because it is good in itself is to choose on the basis of reason—on the basis of a universal and necessary criterion—rather than on the basis of contingent and idiosyncratic desires. We are familiar with such experiences of reason in matters of logic or mathematics: in these cases, it is (1) only because we are free that we can be said to add or to deduce, because these are activities of assenting, but (2) in these experiences our freedom shows itself in the ability to recognize that our assent is compelled. Similarly in morality, our action must be freely chosen, but our freedom must take the form of acknowledging the inherent necessity of the action we choose, acknowledging an obligation, a duty.

I take it that this description of moral experience is basically what Kant has to offer. Kant's concern is to mark the specific sort of behavior that has moral value, and also to show why—namely, because it derives from the very nature of rational freedom—this moral value must be inherently valuable to all free, rational beings. It is because we are human—because we are rational animals—that we can be moral, and as humans we recognize this value.

2. The Hypocrisy of Morality

This discussion of moral value, which I think is true to Kant's basic orientation, focuses attention on the distinctive character of the human sphere: our freedom. As is the case in many defenses of theism against the objection posed by the presence of evil in the world, in this Kantian view of morality the highest value is invested in the sphere of human choice and in the *possibility* this gives for moral conduct. To express this from the point of view of defenses of theism, one would say that the human condition, with its fallibility and its possibility of immorality, is itself good, and God is better to create a world in which moral action is possible than a world in which the "right" thing just gets done automatically by nature. It is its *being chosen* that introduces the worth into the most valuable good, and so God makes a better world by creating beings who can choose—and who could, therefore, choose evil—than he would by, as it were, protecting the world against this possibility by pre-programming reality to conform to some putatively good design. Ignoring the theistic backdrop, we must say essentially the same thing in the context of Kantian moral philosophy: the disharmony of nature and the good is the condition of the possibility of moral value, and, indeed, its source; that is, the greatest value is the human condition of freedom that lets morality be a possibility. It would seem, then, that in its own deepest roots morality must be committed to the ultimacy, and the ultimate value, of this human condition with its characteristic imperfection, particularity, contingency, and disharmony.

This, however, is where the moral view of the world starts to face a tension. Morality, remember, demands that one act on the moral law. The moral law—the categorical imperative—is the good, and, according to the moral law, value is found in bringing one's reality into compliance with this law. According to the explicit doctrine of Kantian moral thought, value is found in my bringing my natural self into rational shape, in bringing my nature into harmony with the good. The very imperative of morality is precisely to fight the disharmony of nature and the good, and instead to transform reality—and oneself—into a situation in which actuality *is* the realization of the good. It is here, I think, that we see the basic contradiction—the basic hypocrisy—that Hegel identifies in the Kantian moral stance. On this analysis, we can see how the moral stance relies on two conflicting models of what has primacy within the realm of moral value: the moral stance must simultaneously *implicitly* grant to the human condition of disharmony the highest value and *explicitly* oppose this human condition in the name of the highest value. The roots of morality are in the valorization of the human lot, but its explicit teachings are anti-human. As Nietzsche might charge, the all-too-human moral philosopher shows her hypocrisy, her *ressentiment*, in this moral doctrine that amounts to a self-mortification.[5] Morality is a betrayal of its own principles, its own founding values, its own conditions of possibility.

Another way to say this is that there is no independence to the realm of reason; that is, reason does not exist independently of naturally existing, self-consciousness agents. The reason that is to be morally autonomous must always be *my* reason; it must be *my* autonomy. If not, whatever moral worth might attach to reason's self-determination would have no significance for my moral worth. Moral worth, thus, enters *into* the world of experience only if it is a phenomenon *of* the world of experience, and thus experience must be the soil and seed of moral value, rather than an alien matter upon which it is overlain. But if this is the case, moral goodness cannot be an independently defined value that can be conferred upon the world of experience but is rather a value conferred upon or opened up within the world by the fact of experience.

This, I take it, is the real idea behind Hegel's critique of Kant. It is the thoroughly "anti-Platonist" insight that the human realm must be self-determining. In this sense, it is an attempt to think along with the Kantian focus on the limits of experience and the value of autonomy. Moral significance is a kind of meaning we find ourselves open to and beholden to within experience, but for this very reason its significance is not unconditional, but is conditioned by the inherent nature of experience as such that is the ground of its possibility. Let me try to make this same basic point from two other angles that may help to bring out the force of this reorientation. We can bring out the weight of this point a bit more fully if we consider how Kant understands the relationship between the moral law and specific duties.[6] Recall that the categorical imperative, the expression of the imperative that our rationality imposes upon us, is that one always act in such a way that the subjective maxim of one's will could be willed as a universal law of nature.[7] The constraint on a universal law of nature, as is indicated by the very expression "universal law," is that it be universal and necessary; so with morality, the moral law must obey the constraints of rationality, namely, that it be a universal and necessary truth that holds true simply by virtue of its form without reference to the contingent details of content. Two plus two is four, regardless of what the twos are that are being added. Similarly, the truth must be told simply by virtue of there being a truth and there being a situation of telling, regardless of the particular details of this truth and the telling. The original source of moral value, Kant argued, was our rationality, and consequently the form moral value must take is this rational form. Specific duties, then—that is, the determination of how we must act in specific situations we face—must be *derived* simply by reference to the demands of rationality itself, and cannot be *developed from* the particularities that happen to attach to any given case. *It must be the moral law that interprets the situation for us, and not the situation that interprets the moral law for us.*[8]

In fact, however, we are never in a position to make this separation and to give to the moral law the primary role in interpretation. It can only ever be our understanding of our own situations that allows us to see how the moral law might apply, since the moral law *specifically does not* articulate itself into the terms of our particular situation. It is precisely out of our lived, particular situations that the terms of our moral dilemmas are posed, for the question is how I, *this* I, am to act in *this* situation, and the very premise that nature is not simply the expression of reason—another version of the disharmony identified above—entails that there must be an activity of translation to determine how the formal terms of the law might be brought to bear. If we imagine translating an English sentence into French, we can see what is involved in such translation.

Whatever I say in English can be said in French only if French is itself inherently able to express the point expressed in English. The translation is not an imposition of an alien meaning, but is, rather, the establishing of a correspondence between the sense of the English and the sense already inherently at play within the French language. It is only from the sense available to the French speaker that the French speaker can find access to the sense of the English speaker, and it is only from the terms opened up by the French language that the meaning of the English sentence can be interpreted.

Analogously, reason can have a sense for our particularity—can enter into contact with our particularity—only insofar as it is made to answer to the terms of our particularity.[9] Thus, once again, the real source of our values—the very sense of moral value—must be *in* the particularities of our human condition—

our human condition of disharmony—even as the moral doctrine explicitly asserts that it is the law of pure abstract reason that has the definitive interpretive role here. In other words, what we again see is that the moral stance tacitly draws on the primacy of the particularities of the contingent human situation for its very possibility of being meaningful, while explicitly it asserts the opposite; that is, it asserts that it confers an autonomous meaning upon those particularities. Let me finally take up this point from one last angle.

In the end, I am arguing (along with Hegel, I believe), that Kantian morality faces the same problem as a Cartesian dualism of mind and body.[10] I must have two identities, and they must be simultaneously reconciled and irreconcilable. In Descartes, the two identities are myself as mind and myself as body. The mind is defined as an autonomous realm of significance, and therefore ontologically independent and irreconcilable with the significances of the body, but it is also that which gives direction to the body, and therefore must be reconciled with it. In Kant, I am arguing, there is an analogous dualism of my rationality and my natural self. It must be me who feels the moral obligation, and this must be the same me who must act in this particular situation; yet equally, the me who feels the obligation must be autonomous reason, able to recognize and interpret the law without taint of particularity. For the moral stance to be operative, we must be able to know our duty—we must be rational—but equally rationality must be that pure, alien existence—with which this particular I can never be identical—that dictates to us without prejudice or particularity.[11] I must both be and not be my particularity, I must both be rational and fall short of being rational.

There are thus two sides to the Kantian moral stance that exist in a logical tension with each other. Thus, I propose, Kant can defend his moral insight only by revising it in one of two directions he does not intend. Either Kant must be true to what I have called his phenomenological roots and accept to reconceive the relationship of reason and particularity, and with that reconceive the very sense of the moral imperative, or he must fall back on a purely rationalist position that starts with the dogmatic presumption of the metaphysical independence of the rational mind. The latter, dualistic stance is, I think, untenable for a variety of reasons, leaving the former, phenomenological stance as the only viable option.

So, Hegel's claim that the moral stance is contradictory because the completion of its project would be its annihilation is not, then, merely formal. It is, rather, a condensed way of expressing the duplicity of a stance that simultaneously draws its life and its value from the particularities of the human situation and adopts a stance of renouncing the primacy of this particularity. The moral stance rightly recognizes the phenomenon of obligation, the phenomenon of the experience of necessity within freedom, and it rightly recognizes that our very character as free beings compels us to recognize the worthiness of the experience of obligation; but the Kantian approach to morality takes up this insight in too dualistic a fashion, with the result that it renounces the very foundation of its life; that is, it ends up an enemy of the very form in which human freedom exists, namely, opacity, particularity, embodiment. It is this last point that I will now pick up on through a brief explanation of what I take to be the Hegelian counter-offer to Kantian morality.

3. Hegel

In a way, Kant's problem rests in the third antinomy, which argues that we have two equally essential but irreconcilable experiences: the experience of causal necessity that comes with cognitive life and the experience of free spontaneity that comes with practical life. This opposition is ultimately formulated as the opposition between the experience of the world of nature and the experience of the world of morality.[12] There is something very daring and very honest in Kant's approach here. Kant's embrace of an unreconcilable contradiction at the foundation of human experience is not a turn to irrationalism; indeed, it is hard to imagine a more rigorous and rational thinker than Kant. On the contrary, the antinomy is a profound attempt to do justice to the form human experience actually takes—it is truly an attempt to be phenomenologically sound.[13] Yet it is here that his philosophy shows its limitations.

Kant finds the different spheres of human experience to be unreconcilable only because he begins with a conception of reason that is too abstract; Kant remains essentially Cartesian in his understanding of reason. Though he understands reason to be self-determining, that is, to give itself a content, and in this sense to be "concrete," Kant still understands reason to be formal and abstract inasmuch as it is independent of the particularities of finite experience to which it must be applied. In another context, I would argue with Hegel that this abstraction of reason from the content to which it applies is of a piece with a dualism of reason and matter that is the foundation of a mechanistic physics, and the dualism of the moral law and the situation to which it applies, that is, that (1) mechanistic causality, (2) abstract morality, and (3) a reason that is lost in antinomies are three reflections of the same fundamental dualistic orientation. Schelling especially makes this clear in his *System of Transcendental Idealism*, when he argues that reason must reconcile the two sides of the antinomy it faces, and that it will do this by recognizing a freedom that is the very life of particularity and a natural causality that is inherently intelligible. Schelling returns to something like an Aristotelian sense of the organic as the fundamental form of natural life, and sees self-conscious freedom as just the most sophisticated form of development of natural life. On this model, reason is understood as a rationality that does not *apply* to things but that is the very soul of things, a reason that is *expressed as* the determinacies of reality.[14] I will not sort out all the issues that are involved here; I introduce the issue in this way only to suggest in outline the route this critique of morality would take us if we pursued it back into the heart of Kant's philosophy. What I will end with, though, is just this notion of a concrete reason, a reason that is not applied to particularities but is, rather, that which is expressed by the particularities.

On Hegel's view, Kant is right to see a fundamental value in rational obligation. Hegel's objection, ultimately, is that Kant has misrepresented the nature of reason. On Hegel's understanding, reason is not something to be found elsewhere than in the particular determinations of reality,[15] and in my discussion of "translation" and "interpretation" above I have tried to indicate something of the phenomenological significance of this claim. Reason is not a set of formal rules for performing operations on any self-identical content. Reason is, rather, the very sense, the very intelligibility, of whatever is real. We do not understand reason by looking away from the world and then bringing back its interpretive powers to the world; rather, to reason is, most truly, to see how our situation makes sense. Respect for reason is not achieved by abstracting from particularity: reason is found precisely in respect for particularity. The basic impetus of moral obligation—to be answerable to the demands of reason—remains intact in Hegel, but it is an obligation to *be dictated to* by the specificities of our situations, not to dictate to such situations. To be moral, according to Hegel, still means to be rational, but being rational means being led by the demands of our determinate situations—it means being unable to withdraw into an a priori morality that would somehow know what to do in independence of knowing the situation. This, I think, is another way of saying what I said at the beginning of this chapter, namely, that our experience always remains fundamentally intuitive.

For this reason, morality as re-envisioned by Hegel is still a matter of finding oneself dutifully beholden to the imperatives of reason, but the discernment of what our duty is much more inductive than deductive. More precisely, I think, the moral stance is the phenomenological stance. Though we can say in advance that we ought to be moral, we cannot give a sense to this imperative except by *beginning* with the orientation toward allowing our situation to *show us* what its rationality—its sense—amounts to.

The Hegelian version of the categorical imperative is to approach situations phenomenologically so as to support them in their own dialectical development, and we might thus reformulate the categorical imperative as something like a dialogic imperative. We must approach our ethical situations the same way the *Phenomenology of Spirit* approaches a shape of consciousness: it discerns the inherent rationality of a situation by a kind of discursive engagement precisely with the particularity of that situation, and through this "dialogue" supports the development of this immanent rationality, typically to the point that the situation can recognize its own contradictions and advance beyond them. I have tried to perform such a "dialogue" here with the moral view of the world, that is, within the immanent norms of the intuition that founds our moral experience. In like fashion, we respect reason in our practical life by working to discern the rationality already at play in our own situation, and to develop this situation to the point where the situation can recognize its own contradictions and advance beyond them. The self-transformative character of moral life thus does not come by renouncing our desires and living a independently determined, rule-governed life; it comes, rather, through working in our world in such a way that our situation brings itself to a more self-conscious state. Moral action is thus ultimately indistinguishable from understanding, but an understanding that progresses only by being a stance of dialogic involvement, a stance that is committed to recognizing the inherent rationality of a world that is *essentially* plural and committed to maintaining the value of such a pluralistic conception of rationality. And thus, as I understand it, the moral imperative of dialectical phenomenology is to practice philosophy Socratically.

eleven

Selfhood, Conscience, and Dialectic

Recognition is fundamental to human self-consciousness.[1] For Hegel, truthfully saying "I" is not something that can be done directly and easily, but is a process that can be fulfilled only through the support of others: to be self-conscious—to say "I"—in the fullest sense will always be something achieved by me in community with others; that is, it is a social act. Thus, what says "I" is always necessarily a "we." Hegel gives a phenomenological argument for this in his *Phenomenology of Spirit,* and I will give an account of the basic logical relations involved to show why it is that Hegel refers to the " 'I' that is 'we' and 'we' that is 'I.' "[2] First I will consider selfhood, and, by gradually bringing out what is implied in the notion of self-conscious selfhood, I will lead to a point at which it is apparent that the conditions for selfhood can be met only in and through a social situation—I will call it a law-governed situation. Second, I will focus on the notion of human society. I will use the implications of this notion of a law-governed situation to show why certain forms of social organization are necessarily inadequate since each is built on a denial of something that is necessary to its own existence; this will allow me to show why a system of conscience is necessary to represent adequately all the *logical* demands of social life. Finally, I will show how Hegelian dialectical method—"absolute knowing"—develops out of the demands of a conscientious relation to "the other," and I will outline briefly why his two main works take the form they do. In sum, then, to be human is to be social, to be social is to be conscientious, and to be conscientious is to engage in absolute knowing.

1. To Be Human Is to Be Social

A conscious self is a being *for itself;* that is, it is defined by a relation to something "other," and that other is in some way *present* to it.[3] This self is aware, and in being aware of things that are other to it, it must implicitly be aware of itself as that which the others specifically are-not. A being that is for-itself, then, is always tacitly aware of itself in being aware of others, and it is explicitly a self-consciousness to the extent that this latent self-awareness does not remain latent, but becomes instead the direct object of its awareness. The completeness of its self-consciousness will vary with the adequacy of its comprehension of what it is. As a being for-itself, it is that in relation to which all that is other to it has a significant being; the being for-itself provides the defining context within which all the others figure, and how they figure is determined by how the self is. Thus, to comprehend adequately the self will be to comprehend it as the determining center that provides the orientation for the totality of being of which it is aware. The fundamental experience of being-a-self, then, is freedom: the experience of being that in terms of which the other is defined.

Put this simply, this account is one-sided, for one does not simply rule the world;[4] it is just as true that one does have the fundamental experience of having to conform oneself to the demands of the world.[5] And yet, this reversal is not complete. The self that can define the world in terms of its values is not simply limited by, or absorbed in, the immediate circumstances of its consciousness, but is, rather, able to "distance" itself from what is immediately present to it, and treat its object in terms of something else, such as, for example, its own desire to eat; thus the fact that the self "is-not" its object has the double meaning that (1) it is differentiated as subject from object, and (2) it is separate as the-power-to-not-be-absorbed-in-it. In fact, the actual saying of "I" is precisely the actualization of this freedom to withdraw, and to change the focus of one's attention and action.[6] Thus, while it is true that any "I" must, in important ways, conform itself to the world, it always remains true that this demand for conforming itself arises only within the sphere of free awareness; that is, the determining power of the self remains superordinate, even in the situation in which the self appears subordinate to its world, and this is because the experienced other to which the self must conform is an other that has already conformed to that point of orientation that is the self.

In expressing both sides of this story, then, we say that to be a self-conscious self is to be able to assert one's freedom, but this assertion of freedom is contingent upon the sanction of that over which one endeavors to make the assertion. One does not, for example, need to tolerate the existence of the neighbor's house, but the ways open to one to overcome its existence are limited by the ways in which it allows itself to be acted upon. It can be burned, but not simply "willed" away. Likewise, I am free to express my point of view, but expression can take place only in particular fashions, and I am free to do as I will only within the limits set by that upon or within which I act. At this level, then, we can already see how the assertion of freedom that characterizes selfhood must always appeal to, or rely upon, the sanction or recognition of its other.[7]

Now if "I" names the actual pivot of my experienced world, it must name that whose determination the objects of my world of experience actually sanction. In saying "I," I announce myself as this free center of the world; but it is not immediately true that this "me," this supposed center that I identify, really is the center. For "my" desire really to count as the determining law of the world requires that it be such as will receive (or has received) the sanction of the other, and thus the "me" I identify when I say "I" will accurately reflect that free self that determines the world only if the desires of that "me" do respect the demands of the world. In other words, what I call the self may not really be that which is running the show. Let me elaborate on this distinction between an apparent self and a real self in human relations, that is, relations in which both the self and the other are self-consciousnesses.[8]

The crucial difference between relations with other self-consciousnesses and relations with beings that cannot be self-conscious is that a self-conscious other is, like the self-conscious self, free to determine what it is in relation to its world. The sanction of the non-self-conscious other amounts to what I can do to it; the sanction of the self-conscious other amounts to what it will allow me to do. Truly to receive the sanction of an other that is self-conscious is to have one's will accord with the choice of that other. I am the center of a world in which there are other self-consciousnesses only if my choices meet with the recognition of their choices. Law is the phenomenon where this recognition is effected.

The crucial point is this: when one chooses to be committed to a law that others likewise recognize as that to which they are committed, then their choices mutually and equally recognize each other. To the extent that each recognizes the judgment made by the law as her/his own judgment, the choices of each are the choices of both and that which each wills is sanctioned— recognized—by the other. What this means is that the self that is sanctioned by the other is the self that is identical with an overarching institution of a society; that is, an "I" is recognizable to the precise extent that the "I" is a we. The very act of sanctioning the other is the act of identifying oneself with the will of the other, so this does not mean that the law must preexist the recognition; rather, it reveals that recognition and being-social are inseparable determinations, and arise together.

I want to make two asides here about this notion of recognition in the law. First, although I have presented this as occurring at the level of self-conscious choice, this need not be so. To the extent that two individuals have both adopted the same habits of unconscious behaving, they will recognize—that is, each will treat as unproblematic for the maintenance of her/his own self-hood—the choices of the other, without this recognition ever becoming thematic or conspicuous: to share habits is thus to recognize the other automatically. Second, the laws I refer to could just as easily be traditional social customs, family practices, or, at the opposite end of cultural systems, works of art, religious practices, philosophical doctrines, and so on. All these are institutions or laws that an individual can identify as her/his "real self" and that can be communally shared. For now I want to leave this account of the necessity of overarching social institutions for selfhood—as it were, the a priori structures of a "we"—and sum up the account of coming to explicit self-consciousness in relation to the need to be social.

I have argued that to be fully self-conscious will require identifying one's apparent self—the "empirical ego"—with what really is one's self. By my "self" is meant the determining center of the world, and the determining center will be only that self that is recognized by the other. Now it is not clear that what I take to be my self really does count as this determining center. Thus, in knowing my empirical ego, I am really knowing myself only if this empirical ego is identical with that real center that is recognized by the other. And we have now determined this "real self" as the overarching self that both I and the other each recognize as our real selves. Let us call this overarching self, this "law," the "transcendental ego." We can now say that a self can be fully self-conscious only if it recognizes itself in and as a transcendental ego, which means precisely the institutional structures of a social relationship, or, in Hegelian language, a "system of right." I want now to look at Hegel's treatment of systems of right in the *Phenomenology of Spirit* in order to determine which is the adequate system of right—the adequate system of social relations—for effecting a comprehensive self-consciousness.

2. To Be Social Is to Be Conscientious

In the end, the only adequate system of social relations is, on Hegel's account, the one that prescribes that the individual become self-conscious,[9] and self-conscious in the sense indicated above, that is, conscious of oneself as founded in a "real" self that is the system of social institutions itself, such that one sees that it is the social system that acts through the singular agents. This will be a system of "conscientious forgiveness." To see why, let me begin by looking at two inadequate social systems, that is, systems that institutionalize relationships of the law and its adherents that are in fact inadequate to the relationships that we have already seen must exist between the law and its adherents.

First, the efficacy of the law—indeed, its very existence as law—rests on its being identified by each singular self as her/his proper self. This means, then, that the legal system essentially depends on the singular selves to actualize it. The analysis above allows us to conclude that it is the law that acts through the singular agents, but equally that the law itself exists only in and through the action of these singular selves. Thus, any social relation (call it "traditional society") that treats the law as something existing in its own right in independence of the singular self-consciousnesses that obey the law is misconstruing its own situation.[10] To say, "these traditions must be carried on, regardless of the expense of individuals," is to misunderstand the value of the traditions, that is, their living role in the struggle for mutual recognition among singular actors. Laws exist as laws only so long as they mediate human relations, allowing the subjects to recognize themselves in and through recognizing others whom the subjects themselves recognize in the law-governed actions. Thus an institutional system that founds that relationship of selves in which the job of "founding the relations of free selves" is denied to institutions in favor of a reverence for the laws that enslaves the singular selves is a self-contradictory system.

Second, just as it is a fiction to think of the law as existing in independence of the adherence to it of singular self-consciousnesses, it is equally false to posit a singular self-consciousness that does not exist precisely as the representative agent of a social system. This was precisely the point of section 1: the self does not first exist as an independent individual and then enter into a society, but is rather constituted as independent only in and through social relations. Thus, a society that believed that one's singular selfhood had the exclusive and distinctive power of and responsibility for making one what one is (as, for example, a communal institution calling for singular acts of faithful conversion to a religion, or for singular acts of enlightened conversion to scientific rationality),[11] would equally be founded on an inadequate institution since, we can now argue, the very thing that constitutes the self-consciousness that is to convert is already mediated by particular social relations that provide the sanctioned goals, methods, and objects that the singular self—the "empirical ego"—takes as given. This is an inadequate social system, for it is a society founded on the self-contradictory institution of denying institutional foundation.

The only adequate system of right, then, will be one that avoids both these "institutionalized self-misunderstandings"; it must, first, acknowledge the overarching primacy of the transcendental ego, but, second, also recognize the essentiality of the singular egos that activate the law.[12] For an individual to be committed to such a law, then, the individual must acknowledge the primacy of the law and its dependence on the support given it by the free choice of its singular adherents. To abide by this law, then, means to recognize my dependence on the others, for the law is my true self, and this, my true self, depends on those others. In fact, we must now recognize that it is this very act of recognizing the dependence on others that is the overarching law. The adequate social system, then, is that system of institutions that recognizes individuals who recognize others. This is the institutional system that Hegel analyzes under the name of "conscience."[13]

The analysis of conscience is the culmination of Chapter VI, Section C, of the *Phenomenology of Spirit*, "*Moralität*," in which section Hegel considers systems of right and recognition that begin from the singular self that develops the universal from out of itself; conscience is the culmination of this dynamic, for it is the attitude of consciousness that can tolerate both the singularity and the particularity of the individual by recognizing them as being of universal value. Rather than develop the whole dynamic of *Moralität* (which, in its preliminary moments, repeats the logical errors of traditional society and the society of self-creation by denigrating one or the other of the logical aspects involved in human relations), we can move directly to the concept of conscience and see how it addresses the demands of the logic of self-consciousness as we have so far developed them. What we must study is the characteristic act that animates conscientious forgiveness; we will see that this act amounts to asking a unifying question. First, we must describe the shape of conscience.

Unlike the simple morality discussed in the first section of "*Moralität*," which posits a formal ground such as Kant's categorical imperative for determining abstract universal principles for behavior that attain their validation precisely through not being intrinsically related to *this* situation, conscience recognizes the primacy of *this* situation, and it recognizes this in three ways. It recognizes the need to respond to a given situation—that is, its duty is a particular duty pertaining to this situation;[14] it recognizes the need to respond in terms of its given powers to determine goals—that is, the universal context of "what ought to be" can be, for it, only the values to which it finds itself committed;[15] finally, in relation to both these issues it recognizes the need for itself to respond—that is, it finds itself responsible for the moment of singular initiative.[16] The conscientious self must respond here and now, both in terms of values and in terms of powers.[17] The Kantian morality is still rooted in something like the ethos of self-creation, in that it posits a self-contained singular self that is abstracted from the particularities of its existence.[18] Conscience, however, while it is animated by the same root commitment to responsible existence as is simple morality, knows it must always act in a particularized (that is, an embodied) fashion.[19]

The basic phenomenon of this conscientiousness is displayed by Martin Luther's "*Hier stehe ich, ich kann nicht anders*,"[20] and it is the recognition of the ultimacy of the justification, "I had to act that way because my conscience demanded it," which means, again, "according to (the limits of) my understanding, with respect to both what is the case and what should be the case, this is how I had to see the situation, and this is how I had to act." It is this claim of lived necessity with respect to both object and method that gives this claim of conscience its ultimacy.[21] Whereas the basic phenomenon of such a lived necessity characterizes all the forms of self-conscious and social relations (indeed, it is our very definition of the transcendental ego), conscience is that form of self-conscious selfhood that *posits* the ultimacy of this justification. Conscience posits the need to act morally, and thereby is the *Aufhebung* of the demand of the society of self-creation that singularity become universal, or that subjectivity become objective; but it is equally the *Aufhebung* of traditional society, in that it recognizes that the objectivity of subjectivity is achieved when its singular judgment is animated by the concrete necessity of ethos rather than the abstract and merely formal necessity of simple reflective reason.

It might initially seem that, since conscience is committed to the ultimacy of the claim of conscientiousness, one can be conscientious simply by saying so; or, again, this might seem like a reversion to a Kantian-style morality according to which only intentions matter. Neither of these routes is adequate to the demands of conscience, however. Indeed, the conscientious "intentions" that count as justification are those that compel the agent to act. Truly conscientious behavior is that which is animated by the commitment to act to the limits of one's ability; it means exerting one's utmost efforts to construe properly one's situation and to construe the method with which to approach it. Yet here again there may seem to be a problem.

There is yet a third way that the attitude of conscience might seem to subvert its own goal and generate inactivity: this would be a situation in which one tries to isolate oneself from the sphere of social action on the ground that, since one cannot know the consequences of one's actions, or how one's actions will affect others, one will always be imposing one's particular will on others, and thereby trespassing, or working against the universal.[22] This is the attitude that conscientiously condemns all other agents as violators of the rights of others. Here again, however, this is not an attitude that adequately represents the logical demands of the standpoint of conscience. This "isolationist" attitude fails to recognize that its stance of immobility is itself a social action with social consequences just as much as is any other; that is, its purported goal of not trespassing by not acting is an unrealizable goal. The institution of conscience, then, is the system of social relating that contains the recognition that, indeed, there is no guarantee of successfully carrying out one's intentions, but there is guaranteed the inescapability of the imperative to act, which means equally the guarantee that one must necessarily trespass upon others, for one is always already a social self. Indeed, the very recognition of others as others is already the inclusion of them into one's field of judgment and existence. Conscience, then, is animated by a logic that posits the inability to isolate singular self-conscious selves from each other.[23]

Conscience, then, in knowing that it has to trespass, has recognized recognition; that is, it has itself come to an operative understanding of the conception of selfhood that we have been developing, in that it knows that the only self that is is a social self;[24] conscience acts, in other words, on the tacit recognition that "those others are not outside me—they are me."[25] This thus imposes a demand on conscience to act within the parameters of its given situation, not because it is wrong to go outside, but because it is impossible. Let me clarify these points.

We have seen in section 1 that the real self is necessarily the social system itself, and our task has been to construe adequately the relations between whole and member within this situation. We have seen in section 2 that the singular self neither can be excluded from the social substance (as in traditional society) nor can be withdrawn from it (as in the society of self-creation), but must be recognized as that very social substance itself in its very act of becoming *für sich* in a singular (or, rather, we may say at this point, "individual") act of willing. Society, therefore, must be understood as a system of monads, where there are no "external relations" precisely because all those things that could naively be said to be "outside" the self are now recognized to be already internal to the self. This was already implied in the doctrine of recognition and in the notion of a social system of right, for what these reveal is the necessity, to the spiritual self, that it recognize "others" as it very own self. Conscience in its final form is that form of experience that has, as the implicit logic that must be invoked in order to explain its behavior, the recognition of this very doctrine of the self and its embodiment in social relations.[26]

Conscience thus knows it must act in this world. It does not act randomly, but must do its best to act as it ought; what determines whether or not it has done so is whether or not it has tried to know what to do to the best of its ability. Further, given that each self is already internally related to all others, it is not possible to act without acting violently.[27] Thus, again, conscience knows it must force its will upon others and, to the extent that it is actually animated by the notion of ultimacy of conscience, it equally must forgive others when they necessarily do the same;[28] as forgiveness, it must accept the actions of others according to the same standards as it uses in its own activity. Conscience must itself recognize the very thing Hegel's phenomenology of the world of self-creation recognizes,[29] namely, that social integration always comes hand in hand with interpersonal exclusion and violence, which is rooted in the constitutive necessity of the moment of particularity to all self-conscious selfhood. In recognizing that, as forgiveness, one is committed to endorsing that which the other is committed to endorsing, one has tacitly recognized that one's real self is constituted by the others. What conscientiously forgiving behavior thus tacitly recognizes, then, is that the self is not in simple and immediate possession of itself, but that it rather finds out who it is through encountering itself as the social world of its otherness.[30] Thus conscience recognizes the intersubjective world to which it belongs as being its own real truth. Let us consider further the presupposed "cognitive" dynamics of forgiveness.

To forgive means to say of the offending other, "she/he had to act that way," that is, forgiveness means seeing the other to be animated by a lived experience of necessity just as one is oneself. Furthermore, in order to forgive the other it is not even required that the other preface her/his actions with the claim of conscience that "I had to act that way," for it is equally necessary to forgive the failure of the other to come to the level of self-consciousness required to make this claim. To forgive, then, means to see the actions of the other as precisely the expression—the being-for-another—of the other's animating selfhood. To forgive, then, means precisely to treat what one faces as the expressive bodiliness of the other, and to do this requires the enacting of two cognitive operations. First, that which is to be interpreted must be posited as a single (extensive) totality; second, it must be posited as intrinsically unified. Since *all* determinate particularity trespasses in one's lived experience, it is the totality of what one faces that must be thus forgiven. Therefore, the process of forgiveness culminates in the interpretation of all one's otherness as an intrinsically unified—a self-determining—totality.

This operation of forgiving, then, requires that the forgiving consciousness take up an investigative stance toward its otherness. Recall that forgiveness is not an activity in which the agent arbitrarily chooses to engage, but is, rather, the act to which it has been driven by its animating drive to be moral. Thus the conscientious self finds itself morally driven to understand the other; that is, its duty is to see the other as in process of self-determination. Recall, too, that the pursuit of duty is the attempt of the self-conscious self to identify its empirical ego with its transcendental ego, that is, to be autonomous; here, in the culmination of conscience in forgiveness, we see that the project of identifying with the transcendental ego—the project of being autonomous—is realized only in identifying my self with the self of the other; that is, I posit as right that which animates the other's behavior. I thus allow myself to be determined by the law that animates the other, or, rather, I sanction this determination that I have always already allowed. In conscientious forgiveness, the right of the other to make and to have made demands upon me is my highest ideal, and the project of autonomy is thus realized only in the most radical heteronomy.

But note, finally, that if I now treat all otherness as the expressive body of the other, and if, further, I treat the other—or, rather, the unity of myself with the other—as my true self, then all otherness must be the expressive body of *my* self; that is, experience is the sphere in which what I am is expressed to me. The adequate form of the institutional relations that constitute self-conscious selfhood, then, is that form in which the institutional basis of social relations is the demand that the self recognize the sphere of its otherness as its own expression. A brief recapitulation will allow us to make the transition to absolute knowing.

In the first section I discussed instituting a law as a "transcendental ego" for a "we," and I argued that by the mutual identification of the respective singular selves with this law they were able to identify with—recognize—each other. In the system of conscience, we now see that the law that provides the real self for each and all of the participant selves is "the law of the other," that is, when you and I relate according to conscience, I do not just have a part of myself identifying with that part of yourself that accepts a certain law; rather, the law of my entire self is to identify with your entire self, and vice versa. This obeying of the law of the other means forgiving the other, which means recognizing the actions of the other according to that standard by which they are *intrinsically governed*. This, clearly, is not an approach like natural science, where a certain abstract law that is known independently of its instances is applied indifferently to a variety of instances, and only to what is "essential" in those instances (e.g., mass in the case of gravity); forgiveness needs, rather, an approach that takes its method from its object—uniquely. To do this will mean to ask of the other's action, "how are these actions the unified expression of an intrinsic law?" and what will be found is a law that cannot be known independently of its instances; forgiveness forgives a whole in which form and content, whole and part, are reciprocally determined and defined. Forgiveness, thus, must ask of the other "what ideals do your actions themselves prescribe for evaluating behavior?" and then turn these ideals on its own actions to see how it is conscientious in the fulfilling of these ideals. To treat the other conscientiously is thus to see her/him *as* someone whose behavior is necessary, but necessary in the (Kantian) sense of being autonomous, or self-determining. The demand to respond to otherness in this fashion could be termed the "dialectical imperative," and it is of this project of heteronomous autonomy that "absolute knowing" is an enactment.

3. To Be Conscientious Is to Engage in Absolute Knowing

To be conscientious in one's treatment of the other, then, requires that one recognize the other as self-determined; but this in turn requires, of course, that one be *able* to effect this recognition. One's own conception of how things can be unified, what kinds of laws of behavior there can be, and so on, will determine the limits of what one *can* recognize *as* a unity, *as* a law of behavior, and so on. To know the other on its own terms, recall, means that one not be imposing an alien standard on that other, but the limitation of one's own ability to recognize the possibilities for unity, and so on, is the most severe alien standard. Hegel's *Phenomenology of Spirit* and *Science of Logic* precisely provide an education in recognizing the forms of unified behavior.

These two works are each the actual practice of what Hegel calls absolute knowing, and each offers a series of studies of behavior to show how these behaviors are conscientious, that is, unified, self-determining processes. The *Phenomenology of Spirit* traces out particular human relationships, and shows how they are unities, while the *Logic* traces out more generally the different ways in which anything can be unified. What each offers, then, are studies in how to forgive the other; the studies, furthermore, are arranged hierarchically, so that as one proceeds through the books one is educated into an ability to appreciate progressively more sophisticated forms of self-determination. Let us focus on this notion of a hierarchy in relation to the *Phenomenology of Spirit*, to bring out a second dimension of Hegel's dialectic, namely, the role of self-contradiction.

Hegel's study of the different forms of behavior is not simply a list, but is a systematic study that shows how it is that the various relations he studies are hierarchically arranged as progressively more adequate attempts to *be* self-determined. In each situation that he considers, he shows how it is that the behavior is self-determined, that is, how it is a unified expression of an intrinsic law, but also how it is that the law that is doing the self-determining is itself inconsistent, and thus criticizable *by its own standards*; examples of this kind of internal inconsistency are the ethos of "traditional society" and of the society of "self-creation," which I considered above, in which the institutions of the situations are at odds with the very notion of there being an institutional situation. The dialectical analysis of a situation shows how it is that the charac-teristic behavior is animated by an intrinsic law, but also how it is that what the behavior ultimately expresses is the self-*criticism* of that very law; so, for exam-ple, Hegel's analysis of these two types of society demonstrates how it is that on their own steam these societies will collapse just through the acting out of the appropriate behavior prescribed by their constitutive institutions. The hier-archization of relationships is thus effected in terms of the ability of the situa-tions under consideration to be self-consistent; in particular, the ordering is produced by showing how each subsequent form resolves—by operating on the basis of a new law—some aspect of the problem faced by the preced-ing form.

This ordering of the forms of human relationships continues until a situa-tion is reached that is animated by a law that is capable of being consistently worked out. What the analysis ends up concluding is that it is only a human relationship based on the conception of human relations that I have articu-lated in this paper that is self-consistent and capable of being stably enacted. I want to conclude with one last point about why the inadequate systems are inadequate, and why the dialectical logic of relationships is able to overcome these problems and be self-consistent.

In each case of an inadequate human situation, the inconsistency in its animating logic will be, as we have anticipated from the start, a misidentifica-tion of the real self. The real self *is* the animating law, and in each inadequate situation there will be a disparity between what the situation *posits* as its animating law, or "transcendental ego," and what the actual behavior ex-presses, that is, the law that is *really* sanctioned by the behavior *as* its animating center. Absolute knowing, then, will be that situation in which the real self properly recognizes itself as the self that it is, or it will be the only situation that actually behaves according to the laws that it believes animate its behavior.

In particular, the distinctive recognition made by absolute knowing is that its whole project has been to achieve this self-knowledge. Following up the project of conscience, absolute knowledge does not just *act in accord with* the principle that it can be itself only by identifying with the other as simple conscience does; rather, for absolute knowing, this goal of self-knowledge in absolute otherness is what it *explicitly* pursues.[31] In other words, it does not just know itself in knowing the other; it *knows that* in knowing the other it is knowing itself. Let me finish with one remark about the details.

In order to ask the other what method its prescribes for its self-evaluation, the questioner must first *have an other to ask*. Thus the act of asking the other has *already* trespassed on the other by forcing it to conform to an *external* imposition of a law that decides what does and what does not count as an other being. In absolute knowing, the questioner recognizes that the other being known is a being upon whom one has already committed a trespass, and that one's attempt to conform to the law of the other is conformance to an other *that has already conformed to one's own law*. But this, of course, was exactly how we defined the relation of the real self to its other in the first section. Absolute knowledge thus becomes the successful fulfillment of the project of self-knowledge by seeing *itself*, that is, its own actions, as the conscientious expression of the intrinsic drive to self-knowledge, and it is only when it thus recognizes how its own intrinsic law—its drive to this self-comprehension—has trespassed on the other as that "real self" to which the other gives its sanction that its project is complete. This is proved in the *Phenomenology of Spirit* by showing how the self-criticism of the various situations considered literally leads to the writing of this very book;[32] it is the concrete *Darstellung* of how its object is animated by the intrinsic goal of being knowable by absolute knowing; that is, the *Phenomenology of Spirit* does not just provide an a priori justification of its method, but shows how this method is concretely sanctioned by the very object it addresses. My account is successful if it has helped explain why the *Phenomenology of Spirit* finds itself compelled to take this form, with respect to both its method and its subject-matter.

Religion

twelve
The Ritual Basis of
Self-Identity

1. Phenomenology and Ritual Identity

Heidegger's *Being and Time* is essentially an analysis of what it is to be human, of what it is to be that kind of being that each of us singly is, namely, a being that can take account of itself. As modern philosophy has insisted, we are indeed reflective, rational, self-conscious beings, but what is most interesting about us, according to Heidegger's analysis, is how these definitive facets of our existence themselves depend on the existence of fundamentally *non*-reflective, *non*-self-conscious, and (in some respects) *non*-rational dimensions in our existence. I make, in part 1, what is perhaps an unexpected connection between this Heideggerean concern for the un-self-conscious project of being-in-the-world and Hegel's argument in the *Phenomenology of Spirit* for the necessity of religious *Vorstellungen,* of myth and ritual, within self-conscious society.[1] I find sacred ritual to be the real matrix for the unreflective life of *Da-sein*—Heidegger's name for human existence—and this allows me, in part 2, to draw two conclusions. First, I argue that it is in ritual life that self-conscious existence is fundamentally established, and that the phenomenological analysis of ritual can mediate in the traditional debate between faith and reason. Second, I argue that it is in the phenomenon of ethnicity that self-conscious

169

existence is fundamentally revealed, and I end by showing how different conceptions of self-conscious selfhood suggest different approaches to ethnicity and cultural pluralism, and that the conception derived from Heidegger and Hegel demands of us that we approach other cultures with the goal of becoming initiated.

a. Heidegger and Self-Consciousness as Being-At-Home

For the most part, our attention is occupied with the things of our world: we are not normally in the condition of explicitly reflecting on our own selfhood. I may be comfortably absorbed in my typing when someone enters and asks, "What are you doing?" My response, "I am typing," demands that I adopt a new attitude to my situation and, rather than continue typing, change my focus into a self-reflection that was precisely *not* in place earlier. But note that the response I give does not take account of any such change, and posits the reflective ego—the "I"—as the agent responsible for the typing: "*I* am typing." Now what is the status of this "I," which my self-reflection posits as having already been running the show all along? On the one hand, this saying of "I" was indeed a permanent possibility throughout the typing experience: at any time I would have given the same answer to the question. On the other hand, the form in which "I" am present in my typing experience is not the same as the form in which "I" am present to myself in self-reflection: this will be confirmed by any serious typist, who will agree, I think, that it is precisely when one tries to let one's self-conscious decision-making powers guide the typing that one makes mistakes. As reflectively self-conscious, then, we posit ourselves *as self-conscious* at the basis of all our activity, and in so doing we misrepresent the reality of our experience.

What does characterize the experience of self-conscious selves, if it is not the fact that an independent ego is always present and running the show? In general, our experience is one of being "at home," in our "world."[2] For the most part, my existence is not a problem: I do not have to adopt an investigative outlook toward everything I encounter, but can usually coast along comfortably without questioning the nature of anything. This is true to such an extent that I can, for example, get up, have breakfast, and take the subway to work, all while conversing with people about other things, reading the paper, and so on. Indeed, these operations can become so habitual and automatic that I may arrive at work and find I cannot really remember the episode of boarding the subway train, or leaving the house. In general, things in our world *work* for us, and our encounters with reality serve much more to remind us that things are indeed as we had thought than they serve to make us inquisitive scientists or philosophers: our experience is much more of a world that confirms our expectations than of one that raises doubts.[3] So what we meet in our affairs is thus something that tells us that we are on track. But notice what I have now said: it tells us that *we* are on track; that is, in our experience of our world we are finding something our about ourselves. According to Heidegger, our fundamental experience of "self-consciousness" is this experience of ourselves that we have in our experience of the things of our world.[4]

How we experience reality is very much a reflection of how we are ourselves; that is, objects as we experience them are indeed structured by the forms of our approach to them; each of us inhabits a world in which the main lines of significance are drawn by the kinds of projects in which we and our companions engage, and where our daily environment is molded by the history of our own activities and is set up to facilitate our pursuit of immediate goals. A gift on my desk keeps a distant friend close to me; I feel relaxed in my office, for it is for me a place where I can doze off with impunity; my car is for me the certain access to my home in another city, and so on: I encounter things *as* oriented by my projects. It is thus metaphysically justifiable to argue that things are in important senses subjectively constituted, and, thus, our experiential certainties are indeed philosophically dubitable, but this *explicit* recognition of the subject's role is absent in day-to-day experience, and in its place is precisely the *comfort* of experiencing the apparent *indubitability* of the apparent nature of things. It is precisely the making over of the world in our own image that makes the world *familiar*, which means its significance seems *obvious*, which makes it seem that our own "take" on the world is indeed the *normal* or the *natural* one. It is the continued smooth flow of experience that constantly confirms our sense that things just are the way we take them to be, and indeed that we are who we take ourselves to be. To be human most fundamentally means being-at-home-in-the-world.[5]

Our comfort can, however, be disturbed. Unexpected car trouble can leave us stranded in an unfamiliar area, and force us to recognize that we are responsible for making the decisions and taking the actions that will get us out of trouble; indeed, the generic form in which explicit self-recognition typically arises according to Heidegger is as such a response to a crisis in the normally inconspicuously functioning world.[6] It is in crisis that our situation reveals to us the necessity for our decisions, and our response may be a resolute acceptance of the responsibility for our actions or a defensive attempt to conceal this responsibility and defer the moment of decision; in either case, it is here that the conditions are encountered that can drive us to *explicitly* recognize ourselves, and in this sense our reflective self-consciousness is in fact derivative of the more fundamental experience of comfort whose disturbance gives rise to reflection. The fully explicit taking of responsibility for one's involvement is, according to Heidegger, the "authenticity" that comes with that most complete of all crises, the recognition of the necessity of one's own death, of one's definitive finitude. But such a taking account of oneself in authentic being-toward-death (which I will not here analyze) is not more *genuine* a self-experience than the average everyday experience of self that characterizes *Dasein*, and it is this latter that we have seen to be foundation for the very possibility of such a fully authentic self-experience in the argument that our world is always offering us a comforting reflection of ourselves.[7]

So it is the inconspicuously established, comforting world that both lets us know implicitly who we are and makes possible any fully explicit taking account of oneself. In finding these unselfconscious layers of experience, then, we are finding the foundations of self-conscious experience. On the basis of what we have seen, we can, in summary, identify three basic stances that have claim to being the experience of self-consciousness.

First, there is the unthematized experience of oneself in the object that comes with the day-to-day experience of comfortably inhabiting a world; this we have said is the primitive experiential root of all self-consciousness, and the ground for more explicit forms.

Second, we have identified the complete and explicit taking of responsibility for oneself as the self that one is, which is "authenticity"; we have seen that any such self-experience must be seen as a derivative from, or modification of, primitive self-experience, and that whatever claim this full self-accounting may have to primacy will not be one of temporal primacy or anything similar.[8]

Third, there is the normal experience of *what we take to be* self-consciousness, namely, that experience of saying "I" wherein one posits oneself as the decision-making agent responsible for actions, which we considered above with the typing example. To this "I," the rest of the world is "outside," and it—the "I"—functions more or less as a parasitic voyeur, observing, but not participating in, the life of the situation. We have seen that the self is really already engaged, and it is on the basis of this engagement that it can reflect, but this reflection, in its most typical form, falsely isolates the self from the very situatedness that constitutes its real substance, and it is this isolating of the ego that develops into the alienating of knowing subject and known object, of mind and body, of self and other selves, and the other dualisms that we associate with seventeenth- and eighteenth-century philosophy. For this reflective ego that has objects outside it, their being *present to its reflection and use* is what constitutes their very reality: they are permanent aliens which one encounters and about which one makes decisions. We see in this a distortion, however, for normally our world is *not* thus "ob-jectified" for us (in the etymological sense of "something thrown in our way"), but is the accommodating situation where we dwell, which is inseparably me and it, subject and object; in being our home, being is as much informed by our animating projects as it is the stuff out of which our own mirror—our self-consciousness—is constructed: we are through it and it is through us.[9]

We will need to remember the characteristics of these three forms of self-consciousness, and especially the distortions of reflective self-consciousness, when we come to the last section of this chapter. Let me now conclude this discussion with one point about this Heideggerean understanding of our situation.

I have just said that being is what it is through our projects, so in an important sense we can talk of our experience as essentially constituted by subjectivity. It is this animating subjectivity that is reflected back to us in the comfort we feel in our inconspicuous dealings with our environment. It is this project, this way of laying out what being counts as, that is communicated in our *language*, and the ease with which our systems of linguistic reference and communication function is precisely a reflection of how far the members of the linguistic community really share the same home:[10] we mutually confirm each other—we are the self-consciousness for the other—by showing each other in and through our communication that we live in the self-same world, the very world that reflects back to us our comfort.[11] Thus it is really in our inconspicuous communication within a community that shares the same metaphysical home that our comfortable self-confirmation is achieved.

b. Hegel and the Habit of Ritual Recognition

The real heart of Hegel's philosophy is found in his account of self-consciousness, especially in his argument that self-consciousness is a collective achievement, won in a dialogue of mutual recognition.[12] For Hegel, the experience of self-conscious selfhood is that of finding oneself at the center of things; but when these things are other self-consciousnesses, this situation is complicated, for to recognize *them* as self-consciousnesses means precisely recognizing that *they* should be at the center, which means to experience oneself as de-centered. Consequently, one's experience is a tension of being a de-centered center, and our sense of selfhood—of being the center—is a kind of hypothesis that needs the other self-consciousnesses—the other centers—to confirm it. The others equally need our confirmation, and this mutual confirmation is achieved through a shared endorsement of what we all count as reality.[13]

Hegel understands social existence in terms of this theme of mutual confirmation through shared commitments. A society is a group of self-conscious agents who have adopted the same standards for evaluating behavior, the same criteria for establishing who one is. *Law* is the basic phenomenon of collective agreement about our codes for how we will confirm or discredit each other's views about who each of us is. If I and another both accept the same law, then I know that my law-abiding action must be recognized by the other in the same way as it is recognized by me, and so on. Hegel is primarily concerned with the kind of law anthropologists call "customary law," that is, that form of social experience in which one is committed to a set of values shared by the other members of one's community, but where these values, these laws, are completely habitual and function without self-conscious reflection or enforcement. Indeed, Hegel sees some form of this habituality of value, this *Sittlichkeit*, as the foundation of any community: it is our habitual adherence to customs that allows us to recognize ourselves as an "us," as a "we," for it is when I act according to the customs we all *automatically* adopt that my action is a representative for all of us. It is these customary laws, then, that define a single identity for the different members of the community by dictating canons of action and of interpretation. This single, shared identity is the real decision-making power behind the actions of the members.

When I behave according to custom, I am doing *what I find myself compelled to do*: how custom functions is precisely by *not* requiring to be explicitly and self-consciously posited, but by guiding action automatically because the agent is thoroughly habituated to the law; thus the experience of custom is the experience of the *need* to act in a particular way just because "that's how it's done."[14] When we share a custom, it means we each recognize a certain system of values as "just the way it is," as the unquestionable, indeed, obvious, character of reality. The custom *dictates for us our action*, and our acting in accordance is our recognition of its legitimacy, just as the shared commitment to this custom by others dictates *their* recognition of the action's legitimacy. In sharing customs, then, we have collectively adopted a source for our actions the meaning and legitimacy of which we all collectively recognize. The dimension of *Sittlichkeit* within communal life, then, is that dimension in which we effectively give ourselves over to a decision-making power that exceeds our singular identities, both in the sense that this is not subject to singular self-conscious choice but operates "behind the back" of each member and in the sense that it is not limited to any particular member, but obtains universally; this decision-making power is custom, which is precisely constituted by the acts of mutual recognition. In this communal life, the custom defines *who I really am*, and *this self is the same for all of us*. Hegel's claim is that the demand of self-consciousness to have its self recognized by others is met in communal acts of mutual recognition in which precisely what is achieved is the instituting of *one and the same real self*, for all the members: I really achieve my "I"-hood only in the situation in which I recognize myself and others as really the same self, as a "we."[15]

So, first, to be a self is to be constantly engaged in a project of self-confirmation, to be waiting upon others to interpret for us who we really are, to interpret whether we are who we take ourselves to be. Second, this pursuit is primarily fulfilled in the collective adherence to a custom, for here we act with the assurance that our act is what we take it to be, for we and our others are equally habitually committed to the same system of interpretive values, which, because they are habitual, are not recognized by the members of the community as anything they are responsible for at all: they do not look to us like values we have adopted, but like the immediately obvious character of reality. Here, then, we have a static view of the smooth functioning of a community of recognition; the last point we need to see, however, is how this is played out dynamically, that is, what is involved in coming to be a member, in coming to have the habits. Here we shall find the foundation of community in sacred ritual, in the establishment of expressive gestures in which the community as a community says, "here is who we are."[16]

Most of us are born into an already well-established community that is going to constitute our identity as reflective selves—that is, we are going to grow up to be members; our task, then, is to *learn who we are going to be*, which means both to take on the traditions and to transform them in a way that will allow them to fit our new and developing situation. The institutions educate each of us into who each of us is, which means they teach us what there is, how to behave, and so on. But to the one growing up, every institution can appear only as a ritual; as children, we do not generate our social customs from ourselves and we do not see other options, but rather find ourselves in a situation that already operates according to customs, that operates according to particular, that is, already determinate, customs.[17]

The new member faces a world determinately structured by an intelligibility to which she is not privy, and must act as a kind of student, asking of her experience how it is that it makes sense. In general, this question amounts to "how should I act," and if the experienced world is turned to for an answer, it will give an answer, namely, it will say, in accordance with its various founding institutions, "act thus." The new member will find that she *is recognized* by the members of the society into which she is born to the extent that her actions conform to their institutions, that is, to the extent that the child animates her actions by the same customs that animate the behavior of the adults (because, *ex hypothesi*, a society's determinate traditions are the only ways the members *can* recognize others). Thus the new member becomes a reflective self-consciousness—and "I"—precisely through the process of becoming habituated to a series of intelligent actions the intelligence of which is not thematic, not self-conscious, to this new self-consciousness. To become a member of the society, then, does not involve coming to understand what it is to be a member of that society; on the contrary, it requires quite the opposite. Becoming a member of a society requires becoming habituated to a series of practices that *do* structure a dynamic of recognition along intelligible lines, but that *do not* appear as such to the practitioner;[18] in other words, becoming a member of the society—becoming self-conscious—really requires *not* knowing who one is, not knowing what it means to be a member of the society, not being explicitly self-conscious in one's social identity. One becomes a reflective self precisely through not being reflectively self-conscious of this process of becoming such.

In the intelligent act that conceals its intelligibility from its practitioner, we have a sacred ritual, a concealedly meaningful performance that must be imitated:[19] for the new member, the institutionalized activities of its new peers count as signs of who they are, of what reality is, and this behavior appears with the imperative that it be imitated, and that through this imitation the would-be member become part of the crowd, one of the initiated.[20] Here we can link our discourse back to our earlier themes of recognition, for primarily what this self-expression and imitation communicates and achieves is the progressive confirmation and development of the anticipative horizons of the project of mutual recognition engaged in by the new member and the old members of the society that is formed through these acts of imitation.[21] This situation of the new member is equally the situation—the continuing situation—of every member of the society.

We have already shifted to the dynamic perspective of the one coming to be a member in a society, but we must construe the dynamism more broadly. Not only is the status of the social member not fixed; the society as a whole is not fixed, but is in a constant state of enacting itself in ever-changing forms. The society has for its substance the organized activity of its members, and as their activity changes, so does the society; the society is not eternal and immutable in the way in which it appears to be to the reflective self-consciousness; that is, it is not the fixed order of things. What one has at any given moment is the complex dynamic of how the different members are taking up the institutional traditions that have been handed over to them, and it is the act of taking them up rather than the material handed down that determines the fundamental shape of the achieved situation.[22] What we have in a social setting is not a fixed substance called "society" and then a bunch of "members" who somehow live in it: rather, we have a number of actors engaged in an ongoing project of mutual recognition, where some set of common institutions has been handed down to all, and how the various agents take up this heritage will determine how—or indeed whether—they can recognize and confirm one another. Thus for all the members, there is an ongoing project of confirming one's expectation of recognition through identifying with the behavior of others, and here, as in the case of the new member, the behavior of others must, at root, appear as ritual.

In sum, then, for the member of society, social institutions are habits, and as such they have lost their meaning; that is, they do not emerge as intelligent products of reflective choice, both in the sense that they do not appear to have their genesis in human reflection and in the sense that the practitioner's adherence to them is habitual and automatic, not reflective.[23] Such institutions are thus signs: signs for teaching a child how to behave, signs for learning what is expected, signs for revealing a community's identity to other communities, but mostly, *signs that we members are confirmed in our identities; that is, they act as continuing endorsements of our horizon of expectation.* That is how they communicate "us" to us, both as learners who are new members and as continuing members. One's culture's rituals, then, are communicative expressions, especially in the pursuit of confirmation: they tell one who one already was in retrospective fashion in that, when one gets them right, one finds out "that's who I was," or "that's who we are," or "that's how it is." To become a member of a society, then, is to imitate those rituals in which a society says "we," in which, precisely as one appropriates and adapts a model to the demands of one's own new situation, one posits oneself as identified with a fixed identity that has already been present all along.[24] This ritual performance in which a community unselfconsciously announces itself as a "we" is what I take to be Hegel's understanding of the core of religion. I want now to pair this up with Heidegger's themes of language and self-consciousness, and then conclude with a discussion of the emergence of science and philosophy in the religious community and with a consideration of where this leaves us politically.

2. Religion as Language

Now, if we take up what I am maintaining is Hegel's line here, and see religion as those rituals in and through which we primarily establish a confirmed identity as a member of a community, then we see in religion the fundamental sphere in which a world becomes comfortably available for us.[25] It is in the ritual laying out of how to behave—which means how I should act, and how things should be acted upon—that what will count as the obvious and immediate significance of things is established. It is the world made significant through ritual that allows the members of a society—that allows self-conscious agents—to find themselves reflected and confirmed in the stuff of their environment. Thus it is in the phenomenon of religious ritual that we see the fundamental realization of what Heidegger calls "the world." I want to make two further links.

First, insofar as religion makes certain forms of behavior necessary, it makes them necessarily *obvious*: precisely what is achieved in the ritual community is a situation of *comfort* in the world. Thus, far from being the experience of *mysterium tremendum et fascinans*, the *core* of religion is precisely the experience of things as *familiar*.[26] Second, insofar as religious rituals, and the world that we integrate into this ritual life, come to signify to us our own identity, it is in these phenomena of religious ritual that we find the proper referent for Heidegger's discussion of language. Language was to be that medium of communication within which the comfortable character of being is made available to us,[27] and we can now see from our account of Hegel that it is the ritual performance that is this medium. There are many directions to go from here, but I want to look at only two: where this leaves us regarding the traditional debates concerning faith and reason, and where this leaves us with the political question of how we are called upon to respond to the religious rituals of others.

a. Faith, Science, and Phenomenology

Let us consider the relation between the ritual foundation of our identity and our reflective projects of investigating our world. Our investigation has shown us that fundamentally we are engaged in a project of establishing an identity for ourselves through ritually communicating with each other who we take ourselves to be. So our identity is fundamentally achieved through a commitment to ritual life—through faith—and the nature of that identity is this very fact that we are in pursuit of self-knowledge; that is, ritual is the foundation of the life of *self-conscious* beings. The very nature or ritual, then, is to be the ground of our pursuit of self-understanding, and our ritual life—

our faith—will itself be fulfilled through our coming to a full-blown self-consciousness.

Now in section 1a, above, I argued that self-*reflection*—the "normal" way we think of self-consciousness—emerges as a response to a felt need; that is, it answers to a crisis in our pre-reflective life. Similarly, our projects of science—the thematic and systematic investigations of our experience[28]—answer to felt needs *within our ritual life*. Our sciences, in other words, must be understood as legitimate and necessary outgrowths of our ritual life; that is, they mark the progressive fulfillment of our project of self-understanding for which the faith of ritual life is the foundation. But notice that we can also see why it is that these two—faith and science—*initially* appear to conflict.

To the extent that our ritual life is in principle non-self-conscious (as I have argued), it appears to be at odds with the very project of self-consciousness that it founds. Ritual thus seems opposed to the scientific pursuit of self-consciousness. But, recalling the distortions of reflective self-consciousness that we diagnosed in section 1a, we can equally see that the science that claims to be revealing to us the truth of our situation itself precisely conceals the nature of our situation to the extent that it treats that being that is truly the *substance* of our lives as if it were fundamentally an *alien* object for reflection, and treats us as *fundamentally* reflective agents, when reflection is in fact a derivative mode of human existence. In other words, *taken in independence of each other*, "faith" and "reason" *conflict*, and *both* fail to live up to their animating projects. These tensions define the role for phenomenology.

As I have developed the account in this chapter, what Hegel and Heidegger show us is that faith and reason *must not be taken in independence of each other*, and that when we see, through our phenomenology of the dynamics of human life, what it is that ritual and science are really achieving, we can see that ritual *completes* itself only *in the science to which it gives birth*; hence it is already intrinsically committed to the integrity of the project of science.[29] Science, in turn, completes itself only in *recognizing the founding primacy of religious life*. Since phenomenology is the investigation of human existence that allows us finally to see this, we must therefore conclude that phenomenology is the act of self-communicative science in which our ritual identity is fulfilled. Let us now use this account of ritual identity to consider how we are called upon to act in a world in which we always find ourselves already involved with a plurality of religious communities.

b. Ethnicity: Initiation and Exotification

In section 1b, I defined religion as the rituals of mutual recognition in which a community says "so that's who we are." The phenomena with which my account of religion as rituals of mutual recognition should be linked are those that we generally lump under the term "ethnicity." It is these customs as communications, as "myths," that provide for a community "the house of being"; indeed it is already not uncommon for people to use such customs as signs of collective identity, and now we have seen why this is right.[30] Essentially what we are called upon to do in our social life, in which we are constantly brought to face others who do not share our own immediate ethnicity, is precisely to recognize the ethnicity of another culture *as* its own act of self-communication as a "we," and thus *as* the act of articulation of the world into a comfortable mirror that reflects that culture's own collective selfhood.

This means that, even though others' gestures are to us initially empty and puzzling, and do not appear as immediately and obviously demanded by the very nature of being, we must recognize that *they are such in principle*, and proceed from there to see *how* they are thus rational. The key to our ability to see this inherent rationality is precisely our ability to recognize that these gestures are players in the universal task (which has been set out in this chapter), which derives from the very nature of self-conscious existence, of seeking mutual recognition and confirmation of identity and of doing this *by* jointly inhabiting a world that in its comfortable availability functions as a confirming mirror for the expectations of normalcy upon which we found our sense of self.[31]

In an ethnically plural society, then, our task is to see what a group takes as obvious, and to see this as the key to interpreting its members' behavior. But to thus interpret means to acknowledge the inherent rationality, and this really means that *we ourselves undergo initiation:*[32] in coming to see the rationality of ethnic rituals, we necessarily find those rituals reflecting back to us our rationality, and they thus become mirrors for our own rational, self-conscious identities, as much as they are mirrors for the original members of the culture. This point is crucial, and I want to describe two experiences that illustrate the kind of relationships I have in mind, and that should be helpful for understanding the significance of this notion of identification and initiation.

I once went to hear a Russian poet giving a reading of his work. He performed some of his works in English translation, and some in the original Russian. I do not speak Russian, and when he read the Russian poems I heard only the sounds. Periodically people in the audience would laugh or applaud, but I could in no way draw the connections between their actions and what he was saying. What I could do, however, was listen to the "music" of the language; that is, I could attend to *how it sounded:* I could notice whether it was full of hard sounds or soft, I could notice frequently repeated sounds, and so on. Then he would speak English, and everything would change. Suddenly I heard *meanings:* a world of human significance was *immediately* communicated to me when he spoke. Not only did I not have to "construct" a meaning out of sounds: I in fact *could not fail* to find his speech meaningful, just as I am sure that my reader cannot fail to find the words of this printed text immediately intelligible. Further, when I tried to isolate the mere audio component to compare English "music" to Russian "music," I could not, and in all honesty I must say that I do not know what English sounds like.[33]

Notice the crucial difference in these two situations of relating to lan-

guage: the Russian language is a set of ritualized sound behaviors that immediately function as shared embodiments of intersubjective meaning for the
Russian-speakers, but for me they were alien and unintelligible practices that
were essentially set-up-in-front-of-me;[34] unlike the Russian language, however,
the English language is *not* an alien that is set up in front of me, but is
inconspicuous, and presents itself to me as the obvious and natural way to
articulate my situation. When English is spoken, I immediately recognize *my
world* in the expression, and even if I disagree with what is explicitly said, I have
already recognized my shared participation with the speaker in *"the"* world,
that is, in what we both accept as our horizon of possible meaningful experience. Here we see, then, what it is like to identify with a language, but equally
how it is that a language with which others similarly identify can appear to us
as an unintelligible alien. With this in mind, let us move on to a second
example in order to understand what it takes to overcome this alienation.

The first time I read Hegel's *Phenomenology of Spirit*, I did not understand
the text; in a way, this now seems to me odd, since it now seems quite clear to
me. Indeed, when students come to me with troubles, I sometimes have to
fight the urge to say, "But can't you see? The text lays this out very straightforwardly: it is self-explanatory"; this, of course, is not how they experience the
text, just as it was not how I first experienced the text. When I first approached
this text, it was simply words on paper that did not communicate to me something understandable; it was, to continue my earlier language, an alien set up
in front of me. Now it was written so as to be understood—indeed, one might
say that it is trying to be understood—and I was trying to understand it, but
both my efforts and the text's efforts were not sufficient, singly or in conjunction, to produce immediately the experience of understanding. I approached
it, however, with the assumption that it would make sense, and eventually,
through study, it did. But notice now what happened to my relations with
the text.

When I came eventually to understand it, I could simply read through it
and say, "I know what it says," that is, "I have the idea that is here expressed."
But at that point, what I saw is that the rationality that characterizes the way the
text has laid itself out is my own, that is to say, to understand it is to see that it
expresses *my* thought. To see the sense of why this sentence follows that, and so
on, is to recognize that that is how the sentences *should* go, that is, to find the
text to be *my self-expression*. In *Metaphysics* A.1, Aristotle says that to reach
understanding is to become one capable of teaching,[35] and this is the reason: at
the point at which one understands a text, a set of practices, or what have you,
one also recognizes oneself in them. At that point one has identified with the
very principle that is responsible for producing the text that one now understands, and at that point one is no longer simply bound to the particular text
one has understood, but one can instead vary one's texts, behaviors, or examples to make what is now *one's own point*. So, once again, the move to compre-

hending adequately that which is expressed in what initially appears as an alien set up in front of one involves, first, recognizing that this other *is* rational, and *is* calling out for understanding, and second, transforming one's own relationship to that other precisely to the point that it is no longer other, but is precisely that in which one recognizes *oneself* being expressed.

It is for these reasons, then, that I say that coming to acknowledge the inherent rationality of another culture's rituals—which is what the phenomenology of self-conscious selfhood requires of us—is precisely for us to undergo initiation, and to come to find in those rituals a mirror of our own identity. The key to the ethics of addressing the other, then, is that the other cannot remain alien, but it must come to be the case that we recognize *ourselves* precisely in our act of recognizing that other. We must each come to identify ourselves in the culture of the other: we must learn how to "speak the language." A politics of ethnic respect would thus be best portrayed as one of ethnic interpretation and initiation.[36] I want to use this idea to make two final points about what we must *not* do in such a situation. What we must not do is content ourselves with treating the social customs of others as alien. The gaze that holds the customs of others up as alien objects for reflection takes two seemingly opposite, but implicitly complementary, forms: the first is a form of critique that might be termed "objection," and the second is a putative form of acceptance that I will call "tolerance."

Other cultures often have practices of which we are critical, and we can have good reasons for our criticism. The way a social custom exists for the attitude of critical reflection is not, however, the way it exists for the agent who achieves a lived, communal self-consciousness through that practice: first and foremost, customary social practices are ritual structures of recognition, and they must be comprehended as such, and not confused with the way they appear as "alien" and contingent practices within the "world" of the criticizing ego. Critique is an essential dimension of our intersubjective life, but the only form of critique that does justice to the human demands of ethnic life is immanent critique: criticism must be something that develops from within the lived ethnic situation itself.

Though a social practice might seem to us "objectionable," we must first see that for the culture suffering our criticism it is *precisely the opposite; that is,* for those who follow the practice it is, if anything, divinely demanded. To even know *what the practice is,* then, we must first come to comprehend the function—the function of establishing recognition—that the practice performs for the members of that community. It is only insofar as we come to recognize this *propriety* of that action within that community that we become someone who "speaks the language," that is, we become someone who *can* really address another person religiously committed to such a form of behavior. Prior to establishing this point of view from which we, the would-be critics, can see the propriety of the action, our objections address a phenomenon that the criticized people *cannot recognize:* they can only see us as failing to comprehend the most basic parameters of reality. Once we have come to see the propriety, however, as I have argued above, we are initiates into the practice.

As initiates, we have rights. As initiates, we have the capacity to speak on behalf of the community to the extent that we speak in accordance with the laws; indeed, this principle was the very basis for the concept of law that we analyzed in section 1b, above. When we speak within the context of the law, we speak in a way *that can be understood* by other members of the same law-governed community, and a criticism made *on the basis of the laws themselves* is thus the form of criticism that can make a claim on the criticized people, for it is a self-criticism. Legitimate criticism, then, is accomplished by establishing the grounds *within the customary practices themselves* for criticizing the form these practices take.

Although the particular forms of such an immanent critique would always have to be worked out determinately on the basis of the particularities of the cultural practices in question, our analysis so far has shown us why such a critique will always be in principle possible. We have seen throughout section 1 that the very foundation of religious practices is to be found in the pursuit, inherent to the very nature of self-consciousness, of establishing a situation of mutual recognition. This is the animating objective of ethnic practices, and such practices are therefore *automatically* self-critical to the extent that they frustrate mutual recognition among self-consciousnesses. Any religion, then, is at root driven by a demand to seek universal recognition, and this is the basis for criticizing the oppressive, exclusionary, or marginalizing consequences of the immediate forms in which it is practiced: as we saw in section 2a, religion, by its own immanent dialectic, faces the imperative to become self-reflective as science; now we see equally that religion faces the imperative to become politically self-critical and to develop its capacities for recognition to the point that they are universally welcoming. The "alienated" cultural critique that does not begin by becoming initiated to the propriety of the other's customs, then, is guilty of the very religious factionalism and intolerance that it seeks to criticize.

The second enemy of this political program of religious respect is something that is often put forward as a friend, but it is really a form of ethnic "exotification." We have seen that as long as the other remains alien to me, it means I have not seen the inherent rationality of the other, which means, really, that I have not seen how the other *already* makes demands upon me, already calls upon me, qua rational, to endorse it. Now it is a fairly common gesture, in the name of pluralism, to insist that we treat others as others, and accept their ways as, perhaps, "interesting," "private" to them, and especially "not the same as ours." But whereas (recalling the three forms of self-consciousness discussed in section 1a) ethnicity is the immediate self-consciousness of a community, and cross-cultural recognition and initiation would be the establishing of an authentic cross-cultural self-consciousness, this exotification that "tolerates the other" is another product of the alienating gaze of the reflective ego, and it fails in two important ways.

First, it makes the other a kind of lesser entity open to our patronizing support, despite our complete rejection of its value as anything other than the cute contingencies of someone else's culture; thus there is an inherent power relation here in which the other is made subordinate to our benevolence and superior reason. Second, it fails to acknowledge that, just as *our* program of tolerance has implications for the other—it contains that other in its view—so too does the ethnicity of this other contain us. Our so-called "democratic" and pluralistic ideal is as much an ethnic expression as that of the other is an ethnicity, and just as our reasons for insisting on ours are rooted in various universal and necessary reasons that thus legitimately make us demand that our others come to recognize these values and that they see the legitimacy of how we have come to express these values, so too do the cultural ideals of others derive from the universal and necessary demands that follow upon the nature of our existence as *Da-sein*, and therefore they equally *require of us* that we come to identify with them.[37]

"Tolerance," then, is really a form of exclusionary complacency, and it is a stance on other cultures that is comparable to the reflective ego's stance on its object, in that it is a stance that falsely portrays the other as comfortably alien rather than seeing that one's very existence is *already* committed to a living involvement with that other.

Ethnicity, then—that is to say, religious ritual—is not to be construed as the unique particularities that "give color" to the life of a culture, but as precisely the point at which that culture engages with its own character as universal and necessary; therefore, ethnicity—whether ours or theirs—is always something that calls to all people *outside* a culture to become initiates. Other cultures are not there for us to "object to" or to "tolerate"; rather, they exist as moral imperatives, as demands to be recognized as determinate achievements of rational self-consciousness. To address a culture in any way other than to try to find in it the rational demands of self-consciousness is thus to belittle it, and to engage in a kind of ethnic bigotry that is not so much "distasteful" as it is at odds with the very nature of our existence as *Da-sein*, that is, as selves in pursuit of self-consciousness.

thirteen
Vision and Image in Hegel's System

In absolute clearness there is seen just as much, and as little, as in absolute darkness.
—Science of Logic, *p. 93*

Twentieth-century philosophy taught us to be wary of the clear-sighted ego, to distrust the ease of daytime vision, to not limit our sights to the waking reality that passes before our eyes. Now, by this dawn of a new century, we have grown suspicious of our easy self-awareness, and we know the need to hunt for ourselves in our dreams, in our diseases, in the darkness of our unconscious, and in the opacity of our bodies. It is figures such as Nietzsche, Heidegger, Sartre, and Merleau-Ponty to whom we would usually think to turn for the discovery that the inconspicuous relationship to the world that we live and that founds the meaningfulness of the obvious and comfortable world of everyday life is the real center of the dynamism of our experience; these are the figures who have turned us to the pre-reflective dimensions of our experience, to the Dionysiac, to being-in-the-world, to the pre-thetic consciousness-(of)-self, to the lived body. It is these figures to whom we would normally turn for the critique of the primacy of the reflective ego. Yet this critique is not new with these figures. This same turning to the subterranean, the non-reflective, the embodied, is equally at the heart of Hegel's dialectical philosophy, and his conceptual analysis is mirrored in his systematic use of visual imagery.

Hegel's vision-based images correspond to distinct positions and logical roles along the path of knowledge, and dealing with Hegel's use of visual images and metaphors will therefore require that Hegel's conceptual critique of the ego be developed alongside the consideration of the images. We will begin with "reflection," which is an image essentially about the alienation of viewer and viewed, the alienation of truth and its medium of manifestation, the alienation of substance and surface, and with "enlightenment," which is an image of a light that is turned on to illuminate an already existent reality to which the light is a superfluous addition, a light that does not light itself up as the source of illumination. Ordinary consciousness presents as its truth the enlightened, reflective ego, and this ego models its life on the completeness of clear vision; the first principle of this purported truth of ordinary consciousness can thus be formulated as "I = Eye." In criticizing this self to which these images of reflection and enlightenment belong, we will be led to images of darkness, of night, of the cunning and deceptive powers that operate out of sight, behind our backs, concealing themselves from our view, creating for us the very illusion of a daylight in which there is the obviousness and clarity of a fully determinate world already given; the ease with which this reality is presented will belie the fact of its being a product of the labor of a communal subjectivity struggling to find for itself an identity. We will see this labor in the inherently idolatrous religious ritual that simultaneously provides for us the images we need for our self-understanding and fails to see its own purpose behind the images it celebrates: religion is a system of ritualized practices that establishes for a community an immediate sensible certainty—a faith in the immediacy of one's vision—that offers both a context in which individuals can develop and also a situation that fails to see its own significance and is oppressive in its conservatism. This tension within religion will point us to the necessity for absolute knowing, and we will move, finally, from the religious imagery of light and revelation to speculation as the image for the perfected vision that apprehends the universal light of concrete reason as both the ground and the goal of even our darkest activities. Hegel's philosophy puts an end to the exotifying gaze of the I = Eye of reflective philosophy, and thereby offers us an inherently multicultural vision with which to enter the twenty-first century.

1. Now It Is Day: Reflection and Enlightenment

"In ordinary consciousness," Hegel writes in his *Differenzschrift*, "the Ego occurs in opposition. Philosophy must explain this opposition to an object."[1] In ordinary consciousness, in other words, the object appears to us to be something intrinsically other than us. Perfected or absolute knowing, however, is the "pure self-recognition in absolute otherness,"[2] that is, philosophy will ultimately teach us to recognize that the apparent other is really ourselves. This gap between ordinary consciousness and absolute knowledge, between the experience of the other as other and the experience of the other as self, marks out the terrain within which our study will situate Hegel's use of visual rhetoric.

The reflective ego is the self whom each of us recognizes from our day-to-day conscious life. When the doorbell rings and I answer, "I'll get it," the subject—both grammatical and experiential—of my sentence is the reflective ego. The reflective ego is the human self as it posits itself—as it recognizes itself—in its explicit acts of noticing itself as a discrete subjectivity. Let us consider what happens when we so reflect: what does experience look like to the reflective ego?

When I say "me," I identify myself in contradistinction to *everything else.* The act of self-positing is the act of announcing the severance of my self from the world. It is thus implicitly the act of announcing the alienness of the world: the act of saying "I" is precisely the act within ordinary experience in which the opposition of self and other, of subject and object, is announced. This portrayal of the situation of the reflective ego has its direct analog in Hegel's portrayal of the structures that characterize sight.

Hegel studies sight in the *Zusatz* of Section 401 of his *Encyclopaedia of the Philosophical Sciences.* His discussion makes it clear why sight is an appropriate metaphor for the rationality of the reflective ego, and why the story of reason can easily be told in images of vision:

> The really material aspect of corporeity . . . does not as yet concern us in seeing. Therefore the objects we see can be remote from us. In seeing things we form, as it were, a merely theoretical, not as yet a practical, relationship; for in seeing things we let them continue to exist in peace and relate ourselves only to their ideal side.[3]

Like the reflective "I," the curious eye takes itself to be encountering an alien reality that is untouched by its gaze. This very alienation of vision from corporeality that gives it the power of ranging universally over a whole field is equally the ground of its inability to really appreciate the reality of its object:

> On account of this independence of sight of corporeity proper, it can be called the noblest sense. On the other hand, sight is a very imperfect sense because by it the object does not present itself to us immediately as a spatial totality, not as *body,* but always only as surface.[4]

Sight, in other words, is not unbiased in its portrayal of its object, but implicitly makes a decision about its nature:

> sight, which is concerned with the object as predominantly self-subsistent, as persisting ideally and materially and which has only an ideal relation to it, senses only its ideal aspect, colour, by means of light, but leaves the material side of the object untouched.[5]

There is thus a parallel between the logic of sight and the logic of the reflective ego in that each portrays its object as an alien and self-subsistent reality that it experiences as a surface and not as a body, and that it portrays as not affected by the gaze that falls upon it or the light that illuminates it.

Hegel's critique of sight as not grasping itself and its other as embodied parallels Hegel's critique of reflection, which in the end is that reflection must unearth a bodily contact that underlies its apparent alienation from its other and that is misrepresented in its immediate apprehension of the other as alien and indifferent. If we now follow the dialectic of the reflective consciousness we will come, ultimately, to see its need to look behind its back to see what unacknowledged truth its own activity is reflecting, to see what life it embodies. We will see this ultimately when we see the need for "external reflection" to recognize its truth as "determining reflection." We turn, first, to the ego's self-description to see how the ego's description of itself as immediately opposed to an alien other is not merely an innocent description that latches on to an already existent division within the nature of being, but is in fact a performative utterance; that is, the announcement of the separation of subject and object is equally the effecting of this very division, and we can see this if we consider the experience of the world as alienated from the self.

As separated from its object, the subject can be only an observer. The key to the metaphysics of the reflective ego is precisely this: since its very definition is to be other to whatever counts as its object, the ego must be an impermeable and independent substance into which nothing alien can ever enter *intrinsically* (that is, its *identity*, its "what it is," is not affected), and which can itself never enter into a real participation in its object. The ego is always isolated, single, alien, and an unchanging onlooker: the ego faces the world like the stereotypic North American faces television.

Now not only is this ego an alien onlooker: it is furthermore in charge of its own destiny, for, *qua* impermeable, it can only look to itself to account for its condition. Thus the self can be only auto-effecting, and, accordingly, it will get its knowledge of things right when it knows itself as the auto-effecting alien who cannot be a participant in any "external" world. Hence the imperative of enlightenment: come to recognize your own truth, and accept the responsibility for your own situation, since you have that responsibility already. Indeed, the enlightenment's charge to the ego is like the charge the academy makes to the stereotypic North American. Advocating something that resembles the image of the light bulb coming on in the head of the inventor, the enlightenment commands the day-to-day self to look at its self: to shine a light—Descartes's "light of nature"—on itself and see what it is really doing.

So the ego on this account is auto-effecting, and it can never encounter, therefore, anything truly alien to itself. Whatever the ego experiences as object, then, can only ever be its own mirror, its own reflection, and this very fact is the basis of consciousness's intrinsic self-imperative to enlightenment, that is, to the self-reflective recognition of itself as something that can only ever be encountering its own self. We began with the experience of subject and object as mutually alien, and our attention to the implications of this metaphysics has led us to see that the reflective ego is never in a real position to talk about an encounter with an alien. Hence the imperative of enlightenment is the imperative for the reflective ego to acknowledge this truth about itself. And we can thus see why the very nature of our consciousness makes enlightenment seem the right stance. Enlightenment says to ordinary consciousness, "wake up," "open your eyes." Ordinary consciousness, then, naturally tends to reflection and enlightenment as to its truth.

Both "reflection" and "enlightenment," in Hegel's discussions, are players implicated in a logic of day-vision, of nonparticipant observation, in the assumed ideal of disinterested, noninvasive access to an (alien) truth that easily reflects off the surface of things. Hegel studies "enlightenment" as a stance, both personal and cultural, that has a systematic place in the development of the potentialities of human experience, and he studies "reflection" as a pivotal logical relationship for understanding selfhood and cognition.

Chapter VI of the *Phenomenology of Spirit* is Hegel's main consideration of enlightenment, and his account is primarily devoted to studying the idea of alienated, self-reliant egohood as a cultural ideal. The world of enlightenment is the world of humanism, the world animated by the scientific revolution, by the spirit of capitalist self-advancement, by the Protestant religion that "builds its temples and altars in the heart of the individual,"[6] by the secular love of culture as the locus and the product of human self-development. This is very much the world into which our generation has been born. It is the world that is built on the assumption that we can easily see what we ourselves are doing, the world that assumes it knows its own identity easily and immediately, the world criticized by Freud and Marx. The key to this vision of reality is the belief that "you can do it," *simpliciter*. The model for this conception of self-reliance is reason. In reasoning, we work out the answers—the truth—for ourselves, by ourselves. When I find the answer to a mathematical puzzle, I need turn to no one other than myself for confirmation that this answer is correct.[7] Similarly, in a scientific experiment, I know the truth of my results because I did the experiment myself; further, I know that any other subject who conducts the same experiment will get the same results. In reasoning, then, we experience ourselves as the bearers of the criterion of truth: rather than having to look to outside authority to justify our views, we know that anyone outside, if they are to claim truth for their views, must conform to what we ourselves know. Hegel's phenomenological description of this view of the self-reliance of the rational being as it functions as a cultural ideal shows that the social institutions built around this ideal destroy themselves precisely because, by recognizing as valuable only what universally and necessarily belongs to all human beings *qua* rational, this cultural ideal negates the value of all human particularity, and thus ends up negating the very basis of our self-identity.[8] I will not trace out the cultural dialectic, but we must note the inadequacy of reflective reason's self-conception on which this cultural self-criticism turns.

In reasoning it is true that in an important sense we hold the initiative, the agency, that accomplishes truth. If someone else solves the puzzle, or if I merely repeat an answer by rote, my action was not reasoning. I am speaking accurately, in other words, when, after solving a mathematical puzzle, I say, "I did that." The crucial question, however, is "who is this 'I'?": is it the same I, for example, that I identify when I say "I like to type"? Is the ego that speaks with the authority of universal rationality simply identical with the idiosyncratic ego of my personal life?

In general, Hegel argues that reflection misdescribes its own experience, for if the ego spoke honestly it would say that it finds its actions can harness rational ability, but can never "own" it: we find ourselves as *products of* the synthetic activities of self-consciousness, but it is only in and as the determinate realization of these activities that we are able to identify ourselves. It is true that I am the synthetic activity of my own consciousness, but this synthesis, this power, is something I receive: I experience myself as given to myself; whatever power I have comes to me from beyond my immediate self, and thus *qua* rational my action is not a *product* of my empirical ego.[9] Thus the self who says "I did that" is right, but that self has not looked carefully enough. This self does not recognize that whatever it defines as itself and its object come *already* given, already as products of a synthetic activity of self-consciousness that here is not one player *within* the system, but is the ground of the whole determinate system. This self-already-in-situation does not see that the very presence to it of its self and an other already outside it marks the work of a positing power; that is, this already determinately situated self does not see that it has already presupposed the distinction of self and other, and it, as the finite self that it takes itself (immediately) to be, cannot therefore be held up as the agent responsible for the distinction. It exists on the basis of presupposition, so *it* is a product, and it must look for the real truth of its experience, the real agency "behind" the scenes, in the power that did the preliminary "supposing," that is, the original positing power for which the *distinguishing* of self and other is its act: this is the determining power for which the determined elements of self and other are its determinate reflection. Hegel's critique of enlightenment thus leads us to look at Hegel's treatment of this determining power that reflects itself in the mutual externality of self and other, each of which reflects back to the other the determinateness—the already determined-ness—of its identity. It leads us to Hegel's treatment of "External Reflection" and "Determining Reflection" in the *Science of Logic*.

"Reflection," used as an image to characterize the structure of truth, suggests that what we directly experience is an optical stand-in for the real thing; in regard to this surface show, which reflects the real essence, we would ask whether the medium of the reflection plays a role, whether the posture of the viewer is relevant, whether the reflection itself has a reality beyond its role as a conveyer of the essence and its role as potential deceiver. As a epistemological structure, Hegel's "reflection" is fundamentally the relationship that characterizes the forms of the *activity* of the cognitive agent (whether this activity is recognized by the cognitive agent or not), and the issues Hegel's analysis raises mirror the issues the image raises.[10]

First (in "positing reflection"), the dialectic of reflection shows that the cognitive agent can never be passive in cognition (or at least not solely passive) for any recognition of determinateness involves an act of *positing*; that is, recognition is itself an activity. Now the enlightened reasoner—the self who has seen the light of her auto-effection—has recognized her own power of positing and is fundamentally characterized by the second stance of reflection, which Hegel terms "external reflection." "External reflection" names the situation in which we recognize ourselves to be active thinkers, and we take ourselves to be performing our thinking on an already formed object that confronts us. The object is outside of us, and our task is to take what is thus "given" and to find out the truth about it. We take the object, in other words, to be unrecognized in its immediate state, and we see the need to recognize it as something that is showing some truth that is more than its immediate self; reflection is "the movement of the faculty of judgment that goes beyond a given immediate conception and seeks universal determinations for it or compares such determinations with it."[11] For reflection, the other is a show (*Schein*). It is on the one hand "merely" a show, for we have yet to penetrate it to the essential truth that is reflected in it; the immediacy of the show is the inessential, the superfluous. On the other hand the immediate is a show precisely in that it is that which shows us the truth, that without which nothing would show up; the dialectic of reflection moves to the recognition of the essentiality of the immediate show itself. For reflection in general, then, the relation to the object is a relation to a structure of show and essence, or, in more familiar terms, appearance (*Erscheinung*) and reality. External reflection, like the enlightened ego, does realize of itself that it is active, and it takes its activity to be the act of transforming the object of its consciousness from its immediate show to its truth; it knows that it seeks the essence that will explain the show it immediately encounters, where this immediacy itself is deemed superfluous.

What this project of finding the essence of a given other entails, however, is that in taking up its object, in trying to determine the essence of its show, the reflecting subject can never break out of its own self. As Hegel says, "the determinations posited by the external reflection in the immediate are to that extent [that is, to the extent that they are posited by external reflection] external to the latter."[12] The alien, given other must remain permanently impenetrable, opaque, a thing-in-itself that defines the self-contradictory ideal of an object that is to be known (that is, to be in relation to a subject) precisely as devoid of any relations. The *activity* of looking for the truth of the other is precluded from succeeding by the very fact of its being an activity; indeed, the superfluous medium that had seemed to be the residue-less mediator of subject to object-as-essence becomes the very point of absolute resistance, the mark of the limit of the ability of the subject's gaze to penetrate to the truth. What we need to see to resolve the problem of external reflection is that its problems emerge from inadequate assumptions that are built into its original posture; this means seeing that its immediate other is not really so immediate and that its activity does not start with the operation upon this given other, but that the very givenness of the other presupposes a logically prior act of positing on the part of reflection. This is what we see in the move to determining reflection.

Hegel makes this presupposing clear in his concluding remarks about external reflection:

> But if the activity of external reflection is more closely considered [*Aber das Tun der äußern Reflexion näher betrachtet*], it is secondly a positing of the immediate, which consequently becomes the negative or the determinate; but external reflection is immediately also the sublating of this its positing; for it *pre*supposes the immediate; in negating, it is the negating of this its negating. But in doing so it is immediately equally a *positing*, a sublating of the immediate negatively related to it, and this immediate from which it seemed to start as from something alien, *is* only in this its beginning.[13]

Hegel's point is this. Initially, external reflection appeared as a relation of self and other in which the other-as-determined (only) reflects back the self and the other in its immediacy becomes inaccessible; what we now realize is that this *whole* relation is the determinateness, the "show," which reflects the determining power of subjectivity as such; that is, the very *relation*, the very *division* of subject and object, is the way the real agency within experience shows itself. The real essence of experience is thus as much subject as object, or, more precisely, the very form in which the players "subject" and "object" are defined in relation to each other is the self-expression, the determinateness, the show, of a single determining power.[14] The relation itself—the very presence to a subject of an immediately alien other—presupposes a single positing power. Hegel calls this total relation "determining reflection."

What we have seen with the observing ego is that it is right to identify the light that shines within its experience to be its self, but what reflection and enlightenment fail to see is that this their very self is not immediately identical with them insofar as they are alienated egos. Enlightenment suffers from a kind of blindness, much like the blindness of an eyeglass wearer to her glasses: the very power that makes a world or an object visible itself slips outside the field of vision, and conceals itself as essence in its very act of showing its power in its establishment of an articulated relation of subject and object. Indeed, real insight comes when we take up the relation of subject and object as the articulate expression of this power, its self-expression, the real act of saying "I": the "I" not as alien eye, but as the total situation of embodied intentionality. Reflection needs to see itself-as-a-totality as the real image of its identity. As

Hegel implies in always insisting we "observe more closely," vision is not as simple as it "presents" itself to be, and we need to see the self-absenting of the perceptive power, the agency that does not put itself in full view in front of our eyes, but that works its cunning machinations behind our backs.[15]

Sight is the natural analog for the rational ego as reflection, and the inadequacy of sight that Hegel notes is that it does not experience its other bodily. We can say the same thing of the reflective ego: it experiences its other only, as Hegel would say, "ideally," which means it does not engage with it as a carnal contact. Equally, the reflective ego holds itself aloof from the object it studies, thereby failing to realize of itself that it is of the flesh, and therefore vulnerable to the other. What the reflective ego needs to learn is that the situation it finds itself in is not primary, but is derivative of a more fundamental dynamism, and this is the structure we have seen in determining reflection. The reflective ego participates in the embodiment of the dynamism that gives rise to both it and its other as apparently immediately alien to one another. This alienation must be overcome, and we will see this in seeing how our knowledge of the other is originally a bodily knowledge, that is, in seeing that our relation to the other begins as an immediate lived participation in a shared system of meanings that are the basis for our being able to act and that are not first known by way of a process of alienated observation. It is our living relation with the other, not our looking at it, that is our fundamental reality and is that upon which the reflective stance is based. Hegel remarks that we would starve if we had to first learn physiology in order to eat, or again that to learn to swim one must abandon the manuals and jump into the water; the manuals and the scientific observation can be only derivative commentaries on what is already a living bodily communion.

What we can now look for is, to continue this image, how we are already "swimming in" our object exactly when we experience it as alien: in turning to the determining reason of which our very relation to the object is the determinate, concrete expression, we turn to our real identity, which is precisely what is embodied as our relation to the other. This discovery that the immediate alienation of self and other is itself a derivative phenomenon is the thread that will allow us to trace a way back through the labyrinth, the night, of the ethical substance in which we are already embodied; we must pursue this route through Hegel's treatment of Sophocles' *Antigone* in order to later pick up this thread of "immediate presence," which is here shown to be the already mediated result of an absent ground. Just as reflection must turn back to the determining power operating outside of its field of awareness, we must now turn to this power that cloaks itself in darkness in order to found our everydayness;[16] we must turn to night's children, the gods that are our earth, the Chthonian gods of *Antigone*. We, like everyday consciousness, thought we began basking in the obviousness of the daylight of enlightenment; but now it is night, and we must see how we had already begun well before daybreak.

2. Now It Is Night: The Ethical Substance

Antigone does not have to find out through a process of alienated reflection whether the right thing to do is to bury her dead brother Polynices: the imperative to so act is inscribed in the very situation of his corpse lying unburied; it is as obvious as the sunshine that Creon's edict that disallows the burial is a violation of the laws that govern the very nature of things. Hegel's analysis of Sophocles' *Antigone* studies this situation of Antigone as paradigmatic for the immediate form of free human social life;[17] his objective is to unearth the dynamic dimensions of our life that constitute for us this appearance of unachieved, unmediated immediacy, that achieve for us the appearance of an immediately present set of ethical values simply inherent "in the nature of things."[18]

Now Antigone can be asked "why is it right to bury Polynices," and she will have an answer: "Because it is so; the gods decree it." Who are these gods? Hegel describes this power that overrides Creon's edict:

> Confronting this clearly manifest ethical power [the human law] there is, however, another power, the Divine Law. For the ethical power of the state, being the movement of self-conscious action, finds its antithesis in the simple and immediate essence of the ethical sphere. . . . This movement which expresses the ethical sphere in this element of immediacy . . . is the Family. The Family, as the *unconscious*, still inner concept, stands opposed to its actual self-conscious existence.[19]

Hegel further develops the portrayal of this power through reference to Sophocles' *Antigone*, and he continues to describe it through images that show this power to be in contrast to the ideal of the clarity and light of enlightenment reflection:

> The feminine, in the form of the sister, has the highest *intuitive* awareness of what is ethical. She does not attain to *consciousness* of it, or to the objective existence of it, because the law of the Family is an implicit, inner essence which is not exposed to the daylight of consciousness.[20]

This divine law, "the power of the nether world (*die unterirdische Macht*),"[21] this "power which shuns the light of day (*eine lichtscheue Macht*),"[22] the "hidden divine law (*das verborgene göttliche Gesetz*),"[23] this law that hides in the dark, is the real power that sets for us the standards by which we see the objects of our daily life. Antigone's view that bodies should be buried is the expression of a value—it is a *product* of an activity of evaluation on her part—but she does not recognize it (posit it) as such: she sees it as a simple fact. Antigone does not first see a corpse and only subsequently decide that it should be buried; rather, for her the very experience of "corpse" is "to be buried"; her vision—her immediate sensing—is intelligent, is understanding; that is, her sensing is not passive and innocent, but is decisive, already committed, already judgmental. She, however, does not see that what she takes as a given other is really the product of a judging—a pre-judging—activity of consciousness *by which* objects become *possible*. In this regard she is the very consciousness that will have to follow the path to enlightenment. But she gives us a clue to the real determining power in things, for in her we see that behind the immediate subject there is a founding power of prejudice by which there is first allowed to be a world, by which "there is" anything at all. It is this power that gives us the given. For Hegel the day is the place of deceptive simplicity; the gift of immediate presence, which, in its claim to clarity and manifestness, conceals the very giving power, conceals the very determining foundation of, equally, the subject and the object.[24] What is this dark power that gives us the light of day? What is this force that cunningly lays out for us a world as if it were already there waiting for us?

With the daytime world of enlightenment culture there goes a conception of self-consciously reflective, abstract reason; the opposed image of the nighttime world of ethicality equally brings with it an opposite concept of a reason that is intuitive and concrete and that shows forth something else while concealing itself. This reason is the *nous* to which Hegel refers in his introduction to his *Lectures on the Philosophy of History:*

> Anaxagoras . . . was the first to point out that *nous*, understanding in general or Reason, rules the world—but not an intelligence in the sense of an individual consciousness. . . . These two must be carefully distinguished. The motion of the solar system proceeds according to immutable laws; these laws are its reason. But neither the sun nor the planets, which according to these laws rotate around it, have any consciousness of it.

Hegel goes on to discuss how Socrates, in Plato's *Phaedo*, embraces this idea of a governing reason that is invisible to that which it governs, but is disappointed with Anaxagoras's use of it:

> It is evident that the insufficiency which Socrates found in the principle of Anaxagoras has nothing to do with the principle itself, but with Anaxagoras' failure to apply it to concrete nature. Nature was not understood or comprehended through this principle; the principle remained abstract—nature was not understood as a development of Reason, as an organization brought forth by it. I wish at the very outset to draw your attention to this difference between a concept, a principle, a truth, as confined to the abstract and as determining concrete application and development. This difference is fundamental.[25]

This is a *nous*—a reason—that cannot have its own identity apart from the elements it organizes, for these very elements are the substance of the *nous*'s self-expressive act: they are not *instances* to which reason is *applied*, but are its embodiment.

The reason of enlightenment and external reflection is the reason that applies to an other. This is the reason for which the paradigm instances are mathematics and formal logic: the very mark of the authority of these systems of reasoning is the universality and necessity that comes from their being solely *formal* truths; that is, these systems of reasoning claim to tell us the truth about any situation *irrespective of the content.* These are truths that are derived simply from the notion of simple self-identity, and they therefore apply to anything *qua* self-identical. This whole conception of reasoning, then, is based on the premise of a distinction between form and content, such that formal truths are never conditioned by the content to which they apply. Such a notion of reason, however, is constitutively incapable of comprehending, therefore, any identity in which form and content are not distinguishable, for the very premise of formal reasoning is the denial of the very essence of that which it would have to understand.[26] The Anaxagorean *nous,* however, is the conception of an organic reason, a reason that is *realized* through that of which it is the rationality. This concrete reason is a reason premised on a reciprocity of determination between form and content, and this reason's own identity cannot be articulated in independence of articulating that of which it is the organizing reason.[27] It is this reason for which its *explananda* are its own articulation, which is the concrete, self-developing reason that grounds our everydayness.

This *nous* then, that is, reason as concrete, is reason for which that which it explains is in fact its own self-expression; it is animative, rather than applied; that is, the relations it explains are its living substance, its body, not its alien object. This reason is the determining power for which the concrete development it explains is its own reflection; thus its other—it differs from its other as *explanans* from *explandum*—is its own self-articulation, and it will adequately explain its other when it explains it as its own self-reflection. This *nous* is the determining power that we sought at the end of section 1 and that is the determining power in ethical life: and we will see that this *nous* precisely is spirit's self-recognition, and it is what is effected uncomprehendingly in and through religion (section 3) and self-consciously in absolute knowing (section 4). But we have seen in Sophocles' *Antigone* that this *nous* that organizes our world, this *nous* that drives our history, hides itself as ground precisely in its manifestation of itself as articulation. The living reality of Antigone's *sittliche Substanz,* of her ethical world, is really the *expression* of such a founding rationality, and the organization of her world reflects the values that characterize this rationale, but *for* her this rationality is not manifest as such; instead, she lives an identity already attuned to a certain perception of the nature of things, already harmonized to determinate values that she experiences as fixed directly in the nature of things. She does not recognize herself and her world to be products of this founding rationality, and thinks, instead, that she innocently reads the manifest meanings that lie open on the surface of things. This is the "cunning of reason," the reason that gets its work done through subjects who do not recognize their own complicity in passing judgment; of this reason, Hegel says in the *Phenomenology of Spirit* that it works "behind the backs" of subjects, and it is this logical structure of unacknowledged behavioral complicity that is reflected in the image of concealment from sight. Like the gods of Antigone's netherworld, this real power in our experience works behind the scenes, out of sight and out of mind, concealing its cunning manipulation of events behind a veil of everyday obviousness.

Precisely what this cunning reason does is produce us as subjects immediately alienated from our objects, and by so producing *us* as *observers* actually effects its *own* project of *participant self-observation. Our* alienation from the object, in other words, is *its* self-relation. It is the *coalescence* of these two sides of our experience that is "absolute knowing," for absolute knowing is precisely the concrete project of recognizing that and how our apparent other is really a reflection of our own true (determining) identity; that is, absolute knowing realizes that it is only by understanding the determinate form of its own *relation* to its object that it will know itself.

In these first two sections, we have examined the basic logical relationships that characterize natural consciousness, enlightenment, ethicality, and absolute knowing, and we have seen that these logical relations are paralleled in Hegel's uses of visual images. Hegel uses images of a vision that takes itself to be unproblematic to characterize the epistemological and psychological stance that advocates the primacy of the independent reflective ego, and the limitations that his arguments reveal in the reflective stance are mirrored in the limitations to vision that he diagnoses in his explicit discussion of sight. In keeping with this system of images, Hegel uses images of that which is not accessible to sight to characterize the stance that advocates the concrete, embodied reason that operates through individual subjects without their explicit recognition of it.

We are now at the point where we can consider how the theme of imagery is itself thematic in Hegel's analysis: Hegel defines religion as the system of ritualized practices that unite a community around a shared "vision," a socially endorsed system of *Vorstellungen*—images—in and as which a society portrays itself to itself. These images are precisely the expression of the concrete reason that we found to be animating the member of the ethical community; in turning now to consider Hegel's philosophy of religion we will learn both why we depend on images and how we should understand them, and we will watch the development of the image for this socially embodied reason from "light" to "revelation" (and, finally, in section 4, to "speculation"). Along the way we will be led to consider what the foundations are of our immediate vision itself and why this "sense-certainty" is always constructed through images. Let us turn now to the dynamics of the politico-religious vision that emerges from this rejection of the I = Eye in favor of the nocturnal reason that uses the obviousness of daylight to veil the subtle machinations by which it enforces its vision of reality.

3. The Veil of Immediacy: The Religious
Foundation of Sense-Certainty

Antigone's own actions function according to a logic she does not see: her ownmost values are not judgments to which she "owns up" (for which reason she represents a stage of consciousness that must still develop to the point of enlightenment). We have seen that her real animating values—the real core of her self-identity—is a cunning reason that operates behind her back: it is a determining power that fundamentally has its reflection in the determinate relation that it establishes between her and her surroundings, in the immediate form of the opposition of the terms "self" and "other." Precisely what this mediating ground does is establish an immediacy, a relationship of presence, the presence of something for someone. This is the logical structure involved (a structure of determining reflection) but we have not yet seen the experiential dynamics of how this is effected.

The enlightened, externally reflecting "I" was alienated from its others and thus alienated from other egos. If *Antigone* shows us an ethical situation in which this alienation of self and other cannot be primary, but where it is only this very relation that is the reflection of the real determining reason, then it must equally be only in the relation of selves that this founding power that is the real source of the identity of these selves is expressed. In particular, the non-alienation of the members of an ethical community is the system of recognition (*Anerkennen*) in Hegel's language, that is, the system by which there is a mutual supporting of identity: we do not hold our own identity within ourselves, but require, rather, the reflections of others to tell us who we are, and Hegel understands social life essentially as this system of interpersonal communication whereby we tell each other who we are.[28]

In an ethical community, an overarching sense of the community's identity is constantly rearticulated through the practices of community life, which means that the actions of the members effect at each time—along with their manifest, particular goals—an annunciation of "we are. . . ."[29] Just as, then, we earlier saw that the very *relation* of subject and object is the expression of the determining power that is the real identity of both, so do we here see how social actions are precisely the point at which the particular identities that all of the members perform through their behavior equally serve to perform for each and all the expression of their shared identity as members of this "we." Thus once again, even in the determinate oppositions that make one person not another, this immediate opposition is *already* more fundamentally a demonstration of a shared identity: the shared identity—the universal—according to its own logic expresses itself through diverse or even opposed finite identities— the particulars—and it is the single self that performs both its particular and its universal identity in each action.

Indeed, it is the very ability of each particular self to *recognize* itself and the other (that is, its ability to notice the self-identity of each and the difference between them and to agree on this), that is the proof of the presence of the universal identity, for it is only because the selves operate with a shared sense of the relevant categories for evaluation of each other that they can share a sense of who they both are. It is precisely the *recognizability* of the world—both other selves and non-selves—that is the shared situation of the members of the ethical world, and it is the actions in which the various agents communicate their sense of how they recognize the world that they communicate to each other that they know who they are: they know who each other is, and they know who they as a whole are.

Now fundamentally, our world offers us openings for various kinds of behavior: it is as presentations of horizons of possible action that we experience the things of our world. Our world shows itself to us as the arena for the conduct of our life, and, as we saw with Antigone's experience of the corpse, the experience of imperatives to act in this way or that is the *immediate* experience of things. Our actions thus communicate how we experience the imperatives in things; that is, our actions communicate the sense we immediately have of how things are "to be done." It is thus in our performance of actions that we perform because we simply experience them as "to be done" that we fundamentally establish for ourselves and for each other our identity. Now actions that are performed because they are immediately experienced as "to be done" are rituals, and it is thus in our ritual actions that we establish for ourselves as members of a community a shared sense of who we are.[30]

At the most general level, then, our actions, *qua* culturally embedded practices, are fundamentally ritualized actions or practices that communicate our sense of self-identity. Now there is a special set of ritual practices that are usually singled out by ethical communities themselves as religious. What is distinctive of these practices is that these are rituals that are *recognized* as rituals; that is, these are practices in which we *explicitly* announce that our identity is based on a shared sense of what is "to be done."[31] This, it seems to me, is how Hegel fundamentally understands religion. Religious actions are the point at which a community enacts its self-consciousness by recognizing a shared set of things "to be done," but the recognition of these values is an immediate recognition, so it is a recognition of a shared identity that does not recognize about itself that in enacting its rituals it is enacting its own communal self-consciousness; religion is inherently "idolatrous" or committed to *Vorstellungen*—images—in that it is the commitment to the repetition of the practice *qua* un-understood and *as* a gesture of membership or "belief." In Hegel's words, religion is self-consciousness in the form of consciousness.[32]

So what is the reason that operates behind the back of the members of the ethical substance? It is their own activity of self-recognition as a "we": there is a reason behind their activities, namely, they are effecting a collective self-recognition, and it is a *determinate* self-recognition—that is, they recognize themselves as this particular community that carries out its relation-to-being in this way and not in that way;[33] this rationality is expressed in all their actions, and it is the reason why these actions need to be performed, yet it is a rationality that is hidden from the view of the agents themselves. The agents thus experience actions as needing to be done without being able to give an account of that very necessity in *precisely* the same way that every reflective ego *must* posit itself in contradistinction to an object, and it must do this *immediately*: this is an ontological and not a moral "must," which means this distinction is the logical *pre*-condition (this positing of difference is a presupposition) for any action by this reflective ego; so even if this ego (following, for example, the path I have laid out in this chapter) should come to understand why it posits an object in opposition to itself, this will be *subsequent* to the positing itself. It is, in other words, only *within the context of* the immediate participation in the ritual rationality that development is possible. Adequate self-recognition, in other words, must *begin* in this inadequate self-recognition, that is, in this ritual self-recognition that does not recognize itself as an act of self-recognition. We necessarily begin, therefore, as idolatrous, as committed to a set of *Vorstellungen* that are the images *within which* the rationality of our existence is enacted, just as we always have a "first language" that is the set of ritually defined vocalic and gestural behaviors that we and our culture accept as the embodiment of communicable meaning.

Now what this tells us is that a culture's rituals—both those recognized explicitly as religious and those that simply constitute the day-to-day "secular" life—are not contingent within a culture but are, rather, the very soil within which that culture's identity can grow, indeed, within which that culture's identity first becomes possible. And, *qua* ritual, these practices, these ways of experiencing the immediate sense of a situation, must be, for the members of the culture, practices whose imperative nature is *lived* and not reflectively posited.[34] The implication of Hegel's argument is thus that a cultural group will necessarily have ritual practices and will necessarily *not* recognize that they are reflections of cultural identity, but will take them instead as demands fixed within the very nature of things: this is, then, a transcendental argument about the necessary conditions for the possibility of culture, and to say that a society must rely upon such unreflective practices is not to say "it should not and must not question them," but that "it cannot come into existence without such a basing of itself upon an unthematized system of ritual recognition." The ritual life of a culture, then, is something the members immediately participate in; that is, it is their living substance, their immediate embodiment, and not something that they experience as an alien set of rules or practices that they reflectively endorse.

To be a human being, then—that is, to be a self-conscious member of a community of recognition—requires first and foremost to be integrated into a determinate ritual life. What we as philosophical anthropologists uncover as the decisions, values, and practices by which the community establishes for itself a communal self-identity constitute, therefore, that necessary dimension of human life that we, as members of the ritual community, experience as the significance that is immediately presented to us through our senses. It is the dialectic of this immediate certainty, which is always our immediate reality but which is equally always inadequate as a final stance on the nature of truth, that Hegel studies in Chapter I of the *Phenomenology of Spirit*, "Sense-Certainty."

Sense-certainty [*die sinnliche Gewißheit*] is the name Hegel assigns to the most immediate form of consciousness, that is, the most immediate form of the presentation to a subject of an object. Sense-certainty is the immediate noticing of an other. Ultimately, the point of Hegel's phenomenological analysis of sense-certainty is that this experience of "other" is not the truth but is really a kind of idolatry: the object of immediate experience is really an integrated moment in an intelligible totality, and it fundamentally functions as a *sign* that points to this total context, but sense-certainty treats it as an uncontextualized, immediately meaningful unit with the precise sense of "alien thing," which is really the very notion of *Vorstellung*, namely, something posited as alien and as immediately meaningful in independence of the context of subjectivity. Sense-certainty itself, on the other hand, precisely takes the immediate experience of its other to be the truth: "this that I sense right now" is what really comprises experience, according to sense-certainty. Hegel's dialectical phenomenology of sense-certainty proceeds by demonstrating that the here and now of immediate presence exist for us only as contextualized by the there and then, the mediating absences that stand out of sight to let the immediate show itself.

Sense-certainty, says Hegel, equally insists that the truth of experience is "now" when "now it is day" is the truth of its experience, and (twelve hours later), when "now it is night" is the truth. At night, a situation that in no way differs in terms of its experiential structures replaces the first situation, for sense-certainty still says the truth is "now," that is, it claims the identical truth for both experiences, and the absolute transformation of all the determinate features of the experience is not recognized in sense-certainty's monotonic intonation of "this, now."[35] Hegel's images are of our most immediate *sensible* opposition (daylight and darkness of night); we *see* this difference, but this very distinction, which is operative at the level of *sight*—indeed, this opposition is the necessary condition for vision—cannot be accounted for by the very vision it enables. Sense-certainty's efforts to account for its experience are an attempt to say the unique, particular moment of immediacy, but it says instead only the most universal and undifferentiated truth about experience, namely, that it always takes the form of a temporal presentation to a subject—"now." And as the universal form of all experience, it cannot mark out distinctions between experiences; that is, the saying of "now" by itself no more specifies this experience than that.[36]

The point is that what really makes our experience determinate and meaningful is the mediation within experience, whereas the way we immediately experience is to find significance appearing seemingly without mediation. In sense-certainty's "now," however, we see how limited would be the recognizable determinacies of experience if it really were the case that the meaningfulness within experience were merely immediate. Our ability to recognize complex determinacies shows that our organization of our experience is actually operating at a level of logical sophistication that is considerably higher than the level that is explicitly—reflectively—recognized by the sense-certain ego; to say "day" or "night" requires understanding, requires the ability to synthesize and judge a manifold of experience. What is "just present" really points outside itself to what it is not—to its context of mediation, to what is absent—to support its meaning; and for us to recognize the present is for us to equally take up an interpretive stance on the absent, which conceals itself in order to make the present obvious and available.

This concealed mediation takes many forms, but the most significant dimension of this mediation for our purposes is that which we have just been studying, namely the categories of recognition that are ritually announced and endorsed by a community that, through adopting these ways of being sense-certain, establishes for itself a shared identity. The immediate form our experience takes, then, is the presentation of itself as being immediately and unproblematically in relation to determinate truth, but the dialectic of sense-certainty shows this to be an intrinsically contradictory stance; it is religion, in fact, that provides for us the mediation that structures into things their immediately recognizable identities; but, like sense-certainty itself, religion gives an inadequate account of itself, and fails to recognize that it is really the forum for a community's performance of itself as a "we." For Hegel, then, the very immediacy of our vision is *constructed* through traditional social practices, which indoctrinate us into a particular vision, a particular set of images, a particular set of visual expectations: our sensing is inherently religious; that is, it is through ritualized practices that we develop intelligent vision, and this means that the meaning we sense is fundamentally to be understood in the context of the intersubjective pursuit of self-consciousness. The essential form this activity takes, finally, is to conceal the very fact that it is such, and to offer up an obvious immediacy that hides the truth of the performance (and it is this contradiction of not being self-conscious in its establishment of self-consciousness that necessitates the overcoming of religion in philosophy).

According to the Hegelian argument, then, religion is that which gives us our already established sense of what the truth of being is, such that this is not in question within experience, but is, rather, the very foundational context that makes experience possible. Religion, then, is that which initially determines what, for us, is true: it is this determining that makes meaningful experience possible for us, that illuminates for us the determinacies of the world, and it does this by giving us a system of images. Truth is thus more *fundamentally* to be identified with the system that provides the *illumination* of our immediately sensible meaningfulness than it is with the activities of those determinacies themselves: this is what is announced in what Hegel's *Phenomenology* posits as the most immediate form of religion, namely, *das Lichtwesen*, the religion that says "God is light."

The most immediate form of religion is precisely the religion that idolizes visual imagery as the ultimate truth. Hegel begins his description by noting the privileging of the illuminating over the illuminated that is equally the privileging of rituality as such over the human members whose self-conscious existence is the living substance—the actuality—of the ritual:

> Spirit as the essence that is *self-conscious*—or the self-conscious Being that is all truth and knows all reality as its own self—is, to begin with, only its *concept* in contrast to the actuality which it gives itself in the movement of its consciousness.[37]

This privileging of the illuminating over the illuminated, the shaping over the shaped, is essentially equivalent to the privileging of the indeterminate over the determinate that characterizes "Sense-Certainty":

> In the immediate, first diremption of self-knowing absolute Spirit its "shape" has the determination which belongs to *immediate consciousness* or to *sense-certainty*. Spirit beholds itself in the form of *being*, though not of the non-spiritual being that is filled with the contingent determinations of sensation, the being that belongs to sense-certainty; on the contrary, it is being that is filled with Spirit. . . . This being which is filled with the concept of Spirit is, then, the *"shape"* of the *simple* relation of Spirit to itself, or the "shape" of "shapelessness." In virtue of this determination, this "shape" is the pure, all-embracing and all-pervading *essential light* of sunrise, which preserves itself in its formless substantiality. Its otherness is the equally simple negative, *darkness*. The movements of its own externalization, its creations in the unresisting element of its otherness, are torrents of light.[38]

The truth, then, is posited as the universal form as opposed to the determinate multiplicity that it informs.

To simply identify the truth with the illuminating, however, is no better than sense-certainty's identification of the truth with "now." Both stances are right, to be sure, but both equally find themselves in the position of articulating only a formal truth, that is, a truth that is merely selfsame in every situation. In each case, the attempt to say the truth is inarticulate; in the case of "God is light" as in the case of "now," the attempt to name the truth of our experience precisely empties our experience of meaning, since the very determinateness—the very substance—of our experience is lost, for it becomes only so many indifferent "examples" of the truth.

> The content developed by this pure *being*, or the activity of its perceiving, is, therefore, an essenceless by-play in the substance which merely *ascends*, without *descending* into its depths to become a subject and through the self to consolidate its distinct moments. The determinations of this substance are only attributes which do not attain to self-subsistence, but remain merely names of the many-named One.[39]

Spirit must come to recognize that it *is* literally the self-consciousness *of* the individual agents who enact it, and religion must come to acknowledge this at the level of the image. The image of the divine must acknowledge the essentiality to the divine of the determinations or articulations. The image must thus be of the divine as self-explicating such that the One illuminates the many and requires in turn that it be illuminated (to itself) by them, that is, that it become conscious of itself in and through them.

> This reeling, unconstrained Life must determine itself as being-for-self and endow its vanishing "shapes" with an enduring subsistence. . . . It is thus in truth the *Self*; and Spirit therefore passes on to know itself in the form of self. Pure Light disperses its unitary nature into an infinity of forms, and offers up itself as a sacrifice to being-for-self, so that from its substance the individual may take an enduring existence for itself.[40]

It is Christianity, or rather, "the revealed religion," that corrects this by having a god that descends into that which it illuminates, and depends upon this for its own resurrection.[41]

Revealed religion still insists on the truth of the divine illumination, but, like Hegel's own argument, it announces the divinity as the determining power that sacrifices itself to that which it makes possible. Further, it recognizes that that which it makes possible is not a merely superfluous reflection of its own self-sufficient truth, but is rather what the divine itself needs for its own completion. Revealed religion is the religion that announces that religion founds sense-certainty: the definitive image of Christ—the divine itself—self-sacrificed and resurrected (in the hearts of the participants in the Christian church) is the image of determining reflection, and of determining reflection understood as the logic of the dynamism of the (self-)experiential life of a religious community. It is the image that recognizes the need of the divine—the determining power—to be *embodied* in that which it determines, to be embodied in the division into immediately experiencing subject and immediately meaningful object, to be embodied in its expressive reflection: the image is the image of the *logos* made flesh, and of the divinity whose embodiment is the community of believers. Just like individual human subjects, the divine light needs to be recognized, and it needs to be recognized in that which it illuminates, as that which it illuminates, and by that which it illuminates. Unlike the light religion, the revealed religion knows the necessity of self-diremption, knows that the alienation of subject and object is *essential*, for the divine needs to be known—needs to know itself—and this requires that it first divide itself from itself in order to be able to return to itself in recognition. Human existence must be the comprehension of itself as precisely the divine comprehension of itself; divinity must be the comprehension of itself as precisely the human comprehension of itself. This is absolute knowing, and this is the truth of spirit's self-comprehension.

The revealed or absolute religion is the religion that ritually endorses the necessity for religion: the absolute religion is the commitment to the essentiality of the image that founds a community; that is, it is the ritual endorsement of the image of images as needing to be realized in and as rational interpretation by a human community in pursuit of self-understanding. It is thus the founding commitment to the necessity for an immediate experience of alienation that presents itself as an encounter with an immediate meaningfulness but that is really a sign—a *Vorstellung*—and a sign that points to the need to explicate the images we live by into rational systems of social self-communication. Sense-certainty, the very experience that seems to us immediately to be a stepping into the light, is in truth a stepping into the dark, a stepping away from the source that really illuminates our experience; but this stepping away is necessary for us to be able to ultimately comprehend our truth. It is precisely the goal of knowledge to reconcile these two directions within our experience and to have our immediate experience of the world be the recognition of the truth that animates our experience; it is this fulfilled self-consciousness that is absolute knowing. But this absolute knowing is thus possible only *because* we have immediate sense experience, and it is only through this route that knowledge can ever complete itself.

We must now complete our story of Hegel's visual images by turning to this absolute knowing that is itself a vision of a universal humanity. In our study of religion we have seen that every community, in order to be a community, is unified around a specific vision, a specific set of images; now we must consider the universality to which each such vision turns. We must turn from human community as imaginative to human community as logical,[42] which will equally mean turning from the specific identity of any community to the universal human identity—upon which religion implicitly depends—as rational self-conscious agents. This is the same human identity that was recognized by enlightenment reflection, but we will now see how Hegel's understanding of the essentiality of the embeddedness of human identity in ritualized cultural practices makes absolute knowing the *Aufhebung* of this enlightenment conception at the same time as it is the *Aufhebung* of religion, precisely by being the synthesis of these two approaches.

4. Speculation, or, Absolute Vision

Self-consciousness, according to Hegel, is the human project; enlightenment reflection tries to gain this too quickly by assuming that its own identity is in clear view; yet, equally, if we rest with the tradition and ritual of "ethical life," our identity is shrouded in darkness, and this, clearly, cannot be the answer to this human pursuit. Indeed, our very analysis of both enlightenment and religion has been performed from a point of view that can be identified with neither.[43]

Enlightenment reflection wants to see the truth, but it fails to live up to its own ideal because its vision abstracts from its very corporeality; custom and ritual seek to establish a self-conscious community of mutual recognition, but fail to live up to their own ideal because they close their eyes to their own reality. Reflection without custom is empty, and custom without reflection is blind; each opposes the other, yet for each the other is precisely what it needs. Enlightenment needs to find rationality in its embodiment, and *Sittlichkeit* needs to recognize that it is the single rational ego who must ultimately carry out the task of establishing real human recognition through understanding.[44] What both thus point to is the necessity for a vision that can be enacted only through the rationality of the single ego, but that sees its own activity as contextualized by the very reality that it "is not," namely the bodily, cultural, historical context that is the substance of its worldly involvement. In other words, there must be a vision that is, and recognizes itself to be, the vision of the bodily reality itself; that is, it must be the self-consciousness of the cultural community itself. The true vision could only be spirit coming to recognize itself as spirit. Absolute vision must be the point of view of the single ego who recognizes that she sees on behalf of her community: she says "I" always as the voice of "we."[45]

Absolute knowing could be characterized as responsible vision: it requires both a commitment to seeing—to bringing into self-conscious explicitude what confronts one—and a commitment to not abstracting only the obvious and clear features of the situation, but instead to taking account of the concreteness that normally remains as the implicit mediation in one's perspective. In his *Encyclopaedia of the Philosophical Sciences*, Hegel employs two vision-based characterizations of this concrete reason: knowing absolutely he calls "speculation," and spirit's recognition of itself as spirit he portrays as the truth of Aristotle's *noēsis tēs noēseōs*.[46]

"Speculation" is derived from the Latin *speculor*, which means to spy out, to examine, or to explore. It is related to the Latin *specula* (watchtower), *speculum* (mirror), and *species* (a seeing, a sight, a form), and the *spec* root that all share indicates a relation to vision.[47] It is cognate with the English "spy," "espionage," and "special." The Greek "*noēsis*" is formed from the verb *noein*, which means to perceive by the eyes (as in *Iliad* III.396), and comes to mean perceive by the mind. It seems to be related to the Greek *nostos*, which means a "return" as typified by Odysseus's return from Troy to his home in Ithaka.[48] In Plato, the proper object for *noein* is form, *eidos*,[49] which, like the Latin *species*, which translates it, means that which is seen, and it is derived from the same *id* root as the "idealism" that Hegel uses to name his own and all true philosophy.

How is speculation—absolute vision—different from reflection? The Latin and Greek words give us a clue. Whereas the reflective gaze is fascinated by the immediate show (*Schein*) and (as external reflection) can never get past this appearance (*Erscheinung*) to the real thing because the object it sees only reflects the reflection's own presupposition of alienation, speculation spies out what is special to the identity of its other in order to return to itself.

Speculation works with what is not immediately present; that is, it must engage in an act of espionage, of investigative unmasking, to find out what the other keeps hidden. According to Hegel's vision-based vocabulary here, we could say that speculation does not stop at the show the other puts up, but explores in the realm of what is not immediately seen. What it sees, however, is that the other is the image of what it (speculation) itself is trying to conceal. The "other," in other words, has as its truth that it is the real substance of the speculating self, and its self-showing as "other" is the crucial concealing mechanism that must be overcome.[50] This is Hegel's version of transcendental philosophy.

Transcendental philosophy is a regressive philosophy that seeks the conditions of the possibility of experience by uncovering the unconscious processes of subjective synthesis. Unlike Kant's approach to studying the logic of subjective synthesis *in abstraction from* all determinate experience, however, Hegel's understanding of the embodiment of reason requires him to approach the structures of subjectivity by way of a *comprehension* of all experience; that is, philosophical enquiry does not *retreat* from experience, but must, so to speak, fight its way through experience in its very *specificity*, and it thus can see its self only when, like Odysseus, it *returns after* the successful siege. It remains true that the self sought is the self that provides the a priori grounds of experience, but we have no way to even conduct this investigation unless we have already developed a sophisticated relationship to the object so that we can *know what we are looking for*. (The *Phenomenology of Spirit* is the story of developing this progressively more comprehensive relation to our object, in which we gradually come to see just what it is that we are trying to see; that is, the last step is just as much the recognition of what our project is as it is the completion of that project.) The completion of this path of gradually coming to make sense of just what the experience of an object is comes when we recognize the object as precisely that which calls out for us to understand it and to recognize that this is simultaneously its calling to us for our help in bringing it to understand itself; that is, we recognize the object only when we recognize it as calling each of us as an "I" to form with it a "we." As the vision-based terms of Hegel's characterization of absolute knowing suggest, absolute knowing thus means seeing the other as calling for this absolute comprehension. This is what marks out speculative vision from both the clear vision of reflection and the self-blinding of custom and ritual.

Reflection produces its solutions *without* going by way of an immersion in the other; like Descartes's project of solitary meditation, reflection seeks a truth that is universal and necessary without being "contaminated" by the particularities and contingencies of actuality. Because of this, enlightenment can never show itself to be the truth that is demanded by its objects, for it has precisely defined itself in exclusion from them.

Religion does not reject the immersion in particularity, and in that respect can show us the essential dimension of human existence that reflection presupposes and forgets, but it is equally unsatisfactory, for it resists admitting that this embodiedness is in the service of self-consciousness. The very premise of customary practices is that they are implicated in a project of mutual recognition, a project of self-consciousness, and for that reason these practices *whose very logic is to be self-concealing* can complete themselves only by undermining themselves, that is, by un-concealing themselves. Ritual life, then, must sublate itself by generating a self-explication in the form of individuals who engage in a self-uncovering discourse in and through which they discover themselves as rational individuals engaged in the universal project of rational self-consciousness within the always necessarily particularized context of natural and cultural embodiment.

Now since the speculative project is to come to recognize oneself *qua* rational in one's very embodiment, speculation, then, like reflection, still encounters only its own image when it encounters its other; but this mirror, this *speculum speculantis*, is not the static and empty reproduction of an already established identity within an unresisting medium. On the contrary, to understand reality as the mirror of the absolute mind is to see reality as a dialectical process in which a single idea is developing itself through a discourse with itself. The process is then completed when this very project—which is a project of self-recognition—can turn upon itself in its very concreteness and diversity and comprehend this specificity as itself. This speculation sees *sub specie aeternitatis* because it can recognize particularity—specificity—as essential, and it sees this essentiality of particularity when it sees these particularities with respect to "eternity," that is, with respect to the universal and necessary— the inescapable—project of any subject who tries to understand, namely, the project of self-understanding. The act of understanding thus ultimately means the act of studying the other as the key to the hidden side of oneself. It is in recognizing the very thing we posit as other as the key to recognizing ourselves that we establish for the first time the possibility of understanding both. Absolute knowing tells us that the truth of this understanding will be that each of us has our specificity precisely as the set of terms in which we are asking to be led to a shared rational self-consciousness, a "we." Therefore the project of understanding must not be the project of reducing all particularity to the same abstract logic, but must be instead the project of leading both ourselves and our others to a shared self-consciousness as rational individuals, wherein the cultural specificities of each of us must serve as languages building the route and wherein we must each become multilingual in order for any of us to be able to succeed in our project of self-understanding.

Hegel says that speculating is reconciling what initially appear as alien realities by way of a dialectical understanding of the human project. This is reflected in his use of *speculation* and *noēsis* because these words suggest a visual paradigm of awareness, but a vision that is identified with going beyond the immediate in a project of unmasking and return. I have argued that these images capture nicely the dialectical project of looking behind the back of our everydayness to see what are the mediating structures that it tries to hide [unmasking] in order to demand of these structures that they fulfill themselves in a self-uncovering that shows itself to be the always already anticipated "homecoming" of the investigative enterprise [return]. Reconciling the explicit vision and implicit blindness of enlightenment reflection with the explicit blindness and implicit vision of custom, speculative *noēsis* is a vision that is devoted to eliminating its own blind spots through a threefold commitment to the essentiality of its own singular viewpoint, to the essentiality of the universality of the human project of rational self-consciousness, and to the essentiality of the *species*, the particularity, of the other.[51]

Conclusion

One might have thought that a philosophy of "absolute knowledge" would have to renounce sensation. On the contrary, we see that absolute knowledge can be effected only through beings who are *essentially* sensing, that is, through beings who are *essentially* constituted by an immediate relation to an apparent other, which is equally to say that we must be embodied. We will always and necessarily be embodied agents, already involved with our others according to a logic that is not immediately apparent, and we will live in a sense-certainty, the implicit intelligence of which conceals its own foundations in the determinate practices that constitute a specific historically embodied community's efforts to say its own identity. This embodiment in determinate cultural ritual means that the truth, for us, will always be expressed in images, in metaphors; but equally our existence as reflective beings means that our task will always be to see how the images a community uses to articulate the truth do offer a route to establishing a universal communication based on the shared human project of rational self-understanding.

Hegel's philosophy of absolute knowledge thus demands of us that we recognize in the practices of those we encounter the expression of truth, but a truth that may well not be understood by the very practitioners. We must approach the cultures of others the way we approach another language; that is, we must recognize that, *qua* self-conscious human agents, we share with our others our destiny of self-comprehension as a community, but that this shared sense of self-identity can be performed only through, so to speak, becoming multilingual, and we can do this only by letting the language of the other show us its own rationality, while equally demanding that that language have room to accommodate the rational demands of our own reflective experience.[52] Hegel's philosophy is thus neither an unthinking reversion to an unreflective *Sittlichkeit* nor a voyeuristic exotification of an uncomprehended other, but is, rather, a conscientious commitment to a single, human, rational discourse of mutually established self-consciousness. Unlike the enlightenment, Hegel demands a political commitment to the rationality of that which appears alien, which means a political vision that begins with the recognition that it is already committed to the essentiality of that which it does not understand; but, unlike traditional custom and religious ritual, this is a commitment to explicit self-consciousness and understanding, and the commitment is thus a demand upon the other that the other equally submit itself to rational discourse. Absolute knowing is therefore a political vision that can endorse only a cross-cultural communication that seeks not only to enlighten but to be educated by the other into a new language of self-consciousness within the context of a mutual pursuit of free rationality.[53]

Hegel's position, finally, is consistently and systematically articulated through his use of vision-centered vocabulary. Hegel differentiates three essential stances—reflection, *Sittlichkeit*, and absolute knowing—and these stances are likewise marked through different images that suggest, respectively (1) an uncritical trust of the obviousness that attaches to a visual ideal, (2) a recognition of the real determining dimensions of existence as operating out of sight, and (3) a responsible investigative vision that knows that it must see, but that this sight requires it to find what is hidden behind the face the other immediately shows us. Hegel's philosophy is a philosophy of vision, but of a vision that has its own path of dialectical development.[54]

fourteen
Deciding to Read: On the Horizon (of Christianity)

What is reading and how should we do it? It is this question that is most provoked by *Glas,* Derrida's study of Hegel and Genet, and it is this question that I will make some effort toward answering.[1] Through my answering of it, we will see that this question really is the question of openness, of decisions, of resurrecting remains, and even of the word that becomes flesh in Christianity. I will not very much address the details of Derrida's text, but I will use it as a spur to reading Hegel, and in particular to reading Hegel's phenomenology of "Revealed Religion," which is itself a central theme of Derrida's text. Though my goal is primarily to understand Hegel, there will be some occasion to reflect on his relationship to Derrida. Let us begin, then, with the question of reading.

1. Reading and Self-Expression

I want to know what it is to read. What is the logic that can comprehend reading? Let us consider the experience. When we sit with our book, we *open* it. Consider how this "opening" happens. First thing to notice: its opening comes with determinacy; until there are words, until there is writing, there is nothing, no opening. But when we get the writing, the words, just as they make a decision—they say which word will be, and by implication which will not[2]—they leave open what is to come. We cannot decide on the basis of the decided words what the form is of the *opening* that they make. Reading, it seems to me, is this opening; I do not say entering the opening since it is as much true to say that it is we as readers who are the opening as it is true to say that the opening is for us another that we enter: to read is thus to be open to. This being open to comes only with being committed to the marks that open; inasmuch as they open us, we are subject(ed) to them, so we could also say that to read is first to risk being opened, and thus to risk being shaped, by the writing. Derrida describes Genet reading the Gospel of John as being "like a miner who is not sure of getting out from the depths of the earth alive";[3] surely this is the risk of reading—by taking on the responsibility of being opened by the words we are committed to, we risk having the reading be a transformation of ourselves. Afterwards [after words], we will still say "I read it," and even that "I was changed." But the very fact of this change means that the "I" before is not the same as the "I" after. The first "I," if it is really changed, has had its old self destroyed and has been given a new life, as it were; to read is to risk resurrection.[4]

Let us return to the openness. The openness is precisely the way the words point beyond themselves to something that is not yet, that is not yet words, but that does not, for that reason, fail to be—it is as intimated. I want to begin by focusing on this intimation—the hinting of language of which Heidegger speaks[5]—and work at establishing how we must deploy our conceptualizing if we are to recognize intimation—how must we conceptualize if intimation is to be recognizable—cognizable—by us. I want to start this by looking at a definition by Husserl of what he calls a horizon, which seems to me to be very similar to what I have called intimation.

In Section 19 of his *Cartesian Meditations*, Husserl discusses the "actuality and potentiality of intentional life." Of the determinations of experience, Husserl says "*every actuality involves its potentialities*, which are not empty possibilities, but rather possibilities intentionally predelineated in respect of content . . . and, in addition, having the character of possibilities [which are] *actualizable*." This means that "every subjective process [*Erlebnis*] has a process 'horizon,' which changes with the alteration of the nexus of consciousness to which the process belongs and with the alteration of the process itself from phase to phase of its flow—an intentional *horizon of reference* to potentialities of consciousness that belong to the process itself." "The horizons are 'predelineated' potentialities." "The predelineation itself, to be sure, is at all times imperfect; yet, with its *indeterminateness*, it has a *determinate structure*."[6] This "horizonal" structure of consciousness means that every determinateness we experience—everything we notice—is always situated by an inexplicit or unnoticed range of possibilities: it is given with the determinateness that "I can" further explicate it by opening up these possibilities. These possibilities are not themselves given in determinate form; what is given is a determinateness that points outside itself, like a promissory note, to further determinateness not yet available, not yet predictable. For an experiential "thing," in other words, there is always a horizon—the experience does not have precise boundaries, but has, instead, a halo of invitation that always recedes as the invitation is taken up, or, as Merleau-Ponty describes it, it is always a figure-ground structure.

We must not let the indeterminateness of the ground lead us to forget the figure, however. The experience *is* inherently indeterminate; at the same time, however, determinateness is determinable, that is. we can decide what it is— this is precisely what it means to be determinate: it is describable, definable, and so on. It is a definiteness, though, a definability, which stands upon an indeterminate; both are necessary—every phenomenon must exist as a determinate-indeterminate, a precise "what" whose very whatness holds at the core a promise of a beyond. As with the reading example, here also it is only with the decided determinatenesses that there is openness. A text then, or any determination of experience (really synonymous expressions) is not decidable *to the exclusion of* undecidability, nor undecidable *to the exclusion of* decidability; rather, there is *necessarily* an undecidability—an indeterminateness that in principle cannot have its sense predetermined—at the heart of decision, and a decision at the heart of undecidability.

What are the categories we must employ to be able to understand this notion of a phenomenon's horizon? Can we say, for example, whether the horizon is or is not? I think not. It cannot be *simply* true to say that it "is," for this neglects the way in which it is precisely the mark of the *absence* of (certain) determinations/determinateness[es] within consciousness; likewise, saying it "is" does not capture the way in which "it" (to the extent that it can be called "it") always eludes our grasp and precisely *is not* where we look for it, for it has always already receded, and in its place we can only ever find determinateness: wherever we look, our very act of looking—of *taking something as our figure*—will ensure that we find determinateness, that we find something already figured, already figural. Similarly, though, to say *simply* that it "is not" misrepresents it: there clearly is a sense in which the horizon is present—it is an absence that makes itself felt *in* the experience; and again, its indeterminateness is not simple barrenness or emptiness, for it is precisely the promise—the guarantee—of *determinateness*, of preciseness, "over the horizon," for what we find when we approach it is *always* determinate.[7] The horizon neither simply is nor simply is not.

The phenomenon of the horizon—its very recognizability—forces us to go beyond our simple categories of is and is not. Just as the determinateness itself cannot be isolated from the other determinatenesses on its horizon that, in some sense, it is not, but that it equally has embedded in its very heart as promises, so can we say of any two phenomena that they cannot be held separate—each by itself neither simply is or is not itself, and neither is it true that either one simply is or is not the other. Indeed the very fact that they can be noticed together shows that they both point to a shared horizon in terms of which their identities can be geared into each other: the very fact of comparison *performs* this sharedness of horizon. To bring them together in an experience is to show precisely how one was over the horizon for the other. To return to the issue of adequate cognition, we should realize from this that we can recognize them aright only if we (retrospectively) see them as having in their identities from the start the possibility (the horizon) of being compared, of being expressly related. Their openness to our gaze and to each other is part of what it is to be each, and we do not recognize either if we don't recognize ourselves and the other within it.

This implication of *ourselves* in each (all) of these determinations is particularly important. The very recognizability—noticeability—of a phenomenon means that it exists within the field of possibilities *for us*—it is on *our* horizon. To even be able to notice that it is an other determination—other than myself, other than some other—means it is already actualizing the possibilities for otherness that I project: to be noticed as "other" is already to be within the same, in that it and I are now the same field, the same shared horizon. Just as nothing either is simply or is not simply, so are no two determinations either simply other or simply not other to each other. Thus any recognizability, any determinateness we can recognize to be a determinateness cannot be [just] outside us: its very recognizability as a determinateness means it is already intrinsic to our identities and to the identities of the other determinatenesses that we acknowledge. We are already inside each other, whether we like it or not, so we do not have an option about deciding whether or not to come into contact with our others, and to affect them (nor do those others have an option about us). We can say equally that every other is already inside every other other and that every self is already outside itself. Each other is already a licensed commentary on us and our world. Intertextuality means we *ourselves* are always subject to definition by what we deem alien; we can find ourselves only by looking to the determinations that constitute our "beyond."

To be a phenomenon, a determination, a text, then, is already to be an interpretation of, a commentary on, all the others. Each determination reveals one side of what is or is not possible for others; it reveals a piece of the world that is on the horizon of each other which that other must take account of, must acknowledge, within itself, within its ownmost identity.[8] They jointly define a world, a *public space* where they are open to criticism or challenge and where each determination counts as a challenge to all others, demanding accommodation. It amounts to a criticism of a thing's self-portrayal to find that that portrayal does not have room for something else that legitimately exists within the world that the first thing projects. In other words, *we lie about who we are if we are not welcoming of everything we encounter*, for each thing just is an expression *of ourselves*, just a making explicit of what was embedded in our own promise, just making determinate the world projected by our own horizons.

Since we cannot exclude what we find, since it is only by reading what we find that we come to know ourselves, then to read any determination will mean reading from it to the totality of determinations that it projects—that it promises—which means, simply, the totality of determinations (including ourselves as the comprehenders). The very nature of reading, then, is to totalize, and to recognize that totality as a unity, and, specifically, to read the totality as being a unity by virtue of being our own self-expression, the realization, the embodiment of our own identity. The transformative power of reading is indeed this discovery that what we read expresses who we really are. Better, we might say that reading always shows us afterwards [after words] what was implicit in our horizons, and lets us always recognize, "Yeah, that's who I was."[9]

2. Christianity as Forgiveness

In the first section, I have tried to show that the very project of reading has *on its horizon* the project of universal welcoming. Reading—opening ourselves—is like making ourselves big mouths that will accept no limit. Unlike in eating, though, the other that is taken in is not just lost in a "night in which all cows are black" or burned to utter obliteration beyond all trace, but is rather taken in only insofar as it takes us in, only insofar as we commit ourselves to recognizing it in its determinacy and allowing it to transform us. We are truly readers when we subject ourselves to our others, and recognize them as the bearers of our own identity, the identity we are seeking. Our "homecoming" is thus not a return to some comfortable, finished place from which we started: it is always a going out, a discovering of our home in something initially strange and uncomfortable. Home cannot be had by holding ourselves in reserve, but only by throwing ourselves beyond our boundaries into our greatest challenges, our greatest exclusions. What initially looks like our enemy is thus what beckons us home, and it is only by learning to recognize the legitimacy of the way the other is making this claim upon us—only by recognizing that the other *already* speaks on our authority—that we learn to read. Notice, then, that *the project of reading is the project of universal forgiveness.*

Now from Hegel's point of view, the doctrine of universal forgiveness is definitive of "the absolute religion."[10] Christian mythology is the story of the spreading of the absolute to the utter depths of finitude: it is the story of the divine, which has always already sacrificed its possession of its own identity and must rely on the recognition of all the world of its creation, all that it itself recognizes as its others, to constitute, for it, its existence. Hegel's criticism of the mythology of historical Christianity is that it understresses that the resurrection of God—Christ's ascension to the right hand of God—exists only as the Holy Spirit, that is, as the community of believers, and this point is crucial to understanding Hegel's notion of the absolute religion: the absolute religion is, for Hegel, absolute only inasmuch as it is the mythology of the dispersal of identity into the universal reciprocal recognition of the totality of the finite. This is the idea of universal forgiveness—the idea that there can be nothing that falls outside God, that falls outside the horizon of truth that is projected by every thing—which marks this, for Hegel, as the mythology that is adequate to our reality.

But our account of reading indicates that this absolute religion is precisely what is projected by any determination *qua* determination. The notion of forgiveness that makes the absolute religion absolute thus also makes it the religion of reading, and we can also notice this correlation at another point.

Let me recall two things about our others. First, the others on our horizon will be the inscription of our identity: they are our self-expression waiting to be recognized as such. Yet we must not project the identities of those others as *already* fixed, as *already* determinate, for until they are recognized, they are horizonal—they are not-yets, indeterminacies, mere potentialities. It is *in* the recognizing, in the performance, that they receive their very determinateness (just as it is at that point that I become determined vis-à-vis them): the transformation of myself that comes with reading them is equally a transformation of them. Second, this performative dimension to self-realization as reading means also that these others do not so much *reflect* my identity as realize it or embody it. What I am exists only as the relation I hold to these others. The text I read is thus equally my body. Taking these two points together, we can notice that it is in reading that I am transformed into my true identity—I am resurrected—but this resurrection of my soul *is inseparable from* the performative transformation of my others into my body, the text of my own identity. In other words, reading is nothing other than the resurrection of the body. The other I encounter is my self-expression waiting to be recognized—my body waiting to be resurrected—through the death of my old self and my conversion to the absolute project of reading as forgiveness.

3. The Beautiful Soul

It might appear that to demand of one's experienced otherness that it conform to one's unifying interpretation is indeed to do the greatest violence to it, rather than to give it adequate recognition. For absolute reading, it is possible to say that "my object is a unified system as an expression of my self-identity"; yet it is precisely the ground of this systematic unification that the act of absolute reading has itself contributed—that is, the performance of its reading has *made* the other its self-expression. It might, then, seem that precisely what is not happening is an identification with the other, that this is precisely a failure to respect the other as other. Its mistake in reading its self-expressive text, it might thus seem, is precisely to treat it as a text, for not only does an act of reading a text engage in interpreting that which it takes as text, but, furthermore, its very act of taking its text *as a text* is an act of interpretive totalization that forces the indeterminacy out of which the text comes to be unified to be this way rather than that; that is, it actualizes only one of many textual possibilities, and, in so doing, excludes the other possibilities, including especially the possibility of not being read at all. Thus totalization, one might say, is totalitarian. This accusation of textual totalitarianism would challenge the right of reading to posit its own self as that which was being supported by that multiple materiality out of which it has constructed its object, which it calls its otherness. We need to see how Hegel's analysis resolves this problem.

Essentially, this critique is launched from the position that Hegel calls the "beautiful soul," that is, the "isolationist" critic whom Hegel considers in connection with conscience and forgiveness.[11] But this beautiful soul makes a mistake in thinking that there is a point of view from which the trespassing upon the other is something that has yet to transpire; rather, trespassing is not something about which one has a choice, but is something that has always taken place already. In relation to this critique of the project of reading, the mistaken characterization is the insistence that it is in and through the adopting of a project of reading the other that the other is forced to conform to the self, and is forced into the totalitarian system of reflecting only the self. In fact, the very existence *for the self* of an other *already* indicates that that other has been inscribed within the experiential system of the self. Within experience it must be the case that a judgmental stance has *already* been taken in order that there might be, for the self, an other upon which to pass further judgments.[12] By its very definition, other-ness can exist only in *definitive* relation to what is other to it (a self), which recognizes it as other;[13] thus, *in advance of* any explicit interpretive operations on the other, there must be a primordial act of positing the other as the not-self, of deciding what the other is. The trespass, then, that is, the act of treating the other as a product of the operation of the self, *has always already happened* by the time the other can be recognized. Reading, in other words, is always already underway. Stepping outside Christianity, for a moment, we can note that this is what is striking about Krishna's discourse with Arjuna in the Hindu *Mahabharata* (the *Bhagavad-Gita*), namely, that Arjuna is shown not to be in a position of beginning innocently and initiating a struggle; on the contrary, he is already implicated in it, and to try to back out would be to make a decisive move, and one that would be irresponsible. Absolute, forgiving reading, then, is not the instituting of an act of violence; it is the attempt to take responsibility for the institution of violence that is necessarily already the foundation of all its experience, all its relations with the other. Reading is always a decision, but it is not one that we could choose not to make; we could only make it differently.[14]

We do not have a choice about making decisions. We do not have a choice about cutting up our experience into determinations. We do not have a choice about being violent to our others, precisely by defining them as our others. Derrida is sometimes treated as backing off from decision, and challenging our making of claims about our others, but if this were his stance he could not hold our philosophical interest: more even than paralysis, this is simply the stance of the hypocrite. Undecidability can even come up as an issue only for one embedded in—embodied in—decisions. Undecidability exists only at the heart of the decided, exists only as the imperative intrinsic to any judger to go beyond the stasis and finitude of its own immediacy and to recognize its own determinateness, its own identity, as a violent *and a necessary* performance, rather than a given.

In fact, Derrida's project/practice in *Glas* is an attempt to be rigorous in its reading of Hegel's text in basically the same way that Hegel's project/practice attempts to be rigorous in its description of experience. Each aims to be led by the immanent force of the object. (Derrida, unlike Hegel, does not give the reader much of an explanatory preface, but more or less just sets to the reading, with the result that only the reader who reads Derrida rigorously will follow what he is doing.) In this way, Derrida is clearly methodologically superior to almost all other commentators on Hegel. His method in reading Hegel attempts to be the method demanded by Hegel's own text, and his actual reading(s) in *Glas* evince a profound sympathy for the demands of dialectic; he is generally successful in appreciating the subtleties of sense rarely encountered in other commentators. Though *Glas* (when it is read) is often taken to offer a litany of criticisms of Hegel, the text in fact does little more than to allow Hegel's own text to raise questions (the "criticisms") and then to show their untenability, or the ways in which *their* sense and putative closure is not secure. Indeed, most of the criticisms of Hegel typically put forth in Derrida's name are precisely the views that Derrida's reading of Hegel shows to be unable to even appreciate their intended object.[15] In fact, Derrida's reading(s) in *Glas* generally serve to demonstrate the immanent necessity of Hegel's articulations, to resurrect Hegel's corpus.

The general concern behind Derrida-inspired challenges to Hegel is that, even though Hegel may recognize various "giving" powers from which we receive the meaningfulness of our experience (from which we receive our very selves), his philosophy supposedly inverts the relationship to them such that these powers are completely "overcome" by the self. The challenge, in other words, maintains that it is from a given (contingent) embodiment and a given language that "there is . . . " for us; for this reason the giving power is always behind and outside the "there is" but is not, for that reason, absent from experience. This non-present—non-presentable—that gives the present must always be outside the grasp of the organizing of meaning that happens within the meaningfulness it gives. Hegel, it is thought, instead aims to "own" this source, to comprehend it so that it is, as it were, tamed by "the system," and contained/controlled by the logic of "the system." This concern, however, is based on a hypostatization of "the system" that Hegel never makes. On the contrary, "absolute knowing" is just the recognition that meaning takes the form of a giving. The *Phenomenology of Spirit* moves through a description of various attitudes or practices that operate upon prejudices that inhibit the ability of those attitudes to recognize the true form of the given. These stances dismantle and reconfigure themselves as the given meaning with which they grapple makes manifest the insufficiencies of their presuppositions. "Absolute knowing" is the name of the final stance of consciousness. That stance is final because it is the stance that recognizes that it must learn the nature of the given from how the given gives itself. This is the stance of dialectical phenomenology, the stance that recognizes the need to wait upon experience to show its own form, to live out its own dialectic. The "resurrection" that is absolute knowing, then, far from offering us some solace, or supplying us with some guarantee in our navigating with our world that would protect us from the impact of the real force of otherness, is instead only the knowledge that we can never have such guarantees, that we must always wait upon experience to tell us its form, and, indeed, to do so in ways that radically transform our self-conceptions.

This need to be driven by what emerges is what Derrida reads in Hegel's text on absolute knowledge. What Derrida's reading of Hegel mostly shows as its "result" is that "Sa" (absolute knowing) can never be a doctrine or a possession; it is precisely the openness to the text, which means there is no "in advance" answer to any reading, to any challenge—there is nothing in advance of the text, no pre-scription, as it were.[16] Sa is the perpetual re-self-definition of an originary reading, a reading that must always read the text to resurrect itself. In the manner of *Glas*, we might say: *Sa* always remains (to be). In the end, Derrida is indistinguishable from Hegel. Derrida is no BS (beautiful soul), but Hegel relieving himself.

4. Beyond the Text

What I, following Hegel, have tried to show in this chapter is that determinateness, by its very nature as determinateness, necessarily always forms itself into a system, and a system of the self-expression of reading/writing as such, for which Christianity is the adequate mythology. Hegel's Christian system is thus epitomized by the expression "everything is text." But notice that this is no different from the recognition of the primacy of the indeterminacy, for it was from the insistence on the horizonal ground of all determinateness that we were able to reach this conclusion.

Now the horizon, recall, always recedes—it exists as a promise, the fulfillment of which only and necessarily exists *as determinateness*: the horizon is precisely the promise of the system. It is on the ground of the horizon that "there is" determinateness, that there is the system, that "everything is text." But "there is" always and only marks determinateness—we can never simply say "there is" a horizon. The horizon, the very ground of the system, itself "is not"—it "is" *only as retrojected by determinateness as its ground* and projected by determinateness as the promise of further determinateness. The horizon, then, is the permanent promise of an outside that never comes into determinateness as such: it "is," or, better, it nihilates its negativity as the outside of the text of which it cannot be said "there is": thus "there is" not (not-ing) outside text.[17]

These expressions—"everything is text" and "there is nothing beyond the text"—seem to say the same, and yet the duality of expression hints at a difference. This difference is undecidable, is undecidability itself, the very undecidability that is a synonym for absolute knowing. Let me explain. Reading is transformative. This means that the text-read—the body resurrected—is no longer strictly identical with the text-to-be. Reading always presents itself as the reading *of* the text—and, indeed, it can point to the text itself for the compelling evidence of its own justice—and thus the text is seen to cause the reading; yet it is equally true that the reading causes the text; that is, it is the act of reading that creates the text *as* that which can be seen to be its (the reading's) cause.[18] The text is necessarily simultaneously that which is presupposed by the reading—that which it cannot give itself, but must accept as a gift—and that which the reading gives itself.[19] Said otherwise, there is no going back. The act of reading matters, makes a difference, and there is no way to find a perspective outside the reading—a pre-read—to justify that reading; on the contrary, all that can be offered are other readings. Absolute knowing is thus simultaneously the self-giving of the text by which the text-to-be itself obliterates itself as other, as unread, and the self-embodying of a non-predictable reading, an *autopoiesis*. The reading always takes its departure from (i.e., begins in and as the negating of) what is given, what there is, and this givenness—this immediacy—of being can never be erased, even as it is transfigured. "The system" is the recognition of the universal meaningfulness of reality (S*a*) at the same time as it is always equally the recognition of the contingency, the non-deducibility, of the given.[20] Absolute knowing is the recognition of the "*Es gibt Sein*" the recognition that, in the terms of Hegel's phenomenology, we must wait on experience to show us what it is, who we are.

5. The *Glas*

The very determinacy that gives a thing its identity also sets the immediate limits to what it will admit as itself. Therefore, even though the horizonal structure of determinateness implicates things in each other, the *immediacy* of each determinateness *is* to-be-opposed-to-others, to encounter aliens. To be a determinacy is always to be crashing up against others. Those determinacies that one especially resists are, of course, those that touch one deeply, "strike a chord" so to speak, create a resonance with us, a *glas*. But this *glas*, which initially appears to be the inarticulate sound of unassimilable aliens tolling the bell on each other, can never remain that way for us, for precisely what this *glas* is is the call to reading, the call to comprehension.

Our words in their determinacy, their "embodiedness," are always figural, always violating others at unexpected points, getting involved in undesired relations (like the *gl-* in *glas*), which they would like to call "merely superficial."[21] This is why in making decisions, which means committing our thoughts to words—committing ourselves to determinateness—we find our nominations inherently embed us in idolatry, precisely start with us identifying word and thing. What this *"glas"* character of all discourse therefore calls us to is a responsibility to our words, to giving account of our own figurality, to making the figure the incarnation of the *logos* rather than a lifeless idol used to oppress those we exclude: the *glas* effect engenders commentary; it means that the need for supplementary words, the need for the system, is on the horizon of every word. *Glas*, then, is precisely the need to read by writing. And, indeed, in all our commentaries in turn we will have to contend with their equal ability, in the imagery of *Glas*, to be gods or judases dwelling in the spots where the columns they adorn have always already receded.

The *glas*, then, is precisely that which can never remain, but exists only as the already surpassed call to which we refer back our project of making articulate, of deciding. Like the horizon, the *glas* has always already receded, never remaining except as the backward glance that seeks it as its impetus to discourse: it exists only as the systematic response to the call of resurrecting the *glas* as articulate speech. As Nietzsche told us in the preface to the *Genealogy of Morals*, by the time we hear the toll of the bell, resurrection, decision, is already underway, and only the process of reading itself exists as a trace of *glas*.[22]

Absolute Knowing

fifteen

Absolute Knowing:
The Structure and Project of
Hegel's System of Science

To call knowing absolute is to call it unconditioned or unqualified. What would it take for knowing to be qualified or conditioned? Knowledge is conditioned if it is true only "on condition that . . . ," that is, knowledge is conditioned when it has a presupposition. To call knowing "unconditioned," on the contrary, is to say there are no preconditions that have to be accepted in order for the knowledge to be accepted as knowledge. The knowing, then, that is without such conditions, or "absolute," is the knowing that is without presuppositions. "Absolute knowing" and "presuppositionless science" are thus synonymous expressions.

This latter expression—"presuppositionless science"—is Hegel's understanding of whatever it is that he does in his two great books, the *Phenomenology of Spirit* and the *Science of Logic*. "Absolute Knowing" is the title of the final chapter of the *Phenomenology*.[1] Given, then, that "presuppositionless science" and "absolute knowing" are synonymous expressions, we should recognize that the subject-matter of the final chapter of the *Phenomenology* is the very experiential stance whose work is realized as the *Phenomenology* and the *Logic*; that is, absolute knowing is the phenomenological, scientific stance itself—the philosophical stance. The chapter on absolute knowing, then, has as its object the experience that is realized as the whole of these two books: that chapter is, we might say, the phenomenology of phenomenology, or the science of science.

It is this notion of the phenomenology of phenomenology or the science of science that I will use as my point of entry into my study of the chapter on absolute knowing; because the subject matter of that chapter is the whole phenomenological and scientific project, my route will be to reflect on the form and content of Hegel's books (primarily the *Phenomenology*) *as a whole*, in order to determine more clearly the character of the phenomenon under study in this final chapter of the *Phenomenology*. I will begin, in section 1, by considering what we—the phenomenological observers—do in taking up the phenomenology of consciousness and self-consciousness in the first four chapters of the *Phenomenology*; that is, I will be describing what *our* experience is when we are describing the experiences studied in these chapters. This will be enough to allow us in section 2 to consider the overall argumentative structure that characterizes the diptych that is constituted by the *Phenomenology* and the *Logic*. This will allow me to conclude, in section 3, that "absolute knowing" names both the project and the structure in these arguments, or, said otherwise, the phenomenology of absolute knowing shows that absolute knowing just is phenomenology and logic; this means, ultimately, that science is the science of communication.

1. Consciousness as Metaphysics and Desire

In his phenomenology of consciousness (*Phenomenology of Spirit*, Chapters I–III), Hegel shows that ontological claims are always paired with epistemological stances; that is, any claim that might be made about the nature of being is always bound by a correlative mode of experiencing. Any claim that says "being is . . . " is always a truth only for some particular stance, and one must always determine *for whom* being appears in that fashion. At the most general and abstract level, such claims take three basic forms: the nature of being is taken to be "this" or simple immediacy by the stance Hegel's calls sensuous certainty; being is taken to be things, or determinate essential beings, by the stance Hegel calls perception; being is taken to be a comprehensive system of forces by the stance Hegel calls understanding. These three stances—sense-certainty, perception, and understanding—are different modes of subjective comportment, different ways of being an experiencing subject, and it is within, and only within, these three stances that being is taken, respectively, as immediate, as essential and multiply determinate, or as systematically comprehensive. Inasmuch as these general positions map the total terrain of possible metaphysical claims, the arguments of these chapters imply that there are no unqualified metaphysical truths: metaphysical claims are always necessarily descriptions of the ways that being *appears*.[2]

Now, this means that the project of metaphysical speculation—the idea that there is a "there is" to be understood—is itself an attitude: indeed, it is the very stance of consciousness itself, the very stance for which there is being. Implicit in any question of being is the stance that takes there to be being, and the stance that takes being to be that the nature of which must be comprehended. Consciousness, we might say, is that which by definition recognizes—or seeks to recognize—being, and being is that which by definition is to be known by consciousness, that which exists as a challenge to consciousness.

Now consciousness itself is also always necessarily the stance of a desiring being, a being that desires to know, that desires to know being. This fact about consciousness is one of the lessons of Chapter IV of the *Phenomenology*, "Self-Consciousness." The practice of recognizing being *qua* object—theoretical consciousness—is one contextualized by the larger practice of fulfilling desire: as Aristotle showed in his analysis of the "practical syllogism," recognition is always mediated by the way a desiring being projects the parameters for possible relevance according to the norms of its own form of life.[3] Our recognition of determinacy is always a recognition of that determination *as* something, where the form of the "as" is given by the interpretive demands of our desires and projects. In Chapter IV, Hegel shows that the particular ideal of a pure recognition—a recognition in accordance with the ideal of "objectivity," a recognition of "truth"—emerges from our particular character as explicitly self-conscious beings. Hegel's analysis shows that self-consciousness necessarily involves recognizing that one must answer to the interpretive parameters of other such self-conscious beings. It is this being answerable to others, this need to defend one's own interpretations, that entails operating according to norms of justification or objectivity. The desire to know—the desire for objectivity—is the desire of a being involved in the intersubjective pursuit of self-consciousness.

Consciousness, this desire to know, is a stance of desire, then, but this expression "to know" means something different than simply "to want" or "to feel" or "to be provoked by." "To know" is a special kind of desire: it is the desire that desires to answer to criteria, a desire that deems itself accountable to reason and evidence, to the demands of answering to others.[4] The project of knowing is a desire that drives a being who recognizes herself or himself to be *essentially* situated in a field of others' gazes, and the "knowings" that this desiring being accomplishes are all attempts to answer to the demands of these other gazes. Knowing, in other words, is always a stance of communication, always a positioning of oneself—of one's desire—in relation to the need to answer to what others require. Let me pursue this a little further.

When we makes claims about reality—when we invoke the term "is"—we submit our take on our situation to public judgment, and makes ourselves answerable to others' legitimate demand that we accurately assess the evidence and consistently construe the implications of this evidence. In saying "is," we put ourselves forward for others' evaluation, thereby communicating to others how we perceive what is equally their situation, and inviting their communication in turn about the adequacy of our take on our own situation. When I say, "we are in a classroom," I am advancing a sharable vision through which we can recognize our mutual participation in a single world by showing that we all see in the same way; or, if you disagree, we can recognize a disparity between us that forces us to revise our interpretations.

But metaphysical claims are just such "is" claims, advanced in their most general form; that is, they are claims about the very nature of is. Metaphysics, therefore, is always *in* the element of communication—for metaphysics is itself a project of knowing and *ex hypothesi* a project of communication—and metaphysics is itself always an implicit element *of* communication—for communication is always effected through "is" claims. Metaphysics is the answer presented by the desire that recognizes its place among others in response to the question posed to it by its recognition of those others. Thus, the stances of consciousness—the stances of metaphysics—are the stances by which the desiring being seeks to accomplish its bringing of itself into accord with the criterion of intersubjective answerability; the different stances of consciousness are enacted and internally evaluated according to their success at realizing this animating desire of answerability. In other words, all the stances of consciousness presuppose and are contextualized by the intersubjective project of communication of which they are the realizations.

My conclusion to this first section, then, is as follows. The object for us— for the phenomenological observer—is the set of experiential shapes where each shape is experienced by us as a paired structure of subjective comportment and metaphysical commitment, where these paired structures are themselves recognized to be practices of interpersonal communication, that is, attempts to answer to the demand that other self-consciousnesses pose to us by virtue of our being explicitly self-conscious beings.[5]

2. Absolute Knowing as Phenomenology and Logic

So, when we do phenomenology, we see what the *experience* is that holds the various specific metaphysical stances; we see how metaphysical positions are structural features within experiential attitudes. Such *correlations* are the object of absolute knowing; that is, absolute knowing is that type of conscious experience that has the shapes of forms of experience for its object.[6] Our phenomenological analysis is of the shapes of experience, but since shapes of consciousness are always metaphysical positions, in order to be able to comprehend such an object we have equally to do metaphysics; that is, we do not have simply to *project our own* metaphysical commitment (as does any stance of consciousness), but metaphysical commitments *as such* must *be our object*. Absolute knowing, in being the phenomenology of experience—in taking subjective comportments as its explicit object—is equally the sorting out the inherent contradictions of the implicit metaphysical stance of each stage of consciousness. So, while all experiences are implicitly metaphysical, absolute knowing is the stance whose nature requires that it explicitly take metaphysics as its object.

In order explicitly to be the phenomenology of experience, then, absolute knowing must implicitly be a science of metaphysics, or what Hegel calls a science of logic. For this reason, the *Science of Logic* is just the developing into its own proper form of the stance that does phenomenology. Let me turn briefly to the *Science of Logic* to show how the structure and project of this book run in tandem with that of the *Phenomenology*.

Logic begins with the question that the most basic stance of consciousness shows that we can (and must) ask—what is? or, what is it to be? What do we mean by this question; that is, what is the understanding of being already necessarily operative if there is to be consciousness? This is what is answered in the *Logic*, though the *Logic* does not answer this question by posing it as the question of experience, that is, as an answer to the demands of consciousness. Rather, the *Logic* just describes the dialectic of the concept of being *as such* (and it is only with the conclusion of the *Logic* that we will see that it was answering the question of consciousness). The *Phenomenology* begins with sense-certainty, the most immediate knowledge, which is itself the certainty of immediacy;[7] inasmuch as this is the original stance of consciousness, there can be no consciousness without a positing of immediacy. This parallels the beginning of the *Logic*—but the *Logic* begins not with an experience of *the positing of* immediacy, but with immediacy itself, and we watch *immediacy's own* dialectic, for the object of absolute knowing as logic is not experience but being. Once we have posed the question of being—and we always necessarily have by virtue of being conscious—being has a dialectic *of its own*, whether we like it or not. There can be no escape from metaphysics, for it is the very nature of consciousness to be metaphysical.

What I mean by this is that metaphysics—the question of being *as such*—is always necessarily a meaningful demand within experience; that is, it is an experiential significance we can never get beyond nor find irrelevant or unintelligible. There can thus be no legitimacy to the claim that Hegel's *Logic* as a project can be severed from the *Phenomenology*, for they are the same project. We *can* ask the question of being, and the category of "Being" that is the immediate way in which this question must be understood is a category the meaning of which is *necessarily* recognizable by us. Our very nature as consciousness secures our inability to doubt the legitimacy of the starting point of the *Logic* in the question of being as such, that is, with the category of being, pure being.

I will not try to run through the argument of the *Logic* as a whole, except to note that it demonstrates that being, on its own terms, vindicates (in the doctrine of being and the doctrine of essence) the claim of the *Phenomenology* to have found in the phenomenology of consciousness the complete system of subjective comportments toward being as object, and (in the doctrine of the concept) the claim of the *Phenomenology* that the very nature of the object is to be self-conscious subjectivity. I will not defend these claims here (which would require an explication of the *Logic*) but will return now to what this shows us about the relation of these two books. I will return to the content of the *Logic*—specifically its end—in my concluding section.[8]

So we have seen how these two works, the *Phenomenology* and the *Logic*, are paired in their content. The pairing is stronger than this, though. I want to note also how the argument of these books requires that absolute knowing take this doubled form, that is, how it is that the argument of the *Phenomenology* remains incomplete without the performing of the argument of the *Science of Logic* as the activity of the stance of absolute knowing.

The relation of these two works has a structure similar to that of a Kantian antinomy. In the antinomies of the dialectic of reason, Kant shows in each case that we are engaged with two equally compelling starting points, and then argues from each to show that these starting points lead to mutually opposed conclusions. What this shows is that the compelling character of either starting point singly is insufficient evidence to justify the truth of its conclusions, for there is an equally compelling argument against these conclusions.[9] Such an argument is possible in relation to any knowledge that has a presupposition—any conditioned knowledge—for it is always possible that the presupposition on which the argument rests can be considered on its own terms and that doing so will lead to a conclusion opposed to the conclusion of the first argument. From our discussion of the *Phenomenology*, we can see that such an antimony is possible inasmuch as the phenomenological description rests on a metaphysics of being that is implicit in the argument but is not the explicit argument of the *Phenomenology*. Absolute knowing in the *Phenomenology* is implicitly engaged in metaphysical analysis, and so this metaphysics must become explicit if absolute knowledge is to justify its claim to absoluteness. In other words, until being has been taken up *on its own terms*, the completeness of absolute knowing remains in question. The *Phenomenology* begins with consciousness—the opposition of subject and object, of consciousness and being—and argues from the side of consciousness to their reconciliation. The *Logic* begins from the other side of this opposition—being—and must similarly witness being demonstrating on its own terms that it is reconciled with consciousness, if the argument of the *Phenomenology* is not to be overturned.[10]

The *Phenomenology* and the *Logic* thus amount to two sides of an antinomial argument. One begins with experience, the other with being, and the very "thesis" of each of these starting points is the exclusion of the other. The only way to reconcile these two opposed claims to exclusive absoluteness is to show that each on its own terms leads to its integration with the other. Thus, without the *Logic*, the *Phenomenology* is inconclusive, for it produces only an external reflection on being, without having had demonstrated that being itself shows itself to be as the *Phenomenology* demands; similarly, the *Logic* on its own is inconclusive, for it produces only an external reflection on the nature of subjectivity, without having shown that subjectivity on its own account shows itself to be absolute being. But the two books do reconcile with each other. Let me turn now to my final section in order to explain this claim.[11]

3. The Metaphysics of Communication

Absolute knowing is the stance that sees metaphysics embedded within experience, and sees metaphysical—experiential—positions as intersubjective communications. This is itself a stance of experience, and the phenomenology of this—the self-reflection of this phenomenological experience or the phenomenology of this phenomenological stance—would have to show how being is for it; that is, if each stance of experience entails a metaphysical position, we should be able to ascertain what is the metaphysics of absolute knowing. Now we have seen that absolute knowing has metaphysics *as its object*—(initially, an implicit aspect of its object)—but, as itself a stance of experience, absolute knowing must also *project* a metaphysical commitment. And what that commitment is, we have already seen: for absolute knowing, being—the "is"—is the enactment of intersubjective recognition itself. To say "is" is to say "successful communication" or "shared perspective." This, in the end, is what being is—it is the reality of intersubjectivity. Thus, from the side of experience, we are led to conclude that the nature of being is intersubjectivity. Yet we have reached this conclusion only indirectly, by following out the dialectic of experience, for which these metaphysical implications are correlative. What we have not done is shown that this conclusion is so from the point of view of metaphysics as such. This is what is in fact accomplished in the *Science of Logic*.[12] Let me speak about why these two conclusions are the same, and conclude with an understanding of the *Science of Logic* as the science of the forms of communication.

I have said that the *Phenomenology* concludes with the recognition that being is communication; that is, all experiences make is-claims that are players within a dialectic of recognition. The *Logic* ends with the "absolute idea," that is, being as dialectic. How are these conclusions the same?

If being is communication, this means that, in our efforts to know what is, we are really trying to reconcile our own experience with the experience of others; the demand of intersubjective self-consciousness is the demand that we answer to others, which means that we can accommodate ourselves to ourselves only as accommodating ourselves to the experiences of others. Now, the experiences of others—like our own experiences—are the experiences of is-claims, which means that others are essentially presentations of reality, presentations of what is. From the point of view of the conclusion of the *Phenomenology*, then, to know being absolutely is the stance of self-consciousness that communes with itself only by being open to the way that reality shows itself as other subjects; that is, it shows itself as an active, self-conscious reality. The stance that would know absolutely must adopt a stance of active patience: to know absolutely requires cohering with oneself only as and by (a) actively looking for the coherence of the situation while (b) patiently waiting for the active self-showing of that reality to set its own terms for how it can be recognized. In other words, the conclusion of the phenomenology is just the recognition that we must approach the world phenomenologically, and wait upon its own dialectic to demonstrate its reality to us, in a way that thereby demonstrates that reality as our own.

But this reality that shows itself through its own dialectic to the self-interpretive posture that is itself—its own reality—is just what Hegel describes as the absolute idea. Under the name of the absolute idea, Hegel describes a reality that exists as a communion with itself as a process of dialectical self-articulation and self-interpretation. This is a reality that exists only as a self-communication, which means a reality that exists only by opposing itself to itself and, through the interaction—the communication—of these opposed sides of itself, establishing for itself a transformed and more sophisticated existence that has the mediation—the communication—of its sides as its very substance. It is a reality that, through its bifurcation, establishes a situation of self-alienation whose reconciliation can never be specified in advance, but must patiently wait upon the intrinsic activity of the opposed sides to originate through their communication—through their mutual recognition—a successful integration. The phenomenon of which this is the logic is exactly the situation we just identified as phenomenology, as absolute knowing as Spirit or mutual recognition.

In other words, the experiential stance of absolute knowing as phenomenology implies the absolute idea as its implicit metaphysics, and the metaphysical stance of being as the absolute idea implies absolute knowing as its implicit phenomenal realization. Put otherwise, the phenomenology concludes with phenomenology, while the logic concludes with dialectic, and these notions are inseparable, as are sense-certainty and the this, perception and the thing, or understanding and force: all phenomenology must be dialectical, all dialectic must be phenomenological. The conclusions of these two books, then, amount to the same reality, described once from the side of experience, once from the side of metaphysics. The antinomial structure of the system of science leads from both of its sides to the same conclusion: the *Phenomenology* and the *Logic* both conclude with being as communication, with, we might say, an is that is we and a we that is is.

NOTES

INTRODUCTION

1. I am not the first writer to pursue such an interpretation, intimated in writers such as Kenneth L. Schmitz, Joseph Flay, and John Burbidge, but I do think that such an approach to interpretation is currently emerging on the scene of Hegel interpretation in a way that it has not appeared before, most powerfully in the work of such writers as Jay Lampert, David Morris, and David Ciavatta.

2. This was a practice taught to me by H. S. Harris.

1. SENSE, TIME, AND MY MEANING

1. See *Encyclopaedia*, para. 258, remark: "Time is the same principle as the I = I of pure self-consciousness, but this principle, or the simple notion, still in its uttermost externality and abstraction—as intuited mere *Becoming*, pure being-within-self as sheer coming-out-of-self." Through the dialectic of the now, we will see this empty externality give itself determinacy. See also M801, W/C524. See also *Encyclopaedia*, para. 257: "Negativity, thus posited for itself, is Time"; "negativity for itself" is intentionality as such.

2. And compare Plato, *Theaetetus*, 151ff.

3. M91, W/C69–70. See also *Encyclopaedia*, para. 400.

4. Compare the two negations of reflection, *Science of Logic*, E 394–400, G II.17–25. On the negations that characterize reflection, see Dieter Henrich, "Hegels Logik der Reflexion: Neue Fassung."

5. See fragment D-K 8, also fragments D-K 2 and 7. By the end of the analysis, this *to eon* will look more like the *chora* of Plato's *Timaeus* (e.g., 52ab). For the interpretation of the figure of the *chora*, see in particular John Sallis, *Chorology: On Beginning in Plato's Timaeus*.

6. See M97, 104, W/C71–72, 74.

7. M101–103, W/C72–74.

8. Cf. M95, 110, W/C71, 77–78. Many commentators confuse Hegel's own position with the position of sense-certainty itself, wrongly attributing to him the view that the singular moment is an ineffable reality outside comprehension in terms of universals. See, for example, Andrej Warminski, "Reading, for Example: 'Sense-Certainty' in Hegel's *Phenomenology of Spirit*." See the sustained critique of this in Nathan Andersen, "Example, Experiment and Experience in Hegel's *Phenomenology of Spirit*," ch. 1. See also Peter Simpson, *Hegel's Transcendental Induction*, ch. 1, and Thomas Kalenberg, *Die Befreiung der Natur. Natur und Selbstbewusstsein in der Philosophie Hegels*, pp. 2–12. Hegel's discussion in M110, W/C77–78 makes it clear that there is a

problem in principle with this way of articulating the issue. As with all of Hegel's writing—or any book, for that matter—this chapter must be read thinkingly. Determining its sense is not a matter of a calculus of words, but a matter of understanding, interpretation and insight. The key to reading this text is to demand that it answer to the immanent demands of the rigorous phenomenology that Hegel claims it to be; this is done by following the experience under description, rather than demanding that his words confirm to a model of perfect exposition. On the issue of the truth of "my meaning," see especially M322, W/C214–216. On reading Hegel, compare Jacques Derrida, *Glas*, pp. 5–6, 76, 198–199 and 227–228.

9. M96–97, W/C71–72, makes this point abstractly; M106–107, W/C75, makes this point concretely. It is the latter paragraphs that are behind my analysis in the following paragraphs. On this issue, compare M150, W/C105–106, in the chapter on Understanding: "Universal attraction merely asserts that *everything has a constant difference in relation to other things.* The Understanding imagines that in this unification it has found a universal law that expresses universal reality *as such*; but in fact it has only found the *Notion of law itself,* although in such a way that what it is saying is that *all* reality is *in its own self,* conformable to law. The expression, *universal attraction,* is of great importance in so far as it is directed against the thoughtless way in which everything is pictured as contingent, and for which determinateness has the form of sensuous independence."

10. M106, W/C75.

11. Compare Plato, *Theaetetus*, 186–189.

12. This analysis of passage in the context of the now should be remembered when considering the distinction between thinking of something as essentially moving and thinking of something as only superficially in motion (discussed in the chapter on understanding, M153, W/C108).

13. Compare Heidegger, *Being and Time*, div. 2, ch. 3, sect. 65, for the notion of the "ecstatic" character of temporal existence, and of the experiential equiprimordiality of past present and future. See also Augustine's discussion of time in *Confessions*, book 11, sects. 14–28, for the notion that time is the way that the mind is stretched beyond itself through retention of the past and anticipation of the future.

14. This capacity to live now in the not-now is the power of imagination. See Kant, *Critique of Pure Reason*, B151, and especially the discussion of the "synthesis of reproduction in imagination," at A100–102. On the notion of imagination in Hegel's philosophy and its significance for the *Phenomenology*, see Jennifer Bates, "Genesis and Spirit of the Imagination (Hegel's Theory of Imagination between 1801–1807)"; John Sallis, "Hegel's Concept of Presentation: Its Determination in the Preface to the Phenomenology of Spirit," and "Imagination and Presentation in Hegel's Philosophy of Spirit"; and Klaus Düsing, "Hegels Theorie der Einbildungskraft."

15. *Encyclopaedia*, sect. 259, *Zusatz*. Compare the definition of time in *Encyclopaedia*, sect. 258, as "being which, in that it is *is,* is *not,* and in that it is *not,* is." Time, in other words, is the phenomenon that directly refutes the Parmenidean description of reality, and, inasmuch as time is the form of all experience, experience itself exceeds the Parmenidean vision of being. Compare note 5, above. Though Dennis J. Schmidt seems to me to criticize a straw Hegel, his analysis of the future is relevant here: "Circles—Hermeneutic and Otherwise: On Various Senses of the Future as 'Not Yet.'"

16. Compare Henri Bergson's notion of duration, especially in *Time and Free Will:*

An Essay on the Immediate Data of Consciousness, ch. 2. Hegel's chapter on sense-certainty could be read as an immanent critique of Bergson's dualism of, roughly, intuitive and discursive time.

17. See especially M107–108, W/C75–76. With the notion of "of," I am anticipating the stance of "perception," that is, the stance that articulates its experience into things and their properties. The dialectic of the now has revealed that sense takes the form of "of," and consequently we must turn, in the next chapter, to a phenomenology of our experience of sensings "of."

This theme of the non-substantiality of the isolated now and its inherent integration into a larger whole is central to Aristotle's discussion of the now in *Physics*, book 4. For a rich discussion of the Aristotle's notion, see Francis Sparshott, *Taking Life Seriously*, especially pp. 6–9. Aristotle's discussion was of significant interest to the later neo-Platonic philosophers, some of whom developed approaches to time that have some significant similarity to Hegel's. For the phenomenology of the experience of now, see especially Pseudo-Archytas (cited in Simplicius, *Commentary on Aristotle's Categories*, 352,24–353,15) and Damascius (*Dubitationes et Solutiones* II, 236,3–237,28, and in Simplicius, *Commentary on Aristotle's Physics*, 796,27–800,16). Damascius in particular develops the notion of the "now that is many nows" (M107, W/C75) and, even further, develops something like the notion of the "thing" inasmuch as he identifies relatively isolatable temporal wholes; (this latter point is in the context of developing a suggestion from Plato's *Parmenides* 156d). For texts and discussion, see S. Sambursky and S. Pines, *The Concept of Time in Late Neoplatonism*.

18. Though their views are in the end different, Hegel's argument can be profitably illuminated by study of Wilfrid Sellar's criticisms of sense-data empiricism in "Empiricism and the Philosophy of Mind." An essentially Hegelian position is presented in Merleau-Ponty, *Phenomenology of Perception*, "The Sensation as a Unit of Experience," pp. 3–12.

19. See M109, W/C76–77: the truth of the moment of sense is a practical truth, evinced in the activity of the animals, who sense reality as "for the sake of" their desire.

20. This is, to be sure, an ontological claim, but it is ontology within phenomenology; that is, this is how the demands of experience itself require that being be recognized. "Body," in other words, names a meaningfulness within experience.

21. See, for example, the discussion of the problem of the "mediator" at M228–231, W/C154–157, and the discussion of the mediation of mind and material at M325, W/C217, and especially in *Encyclopaedia*, para. 389, and *Zusatz*. The need to mediate dualisms is the central idea behind Hegel's doctrine of the syllogism and his discussion of the relations of identity, difference, and ground in the *Science of Logic*. The problem of dualism is a central theme of chapter 8 in this book. On the notion of bodily existence as the necessary mediation between the opposition of subject and object, see M325, 327, W/C217, 218, and *Encyclopaedia*, sect. 410, *Zusatz*. Body is the self's "corporeal articulation" [*seiner körperlichen Gegliederung*] (M327, W/C218.31–32).

22. *On Generation and Corruption*, I.7.323b1–324a9.

23. Indeed, it is by the bodily act of respiration that I first become an independent self: *Encyclopaedia* para. 396, *Zusatz* (Boumann's). This *Zusatz* is rich throughout in its analysis of the bodily conditions of experience. Compare also M315, W/C210, on the role of the hand in shaping our existence. The bodily character of the self is the reason the self can be enslaved (M190, W/C132–133), and also why freedom emerges through work (M194–196, W/C134–136). On the (Aristotelian) understanding of the

way in which progressively more intensive forms of selfhood are progressively more sophisticated forms of embodiment, see *Encyclopaedia*, para. 381, and *Zusatz*.

24. *Critique of Pure Reason*, A22–25, B37–40. Compare Edward S. Casey's helpful discussion of Kant in *The Fate of Place*, ch. 10, especially pp. 205–210.

25. See Aristotle, *On the Soul*, book 2, ch. 12, for a discussion of the body as receptive of form; Franz Brentano gives a very helpful interpretation of this notion of the intentionality of the body in *Die Psychologie des Aristoteles*, pp. 79–81. For Heidegger's discussion of being-in-the-world and spatial experience, see *Being and Time*, sects. 14–22.

26. D-K 51.

27. Compare Aristotle, *On the Soul*, book 1, ch. 2, 403b25–28. See *Encyclopaedia*, para. 396, *Zusatz* (Boumann's) on the coordination of eyes and hands in a context of movement that is necessary for spatial perception, and, in general, of the practical, bodily conditions of perception.

28. Compare Rüdiger Bubner, "Philosophy Is Its Time Comprehended in Thought," in *Essays in Hermeneutics and Critical Theory*.

29. For the way in which Hegel construes the past as having its sense retroactively conferred upon it by the present, see Jay Lampert, "Husserl and Hegel on the Logic of Subjectivity." On the mutual embeddedness of past, present, and future compare M642, W/C421–422.

30. See M802, W/C525–526; compare Plotinus III.8.6.

31. M105, W/C74. Though the explicit topic is different, Jay Lampert, "Husserl's Account of Syncategorematic Terms: The Problem of Representing the Synthetic Connections That Underlie Meanings," is quite helpful for understanding the phenomenological issues embedded in "indexical" terms.

32. This attempt to show that the system of external negations rests on the existence of something characterized by an internal negation is, in the language of Hegel's *Science of Logic*, an argument that the logic of being (immediacy) depends upon the logic of essence (reflection).

33. See Cory Styranko, "Architecture and Philosophy in German Idealism," ch. 2, on the interpretation of the biblical story of Jacob's Ladder.

34. We might thus say, the present is a product of representation and not the opposite, as is typically presumed. Compare Jacques Derrida, *Glas*, p. 94, where Derrida begins to consider the relationship between representation and presence in the dialectical movement between revealed religion and absolute knowing. If the present always depends on a pointer, a non-present, then there is an aspect to experience that by its nature can never be said, never be exhausted in any act of making-present. The progress through the *Phenomenology* will be the gradually more adequate recognition of this way in which meaning in experience is always given from an originary source that can never be taken over by the self, is always that upon which the self must wait, and is thus never able to be deduced or otherwise determined in advance. Analogous themes are taken up especially in chapter 7 and in chapters 12 through 14.

35. The "ladder to the absolute" is described in M26, W/C19–20; the "way of despair" is described in M78, W/C60–62.

36. See especially David Ciavatta, *Hegel on the Family*, chs. 1 and 2, for a discussion of spirit that specially resonates with this account of the now. On the interpretation of time that is entailed by Hegel's *Phenomenology* and particularly the notion of "spirit," see David Morris, "Lived Time and Absolute Knowing: Habit and Addiction from

Infinite Jest to the *Phenomenology of Spirit.*" See also Joseph Flay, "Time in Hegel's *Phenomenology of Spirit.*"

37. Compare M801, W/C524: "Time is the Concept itself that is there (*der da ist*) and that presents itself to consciousness as empty intuition." Time is the form in which the determinate sense of reality—of spirit—presents itself to itself as to be taken up, to be made sense of.

38. Hegel's conception of the future is masterfully studied in Jay Lampert, "Hegel in the Future." See also the substantial study of Catherine Malabou, *L'Avenir de Hegel: Plasticité, temporalité, dialectique,* which, in addition to considering the concept of the future in Hegel, considers the status of Hegel's philosophy in the context of Derrida's philosophy of deconstruction.

2. FROM PERCEPTION TO PHILOSOPHY

1. See Aristotle, *On the Soul,* I.5, 409b25–410a10.

2. M113, W/C81.

3. See Aristotle, *Categories* 5, 4a10–4b18: the admission of contrary qualities within a self-same substance is the thing itself changing.

4. See Aristotle, *Categories* 5, 2a11–13: substance (*ousia*) is neither predicated of a subject nor present in a subject. For the example of the hand, see *On the Parts of Animals* I.1, 640b33–641a5.

5. See especially *Metaphysics* Z (VII).1, 1028a31–34 on the priority in *logos, gnosis,* and *chronos* of *ousia.* For thinghood as an 'also,' compare John Locke, *An Essay Concerning Human Understanding,* book 2, ch. 23, and book 3, ch. 6.

6. Immanuel Kant, *Critique of Pure Reason,* A103–110.

7. Compare Spinoza, *Ethics,* pt. 1, axiom 1: all things that are are either in themselves or in something else.

8. Compare Merleau-Ponty's discussion of the "tacit thesis of perception," in *Phenomenology of Perception,* p. 54: "The tacit thesis of perception is that at every instant experience can be co-ordinated with that of the previous instant and that of the following, and my perspective with that of other consciousnesses—that all contradictions can be removed, that monadic and intersubjective experience is one unbroken text—that what is now indeterminate for me could become determinate for a more complete knowledge, which is as it were realized in advance in the thing, or rather is the thing itself." See also his discussion of the "decisive moment in perception" on p. 53, and the discussion of philosophy and the notion of the transcendental on pp. 60–63. Compare Henri Bergson, *Matter and Memory,* p. 36: "that which distinguishes it as a *present* image, as an objective reality . . . is the necessity which obliges it to act through every one of its points upon all the points of all other images, to transmit the whole of what it receives, to oppose to every action an equal and contrary reaction, to be, in short, merely a road by which pass, in every direction, the modifications propagated throughout the immensity of the universe."

9. Compare Kant's discussion of the "transcendental object = x" in *Critique of Pure Reason,* A104–110, A250–251, and also the first analogy of experience, A182/224–A189/B232. I have taken up this theme in chapter 14, "Deciding to Read": determinations of experience are given *as* demands for integration, and, as such, each projects a comprehensive system of determinations. Compare Jay Lampert, "Leaving the System As Is," pp. 187–206.

10. We could take up this insight by jumping directly to Chapter IV of the *Phenomenology*, "Self-Consciousness," where Hegel pursue the roots of this understanding in desire: it is our desires, our projects, that determine what will count as the axes for defining the identities of things, that is, what will count as the "common ground." Hegel's subsequent argument follows the dialectical development of desire to show why our desire by its own immanent logic ultimately leads to a recognition of the need to see the world in terms of the universal and necessary categories of all human experience, which means, ultimately, our desire is itself fulfilled in understanding.

11. My goal in this chapter is not to explicate Aristotle, Spinoza, and Leibniz, but to use standard interpretations of these figures to make my point about Hegel. In fact, I do believe standard portrayals are, in the main, appropriate, though I think each of these historical figures offers more complexity, subtlety, and opacity than I here portray. In particular, on this point about nature as a whole one could argue that Aristotle's texts contain more than one might expect of the position I am here articulating. (I have explored some related concerns in "Aristotle's Animative Epistemology," and "Self-Consciousness and the Tradition in Aristotle's Psychology.") On the other hand, the definition of *ousia* in *Metaphysics* Z both as "*ti esti*" and as "*tode ti*" does seem to get Aristotle into a bind very close to that which I analyzed from Hegel's "Perception" chapter; see especially the issue of defining the uniqueness of the thing, and the question of whether each thing and its essence are the same (esp. ch. 15).

12. For Spinozistic science, this accounting amounts to the description of a system of forces, not a system of all the specific modes. See *Treatise on the Emendation of the Intellect* paras. 99–100; compare *Ethics*, pt. 1, proposition 23. See also R. G. Collingwood's discussion of the scientist's use of abstract universals in *Speculum Mentis*, ch. 5. On the notion that experience completes itself in science, compare Merleau-Ponty, *Phenomenology of Perception*, p. 63: "Experience anticipates a philosophy and philosophy is merely an elucidated experience."

13. *Science of Logic*, E555, G219.

14. Spinoza, *Ethics*, pt. 1, proposition 29, Scholium.

15. For another analysis of the argument of this section of the *Logic*, see Joseph Flay, "Hegel and Merleau-Ponty: Radical Essentialism." For another analysis of the argument of the "Understanding" chapter of the *Phenomenology*, see Martin J. de Nys, "Force and Understanding: The Unity of the Object of Consciousness."

16. See Spinoza, *Ethics*, pt. 1, propositions 17, 29, 33.

17. See Leibniz, *Discourse on Metaphysics*, proposition 9. (Spinoza himself seems to be driven toward something more like a Leibnizian monadology, at least with respect to minds, by the end of part 5 of the *Ethics*.)

18. G. W. Leibniz, *Discourse on Metaphysics*, proposition 1.

19. See Plato, *Phaedo*, 97b–d. Hegel's *Science of Logic* is the specific study of what reality requires in order to be real.

20. See M17, W/C13–14: "In my view, which can be justified only by the exposition of the system itself, everything turns on grasping and expressing the True, not only as *Substance*, but equally as *Subject*."

21. The later sections of book 2 of the *Science of Logic* also reveal that there are many different kinds of necessity, and the manner of necessity relevant to one sort of phenomena is not necessarily relevant to others. Herr Krug's pen had to be where it was because Herr Krug put it there. See John W. Burbidge, "The Necessity of Contin-

gency," and Stephen Houlgate, "Necessity and Contingency in Hegel's *Science of Logic.*" Compare Leibniz, *Discourse on Metaphysics,* proposition 4.

22. See M164, W/C117–118.

23. On this theme, see Jay Lampert, "Husserl and Hegel on the Logic of Subjectivity." (Lampert has given a more elaborate version of the argument made in this paper in relation to Husserl in *Synthesis and Backwards Reference in Husserl's Logical Investigations.*)

24. In what follows we will see the core of Hegel's rendition of Kant's question how subjectivity can be objective and his revision to Fichte's second principle and doctrine of the *Anstoß.*

25. For Hegel's study of this notion see especially M178–84, W/C127–129, on the concept of recognition, M397–418, W/C261–277, "The Spiritual Animal Kingdom and Deceit, or, *die Sache selbst,*" and M648–671, W/C426–442, on conscientious action, transgression, and forgiveness.

26. See especially the discussion of the need for a "ladder to the absolute," M26–28, W/C19–23.

27. Compare Hegel's discussion of the "Spiritual Animal Kingdom," M397–418, W/C261–277. This section is helpfully discussed by Brian K. Mackintosh, "From Reason to History in the *Phenomenology of Spirit.*"

28. This is the theme behind Hegel's phenomenology of law-giving reason (M419–428, W/C277–281), and Hegel's discussion of conscience (M632–671, W/C415–442). See especially chapters 8, "Reason and Dualism," 10, "The Contradictions of Moral Life," and 11, "Selfhood, Conscience, and Dialectic" in this book.

29. The attempt to stand outside is what Hegel's criticizes under the name of "the beautiful soul"; see especially M666, W/C438. See Benjamin C. Sax, "Active Individuality and the Language of Confession: The Figure of the Beautiful Soul in the *Lehrjahre* and the *Phänomenologie.*"

30. *Nicomachean Ethics* II.2, 1104a3–10.

31. Hegel, *Vorlesungen über die Philosophie der Geschichte,* pp. 20–21, *The Philosophy of History,* pp. 9–10.

32. Jay Lampert's discussion of Hegel's "hermeneutic multiculturalism" in "Hegel in the Future," develops a similar interpretation of Hegel. I develop this theme in my discussion of "initiation" in chapter 12, "The Ritual Basis of Self-Identity."

3. UNDERSTANDING

1. Compare the discussion of the third level of the "Divided Line" in Plato, *Republic,* VI.509d–512a.

2. See R. G. Collingwood, *Speculum Mentis,* especially the chapters on science and history (chs. 5 and 6), for a discussion of the abstract character of scientific law and the attempt to rectify the problems associated with this in the concrete universals of history.

3. Appearance is thus always more than its law, and this excess really does the work. See M150, W/C105–106. This argument here is analogous to Hegel's critique of Kantian morality (on which see chapter 10). Compare Merleau-Ponty's sense of the "primacy of perception" in the first four chapters of the *Phenomenology of Perception.*

4. Indeed, this is what the whole first three chapters of the *Phenomenology of Spirit*

show us: they show us that the way the object appears varies with the changing demands of consciousness. When understanding turns upon itself, it, properly speaking, should perform phenomenology, and this phenomenology (i.e., that which Hegel has conveniently done for us) would precisely show concretely how it is that the object has been formed by the subject. (See chapter 9 for an analogous argument regarding skepticism and ethicality.)

5. I take my interpretation of the argument of this chapter to accord with that of H. S. Harris in *Hegel's Ladder*. Harris's approach, however, is to interpret the chapter through maximal attention to the textual detail, whereas my intention (here, and in the entire volume) is to produce a minimalist reading of the argument of the text, that is, to make it clear that Hegel's argument is a compelling one, which can be removed from various of the specifics of this textual presentation.

6. See Thomas Kalenberg, *Die Befreiung der Natur. Natur und Selbstbewusstsein in der Philosophie Hegels*, pp. 2–12, for a recapitulation of the dialectic of consciousness that sees the emergence of understanding as, roughly, the *telos* of this dialectic.

7. I have considered the dialectic of perception and the emergence of understanding in chapter 2 in this book. I have there also analyzed M134, W/C94, the particularly important paragraph for determining the essence of the stance of understanding. In what follows, I will primarily draw on paragraphs M148–161, W/C103–114. The intervening paragraphs are largely devoted to the complexities of the logic of force, which, while important in their own right, are not essential to understanding the dialectic of understanding. In this chapter, as in others, Hegel first analyzes the logic of the concept and only then proceeds to the phenomenology of the experience. It is in M148, W/C103–104, that this phenomenology begins, and that is where I begin my analysis.

8. For these issues, see *Science of Logic*, E394–399, 500–505, G II.17–25, 150–156.

9. Michael Baur, "Hegel and the Overcoming of Understanding," offers an analysis of Hegel's treatment of understanding in terms of the "scientific" consciousness. Martin J. de Nys, "Force and Understanding: the Unity of the Object of Consciousness," gives a helpful discussion overall of Hegel's discussion of the object of understanding. De Nys's interpretation (61) of the "universal difference" of M148, W/C104, perhaps underinterprets this expression. On this point, see Peter Simpson, *Hegel's Transcendental Induction*, p. 129, n. 20.

10. See M154, W/C108–109.

11. Compare Plato, *Parmenides*, 130b–d, 132d–e, 134c–e, which suggest various ways in which it seems the world of the Forms must repeat the world of Becoming, and various epistemological problems that seem thereby to arise.

12. For the idea that its reality is the law within it, see M149, W/C104–105. On the "left over" that is not itself explained by the supersensible realm, see M150, W/C105–106.

13. See M150, W/C105–106 on the "superficiality" of law.

14. This is essentially the structure of the *chora* that founds the opposition of being and becoming in Plato's *Timaeus*, and of the *Seyn* that founds the opposition of *Sein* and *Seiendes* in Heidegger's *Contributions to Philosophy*. See John Sallis, *Chorology: On Beginning in Plato's Timaeus*.

15. On the carrying over of hypostasizing presumptions, see M156, W/C110–111. On "simple difference" see M149, 151, 154, W/C104–105, 106, 108–109, and *Science of Logic*, E 417–421, 502, G II.46–52, 151.

16. It has often been noticed that Hegel's argument here is incorporating the Kantian turn to the transcendental conditions of experience into the dialectic of understanding. For a particularly strong and sustained study of the relationship of Hegel's philosophy to Kantian epistemology, see Robert B. Pippin, *Hegel's Idealism: The Satisfactions of Self-Consciousness*. I have taken up related themes in chapter 7.

17. See Joseph Flay, "Hegel's Inverted World," and H.-G. Gadamer, "Hegel's 'Inverted World,'" in *Hegel's Dialectic: Five Hermeneutical Studies*.

18. On this notion of self-differentiation, see Peter Simpson, *Hegel's Transcendental Induction*, p. 27.

19. See note 4, above.

20. *Posterior Analytics*, book 2, ch. 19, *Metaphysics*, book A, chs. 1–2. I consider these texts and issues in an analogous fashion in chapter 14. See also the concluding section of chapter 7 in this book.

21. And in an Aristotelian (and also Hegelian, but not Kantian) understanding of ethics, this is also what is involved in ethical action. What is called for is insight into the demands of a particular situation, rather than the imposition of a rule upon a "type" of situation. On this moral issue in the context of Hegel's critique of Kantian ethics, see chapter 10 in this book.

22. "Thing," here, might be best understood as a rendering of the Greek *to pragma*.

23. Similarly, one who has insight can see the identity of things that others see as different. One can witness a quiescent identity maintaining itself as what others see only as a disconnected multiplicity. I understand this to be a traffic jam. I understand this to be a standard breakfast. I understand this to be a university campus. In each of these three examples, what I am presented with is a complex, varied multiplicity in which none of the constituents on its own is sufficient to indicate to the "uninitiated" the necessity that it belong with the others. Bacon by itself does not entail eggs, and there would be many people from non-British cultures who would see eggs beside bacon on a plate and see no more "unity" here than eggs and pickles, bacon and jam, or pickles and jam. To an average American, however, it is obvious that the eggs and the bacon belong together on the plate, and it is obvious that they also belong with the toast on a separate plate, which obviously does not belong with the separate plate of French Toast that is also sitting on the table in front of another patron. In looking at this assemblage of plates and food items, I immediately recognize, "standard breakfast." Again (recalling Ryle's classic example), I recognize the unity of these buildings, these teenagers, these slightly crazed-looking gray-haired men and women, these playing fields, these books, and these food service employees: they are the appearance of the university. And as these individuals leave and are replaced by others, I recognize the continuing presence of that self-same university. The unity is the recognizable, quiescent identity that pervades this varied and changing multiplicity. Understanding is this insight into the quiescent unity that is present in and as the varied and changing multiplicity. The unity *is there*, but not everyone can recognize it.

24. This *palintropos harmoniē* is what Hegel calls the second law of understanding: that everything differs from itself (M156, 158, W/C110–111, 111–112). The first law is that everything is lawlike; that is, everything maintains a constant difference with respect to everything else (M150 W/C105–106). These first and second laws are themselves opposed, and are in fact the two moments of the dynamism of the first law; that is, they are the two moments of the immanent dialectic of understanding. One can see that the first law—the law of the first supersensible world—corresponds roughly to the

principle of what philosophers in the Kantian tradition refer to properly as *"Verstand,"* whereas the second law—the law of the second supersensible world—corresponds to the principle of *"Vernunft."* *Verstand* is understanding conditioned by "sensible" presuppositions, whereas *Vernunft* is unconditioned cognition. It is universal and necessary cognition that is under analysis in this context. In Hegel's *Phenomenology*, the dialectic of "understanding" (Chapter III) moves us from the one-sided approach to universality (in the reliance upon presupposed, static, conceptual classes) to the dialectical life of immanent necessity; the dialectic of "reason"(Chapter V) moves us from the one-sided approach to necessity (in the reliance on structures of formal principles of deduction) to the same dialectical life of immanent necessity.

I take my understanding of the *palintropos harmoniē* from Abraham Schoener, "Heraclitus on War." I have discussed the *palintropos harmoniē* in "Eros and Education: Plato's Transformative Epistemology," and in "We Sense That They Strive: How to Read (The Theory of the Forms)."

25. D-K 51.

26. That understanding should be understood in terms of a logic of question and answer is a point especially developed by R.G. Collingwood, *An Autobiography*, ch. 5, and taken up by H.-G. Gadamer, especially in *Reason in the Age of Science*.

27. This entails that it is in the essence of the object to be understood.

28. This identity of subject and object, in other words, is governed by precisely the sort of logic Hegel describes as the reciprocal solicitation of forces in the opening paragraphs of this chapter; see M137–141, W/C96–100. Compare M166, W/C120.

29. Chapter 4, "Death and Desire in Hegel's Epistemology," will show more precisely how the dualism of theoretical and practical is overcome.

30. See sects. 41–53, esp. 44, 47–48. I must make my body my own by making it the medium for realizing and expressing my will. See also *Encyclopaedia*, sect. 401, *Zusatz*.

4. DEATH AND DESIRE IN HEGEL'S EPISTEMOLOGY

1. See *Critique of Pure Reason*, A444–453, B472–481. That this is an organizing text for German idealism is seen most clearly in Schelling's *System of Transcendental Idealism* of 1800, introduction, sect. 3, "Preliminary Division of Transcendental Philosophy." In contemporary philosophy of mind one can see this same set of themes played out in Donald Davidson, "Mental Events," in *Essays on Actions and Events*, and M. Merleau-Ponty, "The Body as Object and Mechanistic Physiology," in *Phenomenology of Perception* (the latter replays an idealist resolution of the third antinomy in terms of the phenomenon of the phantom limb of Descartes's sixth meditation.)

2. On the theme of death in Hegel, see Georges Bataille, "Hegel, Death and Sacrifice," Alexandre Kojève, *Introduction to the Reading of Hegel*, first lecture, and John W. Burbidge, "Man, God and Death in Hegel's Phenomenology."

3. Hegel is often seen as a philosopher in the tradition of Descartes and Kant, a tradition that stresses the *activity* of the subject in knowing: for this rationalist tradition, consciousness is always self-consciousness. This is very much true, but we must also see how Hegel is a defender of the empiricist tradition against continental rationalism, a defender, like Hume, of the claim that self-consciousness is consciousness. In this chapter I am investigating the beginnings of the dialectics of consciousness and self-consciousness in order to see how these issues of activity and passivity emerge and

develop. On the sense in which Hegel is an empiricist, see, for example, Tom Rockmore, *Cognition: An Introduction to Hegel's Phenomenology of Spirit*, especially p. 197.

4. See *Science of Logic*, book 1, sect. 1, ch. 1: "Being," E82–108, G I.82–115. The analysis of sense and determinacy that I will discuss in relationship to the *Phenomenology* is analogous to the argument of this chapter of the *Logic*.

5. See *Critique of Pure Reason*, A19–20/B33–34, A50–52/B74–76, A98–100.

6. Compare "With What Must the Science Begin?" in *Science of Logic*, E 67–78, G I.65–79.

7. See, for example, *Science of Logic*, E 398, G II.22.

8. Hegel analyzes desire at the beginning of Chapter IV, "The Truth of Self-Certainty," M166–177, W/C120–127. Hegel's treatment of desire is especially well discussed by David Ciavatta, "Hegel on Desire and Recognition."

9. See, for example, *Civilization and Its Discontents*, ch. 2.

10. See M186, W/C129–130.

11. See M149, 156, 160, W/C104–105, 110–111, 114, and *Science of Logic*, E 417–421, G II.46–52.

12. M186–189, W/C129–132. On the life and death struggle, see Peter Preuss, "Selfhood and the Battle: The Second Beginning of the Phenomenology"; Ludwig Siep, "Zur Dialectik der Anerkennung bei Hegel"; Jacques Derrida, *Glas*, pp. 134–141, and chapters 5 and 6 in this book.

13. For this reason, simple life (the realm of nature) is blind to its own history. I have studied this theme in *The Self and Its Body in Hegel's Phenomenology of Spirit*, pp. 54–61.

14. This theme is powerfully taken up in the introduction to Fichte's *Science of Rights*. The relationship of Fichte's position to that of Hegel is comprehensively studied in Robert R. Williams, *Recognition: Fichte and Hegel on the Other*.

15. See M95–96, 98, W/C71, 72.

16. See M95–97, W/C71–72. Compare Descartes's "wax" argument in his *Meditations on First Philosophy*, meditation 2, and Kant's argument for space and time as the pure forms of intuition, *Critique of Pure Reason*, B37–40, B46–48, for similar revelations of the structures of universality and necessity within experience.

17. *Critique of Pure Reason*, A98–111.

18. Jean-Paul Sartre, *Being and Nothingness*, e.g., p. 107.

19. "Authentic resoluteness" and "absolute knowing" are both stances of identifying oneself with the whole of one's situation, stances that recognize that we always exist "*in medias res*," and embrace this as their essential reality (though the Heideggerean category is a formal category that could correspond to any of the attitudes Hegel includes under the heading of *Moralität*). See Heidegger, *Being and Time*, div. 2, chs. 1 and 2. "Absolute knowing" could be understood as Hegel's *Aufhebung* of the stoic imperative to conform one's will to the nature of things (e.g. Epictetus, *Handbook*, #8).

20. See chapter 6 in this book.

21. See especially chapter 11 in this book.

5. READING AND THE BODY

1. Daniel J. Cook, *Language in the Philosophy of Hegel*, focuses on Hegel's explicit remarks about language in the *Phenomenology*, and Jacques Derrida, "The Pit and the Pyramid: Introduction to Hegel's Semiology," focuses on Hegel's explicit remarks in the

Encyclopaedia. Raymond M. Herbenick, "Hegel's Concept of Embodiment," and Alasdair MacIntyre, "Hegel on Faces and Skulls," focus on explicit remarks about the body in the *Phenomenology*; Jan van der Meulen, "Hegels Lehre von Leib, Seele und Geist," focuses on explicit remarks in the *Encyclopaedia*, as does James Dodd, "The Body as 'Sign and Tool' in Hegel's *Encyclopaedia*." Charles Taylor, *Hegel*, gives a more programmatic approach and relates embodiment to expression and language, but does not see the systematic, dialectical connection of these issues. Crawford L. Elder, "Hegel's Teleology and the Relation between Mind and Brain," addresses only the issue of neurophysiology. I have tried to develop systematically a Hegelian conception of the body in *The Self and Its Body in Hegel's Phenomenology of Spirit*.

2. It would be more accurate to say that the institution of slavery has, as its transcendental conditions of possibility, a situation of selfhood animated by the kinds of principles that animate the selves in the struggle to the death, but a situation that is precisely a solution to a problem faced in the struggle: there is not, in other words, a chronology here, but a logical relationship. I present it is a temporally continuous story for ease of comprehension.

3. The account of the struggle to the death and the emergence of mastery and servitude is in M186–189, W/C129–132. Useful analyses of the struggle can be found in Hans-Georg Gadamer, "Hegel's Dialectic of Self-Consciousness," in *Hegel's Dialectic: Five Hermeneutical Studies*; Jean Hyppolite, *Genesis and Structure of Hegel's Phenomenology of Spirit*; Alexandre Kojève, *Introduction to the Reading of* Hegel—note especially his discussion of the need to provoke a fight; Peter Preuss, "Selfhood and the Battle: The Second Beginning of the Phenomenology," which claims to be a critique, but is really a commentary, and which is interesting for disputing the notion that prestige is the goal of the fight. See also John Burbidge, "Language and Recognition."

4. On the concept of the "we," and on the embodiment of this "we" in social institutions, see chapter 11 in this book.

5. I thus disagree with Guy Debrock, who argues, in "The Silence of Language in Hegel's Dialectic," that what is distinctive about Chapter IV of the *Phenomenology of Spirit* is the absence of language; on the contrary, what is most distinctive of the dynamic of self-consciousness is the constitutive role that language must play in its institution. My argument also makes untenable Kojève's claim (*Introduction à la Lecture*, p. 171, n. 1) that speech is "born in and from the Slave's Self-Consciousness (through Work)," and the distinction that Lewis P. Hinchman draws between language and gesture in *Hegel's Critique of the Enlightenment*, p. 113. For more on the theme of language as the middle term between the isolated singular and the acknowledged self-consciousness, see M651–654, W/C428–430 in the section on "Conscience."

6. Note, then, that to read is also to write, for it involves treating the body as expressive. Here, however, it appears to be the other's body that is being read; in the next section I will consider how one can always read only one's own body.

7. These two acts are the twin negations of "Reflection" in Hegel's *Science of Logic*, and the characters "signifier" and "signified" are, respectively, "show" and "essence." See *Science of Logic*, E 394–408, G II.17–35. The whole *Science of Logic* can be seen to be organized around this notion: the dialectic of book 1 leads to the conclusion that being is a sign; book 2 is the dialectic of the sign on its own, which leads to the conclusion that the sign must have a comprehensiveness characterized by universality and necessity; book 3, finally, reveals that the sign must be a self-reader, which is ultimately the conclusion this chapter will reach.

8. Michael Rosen, *Hegel's Dialectic and Its Criticism*, gives an interpretation of Hegel's approach to meaning and interpretation that can usefully be compared with my remarks. Joseph Flay, "Pragmatic Presuppositions and the Dialectics of Hegel's *Phenomenology*," bears on my treatment of the criterion of meaningfulness. Compare Hegel's discussion of the cunning of reason in *Vorlesungen über die Philosophie der Geschichte*, p. 49, *The Philosophy of History*, p. 33; see M87, W/C67–68 for the notion of the meaningfulness that is operative behind the back of consciousness.

9. Pp. 37–39: "With every tool man is perfecting his own organs, or removing the limits to their functioning. . . . Man has, as it were, become a kind of prosthetic God."

10. M446–476, W/C292–316. For discussion, see, for example, Judith Shklar's account of Chapter VI, Section A, as a "lament for Hellas" (*Freedom and Independence: A Study of the Political Ideas of Hegel's Phenomenology of Mind*, pp. 43–44, 69–95); although good in some of its details, Shklar's account is one-sided in its overall orientation, because she does not see this as the self-developing (and hence self-destroying) immediate first position in a dialectical argument about the philosophy of systems of equal recognition, and thus seems not to notice that Hegel's account in VI A (especially section b) is primarily about why this social system, which Hegel calls *Sittlichkeit*, is inadequate. For a corrective notion of social systems as systems of equal recognition, see David Kolb, *The Critique of Pure Modernity: Hegel, Heidegger and After*, pp. 23–31, 99–101, and for the notion of the immediacy of *Sittlichkeit*, see p. 66; Kolb's analyses are rooted in the *Philosophy of Right*, rather than the *Phenomenology of Spirit*, but his results are easily transferable. Without a doubt, the most precise, philosophically insightful, and textually grounded reading of these pages is Jacques Derrida, *Glas*, passim, but especially pp. 141–151, 162–176, 186–188. My analysis has especially benefited from reading H. S. Harris, "Hegel and Antigone's Unwritten Laws." For a discussion of the literary-critical issues of Hegel's treatment of Sophocles' tragedy, see Martin Donougho, "The Woman in White: On the Reception of Hegel's Antigone."

11. See Hinchman, *Hegel's Critique of the Enlightenment*, pp. 99–100, for a comparable discussion of the relation of the singular self to social institutions in the realm of *Sittlichkeit*.

12. Compare the discussion of related themes in Friedrich Schiller, *On the Aesthetic Education of Man*, fourth letter, para. 2. This Kant- and Fichte-inspired discussion uses language very similar to my own.

13. The divine law itself speaks in two ways, for it also insists that the women stay at home, and leave the political action to the men. This is the side of the divine law that animates Ismene's reading, and it is this double-sided commitment within the divine law that makes conflict possible.

14. M463, W/C303–304, summarizes how the two systems are supposed to function harmoniously; M473–475, W/C311–315, describes the conflict of the two systems. The reason for the breakdown can also be described in terms of the very concept of law. What is distinctive of this whole social situation is that the entire understanding of law is derived primarily from the notion of immediate natural propriety. Even though it is recognized that human law requires explicit reflection, choice, and so on, *that* such a law is needed, and the basic conception of how it should function, is still accepted as the way human life should naturally be. At the level neither of human nor of divine law is the question asked "what is law?" There is likewise no element within either set of laws that aims at the development or transformation of the society in such a way as to produce individuals who could answer "what is law?" Rather, it is a self-satisfied society

that takes itself to simply be itself, naturally: it does not see humanity as an achievement. Thus it equally does not see human action as its own foundation and goal. It is this essential *stasis*—the inability to countenance conflict—that marks the situation, and that reveals why the situation collapses precisely when a conflict arises in the society.

15. M470, W/C309–310.

16. That is, they force a subject who has her method of reading imposed, to the extent that she *sees the commitment to law as necessary*.

17. This is at the core of the claim that philosophy must become systematic science in the preface, M1–29, W/C3–24. "The Absolute Idea" in the *Science of Logic* also discusses dialectical method in terms of the overcoming of contradiction.

18. On reading the text as leading up to oneself, see M5, W/C6.

6. HERMENEUTICAL PRESSURE

1. The slave is free in principle (*an sich* or implicitly), but not in fact (*für sich* or explicitly).

2. See M190, W/C132, lines 32–37, on the chain of nature that binds the slave.

3. See M189, W/C132 for the slave as the one who values life.

4. Compare Fichte's 3rd Fundamental Principle in the *Science of Knowledge*. (Both in Fichte and in Hegel's analysis of the slave, the first necessity is universality, the second, particularity, and the third, singularity.)

5. While killing the slave would not violate the explicit rules of her identity, it would realize a change in her identity, for there would be no one left to recognize the master as master. This points to the central contradiction in the master's identity, namely, that she depends on the recognition of the slave in order to be defined as independent. See M191–2, W/C132–134. This is the complementary contradiction to that which we will find in the slave identity: the slave's singular initiative is implicitly essential but explicitly denied within the relation of master and slave.

6. See M190, W/C132, on the notion that the slave must work, and in so doing engage with the things of the world *qua* independent, whereas the master engages them *qua* dependent (upon her desire). On this theme, see Hans-Georg Gadamer, "Hegel's Dialectic of Self-Consciousness" in *Hegel's Dialectic*.

7. On the idea that this is in fact a necessary condition for making the transition from the struggle to the death into slavery, see chapter 5 in this book.

8. Compare Jean-Paul Sartre, *Being and Nothingness*, pp. 5–6.

9. This entails already recognizing one's *self* as constrained by sensation—"that hurt is *me*." This is the synthesis of apprehension in intuition, which amounts to recognizing that one is the body that is vulnerable to impression, that is, sensitive. For a thorough and extremely helpful study of the syntheses of conscious life, see Jay Lampert, *Synthesis and Backwards Reference in Husserl's Logical Investigations*.

10. Immanuel Kant, *Critique of Pure Reason*, A98–110.

11. On the role of Kant's transcendental argumentation in Hegel's "Consciousness" chapters, see chapter 7, note 35; compare Charles Taylor, "The Opening Arguments of the *Phenomenology*." For a sustained study of the relationship of Hegel's philosophy to Kant's epistemology, see Robert B. Pippin, *Hegel's Idealism: The Satisfactions of Self-Consciousness*.

12. Compare Aristotle, *On the Soul*, book 3, ch. 9, 432a15–432b7.

13. On reason as the *Aufhebung* of desire, see chapter 8 of this book, especially section 1. See also Gadamer, "The Idea of Hegelian Logic" in *Hegel's Dialectic*.

14. Compare Sartre's discussion of "the look" and "the body for others" in *Being and Nothingness*, pp. 340–400, 445–460.

15. On the logical relationships involved in self-consciousness and their implications for the notion of intersubjectivity, see chapter 11 in this book.

16. Compare Freud's discussion of the "pleasure principle," for example in *Civilization and Its Discontents*, ch. 1.

17. This is the "Struggle to the Death," M186–189, W/C129–132.

18. See M191–192, W/C132–134, on the inequality of recognition.

19. Compare the roles of the synthesis of "the transcendental object = x" and "the transcendental unity of apperception" within Kant's discussion of the synthesis of recognition in a concept, *Critique of Pure Reason* A103–110.

20. These two—reading and writing—cannot really be distinguished, for to read is to ascribe (ad-scribe) to the other the text of our interpretation; precisely what the slave has been doing is writing the desire of the other. I will use the opposition of reading and writing here only to indicate the difference of direction between (1) explicitly portraying oneself as answering to another and (2) implicitly putting oneself forward. On the indistinguishability of reading and writing, see chapter 5. See also chapter 14 on the logic of reading.

21. This is the stance of "Stoicism" (M197–201, W/C136–140) the first of the stances studied by Hegel under the heading, "The Freedom of Self-Consciousness," the other stances being "Scepticism" and "Unhappy Consciousness." This and the final section of this chapter will make an argument that parallels the dialectical advance through this section of Hegel's text.

22. M419–437, W/C277–287, especially M437, W/C286–287.

23. That it is in the experience of necessity that our freedom is most fully realized is a theme that runs throughout Kant's *Groundwork of the Metaphysics of Morals* and *Critique of Practical Reason*. Compare Descartes, *Meditations on First Philosophy*, meditation 4.

24. See *Civilization and Its Discontents*, especially ch. 8, and "The Transformations of Puberty," in *Three Essays on the Theory of Sexuality*, for Freud's explanation why the roots [routes] of civilization and of neurosis are one and the same.

25. Note especially the description of the laws: "They *are*. If I inquire after their origin and confine them to the point whence they arose, then I have transcended them; for now it is I who am the universal, and *they* are the conditioned and limited" (W/C286.34–37).

26. See M177, W/C127.19–24, for the notion that self-consciousness realizes its proper form in the "I" that is "We" and the "We" that is "I." On the idea that the mutual endorsement of traditional law is the establishment of an equality of recognition, see chapters 11 and 13 in this book.

27. I choose this example partially because it alludes to the accepting of traditional sex-roles that characterizes the *Sittlichkeit* of Antigone; see, e.g., M457, 459, 465, W/C300, 301, 305. On this issue, see Kenley Dove, "Phenomenology and Systematic Philosophy," p. 37. On the sex-roles of "man" and "woman" in contemporary culture as exemplary of the Hegelian roles of master and slave, see Simone de Beauvoir, *The Second Sex*, especially pt. 7. On the stoic ideal of masculine identity, and its embeddedness in the political system of which fascism is the culmination, see Klaus Theweleit,

Male Fantasies. See also Monique Wittig, "One Is Not Born a Woman," and Maurice Merleau-Ponty's discussion of "psychological rigidity" in "The Child's Relations with Others."

28. This theme is taken up in greater detail in chapters 12 and 13 in this book.

29. The skeptic is studied in M202–205, W/C140–143, and throughout the introduction to the *Phenomenology*.

30. M206–231, W/C144–157. I have defended this interpretation of "unhappy consciousness" in *The Self and Its Body in Hegel's Phenomenology of Spirit*, ch. 1; see chapter 7 in this book. My language here alludes to Heidegger's description of *Da-sein* in *Being and Time*.

7. THE "FREEDOM OF SELF-CONSCIOUSNESS" AND EARLY MODERN EPISTEMOLOGY

1. Hegel, *Vorlesungen über die Ästhetik* I, p. 59: "For rational intelligence does not belong like desire to the single subject as such, but to the single as equally in itself universal."

2. Alexandre Kojève, *Introduction à la Lecture de Hegel*, pp. 180–182. Also adopted, for example, by Shklar in *Freedom and Independence: A Study of the Political Ideas of Hegel's Phenomenology of Mind*, e.g., pp. 43–44.

3. This is how I have understood Harris's position in *Hegel's Ladder*. See Quentin Lauer, *A Reading of Hegel's Phenomenology of Spirit*, pp. 113–124, and J. N. Findlay, *Hegel: A Re-examination*, pp. 100–102 (see following note).

4. John Burbidge, "Unhappy Consciousness in Hegel: An Analysis of Medieval Catholicism?" See also Jean Hyppolite, *Genèse et Structure de la Phénoménologie de l'Esprit de Hegel*, I, pp. 172–173, 189; his inadequately defined notion of history at I, pp. 214–218, however, makes his position unclear. Despite the view expressed in *Hegel: A Re-examination* (see previous note), Findlay seems to share the view that the argument is transcendental in his analysis of M230 (on p. 527 of Miller's text).

5. The three forms are articulated in M210, W/C145.29–39. I have presented my analysis in *The Self and Its Body in Hegel's Phenomenology of Spirit*, ch. 1.

6. In noting the primacy of unhappy consciousness, I am working in the tradition of such French commentators as J. Wahl, A. Koyré, and J. Hyppolite. See, e.g., Hyppolite, *Genèse et Structure*, I, p. 184.

7. My understanding of the relation between unhappy consciousness and reason is primarily developed from a reading of *Encyclopaedia*, sects. 436–439.

8. See M197, W/C137.35–39.

9. See M200, W/C139.26–31.

10. See M200, W/C139.10–13.

11. See M197, W/C137.39–140.8; M199, W/C138.18–27; and M200, W/C139.5–140.4. See Hyppolite, *Genèse et Structure*, I, pp. 172–175.

12. Compare M73, W/C57–58, in the introduction, which discusses the conception of knowledge as an "instrument," and the problems this raises; the two possible unsuccessful strategies for dealing with this bear closely on the problems I am discussing here.

13. M202, W/C140.15–21; M202, W/C140.36–38; M204, W/C141.24–25. In the introduction, Hegel compares his own philosophical method with skepticism, and, in the context of this discussion, he notes as the positive contribution of skepticism that

it achieves that transformation whereby "what first appeared as the object sinks for consciousness to the level of its way of knowing it" (M87, W/C67.32–33). Compare Jay Lampert's discussion regarding what both Hegel and Fichte put forward as the basis of immediate right in "Locke, Fichte and Hegel on the Right to Property."

14. M205, W/C142.8–18; Hume, *A Treatise of Human Nature*, book 1, pt. 4, sect. 6, p. 252. I thus disagree with those commentators (including Hyppolite, *Genèse et Structure*, I, p. 179, and Forster, *Hegel and Skepticism*, pt. 1) who maintain that this section of the *Phenomenology of Spirit* addresses only ancient skepticism and not the supposedly less skeptical modern skepticism; on this issue of selfhood, I can see no difference, and, in general, I am not convinced by the interpretation given to Hume's skepticism. See, on this point, Hanna's review of Forster, p. 631. I am thus also unsatisfied with Pippin's treatment in his excellent *Hegel's Idealism*, p. 95. A discussion of related issues by a younger Hegel can be found in "Relationship of Skepticism to Philosophy, Exposition of Its Different Modifications and Comparison to the Latest Form with the Ancient One." As I discuss in chapter 9, there are grounds for deeming modern (Humean) skepticism to be less skeptical than ancient skepticism in that modern skepticism involves unjustified presuppositions concerning the nature of experience; on this point, see Forster, *Hegel and Skepticism*, pp. 11–15, 17, 25–27. These differences do not alter modern skepticism's relevance to this section of the *Phenomenology* or, especially, to the introduction.

15. In *Human Experience: Philosophy, Neurosis and the Elements of Everyday Life*, I have drawn upon the logic of stoicism, skepticism, and unhappy consciousness as a model for understanding mental health in terms of neurosis, psychosis, and phenomenology as therapy.

16. M205, W/C142.25–28. Compare the dialectic of the thing and its properties in Chapter II, "Perception," where a comparable issue of the relation of thinghood as an essential and exclusive oneness to thinghood as a mere locus for the coming together of multiple properties is played out.

17. See Dieter Henrich, "Hegels Logik der Reflexion: Neue Fassung," on the notion of "absolute" negation.

18. M205, W/C143.3–5: "es spricht das absolute *Verschwinden* aus, aber das *Aussprechen* IST, und dies Bewußtsein ist das ausgesprochne Verschwinden." See Hyppolite, *Genèse et Structure*, I, pp. 180–183, especially p. 182, for a good account of this tension within the skeptic self. Compare the dialectic of the "now," M106–107, W/C75.

19. M205, W/C143.9–12: "Sein Tun und seine Worte widersprechen sich immer, und ebenso hat es selbst das gedoppelte widersprechende Bewußtsein der Unwandelbarkeit und Gleichheit, und der völligen Zufälligkeit und Ungleichheit mit sich." See M205, W, 142.32–143.12 in general.

I take Lauer's account of the breakdown of skepticism in A *Reading of Hegel's Phenomenology of Spirit*, p. 116, to be mistaken. Lauer claims that "it [skepticism] is self-contradictory, not in the sense that it involves logical contradiction, to which it is indifferent, but in the sense that the way it thinks contradicts the way it lives," that is, "it *does* what it *claims* has no validity." See also Findlay, *Hegel: A Re-examination*, pp. 99–100, Forster, *Hegel and Skepticism*, pp. 39–40. It seems to me that this is not Hegel's argument, at least not in the sense these commentators give to their words. Indeed, it seems to me that Lauer has not adequately grasped his own valuable insight that the value of skepticism is its proof that "[o]nly what consciousness produces from within itself counts" (pp. 115–116), for this latter point is precisely why Hegel's demonstration of the *internal* contradiction of skepticism "counts" whereas this *external* critique offered by Lauer, Findlay, and Forster will never overcome the skeptic, since it presupposes a reality to appearances that the skeptic will never accept. The critique seems unsuccessful both as an argument against skepticism and as a reading of Hegel's text, for all three commentators, I believe, have a mistaken view of what Hegel would count as a "deed" or a "word." The whole point of stoicism and skepticism, and the reason they advance the dialectic, is that they are the first forms in which the self-conscious self fulfills the potentiality, implicit in slavery, of recognizing itself in its *products*, that is, its *deeds*; the "deed" of stoicism is precisely to think abstract thoughts (and the skeptic simply universalizes this by recognizing all determinations of consciousness as being such "deeds" of self-consciousness); the claims of Lauer, Findlay, and Forster make sense only if one posits a dualism of thought and action that is alien to Hegel's argument. (The "word" of Hegel's text refers to what skepticism explicitly takes itself to be.) The same criticism can be made of Kojève's claim (*Introduction à la Lecture*, pp. 180–181) that the stoic does not do anything; his claim (often repeated by others) that stoicism collapses because it is boring, while based on Hegel's remark at M200, W/C139.38–140.4, is a misunderstanding: what is wrong with stoicism is that the rigorous pursuit of its own principles necessarily leads to skepticism. Shklar's claim (*Freedom and Independence*, p. 64) that it is an *emotional* tension that makes or lets the unhappy consciousness take over from the skeptic seems to me to entirely misunderstand the epistemological issues involved in Hegel's argument.

20. See M82–84, W/C64–65.

21. Typically, commentators consider only inadequate forms of unhappy consciousness, and want to limit the use of this term to those forms. In so doing they fail to notice that the third form of unhappy consciousness (to be discussed below) is not inadequate. It is true that Hegel himself tends to use the expression "unhappy consciousness" to refer to the inadequate forms, but this is no different from terms such as *Verstand* and *Vernunft* in his vocabulary that can function either to name a particular, limited form of experience, or to name the essence of experience as such. See chapter 3, n. 24 in this book.

22. M210, W/C145.29–39. Hegel here articulates the three forms, and then goes on to discuss only the first briefly and the second in detail. This second form is itself broken down into three sub-forms, and it is important not to confuse the third sub-form here with the third stage described in M210 (a mistake made by almost all commentators on this section, including Hyppolite and Burbidge). The third form of unhappy consciousness articulated in M210 is really the protagonist for the remaining four chapters of the *Phenomenology of Spirit*. The third form is described in M231, the first paragraph of the "Reason" chapter, and this paragraph is better read as the final paragraph of Chapter IV. In my study of the unhappy consciousness, I have especially benefited from Jennifer Bates, "The Breakdowns of Unhappy Consciousness."

23. Cf. the possibility and necessity of a "ladder to the absolute" in the preface, M26, W/C19–21.

24. I notice four interesting features here, each of which is exploited in later idealism. First, the very fact of the experience has consequences; this notion that the very enactment or performance has implications is the basis of transcendental argumentation as it will appear in Kant and Fichte, where the very fact of coherent experience guarantees that the conditions that must be in place for there to be coherent

experience are actual. This is evident throughout Kant's Transcendental Aesthetic and Analytic; it is the basis of Fichte's familiar refrain in the *Science of Knowledge,* upon discovery of an antithesis in the constitutive principles of consciousness: "The two principles annul one another. . . . But if it is annulled, so is the major principle that contains it and with that in turn the unity of consciousness. So it cannot annul itself, and the opposites it contains must be capable of reconciliation" (*Science of Knowledge, Werke* I 132, etc.). The second interesting feature is that the *ego, cogito* argument is performed precisely in and as an act of self-reflection, which means the truth is discovered by a method of *phenomenological description* in which the two roles are discerned of the consciousness being observed, and the consciousness observing, which will lead to Hegel's "for itself" and "for us." Third, the argument places the reader in the same position as that of the narrator of the text, and so the successful reading of the text involves recognizing that it is one's own consciousness that is being observed. This theme comes to be exploited in Fichte's insistence that the student will grant all Fichte's arguments, that is, "I bring you no new revelations. What I can teach you you already know. I cannot deceive you, for you will grant me everything I say" (*The Vocation of Man, Werke* II 199); it is further exploited in Hegel's insistence that the *Phenomenology of Spirit* must, and does, provide each single consciousness with a "ladder to the absolute" (M26, W/C19–21). Finally, notice that the response to skepticism comes through an attention to the unique demands that derive from the determinate form of that being investigated: only if one maintains an "abstract" skepticism that does not notice *what* it is doubting, but insists, instead, on the independent, universal validity of doubting, can one doubt the existence of the doubter, for as soon as one *understands* what is being said here; that is, as soon as the doubt has *meaning,* it becomes impossible. This is, then, the beginning of the insistence on the necessary concreteness of reason. See M78–84, W/C60–65.

25. Trans. Donald A. Cress. The emphasis is mine, and the emphasized text reads in the Latin, "*in quibus scilicet repugnantiam agnosco manifestam.*" Here again, the skepticism cannot be maintained in the face of an actual recognition of the determinateness of the object being doubted. This whole paragraph of Descartes's text is interesting because it sets up the basis for a dialectical argument in the form characteristic of Fichte: two equally compelling but opposed claims are presented; since neither can be rejected and since the conflict cannot be the proper form for their existence, we can be certain that there is a way to reconcile the two.

26. Compare Husserl's discussion of the relation of the empirical and the transcendental "I" and "We" in his *Encyclopaedia Brittanica* article, "Phenomenology," pt. 2, sect. D, p. 85.

27. On this issue, see the second meditation, paras. 3ff., and the first part of Arnauld's objections to the *Meditations* (*Fourth Set of Objections*) with Descartes's response.

28. This is the argument that I have taken up in *The Self and Its Body in Hegel's Phenomenology of Spirit.*

29. Para. 11ff.

30. I am arguing that all the roles "God" is made to play in these arguments are completely consistent and indeed necessary roles for an argument about transcendental subjectivity. Just at the level of argument, then, Descartes's position is fine, indeed compelling, and involves no illicit appeal to any God other than the very concept of reason (hence the accusation that he reasons in a circle from reason to God to reason is

a true statement that misses the point). There remains a question, however, of how Descartes imagined this God, that is, whether he took God to mean something other than reason. On this point I have no strong view, but I would note that in the *Principles* I.51 God already looks a great deal like Spinoza's substance. At any rate, even if Descartes does mean something else, this is *logically* discardable because the argument does not depend on it; indeed, his claim is to be rationally rigorous, and our job is to follow the *argument* rigorously, so we are really compelled by the argument to understand the God of meditations 3 and 5 as reason.

31. See M26, W/C19–21, in the preface to the *Phenomenology of Spirit*, where the recognition of the self in the other is the hallmark of real science. It is because they are all forms of such recognition that "Reason," "Spirit," "Religion," and "Absolute Knowing" are all included as Section C of the *Phenomenology*.

32. Compare the dialectic of "external reflection," *Science of Logic*, E 403–404, G II.28–40.

33. On this point, note that Hegel accuses Kant of ultimately being a skeptic. Note also that Kant's dialectic is itself portrayed by Kant in the "Antinomies" as a *"sceptical method,"* while what is clearly a development of this same method is portrayed by Fichte in the second introduction to the *Science of Knowledge* (and, in turn, by Hegel in the introduction to the *Phenomenology*) as the direct observation of the truth. See Kant, *Critique of Pure Reason* A423/B451, Fichte, *Science of Knowledge*, Werke I 454.

34. This "check" first appears at the end of the first discourse (on theoretical knowledge), *Werke* I 210, and the attempt to resolve the dualism *in action* is the subject matter of the discourses on the practical that close the *Science of Knowledge*.

35. The first three chapters of the *Phenomenology of Spirit* clearly focus on the structures of the *object* of experience, yet these all translate into structures of what Kant would call transcendental subjectivity; indeed, the progress through these three chapters essentially parallels Kant's laying out of the "layers" of synthesis in the *Critique of Pure Reason*, A98–110. "Sense-Certainty" begins as the "synthesis of apprehension in intuition," and the dialectical argument of the chapter leads us to see that this synthesis already depends upon memory, and the holding together of sensations within a realm of possibility, that is, "the synthesis of reproduction in imagination." This synthesis is the basic "thesis" of "Perception," and the dialectical argument of this chapter reveals that the recognizable unities we face are necessarily already the products of a conceptual synthesis, that is, "the synthesis of recognition in a concept." Thus the first three chapters move us dialectically from sensation to imagination to understanding, in each case revealing that the earlier presupposes the later. Finally, the chapter on "Understanding" starts with the thesis of the "synthesis of recognition in a concept" and argues that this stands on the presupposition of a posited unified field of objectivity (the synthesis of "the transcendental object = x") and further on the yet more fundamental synthesis of an overarching subjectivity, the unified experience of which is the ground of the unity of the object and all the other syntheses that depend upon it (= the "transcendental unity of apperception"). Compare Charles Taylor, who in "The Opening Arguments of the *Phenomenology*" also considers the transcendental argumentation of the first three chapters.

36. Compare Jay Lampert's discussion of the culmination of property as the need to be stolen in "Locke, Fichte and Hegel on the Right to Property."

37. I have developed this theme of Aristotle's active empiricism in "Aristotle's

Animative Epistemology," and "Self-Consciousness and the Tradition in Aristotle's Psychology."

38. See Stephen Houlgate, "World History as the Progress of Consciousness: An Interpretation of Hegel's Philosophy of History," pp. 79–80: "the future, in Hegel's view, is open. What will happen, we cannot predict. However, that future cannot confront us with anything which we are not equipped to understand."

8. REASON AND DUALISM

1. This dualism has two important anticipative precedents in Chapter IV, "Self-Consciousness." The most immediate form of a dualism of self and body appears in the dynamic of desire at the beginning of Chapter IV, "Self-Consciousness"; here the positing of self as independent and immediately self-present reality is non-reflective, and the body from which it is differentiated is all otherness. The second dualism that anticipates reason appears as stoicism; here the self is explicitly posited as an independent determinate being, and the body of nature from which it is differentiated is equally posited as a self-contained determinate being. "Reason" is the ultimate form of this dualism because the self as independent reality is posited as in principle equal to all reality. These three shapes of dualism form a logical progression of, roughly, the self as pure being to the self as determinate being to the self as the infinite (according to the categories of book 1 of the *Science of Logic*), or, again, positing reflection to external reflection to determining reflection (according to the categories of book 2). There is also a fourth crucial appearance of a dualism of self and body in the *Phenomenology*, and this is the whole dynamic of *Bildung* in Chapter VI, *"Geist."* This is the society that institutionalizes the principles that animate reason, and the body from which this rational self is differentiated is the body of social institutions; the theme of the body as institutions will come up for consideration in section 3 of this chapter.

2. Note that this is close both to the logic by which stoicism is seen to culminate in skepticism, and to the logic that marks the problem of the first form of unhappy consciousness as studied in chapter 7 of this book.

3. See *Encyclopaedia*, para. 389 (*Hegels Philosophie des subjectiven Geistes*, Bd. 2, p. 4.24–34, p. 5.26–35), and see M325 W/C217 on the issue of material mediation of mind and matter (as in the text-book portrayal of Descartes's proposal of the pineal gland as the mediating organ). We will see various forms of the problem of dualism and the attempt to defer resolving the problem through an infinite multiplication of inadequate middle terms emerge in the course of the dialectic of observing reason.

4. M233, W/C158–159.

5. *Aufheben* is the verb Hegel uses to characterize the transformation by which a constitutive feature of a relatively primitive form of relationship is maintained in a modified form within a more sophisticated relationship. To say that the equivalent feature in the more sophisticated relationship is the "sublimation" of the feature in the more primitive comes close to capturing this relationship except insofar as the notion of sublimation carries with it the sense of misleading distortion: rather than being a repression of the feature's rightful position, the feature as *aufgehoben* is, according to Hegel's argument, the bringing of the feature closer to its proper form; in many ways, "developed" would be a closer translation of *aufgehoben*. See M113, W/C80.14–19 and *Science of Logic*, E106–108, G I.113–115.

6. As such scholars as Hyppolite, *Genèse et Structure*, I p. 224, Harris, *Hegel's Ladder*, and Findlay, *Hegel: A Re-examination*, p. 107, have noted, the historical figures whose ideas provide the raw material for Chapter V, Section A, "Observing Reason," range from Bacon and Descartes to Kant and Schelling. It is certainly true that the simple conception of a substantial identity that excludes difference more obviously accords with Descartes's metaphysics than with the much more sophisticated metaphysics of the *Naturphilosophen*, but precisely what this section of Hegel's text reveals is that even the later figures remain ultimately Cartesian in their projects. The same point can be made, *mutatis mutandis*, for the other two sections of Chapter V, "Reason." For the disparity that exists between reason's posited identity with all reality and the necessary dualism that comes with this conception of substantial identity, see Flay, *Hegel's Quest for Certainty*, pp. 118–119, and the discussion of relative and absolute otherness.

7. Hegel makes this point explicitly in his *Science of Logic*: "for reflection, the omnipresence of the simple in a multiple externality is an absolute contradiction, and, in so far as reflection at the same time must take this omnipresence from the perception of Life and must thus admit the actuality of this Idea, it is an incomprehensible mystery [*unbegreifliches Geheimniß*]" (trans. Johnson and Struthers, Vol. II, p. 403.34–39, *Wissenschaft der Logik*, II, pp. 181.23–27). The task facing reason, and that to which it will be logically driven in the course of our phenomenological investigation, is the self-conscious recognition of a unity in and through difference. A similar situation characterized the dialectic of understanding in Chapter III, "Force and the Understanding."

8. For Chapter V, Harris, *Hegel's Ladder*, and Hyppolite, *Genèse et Structure* are particularly helpful. Findlay, *Hegel: A Re-examination*, is helpful for Chapter V, Sections A and C, but poor on the logical structure of the chapter as a whole, especially Section B; Taylor, *Hegel*, explicates themes of Sections B and C in his general discussions of enlightenment culture.

9. M245–247, W/C166–169, "*Beschreiben überhaupt, Merkmale.*"

10. M254–297, W/C173–200, especially from M265, W/C180, "*das Innre*" to M290, W/C194–196, on "*spezifische Schwere.*"

11. M245–247, W/C166–169.

12. M286–290, W/C192–196.

13. M298–308, W/C201–206, especially M300, W/C202, and M303, W/C203–204.

14. M309–346, W/C206–233.

15. M242, 244, W/C164–165, 166.

16. Note that this is reason acting in the general mode of "Consciousness" as this is defined in Chapters I–III of the *Phenomenology of Spirit*. In Section B of Chapter V, we will move on to reason operating in the mode of self-consciousness, and we will conclude, in Section C of Chapter V, with reason finally struggling to adopt its own proper form as reason. See M348, W/C233–234.

17. See M232, W/C157–158.

18. The coming to self-consciousness of this animating imperative is what is developed at the end of Chapter V, "Reason," in the dialectic of "Individuality real in and for itself," and the full implications of this move are worked out in the remaining three chapters of the *Phenomenology of Spirit*. That reason itself is not aware of its implicit imperative is simply another way of expressing the remark of M233, W/C158–159 that reason does not recognize its own history. M233 and 234, W/C158–160, discuss the difference between the *lived practice* of reason (science) that operates with the *as-*

surance (*Versicherung*) that it is all reality, and the *philosophy* of reason (idealism) that makes the *assertion* (*Behauptung*) that it is all reality. Miller's translation obscures this point by translating both these terms as "assertion." Hyppolite offers some discussion of the relation of reason and idealism in *Genèse et Structure*, I, pp. 217–224. For the "instinct" of reason, see M246, W/C168.6–8; the term *Vernunftinstinkt* first appears at M248, W/C169.35.

19. See M238–239, W/C162–163, for the statement of this problem as it appears in the *philosophy* of reason, *viz.*, idealism.

20. These basic moves are contained in M245–254, W/C166–173; the remainder of the observation of nature is devoted to various developments within the observation of the organic.

21. The move out of the observation of nature to the observation of self-consciousness, and beyond that to the observation of the relation of self-consciousness to its immediate actuality, are likewise moves which represent the recognition of a more appropriate object within which to find a reflection of reason, but the basic problems that attach to the observational method are all manifest by the time we reach the observation of organic nature, for life has the logical form of the infinite (see M162, W/C115.16–17), and thus already demonstrates the situation in which reason should see its own reflection, but is limited by its method. Consequently, my analysis of the problems of observation will focus only on the observation of nature. On the hierarchy of subjects for observation, see Flay, *Hegel's Quest for Certainty*, pp. 122–136; for biology's limited reflection of reason, see pp. 124–125.

I will thus not here analyze Hegel's discussion of physiognomy and phrenology, where the human body is subjected to observation, for it makes no essential advance in the study of self-identity and difference in relation to the rational self. In this section, however, Hegel does make interesting editorial comments about the nature of the body, and these are discussed in Herbenick, "Hegel's Concept of Embodiment," and by MacIntyre, "Hegel on Faces and Skulls." See also Donald Phillip Verene, *Hegel's Recollection*, pp. 80–91.

22. For chemistry, see M246, W/C167–168. Hegel's philosophy of chemistry is exhaustively studied by John W. Burbidge, *Real Process: How Logic and Chemistry Combine in Hegel's Philosophy of Nature*.

23. See, for example, M254, W/C173.

24. This is recognized by Hyppolite, *Genèse et Structure*, I, pp. 223–224, 234–236, 239–249, although Hyppolite treats "Observation of Nature" as if it actually presented Hegel's philosophy of nature, whereas in fact the argument bears on Hegel's philosophy of nature, but is not that philosophy's systematic presentation; Hegel's philosophy of nature is not a constitutive moment of the *Phenomenology of Spirit*.

25. Cf. Ryle, *The Concept of Mind*, p. 16.

26. See M251–252, W/C171–173, for reason's attempt to observe laws.

27. See M258, W/C176–177, for the positing of the end in an alien intelligence. On this issue of end, compare *Philosophy of Nature*, sect. 360.

28. See M251–252, W/C171–173, on the issue of the observability of laws; for teleology, and the limits of observational reason, see M256, W/C175–176.

29. Shklar, *Freedom and Independence*, p. 32 articulates something similar when she argues that, in its continued attempts to observe, reason "gets thrown back on the solipsistic dead end of 'ego = ego,' from which it . . . turns away . . . by discovering a new science."

30. The detailed articulations of the different variants of the logic of immediate being and the logic of reflection are the subject-matters of, respectively, the "Doctrine of Being" and the "Doctrine of Essence" in Hegel's *Science of Logic*.

31. That is, its self-observation produces the logical laws of simple identity, or tautology, which we have seen to be the truth of its method (see M299, W/C201–202).

32. *Contra* Findlay (*Hegel: A Re-Examination*, p.109), who calls the transition from Section A to Section B, "one of the most arbitrary somersaults in the whole course of [Hegel's] dialectic," and Shklar (*Freedom and Independence*, p. 98), who says, "One may well wonder why Hegel called these highly irrational expressions of subjectivity reason at all."

33. Here again, however, self-actualizing reason will still posit the achieved *state* as what is rational, and will again fail to adequately comprehend the primacy of action.

34. Note that the self-actualizing *"vernünftigen Selbstbewußtsein"* of the title is ambiguous: it refers, on the one hand, to the singular agent who carries out the revolution (for this agent is making her essence actual), and, on the other hand, to the society that is thus revolutionized (for the very thesis of the revolutionary is that she is only enacting the latent essence—the destiny—of the self-consciousness that is her object). It is this very ambiguity of the individuality that, in its fulfillment, is identical with both the singular and the universal, which self-actualizing reason will not adequately comprehend; self-actualizing reason will vacillate between the two identifications because it will hold fast to the distinctness and self-containedness of the identity of each, again falling into the error of observing reason of positing what are merely moments of a process as inert substances.

35. M360–366, W/C240–244.

36. M359, 361, W/C239, 240.

37. M362, W/C240–241. See Hyppolite's discussion, at *Genèse et Structure*, I, pp. 155, 158, of the distinction between *désir* (Hegel's *Begierde*) and *l'amour* (and compare Gadamer, *"Hegels Dialektik des Selbstbewußtseins,"* p. 55, n.4).

38. M360, W/C240.

39. M360, W/C240.

40. M362, W/C240–241.

41. M364–365, W/C242–243.

42. M363; W/C242.12–15: "Was dem Selbstbewußtsein also in der genießenden Lust als sein Wesen zum *Gegenstande* wird, ist die Ausbreitung jener leeren Wesenheiten, der reinen Einheit, des reinen Unterschiedes, und ihrer Beziehung."

43. M363; W/C242.26–29: "Einheit, Unterschied und Beziehung sind Kategorien, deren jede nichts an und für sich, nur in Beziehung auf ihr Gegenteil ist, und die daher nicht auseinander kommen können."

44. M369, W/C244–245. Compare Freud's analysis of St. Francis in *Civilization and Its Discontents*, p. 49.

45. M375–377, W/C248–250.

46. M381, W/C251–252.

47. M385, W/C254.

48. M381–382, W/C251–253.

49. M389, W/C256–257.

50. M392–393, W/C258–259.

51. M391, 382, W/C258, 252–253.

52. *Die Individualität, welche sich an und für sich selbst reell ist.*

53. Findlay's translation of "*Das geistige Tierreich und der Betrug*" as "The Spiritual Zoo and Humbug" (*Hegel: A Re-Examination*, p. 112), nicely captures the notion, in M402–404, W/C265–266, that the different real individuals are differentiated in terms of their eccentricities and "energy of will" rather in the fashion of museum pieces or animals in a zoo.

Die Sache selbst is notoriously hard to translate in this situation, primarily since a periphrastic translation that would suit parts of Section C would not suit others, and certainly would not be suitable outside this section of the text. A simple rendering of it as "the fact itself" really conveys nothing to the English reader. Miller's "the matter in hand" seems far too casual and also does not easily lend itself to translating the difference between *seine Sache* and *die Sache selbst*, as in M415, W/C273, where the real individual is revealed to be pursuing merely idiosyncratic rather than essential, universal interests. Baillie's "the real intent" seems better in that it captures the sense of real versus apparent, and because intent really is the focal issue in this particular stage of real individuality; this translation is limited, however, in that, by being usefully interpretive of this stage of the development, it is quite out of order with other stages, even within Section C, such as M420, W/C277–278, where *die absolute Sache*, the direct descendent of *die Sache selbst* is now *die sittliche Substanz*. The sense of *die Sache selbst* that must be captured is really "the Good," but such a translation would be too vague here, and would again not easily adapt to variants that would accord with the other uses of *die Sache*. "The real thing," which can be opposed to doing "one's own thing" (used by Harris) is perhaps the best one can do in English. I will leave the phrase untranslated in my text.

The concept of *die Sache selbst* is given extensive coverage by Shannon, *The Question Concerning the Factum of Experience: The Ontological Dimensions of Hegel's Thought*.

54. M398–401, W/C261–265.

55. M400, W/C262–263.

56. See M401–403, W/C263–266.

57. M409–415, W/C269–273. Compare Sartre's account of the vacillation between facticity and transcendence, in "*La mauvaise foi*" in *L'être et le néant*, pp. 82–107.

58. This was the conclusion of "Virtue and the Way of the World," and it is summed up in M394, W/C259–260.

59. M419, W/C277.

60. M419–422, W/C277–278.

61. M420–421, W/C277–278.

62. M424, W/C278–279.

63. M425, W/C280.

64. See M426, W/C281.

65. M427, W/C281.

66. See M419, W/C277.

67. M428, W/C281.

68. M429–430, W/C281–283.

69. M430–431, W/C282–284; Hegel also shows in this same analysis that, using his own notion of concrete reason, *neither* of these laws is simply self-identical, but both are, rather, intrinsically self-contradictory, but this is more than the abstract reason of the real individual can observe.

70. M434–436, W/C284–286.

71. M436–437, W/C285–287; this law that already constitutes self-conscious actuality will be what we study when we come to Chapter VI, "Spirit."

9. SPIRIT AND SKEPTICISM

1. It was through discussions with Peter Simpson that I was initially led to this interpretation of Hegel's treatment of skepticism. His *Hegel's Transcendental Induction* offers many helpful insights regarding Hegel's epistemology.

2. Hence it is hard to take seriously older "interpretations" of Hegel that did not recognize him to be involved in an epistemological endeavour or to be responding to skeptical challenges. Such interpretations are discussed and challenged in Michael Forster, *Hegel and Skepticism*, especially ch. 6.

3. The differences between modern and ancient skepticism, and Hegel's relationship to these differences, is substantially discussed in Forster, *Hegel and Skepticism*, especially ch. 1. Forster discusses reasons (derived from Hegel) for considering modern skepticism to be less skeptical than that of the ancients, especially on pp. 11, 13–15, 17, and 25–27. Forster also catalogues Hegel's views on skepticism as they are presented throughout his writings.

4. See, for example, Diogenes Laertius, 9.78–89. The question-begging character of the selection of criteria is better articulated in the five modes of Agrippa.

5. See M205, W/C142–143.

6. M205, W/C142–143.

7. M205–207, W/C142–144; compare Aristotle on the common power of sensing (*On the Soul* III.2). Though Forster rightly notes that Hegel discerns a self-contradictory character to skepticism, he is not successful in identifying this self-contradiction in a compelling manner; see *Hegel and Skepticism*, pp. 39–40. His discussion of Hegel's response to skepticism is primarily to be found on pp. 107–108. Forster maintains that Hegel is not obliged to answer the modern skeptic (p. 103), which is a claim that sits oddly with Hegel's specification of the need for philosophy to provide the natural consciousness with a "ladder to the absolute" (M26, W/C19–20); Forster does take up this notion in his discussion of the distinctive character of the *Phenomenology of Spirit* and its response to skepticism (pp. 161–170). For more on this theme, see chapter 7 in this book.

8. Compare J. G. Fichte, *Science of Knowledge*, 2nd introduction.

9. M437, W/C286–287.

10. In the sections "Reason as Lawgiver" and "Reason as Testing Laws." These sections are helpfully discussed by Brian Mackintosh, "From Reason to History in the *Phenomenology of Spirit*."

11. Contra Jonathan Robinson, *Duty and Hypocrisy in Hegel's Phenomenology of Mind: An Essay in the Real and Ideal*, who portrays Hegel as a reductive empiricist on this matter.

12. See David Ciavatta, "Hegel on the Family," ch. 1.

13. M177, W/C127. This theme of the "I that is We" is profitably studied throughout Robert R. Williams, *Recognition: Fichte and Hegel on the Other*.

14. M354, W/C236–237.

15. M347, W/C233.

16. M355, W/C237.

17. M356, W/C237–238. Compare Heidegger, *Being and Time*, sect. 27.

18. M444, W/C291.

19. On this opposition of natural causality and freedom in human experience, see especially Kant's third antinomy: *Critique of Pure Reason*, A 444–453, B 472–481. (I have considered the significance of this antinomy in some detail in chapter 4 of this book.)

20. See, for example, M463, W/C303–304.

21. See M349, W/C234.

22. See M473, W/C311–312.

23. See M476, W/C315–316.

24. M488, W/C323–324.

25. M499, W/C331.

26. M491, W/C326.

27. Compare Lewis P. Hinchman, *Hegel's Critique of the Enlightenment*, p. 173.

28. M597, W/C395.

10. THE CONTRADICTIONS OF MORAL LIFE

1. A helpful discussion of the debates regarding Hegel's criticism of Kant is C. Allen Speight, "The Metaphysics of Morals and Hegel's Critique of Kantian Ethics."

2. M621, W/C408.

3. R. Z. Friedman, "Hypocrisy and the Highest Good: Hegel on Kant's Transition from Morality to Religion." H. S. Harris, *Hegel's Ladder*.

4. The points I will make here can most easily be found throughout the first two chapters of the *Groundwork for the Metaphysics of Morals*. The argument that our very capacity to enter into discussion about duty already makes us subject to duty could also be found in the opening sections of the *Critique of Practical Reason*. See also *Critique of Pure Reason*, A551/B579, A547/B575. For discussion, see Sally Sedgwick, "Metaphysics and Morality in Kant and Hegel," esp. pp 309–310.

5. I take this to be the core of the argument in M621–3, 628, 630, W/C408–410, 412–414; cf. M602, W/C397–398.

6. These themes are discussed in M626–8, W/C411–13; cf. M606, W/C401. My argument will also draw on Hegel's discussion of "Law-Giving Reason" in Chapter V, "Reason," M419–428, W/C277–281.

7. On the difficulties this analogy to nature poses for this formulation of the moral law, see Gregory Recco, "The Experience of Analogy."

8. See M424–426, W/C278–281.

9. See M630, W/C413–14. This problem is another version of the problem of schematization that Kant addresses in the *Critique of Pure Reason*, A137/B176–A147/B187. Compare the need for the slave to interpret the orders of the master; M194–96, W/C134–36. See also Aquinas, *Summa Theologiae*, I q. 75 a. 5 resp., and Plato, *Phaedo*, 99b. This is the real significance of Hegel's claim that Kant's categorical imperative is "formalist" and therefore "empty." Attempts to defend Kant against this charge tend to stress the real role of empirical content in Kant's ethics, especially as found in the *Metaphysics of Morals*; see, for example, Henry Allison, "On a Presumed Gap in the Derivation of the Categorical Imperative," p. 143. As Sally Sedgwick has

rightly pointed out (in "Metaphysics and Morality in Kant and Hegel," especially pp. 312–314), such defenses miss the point, for it is precisely the dualism of form and content that is the object of Hegel's challenge.

10. That Hegel's ultimate criticism of Kant addresses its dualistic nature is stressed by Sally Sedgwick in "Metaphysics and Morality in Kant and Hegel," passim.

11. See M606–609, 626–629, W/C401–402, 411–413. Compare Aquinas, *Summa Theologiae*, I, q. 76 a. 1 resp.

12. The third antinomy is in the *Critique of Pure Reason*, A445/B473–A451/B479. The significance of this antinomy for our understanding the rationality of nature is especially the theme of the "Critique of Teleological Judgment" in the *Critique of Judgment*.

13. A gesture repeated in Wilfrid Sellars, "Empiricism and the Philosophy of Mind," and Donald Davidson, "Mental Events."

14. F. W. J. Schelling, *System of Transcendental Idealism*, pp. 10–12; *System des transzendentalen Idealismus*, pp. 15–19.

15. Compare Sally Sedgwick, "Metaphysics and Morality in Kant and Hegel," pp. 320–321. On "Mind" as the very sense of the particularities of the real, see John McDowell, *Mind and World*.

11. SELFHOOD, CONSCIENCE, AND DIALECTIC

1. M178–184, W/C127–129. The most substantial study of recognition in Hegel is Robert R. Williams, *Recognition: Fichte and Hegel on the Other*. See also Andreas Wildt, *Autonomie und Anerkennung: Hegel's Moralitätskritik im Lichte seiner Fichte-Rezeption*.

2. M177: "What still lies ahead for consciousness is the experience of what Spirit is—this absolute substance which is the unity of the different independent self-consciousnesses which, in their opposition, enjoy perfect freedom and independence: 'I' that is 'We' and 'We' that is 'I'" (trans. Miller); W/C127, lines 19–24: "Was für das Bewußtsein weiter wird, ist die Erfahrung, was der Geist ist, diese absolute Substanz, welche in der vollkommenen Freiheit und Selbstständigkeit ihres Gegensatzes, nämlich verschiedener für sich seiender Selbstbewußtsein, die Einheit derselben ist; Ich, das Wir, und Wir, das Ich ist."

3. In this first section I will develop the logic of selfhood that is worked through phenomenologically in Hegel's Chapter IV, "Self-Consciousness."

4. Living out this one-sided view is "life" and "desire," analyzed in the unnumbered first section of Chapter IV, M167–177, W/C120–127.

5. It is the desiring self's coming to learn this lesson that is described in Chapter IV, Section A, "Independence and Dependence of Self-Consciousness," M178–196, W/C127–136.

6. The self-conscious taking up of this facet of self-conscious selfhood is the life of "Stoicism," M197–201, W/C136–140.

7. That the dynamic of self-conscious selfhood revolves around the concept of recognition is articulated in M178–184, W/C127–129.

8. That the logic of self-consciousness culminates in a dynamic of real and apparent selfhood is the point of the section called "Unhappy Consciousness," M207–230, W/C144–156. The key to the interpretation of this oft-misunderstood section of the

Phenomenology of Spirit is found in M210, W/C145–146, where Hegel lays out the entire logical dynamic of unhappy consciousness in terms of the three essential forms through which unhappy consciousness develops. In the remainder of the section, however, Hegel considers only the first two of these relations, while the third is the proper subject-matter of the remainder of the book. Confusing the last *page* of Chapter IV with the *logical* end of the dynamic of unhappy consciousness is a mistake made by almost all commentators. Even Hyppolite, who, in *Genèse et Structure de la Phénoménologie de l'Esprit de Hegel,* rightly notes the primacy of unhappy consciousness, and who notes the triad of M210, still confuses the concluding paragraphs of the chapter with the culmination of the logical dynamic (see vol. 1, pp. 184, 194, 205–208). Two of the most extreme misreadings are Shklar, *Freedom and Independence: A Study of the Political Ideas of Hegel's Phenomenology of Mind,* who does not see any essential connection between the logic of unhappy consciousness and the logical dynamic of self-consciousness per se and consequently draws the disastrous conclusion that for Hegel it makes no difference whether God is known as Father, Son, or Holy Spirit (pp. 66, 93), thus completely missing the significance of the triadic form of unhappy consciousness outlined in M210; and Kojève who, throughout *Introduction à la Lecture de Hegel,* models the dynamic of selfhood on the dualistic logic of master and slave, thus forever precluding his analysis from comprehending the essentially triadic dynamic of spirit. It is probably Findlay's discussion of the transcendental dimension of the ego in *Hegel: A Re-examination* that comes closest to appreciating the dynamic of real and apparent selfhood that is the substance of unhappy consciousness and the culmination of the logic of self-consciousness (pp. 39–52).

9. And, as we shall see, to become scientific in knowing the world (but, of course, this is just an implication of the first, since the world is also my "self").

10. This is *Sittlichkeit* or the society of "true spirit" in Section A of Chapter VI of the *Phenomenology of Spirit,* M444–483, W/C291–320.

11. This is the world of *Bildung* in its two forms of the world of faith and the world of the enlightenment in Section B of Chapter VI of the *Phenomenology of Spirit,* M484–595, W/C320–394.

12. This will be *Moralität,* whose dynamic is found in Section C of Chapter VI of the *Phenomenology of Spirit,* M596–671, W/C394–442.

13. M632–671, W/C415–442.

14. This could be called the *material condition.*

15. This could be called the *formal condition.*

16. Where the particularity provided the material condition *for the conscientious action,* and the universality provided the formal condition *for the conscientious action,* singularity could be said to provide the moment of *activity;* this synthesizing action thus initiated is the *self*-conditioned (that is, "absolute") self-activity of the *individual.*

17. Compare Hegel's discussion of "*hic Rhodus, hic saltus*" in the preface to the *Philosophy of Right.*

18. Pinkard, "Freedom and Social Categories in Hegel's Ethics," especially pp. 213, 221ff., argues that Hegel's response to Kant primarily amounts to using *Sittlichkeit* to provide the proper objects of will that Kantian formalism cannot provide; this focus on the objects of will is right, but it is incomplete if "object" here is construed in abstraction from the method of evaluation of the object. See also Kolb, *The Critique of Pure Modernity: Hegel, Heidegger and After,* pp. 99–100. Here he argues that custom

(that is, the institutionalized structures of recognition) provides the objective content for the self-determination of the rational will; again on p. 101: "the rational content of the social whole is to be found within its structures of mutual recognition."

19. While body, that is, a *particular* involvement in existence, has traditionally been seen to preclude access to the universal, with respect to being, knowing, or doing, we here see clearly that Hegel's project is rooted in the rejection of this notion of the "taint" of particularity—of bias—and is engaged in generating universality *concretely* on the basis of particularity.

20. Supposedly spoken in the speech at the Diet of Worms, April 18, 1521; see Bainton, *Here I Stand: A Life of Martin Luther*, pp. 144–145.

21. Insofar as these judgments are *necessary*, they achieve for conscientious subjectivity the equivalent of Kantian objectivity.

22. This is the shape of consciousness studied by Hegel under the name of "the beautiful soul." See chapter 14 in this book for further consideration of "the beautiful soul."

23. Here we are addressing that moment of conscience that is the self as necessarily already guilty or "evil"; our account will be concluded when we develop the last moment of conscience, which is the moment of forgiveness that itself derives from the concept of conscience as necessarily evil. It is by developing this last moment of forgiveness that we will be enabled to make the transition to absolute knowing.

24. See Hinchman, *Hegel's Critique of the Enlightenment*, p. 171: "to be a self and to be moral or conscientious are one and the same."

25. See Hinchman, *Hegel's Critique of the Enlightenment*, p. 173: "Morality [i.e., as conscience] is thus not so much a relation between my specific situation and a universal law, but between me and you. It becomes a reality when we recognize each other as free individuals and are aware of that mutual recognition as the essence and source of our obligation." Although it is indeed true that the analysis of conscience is very much a critique of the abstractness of the Kantian-style morality as portrayed in the immediately antecedent sections of Hegel's text, it is important not to make the mistake of thinking that this program of morality has been abandoned; rather than being a rejection of the notions of autonomy and of the categorical imperative, conscience is deeply committed to these ideals. The difference between the ideal of autonomy in the moral view of the world and the ideal of autonomy in conscience is that the former is premised on an abstraction from difference (which likewise characterizes the "category" throughout Chapter V, "Reason"), whereas conscience recognizes that the autonomy of the will is achieved only in and as radical heteronomy—that is, the self must identify with its otherness. Robinson, *Duty and Hypocrisy in Hegel's Phenomenology of Mind: An Essay in the Real and Ideal*, p. 101, rightly claims that only someone who has taken the ideal of the moral point of view very seriously can be a person of conscience (although his account is in other ways problematic). Knox, "Hegel's Attitude to Kant's Ethics," and Pinkard, "Freedom and Social Categories in Hegel's Ethics," also portray Hegel as continuing in the Kantian tradition. Other excellent studies of conscience are found in Jay Bernstein, "Confession and Forgiveness: Hegel's Poetics of Action," and "Conscience and Transgression: The Exemplarity of Tragic Action," and Daniel Dahlstrom, "The Dialectic of Conscience and the Necessity of Morality in Hegel's *Philosophy of Spirit*."

26. See M666–671, W/C438–442.

27. This is seen from another angle in the impossibility of *not* acting on particular interests described in the transformation of absolute freedom into terror; see M659–666, W/C433–438; M588–589, W/C388–389. Hinchman, *Hegel's Critique of the Enlightenment*, p. 181, discusses this notion that one is always "guilty," because isolated, but that, equally, this isolation cannot be separated from social integration.

28. M666–667, W/C438–439.

29. In the dialectic of "absolute freedom and terror," M582–595, W/C385–394; see above, note 27.

30. This should be compared with the problem faced by the "spiritual animal kingdom" in Chapter V, Section C.

31. See M26: "A self having knowledge purely of itself in the absolute antithesis of itself, this pure ether as such, is the very soil where science flourishes, is knowledge in universal form" (trans. Baillie); W/C19, lines 22–24: "Das *reine* Selbsterkennen im absoluten Anderssein, dieser Äther *als solcher*, ist der Grund und Boden der Wissenschaft oder das *Wissen im Allgemeinen.*"

For the notion that systematic science is the culmination of conscience, and, in general, for the need for knowledge to take the form of science, see M793, W/C519, M805, W/C528–529, M5–6, W/C6–7, M18–25, W/C14–19, M24, W/C18, M56, W/C42, and especially M88–89, W/C68. An illuminating discussion of Hegelian absolute knowing and philosophical science is found in Lampert, "Husserl and Hegel on the Logic of Subjectivity."

32. See M27–29, W/C21–24. On this point—that Hegel's argument is that only his act of writing the *Phenomenology of Spirit* (or its equivalent) can count as the responsible, political action that lives up to the full demands of conscience—see Shklar, *Freedom and Independence*, pp. 56, 187–188, who seems to recognize that philosophy is the end of conscience, and Hinchman, *Hegel's Critique of the Enlightenment*, p. 154, who directly sees Hegel's submission of his work as the legitimate response to the task.

A comparable move is made in the *Science of Logic*, by showing how the self-criticism of the various metaphysical conceptions of self-consistency ultimate develop, on their own steam, to the notion of dialectical self-cognition as the only self-consistent form of unity.

12. THE RITUAL BASIS OF SELF-IDENTITY

1. The account of Heidegger will depend primarily on div. 1, chs. 3, 4, and 5, and div. 2, ch. 5, of *Sein und Zeit* (referred to hereafter as SZ followed by page number), translated as *Being and Time* (referred to hereafter as BT followed by page number), to sect. 15 of *Die Grundprobleme der Phänomenologie*, translated as *The Basic Problems of Phenomenology* (hereafter BPP), and "Brief über den Humanismus" (hereafter "Brief"), translated as "Letter on Humanism" (hereafter "Letter"). The account of Hegel will depend primarily on Chapters IV, VI, and VII of the *Phenomenology of Spirit*.

2. Heidegger refers to his concept of "the world" as his greatest contribution to philosophy. It is discussed in *BT* sects. 17–18, and in *BPP* sect. 15; the relation of "world" and "earth" is the focus of discussion in "Der Ursprung des Kunstwerkes," especially pp. 25–43 and 49–55, translated as "The Origin of the Work of Art," especially pp. 39–57 and 62–69.

3. Certainly Descartes himself notices this in this first meditation, for he precisely sees his task as to introduce doubt where our habits usually resist this; again, Hume adopts a similar view of normal experience in arguing that what skepticism really has to resist is the views that we adopt automatically through custom and habit. As we shall see below in the discussion of crisis, the seeds of philosophic inquiry are already laid in the very way we exist as "at home." For the theme of the roots of metaphysical inquiry in the very nature of *Da-sein*, see Frank Schalow, "Re-opening the Issue of World: Heidegger and Kant," especially pp. 191–192.

4. *BPP* 75: "Proximally and for the most part, Dasein understands itself in terms of that which it encounters in the environment and that with which it is circumspectively concerned." This is why "authenticity is an existentiell modification of *das Man*" (*BT* 168, *SZ* 130); this is *Da-sein*'s "thrownness" (*Geworfenheit*) (*BT* 174, 219–224, *SZ* 135, 175–180). Compare M26, W/C19: "*Pure* self-recognition in absolute otherness . . . is the ground and soil of Science or *knowledge in general*." This "absolute knowing" that completes Hegel's philosophical project is precisely the self-consciousness that recognizes itself as founded in a lived world that reflects its own identity.

5. W. Morriston, "Heidegger on the World," is a concise discussion of Heidegger's treatment of world in *Being and Time*. Richard Holmes, "The World according to Husserl and Heidegger," gives a good discussion of the existential-epistemological themes involved here, showing Husserl and Heidegger to be really in agreement, and doing this by way of articulating their joint response to Descartes's wax argument. See also Frank Schalow, "The Anomaly of World: From Scheler to Heidegger," and John Russon, "Embodiment and Responsibility: Merleau-Ponty and the Ontology of Nature," especially sect. 2.

6. *BT* sect. 16 discusses the way our habitual absorption in the "ready-to-hand" world can be interrupted and a reflective posture adopted, using "conspicuousness," "obstinacy," and "obtrusiveness" as phenomenological descriptions of lived crisis (*BT* 102–105, *SZ* 73–74). Compare the discussion of crisis in the basic concepts of a science (*BT* 29–31, *SZ* 9–11).

7. "Authenticity" is analyzed in *BPP* sect. 15, and *BT* div. 1, ch. 4. "Being-towards-death" is taken up in *BT* div. 2, ch. 1. "Resoluteness" is developed in *BT* div. 2, ch. 2. On the issue of the emergence of responsible self-consciousness through facing the possibility of one's own death, compare Hegel's discussion of the dynamic of the self-consciousness of the slave in M192–196, W/C133–136, and of the emergence of "Morality" following the dialectic of "Absolute Freedom and Terror," M592–598, W/C391–395.

8. On the issue of the primacy or derivativeness of authenticity, see J. Stambaugh, "An Inquiry into Authenticity and Inauthenticity in *Being and Time*," and C. B. Guignon, "Heidegger's 'Authenticity' Revisited," especially pp. 329–338.

9. *BT* 255, *SZ* 212: "Of course only as long as Dasein *is* (that is, only as long as an understanding of Being is ontically possible), 'is there' Being." See also *BT* 272–273, *SZ* 230, and "Brief," 331–333, "Letter," 214–217.

10. "Letter," 193: "Language is the house of Being"; and 206: "Language is the lighting-concealing advent of Being itself." "Brief," 311: "Die Sprache ist das Haus des Seins"; and 324: "Sprache ist lichtend-vergebende Ankunft des Seins selbst."

11. Compare Maurice Merleau-Ponty, *Phenomenology of Perception*, p. 185, who concludes his account of discourse by saying of it, "there is a mutual confirmation between myself and others."

12. See M177–178, W/C127–128, for the " 'I' that is 'we' and the 'we' that is 'I,' " and the notion that self-consciousness is achieved through recognition. A comparable dialectic of mutual recognition is outlined in Thomas Nagel, "Sexual Perversion."

13. The phenomenological analysis of this in Hegel's *Phenomenology of Spirit* leads us along two routes. First, we watch the emergence of self-conscious selfhood from the primitive desire of destructive immediate self-consciousness as it reveals itself to be necessarily already social, and to institute its identity through social habits through its own immanent dynamic. Second, we start from the established reflective ego in stoicism and see how it is driven to distinguish empirical and transcendental selfhood, and then we observe how the dynamic of this distinction, and especially of the notion of transcendental selfhood, leads equally necessarily to the need to recognize oneself in and as one's social others. In this chapter, I give only the completed statement of Hegel's position as it can be stated after one has performed the phenomenological observations that see the experiences themselves demonstrate it dialectically. The conceptual story as I articulate it here is especially indebted to the section of Chapter V, "Reason," called "The Spiritual Animal Kingdom and Deceit, or, *die Sache selbst*"; the analysis of the "Beautiful Soul," in Chapter VI, "Spirit"; and the analysis of the identity of being-for-self and being-for-other in the determinateness of the thing in Chapter II, "Perception."

14. See M437, W/C286–287, for Hegel's description of the relation to law in *Sittlichkeit*. Hegel here quotes Antigone's description of "the gods' unwritten and unfailing law": "Not now, indeed, nor yesterday, but for eternity it lives, and no man knows its origin in time" (*Antigone*, II 455–457). Compare the notion of "habitus" in Pierre Bourdieu, *Outline of a Theory of Practice*, especially p. 80, and the discussion of ritual in Clifford Geertz, *The Interpretation of Cultures*, especially p. 112.

15. Recall that this set of actions of mutual recognition in custom need not, in fact, *must* not happen reflectively. This means that, *while my actions reveal themselves to be positing an identity between myself and yourself, I do not realize this,* and continue to insist on my own independent selfhood. Roughly, Hegel's critique of the notion of the independent rational self takes the form of showing that the very acts of self-assertion that characterize the ego's positing of itself as isolated and independent are possible only in the context of a social dynamic of recognition that has sunk to the level of habit and is, consequently, not recognized as such by the reflective ego. I do not want here to pursue this critique, however, so much as to continue to build on what the life of self-consciousness must be like given this social dynamic of recognition in custom.

16. Compare Hegel, *Encyclopaedia*, sect. 552: "genuine religion and genuine religiosity emerge only from *Sittlichkeit*, and religion is the thinking *Sittlichkeit*, i.e., the *Sittlichkeit* which is becoming conscious of the free universality of its concrete essence. . . . Therefore it is vain to seek true religion and religiosity outside the *sittlich* spirit."

17. We accept to enact something that can only be called, for us, a ritual. *In so doing*, without explicitly choosing it, we take sides, make commitments; we adopt a determinate course of action, but without seeing other possibilities. See W. Morriston, "Heidegger on the World," and his discussion of *Befindlichkeit* (458): "There is no point in time when Human Being decides for the first time how it will dispose of its being, and correlatively, what sort of world it will project for itself. As soon as it *is*, it is *already* thrown into certain possibilities and cut off from others"; see BT 183, SZ 144. My account of the necessity of adopting a determinate ethnicity is a specialized case of the necessary thrownness (*Gerworfenheit*) that is an ontological characterization of *Da-*

sein. For Heidegger on "tradition" and "heritage," see C. B. Guignon, "Heidegger's 'Authenticity' Revisited," pp. 335–336. My use of Hegel to interpret Heidegger should be compared especially with *BT* 434–439, *SZ* 382–387 (sect. 74). Compare *BT* 41: "Dasein has grown up both into and in a traditional way of interpreting itself"; *SZ* 20: "Das Dasein . . . in eine überkommene Daseinsauslegung hinein—und in ihr aufgewachsen." For a somewhat different interpretation of this sentence than the one my essay suggests, see Charles Scott, "The De-Struction of Being and Time in *Being and Time*," 97.

18. Compare Aristotle, *Nicomachean Ethics*, II.1.

19. On the theme of ritual repetition as the foundation of emotional life, compare Freud's definition of emotions in terms of repetition in "The Unconscious," and Heidegger's discussion of repetition and *Befindlichkeit*, *BT* 388, *SZ* 339. See also Charles Guignon, "Moods in Heidegger's *Being and Time*," especially p. 236.

20. Regarding this notion of ritual, compare Walter Burkert, *Homo Necans: The Anthropology of Ancient Greek Sacrificial Ritual and Myth*, p. 23: "Since the work of Sir Julian Huxley and Konrad Lorenz, biology has defined *ritual* as a behavioral pattern that has lost its primary function—present in its unritualized mode—but which persists in a new function, that of communication." It is how this ritualized activity functions as communication that will now be the focus of our concerns. Regarding the notion of the sacred, see the excellent discussion of the roots of the concept of religion in Kenneth L. Schmitz, "Philosophy of Religion and the Redefinition of Philosophy," especially pp. 58–59.

21. "Anticipative horizons" refers to Husserl's account of the dynamics of conscious life, according to which meaningfulness—determinateness—in experience is always contextualized by our projects, and that consequently experience always operates according to a structure of anticipation and fulfillment. In other words, an experience is meaningful to the extent that it answers to projected possibilities (anticipations) established through past experience, and new experiences in turn open up possibilities for meaning that subsequent experiences will fulfill. These anticipations, however, do not lay out determinately in advance all the actual meanings that could follow, but rather project directions that point to possible developments, and it is how subsequent experience engages these indeterminate horizons that retrospectively makes the anticipative structures determinate. See the concise discussion in *Cartesianische Meditationen*, pp. 46–48, translated as *Cartesian Meditations*, pp. 44–46. An excellent account of intentionality in Husserl that pivots on this notion of the dynamics of anticipation and fulfillment is Jay Lampert, "Husserl's Account of Syncategorematic Terms: The Problem of Representing the Synthetic Connections That Underlie Meanings."

22. On this notion of the act of taking-up that retrospectively determines the nature of a situation that was prospectively indeterminate, compare Bernard P. Dauenhauer, "Heidegger, Spokesman for the Dweller," especially p. 190 on the nature of the "leap" that "bridges" what, prior to the act of bridging, did not exist as fixed termini, and Jay Lampert, "Husserl and Hegel on the Logic of Subjectivity," which focuses on the logic of "referring back," by which experiential determinateness retrospectively confers on its conditions the possibility of being its conditions. Wayne D. Owens, "The Way-Making Movement of Thinking: Heidegger and George's 'The Word,'" discusses retrospection in relation to language (pp. 136–138), and the need for thinking to follow the path laid out pre-reflectively by language (p. 146). Parallel themes are also taken up in

the discussion of the concept of race in Anthony Appiah, "The Uncompleted Argument: Du Bois and the Illusion of Race."

23. Compare Hegel's discussion of the experience of the world as governed by divine law with the "ethical substance," M445, 448–449, W/C291–292, 293.

24. As Werner Sollors, "Introduction: The Invention of Ethnicity," puts it: "Ethnic groups are typically imagined as if they were natural, real, eternal, stable and static units. They seem to be always already in existence" (pp. xiii–xiv).

25. See C. B. Guignon, "Heidegger's 'Authenticity' Revisited," p. 333: "Only because we have been initiated into a shared 'we-world' can we handle ourselves in coherent normalized ways" (in the context of discussing authenticity and *das Man*). For the primacy of religion in Hegel's philosophy, see Emil Fackenheim, *The Religious Dimension in Hegel's Thought*, pp. 8–10 and *passim*.

26. This is not to deny the importance of this phenomenon studied in Rudolph Otto, *The Idea of the Holy: An Inquiry into the Non-rational Factor in the Idea of the Divine and Its Relation to the Rational*; indeed, this experience is, I would argue, central to the *authentic* appropriation of one's own religion. On this notion, compare the discussion in Schmitz, "Philosophy of Religion and the Redefinition of Philosophy," pp. 58–59. My point is rather that the experience of *mysterium tremendum et fascinans* does not capture what is *logically primary* in religious lie. Indeed, I am defining faith as the ground that makes *possible* such an experience. It is in our self-conscious attempts to be conscientious in our faith and to respond to the integrity of the demands that it makes upon us that this experience arises.

27. Hans-Georg Gadamer, in *Truth and Method*, p. 432, defines language along Heideggerean lines simply as "being that can be understood"; *Wahrheit und Methode*, p. 450: "Sein, das verstanden werden kann, ist Sprache." Gadamer discusses this remark in "Aesthetics and Hermeneutics," pp. 103–104.

28. See *BT* 408–415, *SZ* 356–364.

29. On the issue of the integrity of the projects of science, religion, etc., compare Eric von der Luft's discussion of the "uncompromising sincerity" of the enterprises of philosophy, religion, and art in "Would Hegel Have Liked to Burn Down All the Churches and Replace Them with Philosophical Academies?" p. 45. See also Hegel, *Faith and Knowledge*, p. 55: "Enlightened Reason won a glorious victory over what it believed, in its limited conception of religion, to be faith as opposed to Reason. Yet seen in a clear light the victory comes to no more than this: the positive element with which Reason busied itself to do battle, is no longer religion, and victorious Reason is no longer Reason."

30. Notice, then, that issues such as bloodlines, skin color, and so on are not *in themselves* definitive of ethnic participation, but are such only insofar as they are themselves ritually recognized; that is, there are no *natural* bases for ethnicity. Compare the treatment of the concept of "race" in Appiah, "The Uncompleted Argument: Du Bois and the Illusion of Race." See also Orlando Patterson, "Context and Choice in Ethnic Allegiance: A Theoretical Framework and Caribbean Case Study," who defines ethnicity as: "that condition wherein certain members of a society, in a given social context, choose to emphasize as their most meaningful basis of primary, extrafamilial identity certain assumed cultural, national, or somatic traits" (308). He continues, "the fact that ethnicity is a chosen form of identification cannot be overemphasized. An ethnic group only exists when members consider themselves to belong to such a group:

a conscious sense of belonging is critical" (309). I think this to be a good approach, depending on how explicit the "choice" and "conscious sense of belonging" are taken to be, for my argument about self-consciousness would accept a sense of belonging that makes itself explicit only when challenged, and my account would also demand that, because the definition is in terms of *perceived* identities, one could be *legitimately* included in an (other's) ethnic group *from another's point of view* even though one did not so regard oneself. On this last theme, see Donald L. Horowitz, "Ethnic Identity."

31. On how to understand "rationality" in the context of the Hegelian dialectic of recognition, see chapter 8 of this book.

32. By no means do I intend to suggest either that this is easy or that it is always in fact possible for the relevant agents concerned; my intention here is rather to identify the proper conceptual ground for understanding what is really at stake in such situations, and what is therefore necessary in principle. The argument about recognition also established why in principle it would be possible to succeed here *in ideal conditions*, but this, again, does not guarantee for any situation that mutually fulfilling relations can be harmoniously and comfortably achieved. Compare Barbara Tedlock's account of her process of initiation into dream rituals in the context of her anthropological research in "The New Anthropology of Dreaming"; cf. Graeme Nicholson, "The Politics of Heidegger's Rectoral Address." Compare also the notion of women "apprenticing" with other women in contemporary feminist discourses.

33. See *BT* 207, *SZ* 163; compare Hans-Georg Gadamer, "Man and Language," p. 65.

34. I use this expression to invoke Hegel's use of the term *Vorstellung*, which he uses to describe religious practices that are not recognized for the communal acts of self-consciousness that they really are; see M677–678, W/C444–445.

35. *Metaphysics*, A.1.981b7–9; cf. *Posterior Analytics*, II.19 and *De Anima*, III.4. Cf. John Russon, "Aristotle's Animative Epistemology."

36. What I articulate in the language of initiation and interpretation could also be articulated in the language of forgiveness. See chapter 11 of this book and Dauenhauer, "Heidegger, Spokesman for the Dweller," p. 194. See also von der Luft, "Would Hegel Have Liked to Burn Down All the Churches and Replace Them with Philosophical Academies?" who considers the primacy, for Hegel, of the notion of reconciliation (*Versöhnung*); a propos this notion of forgiveness, von der Luft notes: "every aspect of spirit, however repulsive, must be given its due. This is what *Aufhebung* means" (52).

37. Cf. Jacques Derrida, "Structure, Sign, and Play in the Discourse of the Human Sciences," p. 282, on the inescapability of ethnocentrism; my argument is indeed that ethnocentrism is inescapable, but that any ethnicity has as its animating principle the drive to universality through mutual interpretation. Interpretation is fruitfully discussed in Charles Taylor, "Understanding and Ethnocentricity." As in my account, Taylor's account focuses on interpretation as a dialogue in which *both* participants achieve their self-definition through the dialogue. The crucial point is on page 125: "Aren't we unavoidably committed to ethnocentricity? No, I want to argue, we are not. The error in this view is to hold that the language of a cross-cultural theory has to be either theirs or ours. . . . But as a matter of fact, while challenging their language of self-understanding, we may also be challenging ours. . . . In fact, it will almost always be the case that the adequate language in which we can understand another society is not our language of understanding, or theirs, but rather what one could call a language of perspicuous contrast. This would be a language in which we could formulate both their

way of life and ours as alternative possibilities in relation to some human constants at work in both" (and see especially his concluding paragraph on p. 133). It is these "human constants" that I have worked to disclose in this chapter: the phenomenological account of self-consciousness gives us the adequate logic within which to comprehend self-consciousness, and this logic is unrevisable, even if our cross-cultural dialogue transforms our ethnic identities. It is for this reason that I disagree with Vincent A. McCarthy's claim, in *Quest for a Philosophical Jesus: Christianity and Philosophy in Rousseau, Kant, Hegel, and Schelling,* that Hegel's philosophy should have led him to reject any final theology (p. 159). My argument, on the contrary, is that it is precisely the finality of theology that allows for the legitimacy of a plurality of religious traditions and systems.

13. VISION AND IMAGE IN HEGEL'S SYSTEM

1. *The Difference between Fichte's and Schelling's System of Philosophy,* p. 119. See *Science of Logic,* E 49, 404–405, G I.43, II.30–32.

2. "Das reine Selbsterkennen im absoluten Anderssein." M26, W/C19. In quoting the *Phenomenology,* I will consistently alter Miller's translation of *Begriff* from "Notion" to "concept."

3. This and the following quotation are from *Philosophy of Mind,* trans. William Wallace and A. V. Miller, p. 78; *Enzyclopädie der Philosophischen Wissenschaften im Grundrisse,* p. 104.

4. Hegel's account here does not ultimately do full justice to his own principles. He knows in general that any coming to unity transforms the identity of its constituent parts, but he does not here treat the various sense modalities as undergoing redefinition from their participation in a unified sensing subject: he needs to see that (as Merleau-Ponty puts it in *Phenomenology of Perception,* pp. 207–215), we see sounds and hear colors. Likewise, to say we see only the two dimensions, and so on, is just phenomenologically inaccurate, and it is related to an analytic mistake that Hegel criticizes in the preface to the *Phenomenology,* namely, that anatomy studies a corpse and mistakes its object for the human body. Hegel's account is reasonable for what each sensory modality is singly as a sensitive system, but the senses do not function singly, so he should not talk of actual sight this way, for the senses exist this way only for dismembering reflection. It is also important for Hegel to remember that when he says sight does not affect its object but leaves it at peace, this is a claim about how things work within the parameters established by sight; metaphysically, sight does alter its object, and this is precisely the point of the Aristotelian epistemology/ontology that Hegel adopts here; that is, sensation is a simultaneous actualization of seer and seen: we affect the object in that we answer its call to be seen, and thereby fulfill it. For an account of vision that Hegel should endorse, see Varela, Palacios, and Thompson, "Ways of Coloring: Comparative Color Vision as a Case-Study for Cognitive Science."

5. *Philosophy of Mind, Zusatz* to sect. 448, p. 197; *Enzyclopädie,* p. 251.

6. *Faith and Knowledge,* p. 57.

7. On this point, and the sense in which even reasoning is rooted in confirmation by others, see chapter 8 of this book.

8. This is particularly illustrated through his analysis of the French Revolution, *Phenomenology,* M582–595, W/C385–394. The revolution is based on the principle of universal rational equality, which means it grants recognition to—accepts as legiti-

mate—individuals *qua* rational, which here means *qua* egos abstracted from all conditioning circumstance, that is, abstracted from all particularity; but only particularity gives distinct identity. Consequently any distinct identity, by being non-universal, runs counter to the principle of universal rationality that drives the revolution. The revolution is thus the foe of any distinct individuality, and this abstract goal of universal rational freedom thus reveals its truth in the terror in which all are immediately guilty. See chapter 11 of this book.

9. This is the truth behind "the unhappy consciousness," which Hegel analyzes as the culminating form of self-conscious selfhood; it is the third form of the relationship that Hegel lays out in M210, W/C145–146, and that is illustrated in M231, W/C157.

10. Hegel's study of the logic of reflection is not primarily a study in epistemology, for he is interested in a type of organization of elements that is equally present in beings other than self-conscious agents; life, for example, demonstrates the logic of reflection (and, indeed, the more sophisticated logic of "the idea"), as does any relationship of a whole and its parts. Still, it is in cognition that reflection has its paradigmatic realization, and it is as a portrayal of a cognitive stance that I will present reflection. See *Science of Logic*, E 404, G II.30–31.

11. *Science of Logic* E 404.15–18, G II.30.12–15.

12. *Science of Logic* E 403.-20—.-19, G II.29.10–12.

13. *Science of Logic* (translation modified), E 403.-8—404.1, G II.29.-14—.-6.

14. Compare Merleau-Ponty's discussion of the "tacit cogito" in *The Visible and the Invisible*, pp. 170–171, 175–176, 179, and in *Phenomenology of Perception*, e.g., p. 402; see also p. 394 for his related discussion of *Fundierung*.

15. Theodor W. Adorno, in "Skoteinos, or How to Read Hegel," makes the excellent parallel point that just as much as Hegel's philosophy criticizes the content of rationalism, so is Hegel's style anti-Cartesian. The reflective ideal demands a clear and distinct presentation of a clear and distinct idea (pp. 96–99), but Hegel's text offers instead a demand for an active student who does not "simply look on" (p. 94) but instead becomes immersed in the obscurities of Hegel's text and, adopting a critical stance, works to "illuminate him from behind" (p. 92). See pp. 122–123, 145. For Adorno's own treatment of the images of clarity and enlightenment, see the note to pp. 96–97.

16. Compare Plato, *Republic*, book VII, 518 d 3–4, on education as "the art of turning around." In general, the account I am here giving of the relation between Hegel's argument and his visual images could equally serve as a commentary on the analogy of the sun in *Republic* books 6 and 7.

17. M444–476, W/C291–316. Strictly speaking, it is only Hegel's allusions to *Antigone* in the *Phenomenology* that we are here considering; his explicit analysis of the tragedy in his *Aesthetics* has slightly different concerns.

I refer to human social life that is "free" to indicate that this is a situation premised on equality of recognition between social members, and not a relationship of master and slave, which Hegel calls not a matter of freedom (*Freiheit*) but a matter of dependence and independence (*Unselbstständigkeit und Selbstständigkeit*); see the titles of *Phenomenology*, Chapter IV, Section A (before M178, W/C127) and Section B (before M197, W/C136). On freedom as equality of recognition, see chapter 11 in this book.

18. I have taken this up directly in chapter 5.

19. M449, 450, W/C293–294.

20. M457, W/C299.

21. M460, W/C301.39–40.

22. M469, W/C309.22.

23. M477, W/C316.12–13.

24. Compare Pierre Bourdieu, *Outline of a Theory of Practice*, p. 72, on the need "to pass from the *opus operatum* to the *modus operandi*, . . . to the principle of the production of this observed order."

25. This and the preceding passage are from *Reason in History*, pp. 13–14; *Vorlesungen über die Philosophie der Geschichte*, pp. 23–24. These concepts of "the concrete" and of "development" are also given special focus in Hegel's introduction to the *Lectures on the History of Philosophy*, in Part A, "The Notion of the History of Philosophy," Section 2, "Explanatory Remarks upon the Definition of the History of Philosophy."

26. Consequently, we can see that the very attempt to separate form and content itself is an approach to form that does specify a content. Hegel discusses this in *Phenomenology of Spirit*, Chapter V, "Reason," in the section of "Observing Reason" entitled "Observation of Self-Consciousness in Its Purity and in Its Relation to External Actuality: Logical and Psychological Laws," M299–300, W/C201–202. See also *Science of Logic*, E 43–45ff., G I.36–38ff.

27. Indeed, this articulation is what each of Hegel's systematic books does: the *Phenomenology* articulates its own principle only through the exposition of that which this principle explains; the *Logic* develops the idea of logic only as it develops its determinations; the *Philosophy of Nature* shows how the very concept of nature comes to be articulated only through the development of the determinations of nature; and so on.

28. To have the experience of other selves (*as* selves) is to have the experience that I am subject to the judgment of others, just as they, and the rest of the stuff of the world, are subject to my judgment, my consciousness. The presence within my experience of other self-conscious selves means, thus, that my actions in the world are always necessarily public. *What I do* defines who I am, but it is not simply up to me to decide what I did. My actions and my experience *are* the very stuff of my existence, and *who I really am* is whatever the source is that will adequately explain this. We are what our actions show us to be, and one of the most important sides of our action—what makes it what it is, when we are in a social context—is how it has impact on others. But if one's substance, one's "stuff," itself is all "public domain" material, then what it is of which the real "I" is the source has its reality established publicly. What that stuff *is* is how it functions in the experience of those others who equally have it as their substance. It is all of our substance, and one's real self will be that which is the explanatory source of *what it turns out to be* (or to have been) in this public context. But that means *my reality* is established socially, and whether my intent or my interpretation—who I *appear* to be—is who I *really* am depends on my ability to interpret and intend what actually is. It is when I see things as my fellows must see them that my view of me is right. On these points, see especially *Phenomenology*, Chapter V, pt. C, sect. A, "The Spiritual Animal Kingdom and Deceit, or, *die Sache selbst*."

29. Compare Bourdieu, *Outline of a Theory of Practice*, p. 22, on the double goal in rule-following of both accomplishing the manifest objective of the rule and winning the honor of living up to the rules, and p. 81, on the notion that "interpersonal" relations are never strictly "individual to individual" but involve the mediation of a sense of the objects that is communally established through traditional systems of practice.

30. Compare Bourdieu on the notion of "habitus," which he defines as "systems of durable, transposable *dispositions*, structured structures predisposed to function as structuring structures, that is, as principles of the generation and structuring of practices and representations which can be objectively 'regulated' and 'regular' without in any way being the product of obedience to rules" (p. 72). See especially p. 80: "one of the fundamental effects of the orchestration of habitus is the production of a commonsense world endowed with the *objectivity* secured by consensus on the meaning (sens) of practices and the world, in other words, the harmonization of agents' experiences and continuous reinforcement that each of them receives from the expression, individual or collective (in festivals, for example), improvised or programmed (commonplaces, sayings), of similar or identical experiences." See also Clifford Geertz, *The Interpretation of Cultures*, p. 112: "For it is in ritual—that is, consecrated behavior—that this conviction that religious conceptions are veridical and that religious directives are sound is somehow generated. It is in some sort of ceremonial form . . . that the moods and motivations which sacred symbols induce in men and the general conceptions of the order of existence which they formulate for men meet and reinforce each other." Hegel's understanding of the origins of ritual in the dialectic of recognition has the advantage of being able to answer the question of motivation for religious participation that Geertz (p. 109) describes as being "of all the problems surrounding attempts to conduct anthropological analysis of religion . . . the one that has perhaps been most troublesome and therefore the most often avoided." Like Geertz (pp. 109–110), Hegel locates the source in a cultural demand for faith in its values and images.

31. See Geertz, p. 113, for a comparable distinction.

32. M677–682, 788, W/C444–449, 516–517.

33. Precisely this determinateness is the core of the self-contradiction of religion. The very thesis of religion, as I have here argued, is that it serves to establish a shared recognition, a communal self-consciousness. Yet precisely what the determinateness of a society's ritual practices creates is a situation in which those who do not practice the same rituals cannot be recognized. Consequently, the very same practices that make a shared self-consciousness possible within a community preclude its possibility outside the community. Religious rituals thus establish boundaries between communities and actually hinder their own constitutive project of establishing a universal self-consciousness. This last can only be done in the absolute knowing that moves beyond the insistence on the immediacy of the ritual practice, the immediacy of the image in which the spiritual self-consciousness is established, and endorses instead the mediation, the universal rationality of self-consciousness, that gives the image its power.

34. Compare Bourdieu, pp. 5–6, on why a ritual practice requires to be not understood, p. 80, on the production of a "commonsense" world, and pp. 166–167, on what "goes without saying."

35. M95, W/C71.

36. M96–100, W/C71–72.

37. M685, W/C452.

38. M686, W/C542–453. Jacques Derrida, *Glas*, offers a valuable reading of these texts. See especially pp. 237–242.

39. M687, W/C453.

40. M688, W/C453–454.

41. M748–787, W/C488–515.

42. Treating religion thus as spirit's "imagination" is Hegel's appropriation of

Aristotle's claim that all thought takes place in a *phantasm*; see Aristotle, *De Anima*, III.8.432a8–9.

43. Compare Andrew Buchwalter, "Hegel's Concept of Virtue," who shows, within the context of Hegel's *Philosophy of Right*, that Hegel's speculative return to a Greek notion of virtue cannot be understood as a rejection of the modern notion of the primacy of individual subjectivity, but is in fact premised upon the respect for individual rational autonomy; Hegel's position is thus the speculative synthesis of the otherwise opposed ideals of Enlightenment and *Sittlichkeit*. See especially pp. 552–553, 562, 576. See also chapter 5, n. 14, in this book. Adorno makes a comparable point: "But once it is acknowledged that clarity and distinctness are not mere characteristics of what is given, and are not themselves given, one can no longer evaluate the worth of knowledge in terms of how clearly and unequivocally individual items of knowledge present themselves. . . . Of course one cannot grossly neglect the demand for clarity; philosophy should not succumb to confusion and destroy the very possibility of its existence. What we should take from this is the urgent demand that the expression fit the matter expressed precisely" (p. 100).

44. See Buchwalter, pp. 563–564.

45. M177, W/C127.

46. Hegel discusses speculation in *Enzyclopädie*, sect. 82. In the *Zusatz* to this section, Hegel discusses the meaning of the word in terms of transcending what is immediately given, and in terms of uniting into a concrete totality the determinations that the reflective understanding holds in mutual alienation. Compare his discussion of speculation in *The Difference between Fichte's and Schelling's System of Philosophy*, pp. 102–103; this passage is discussed by Adorno, pp. 90–91. The reference to Aristotle is in *Enzyclopädie*, sect. 577. Here Hegel discusses how the unity of absolute mind is revealed in a duality of appearances.

47. It is derived from the Indo-European root *spek* and is cognate with the Greek *skeptomai*, from which we get such words as "skeptic," "scope," and "episcopal." It is also related to other words for "seer" such as, for example, *haruspex*, which is the name for one who looks at the entrails of animals. See *The American Heritage Dictionary of Indo-European Roots*; *Origins: A Short Etymological Dictionary of Modern English*; *A Latin Dictionary*; *Greek-English Lexicon*.

48. On the connection of *noein* with *nostos* and with the Odyssey in general, see Douglas Frame, *The Myth of Return in Early Greek Epic*.

49. *Republic*, 6.511b3–c2.

50. See *Science of Logic*, E 826–827, especially p. 826.-3 to .-4, G II.551–553.

51. Hegel's project thus dovetails with Geertz's "semiotic" approach to culture, according to which "the aim of anthropology is the enlargement of human discourse" (p. 14).

52. See Geertz, p. 13: "We [anthropologists] are not . . . seeking either to become natives . . . or to mimic them. . . . We are seeking, in the widened sense of the word in which it encompasses very much more than talk, to converse with them, a matter a great deal more difficult, and not only with strangers, than is commonly recognized." In this project we cannot simply trust our own sense of what another's images "obviously" mean, and *neither can we immediately trust the account that is given by the reflective ego of the other*: that account is not the truth of these images, but is itself part of the system of images—a piece of evidence, but not the solution. Compare Bourdieu, pp. 18–19, on why the vision of a native of some culture upon that culture is not necessarily adequate;

in particular, such an "informant's" discourse "tends to draw attention to the most remarkable 'moves' . . . rather than to the principle from which these moves and all equally possible moves can be generated and which, belonging to the universe of the undisputed, most often remain in the implicit state."

53. Compare Adorno, p. 94: "Hegel's logic is not only his metaphysics; it is also his politics."

54. Compare Geertz's discussion of the difference between the religious, the scientific, the commonsense, and the aesthetic perspectives in terms of "seeing," on pp. 110–112.

14. DECIDING TO READ

1. See especially Jacques Derrida, *Glas*, pp. 5–6, 76, 198–199, and 227–228.

2. Each word implies of all others that they will not be where it is, and also more particularly differentiates itself from other comparable choices (within the same so-called paradigm).

3. Jacques Derrida, *Glas*, p. 8.

4. "Resurrection," though, has no particularly pleasant connotation here: as is well known in existentialism, the transformations in which we allow ourselves to be re-defined by the demands we find pressed upon us by our freedom are conducted in anxiety, in a process in which all our familiar guarantees and anchors are lost. Compare M78, W/C60–62 on dialectical phenomenology as the "way of despair."

5. Martin Heidegger, "A Dialogue on Language," p. 24.

6. Edmund Husserl, *Cartesian Meditations*, pp. 44–45; *Cartesianische Meditationen*, pp. 33–34.

7. We can make similar points about the nature of determinateness with respect to time. Necessarily we are always already *in medias res*. A presence, a determinateness, can never be first: by virtue of being necessarily logically mediated (e.g., by the categories of being and nothing, or by an intrinsic relation of already differentiated "elements" that are other to each other) it must already *have* begun, it is already second. It is thus already mediated by, points to, a past, even a logical one, and announces itself as therefore not fully present. Indeed, by being situated already with respect to other possibilities (the very notion of the horizon) it effectively says "you can only get here from there," meaning it *is* only if those others already *are*: determinateness claims about itself that it can never be first. Thus every determinateness, in its very being, points outside itself, defines itself as already situated. It already has a being that is spread out. The past thus exists as something projected backward from the present in order to make itself possible: it is the past *of* the present, the making determinate of which exists only as a future project. Compare Hegel's discussion of the "now" in M106–107, W/C75. On memory as a promise, cf. Jacques Derrida, "But, beyond . . . (Open Letter to Anne McClintock and Rob Nixon)," p. 359. On the inadequacy of the categories of being and nothing to conceptualize a beginning or any becoming, see *Science of Logic*, E82–108, especially 82–83, G82–115, especially 82–83. Dieter Henrich, "Anfang und Methode der Logik," is a helpful commentary.

8. Compare Henri Bergson, *Matter and Memory*, p. 36: "that which distinguishes it as a *present* image, as an objective reality, from a *represented* image is the necessity which obliges it to act through every one of its points upon all the points of all other images, to transmit the whole of what it receives, to oppose to every action an equal and

contrary reaction, to be, in short, merely a road by which pass, in every direction, the modifications propagated throughout the immensity of the universe."

9. This structure of retrospective recognition is studied in detail throughout Maurice Merleau-Ponty, *Phenomenology of Perception*, and Gilles Deleuze and Félix Guattari, *Anti-Oedipus: Capitalism and Schizophrenia*. See also Jay Lampert, "Husserl and Hegel on the Logic of Subjectivity."

10. This is the point made throughout G. W. F. Hegel, *Lectures on the Philosophy of Religion*, vol. III, *The Consummate Religion*.

11. M658–660, W/C432–434. See also M7–11, W/C7–10, for a discussion of criticisms of systematic science (primarily "intuitionism") that closely resemble the logic of the beautiful soul. See M795, W/C520–521, for the notion that it is in the response to the beautiful soul (the dialectic of evil and forgiveness) that the Concept is realized.

12. This is the relationship that holds between "Determining Reflection" and "External Reflection" in Hegel's *Science of Logic*, E 402–408, G II.28–35. I have discussed this relationship in greater detail in chapter 13.

13. There is not so much an opposition of reading and non-reading as there is an immanent dialectic to reading itself, different forms of reading that answer to reading's own needs and possibilities to a greater or lesser extent; compare the related claims in *Glas*, pp. 168, 199, regarding desire and difference.

14. See *Science of Logic*, E 117–119, G I.125–127.

15. A helpful introduction to *Glas* that draws on what might be called a "standard" view of Derrida can be found in Simon Critchley, "A Commentary upon Derrida's Reading of Hegel in *Glas*." A reading of Derrida much closer to my own can be found in Jay Lampert, "Leaving the System As Is." Readings of *Glas* typically isolate particular sentences and interpret them as asserting the author's intention; while it is true that Derrida's reading regularly produces provisional interpretive totalizations of the textual process, these interpretations themselves return into the (dialectical) flow of interpretation and are thus overturned or transformed in their significance. For an orientation to the reading as a whole (and many such orientations are possible), one might begin on p. 33, with the question whether the Christian mythology is the only possible mythological model for absolute knowledge (see also p. 45), and with the analogous question whether the monogamous, heterosexual couple is the only model of sexuality and the family acceptable to "the" so-called "system." One could read in Derrida's text a demonstration of the emergence of dialectics and of *Sa* from a Jewish mythology and, in the elaborate study of Genet that occupies half the book, in a non-monogamous, homosexual environment. I have taken up the relation of Hegel and Derrida in "Reading: Derrida in Hegel's Understanding." David Kolb challenges Hegel on the ground of his purported insistence on the exclusive place of Christian mythology in Hegel's system in "The Final Name of God"; John Burbidge challenges this interpretation of Hegel in "Hegel's Open Future."

16. For a comparable interpretation of Hegel, see John Burbidge, "Hegel's Absolutes."

17. Derrida, "But, beyond . . . ," p. 366.

18. This relation is beautifully illustrated by the example of recognizing a ship on the beach in Merleau-Ponty, *Phenomenology of Perception*, p. 17.

19. See *Glas*, pp. 229, 94–96.

20. Though the logical relationships we are dealing with here are properly issues

of "the Concept," an analogous point is well-presented in the logic of "Essence" in the *Science of Logic,* in the discussion of "Substance and Accidents," in the logic of "the Absolute Relation," and, indeed, in the immediately preceding discussion of necessity and contingency.

21. Compare Julia Kristeva, *The Revolution in Poetic Language,* pt. 1, ch. 12, "Genotext and Phenotext," on the notion of "genotext," and Gilles Deleuze and Félix Guattari, *Anti-Oedipus: Capitalism and Schizophrenia,* ch. 1, "The Desiring Machines," on the synthesis of "and . . . and . . . and. . . ."

22. Friedrich Nietzsche, *On the Genealogy of Morals,* preface, sect. 1.

15. ABSOLUTE KNOWING

1. My interpretation of this chapter will follow in the general tradition of John W. Burbidge, "Hegel's Absolutes," and Jay Lampert, "Hegel in the Future."

2. See M788, W/C516–517: "Equally, consciousness must have related itself to the object in accordance with the totality of the latter's determinations and have thus grasped it from the standpoint of each of them." (This point is further elaborated in M789, W/C517.) Here we see what I will go on to show is the need for the *Logic:* that these positions map the total metaphysical terrain has to be shown on being's own terms. Cf. M802, W/C525–526: "nothing is *known* that is not in *experience.*"

3. Aristotle, *On the Movement of Animals,* chs. 1–7, *On the Soul,* book 3, chs. 9–10; M167, W/C120–122.

4. See chapters 6 and 8 of this book.

5. This is the significance of what Hegel says in M788, W/C516–517 (recalling that self-consciousness names the situation of intersubjective recognition, i.e., Spirit): "This surmounting of the object of consciousness is not to be taken one-sidedly to mean that the object showed itself as returning into the Self, but is to be taken more specifically to mean not only that the object as such presented itself to the Self as vanishing, but rather that it is the externalization of self-consciousness that posits the thinghood and that this externalization has not merely a negative but a positive meaning, a meaning which is not only for us or in itself, but for self-consciousness itself. The negative of the object, or its self-supersession, has a positive meaning for self-consciousness, i.e. self-consciousness *knows* the nothingness of the object, on the one hand, because it externalizes its own self—for in this externalization it posits *itself* as object, or the object as itself, in virtue of the indivisible unity of *being-for-self.* On the other hand, this positing at the same time contains the other moment, viz. That self-consciousness has equally superseded this externalization and objectivity too, and taken it back into itself so that it is in communion with itself in *its* otherness as such. This is the movement of *consciousness,* and in that movement consciousness is the totality of its moments. Equally, consciousness must have related itself to the object in accordance with the totality of the latter's determinations and have thus grasped it from the standpoint of each of them. This totality of its determinations establishes the object as an *implicitly* spiritual being, and it does truly become a spiritual being for consciousness when each of its individual determinations is grasped as a determination of the Self, or through the spiritual relationship to them that was just mentioned."

6. See M797–98, W/C522–523: "Our *own* act here has been simply to *gather together* the separate moments, each of which in principle exhibits the life of Spirit in its entirety, and also to stick to the Concept in the form of the Concept, the content of

which would already have yielded itself in those moments and in the form of a *shape of consciousness*. This last shape of Spirit—the Spirit which at the same time gives its complete and true content the form of the Self and thereby realizes its Concept as remaining in its Concept in this realization—this is absolute knowing; it is Spirit that knows itself in the shape of Spirit, or a *comprehensive knowing*." This means that the *Phenomenology* and the *Logic* are the *Darstellung* of the experience of absolute knowing itself.

7. M806, W/C529.

8. Though many scholars note that the *Phenomenology* and the *Logic* are importantly paired in their content, views of how this is so tend to be rather simplistic. See, for example, H. F. Fulda, *Das Problem einer Einleitung in Hegels Wissenschaft der Logik*, pp. 163–164.

9. This is Kant's argument against the Cartesian argument (implied in the second and third meditations and formulated explicitly in the sixth meditation) that the compelling character of reason makes global skepticism impossible. Kant takes Descartes's own premise—reason—and shows that on its own terms it leads to skepticism because its operation contradicts itself. (For Hegel, what this ultimately shows is only that reason as Descartes and Kant understand it is formal and abstract, and cannot supply its own starting points.) Compare the method that Parmenides teaches to Socrates in *Parmenides*.

10. Contra, for example, the interpretation of this relationship in Michael Forster, *Hegel and Skepticism*, pp. 139–140. Compare my fuller analysis of the antinomial structure of the argument of the *Phenomenology* in chapter 4, "Death and Desire in Hegel's Epistemology." I have also shown the implicit antinomial structure of Hegel's argument with respect to "Lordship and Bondage" in chapter 6, "Hermeneutical Pressure: Intersubjectivity and Objectivity" in this book.

11. We have now situated absolute knowing at the pivot point in the system of science as a whole (and have thereby established something of the relationship between the *Phenomenology* and the *Logic*). We have seen that "absolute knowing" names what is necessarily both the project and the structure of the system of science.

12. It is the system of shapes of experience *thought as system*. See M793, W/C519: "These are the moments of which the reconciliation of Spirit with its own consciousness proper is composed; by themselves they are single and separate, and it is solely their spiritual unity that constitutes the power of this reconciliation. The last of these moments is, however, necessarily this unity itself, and, as is evident, it binds them all into itself." See also M794, 797, W/C519–520, 522.

BIBLIOGRAPHY

Primary Texts

German Texts

Hegel, G. W. F. *Enzyclopädie der philosophischen Wissenschaften im Grundrisse.* Teile I, II, and III. *Werke in zwanzig Bänden,* Bde. 9, 10, 11, ed. Eva Moldenhauer und Karl Markus Michel. Frankfurt am Main: Suhrkamp Verlag, 1970.

———. *Grundlinien der Philosophie des Rechts.* 4. Auflage, hrsg. v. Johannes Hoffmeister. Hamburg: Felix Meiner Verlag, 1955.

———. *Hegels Philosophie des subjektiven Geistes/Hegel's Philosophy of Subjective Spirit.* Bde. 1 and 2. Text, translation, and notes by M. J. Petry. Dordrecht, Holland: D. Reidel Publishing Company, 1978.

———. *Phänomenologie des Geistes.* Hrsg. v. Hans-Friedrich Wessels und Heinrich Clairmont. Hamburg: Felix Meiner Verlag, 1988.

———. "Ueber das Wesen der philosophischen Kritik überhaupt, und ihr Verhältniss zum gegenwärtigen Zustand der Philosophie insbesondere." *Kritisches Journal der Philosophie,* Bd. 1, Stück 1, *"Einleitung,"* *Gesammelte Werke,* Bd. 4, hrsg. v. Hartmut Buchner und Otto Pöggeler, pp. 117–128. Hamburg: Felix Meiner Verlag, 1968.

———. *Vorlesungen über die Ästhetik* I. *Werke in zwanzig Bänden.* Bd.13, hrsg. v. Eva Moldenhaur und Karl Markus Michel. Frankfurt am Main: Suhrkamp Taschenbuch Verlag, 1986.

———. *Vorlesungen über die Philophie der Geschichte. Werke in zwanzig Bänden,* Bd. 12, hrsg. v. Eva Moldenhauer and Karl Markus Michel. Frankfurt am Main: Suhrkamp Taschenbuch Verlag, 1986.

———. *Vorlesungen über die Philosophie der Religion,* Teil 3. *Vorlesungen: Ausgewählte Nachschriften und Manuskripte,* Bd. 5, hrsg. v. Walter Jaeschke. Hamburg: Felix Meiner, 1984.

———. *Wissenschaft der Logik,* Bde. I and II. *Gesammelte Werke,* Bde. 11 and 12, hrsg. v. Friedrich Hogemann und Walter Jaeschke. Hamburg: Felix Meiner Verlag, 1978 (Bd. 11) and 1981 (Bd. 12).

English Translations

———. *The Difference between Fichte's and Schelling's System of Philosophy.* Trans. H. S. Harris and Walter Cerf. Albany: State University of New York Press, 1977.

———. *The Encyclopaedia Logic, with the Zusätze.* Trans. T. F. Geraets, W. A. Suchting, and H. S. Harris. Indianapolis/Cambridge: Hackett Publishing, 1991.

———. *Faith and Knowledge.* Trans. Walter Cerf and H. S. Harris. New York: State University of New York Press, 1977.

———. *Lectures on the History of Philosophy.* Trans. E. S. Haldane and Frances H. Simson. Atlantic Highlands, N.J.: Humanities Press, 1974.

———. *Lectures on the Philosophy of Religion.* Vol. 3. Ed. Peter C. Hodgson, trans. R. F. Brown, P. C. Hodgson, and J. M. Stewart, with the assistance of H. S. Harris. Berkeley: University of California Press, 1985.

———. *Logic, Being Part I of the Encyclopaedia of the Philosophical Sciences.* Trans. William Wallace. 3rd ed. Oxford: Clarendon Press, 1975.

———. *Phenomenology of Mind.* Trans. J. B. Baillie. New York: Harper and Row, 1967.

———. *Phenomenology of Spirit.* Trans. A. V. Miller. Oxford: Oxford University Press, 1977.

———. *The Philosophy of History.* Trans. J. Sibree. New York: Dover Publications, 1956.

———. *Philosophy of Mind, Being Part III of the Encyclopaedia of the Philosophical Sciences.* Trans. William Wallace and A. V. Miller. Oxford: Clarendon Press, 1971.

———. *Philosophy of Nature, Being Part II of the Encyclopaedia of the Philosophical Sciences.* Trans. A. V. Miller. Oxford: Clarendon Press, 1970.

———. *Philosophy of Right.* Trans. T. M. Knox. Oxford: Oxford University Press, 1967 (paperback).

———. *Reason in History.* Trans. Robert S. Hartman. Indianapolis: Bobbs-Merrill, 1953.

———. "Relationship of Skepticism to Philosophy, Exposition of Its Different Modifications and Comparison to the Latest Form with the Ancient One." Trans. H. S. Harris. In George di Giovanni and H. S. Harris, eds., *Between Kant and Hegel: Texts in the Development of Post-Kantian Idealism,* pp. 313–362. Albany: SUNY Press, 1985.

———. *Science of Logic.* 2 vols. Trans. W. H. Johnson and L. G. Struthers. London: George Allen and Unwin, 1929.

———. *Science of Logic.* Trans. A. V. Miller. New York: Humanities Press, 1976.

Other Works

Adelman, Howard. "Hegel's *Phenomenology:* Facing the Preface." *Idealistic Studies* 14 (1984): 159–170.

Adorno, Theodor W. *Negative Dialektik.* Frankfurt am Main: Suhrkamp Verlag, 1966. Translated into English by E. B. Ashton as *Negative Dialectics.* New York: Seabury Press, 1973.

———. "Skoteinos, or How to Read Hegel." In *Hegel: Three Studies,* trans. Shierry Weber Nicholson, pp. 89–148. Cambridge, Mass.: MIT, 1993.

Allison, Henry. "On the Presumed Gap in the Derivation of the Categorical Imperative." In *Idealism and Freedom,* pp. 143–154. Cambridge: Cambridge University Press, 1996.

Andersen, Nathan. "Example, Experiment and Experience in Hegel's Phenomenology of Spirit." Dissertation, Pennsylvania State University, 2000.

Appiah, Anthony. "The Uncompleted Argument: Du Bois and the Illusion of Race." In Gates, ed., *"Race," Writing and Difference,* pp. 21–37.

Aquinas, Saint Thomas. *Summa Theologiae.* Leonine ed. Madrid: Biblioteca de Autores Cristianos, 1978.

Aristotle. *The Complete Works of Aristotle*. 2 vols. Ed. Jonathan Barnes. Princeton, N.J.: Princeton University Press, 1984.

Augustine, Saint. *Confessions*. Trans. John K. Ryan. New York: Image Books, 1960.

Bainton, Roland H. *Here I Stand: A Life of Martin Luther*. New York: Mentor, 1950 (paperback).

Bataille, Georges, "Hegel, Death and Sacrifice." *Yale French Studies* 78 (1990): 9–28.

Bates, Jennifer. "The Breakdowns of Unhappy Consciousness." Unpublished.

———. "Genesis and Spirit of the Imagination (Hegel's Theory of Imagination between 1801–1807)." Doctoral dissertation, University of Toronto, 1996.

Baugh, Bruce. "Sartre and James on the Role of the Body in Emotion." *Dialogue* 29 (1990): 357–373.

———. "The Unhappy Consciousness: Hegel in France from Wahl to Derrida." Unpublished.

Baur, Michael. "Hegel and the Overcoming of Understanding." *Owl of Minerva* 22 (1991): 141–158.

Baur, Michael, and John Russon, eds. *Hegel and the Tradition: Essays in Honour of H. S. Harris*. Toronto: University of Toronto Press, 1997.

Bergson, Henri. *Matter and Memory*. Trans. Nancy Margaret Paul and W. Scott Palmer. New York: Zone Books, 1991.

———. *Time and Free Will: An Essay on the Immediate Data of Consciousness*. Kila, Mont.: Kessinger Publishing, n.d. (reproduction).

Bernstein, Jay. "Confession and Forgiveness: Hegel's Poetics of Action." In Richard Eldredge, ed., *Beyond Representation: Philosophy and Poetic Imagination*. New York: Cambridge University Press, 1996.

———. "Conscience and Transgression: The Exemplarity of Tragic Action." In G. K. Browning, ed., *Hegel's Phenomenology of Spirit: A Reappraisal*, pp. 79–97. London: Kluwer, 1997.

Berthold-Bond, Daniel. *Hegel's Grand Synthesis: A Study of Being, Thought, and History*. Albany: State University of New York Press, 1989.

Bourdieu, Pierre. *Outline of a Theory of Practice*. Trans. Richard Nice. Cambridge: Cambridge University Press, 1977.

Brentano, Franz. *Die Psychologie des Aristoteles*. 1867. Darmstadt, Germany: Wissenschaftliche Buchgesellschaft, 1967 (reproduction).

Bubner, Rüdiger. "Philosophy Is Its Time Comprehended in Thought." In *Essays in Hermeneutics and Critical Theory*, trans. Eric Matthews, pp. 37–61. New York: Columbia University Press, 1988.

Buchwalter, Andrew. "Hegel's Concept of Virtue." *Political Theory* 20 (1992): 548–583.

Burbidge, John W. "Hegel's Absolutes." *Owl of Minerva* 29, no. 1 (1997): 23–37.

———. "Hegel's Open Future." In Baur and Russon, eds., *Hegel and the Tradition*, pp. 176–189.

———. "Language and Recognition." In Westphal, ed., *Method and Speculation in Hegel's Phenomenology*, pp. 85–94.

———. "Man, God and Death in Hegel's Phenomenology." *Philosophy and Phenomenological Research* 42 (1981): 183–196.

———. "The Necessity of Contingency." In *Hegel on Logic and Religion*, pp. 39–51. Albany: State University of New York Press, 1992.

———."Unhappy Consciousness in Hegel—An Analysis of Medieval Catholicism?" *Mosaic* 11, no. 4 (1977–78): 67–80.

Burkert, Walter. *Homo Necans: The Anthropology of Ancient Greek Sacrificial Ritual and Myth.* Trans. Peter Bing. Berkeley: University of California Press, 1983.

Casey, Edward S. *The Fate of Place: A Philosophical History.* Berkeley: Ujiversity of California Press, 1998.

Ciavatta, David. "Hegel on Desire and Recognition." Unpublished.

———. "Hegel on the Family." Doctoral dissertation, Pennsylvania State University, 2003.

Collingwood, R. G. *An Autobiography.* Oxford: Oxford University Press, 1939.

———. *Speculum Mentis.* Oxford: Clarendon Press, 1924.

Cook, Daniel J. *Language in the Philosophy of Hegel.* The Hague: Mouton and Co., 1973.

Cooper, Barry. *The End of History: An Essay on Modern Hegelianism.* Toronto: University of Toronto Press, 1984.

Copleston, Frederick. *A History of Philosophy.* Vol. 7: *Fichte to Hegel.* Garden City, N.Y.: Image Books, 1965 (paperback).

Critchley, Simon. "A Commentary upon Derrida's Reading of Hegel in *Glas.*" *Bulletin of the Hegel Society of Great Britain* 18 (1988): 6–32.

Dahlstrom, Daniel. "The Dialectic of Conscience and the Necessity of Morality in Hegel's *Philosophy of Spirit.*" *Owl of Minerva* 24, no. 2 (1993): 181–189.

Dauenhauer, Bernard P. "Heidegger, Spokesman for the Dweller." *Southern Journal of Philosophy* 15 (1977): 189–199.

Davidson, Donald. "Mental Events." In *Essays on Actions and Events,* pp. 207–225. Oxford: Clarendon Press, 1980.

de Beauvoir, Simone. *The Second Sex.* Trans. and ed. H. M. Parshley. New York: Vintage Books, 1989.

Debrock, Guy. "The Silence of Language in Hegel's Dialectic." *Cultural Hermeneutics* 3 (1973): 285–304.

Deleuze, Gilles, and Félix Guattari. *Anti-Oedipus: Capitalism and Schizophrenia.* Trans. Robert Hurley, Mark Seem, and Helen R. Lane. New York: Viking Press, 1977.

de Nys, Martin J. "Force and Understanding: The Unity of the Object of Consciousness." In Westphal, ed., *Method and Speculation in Hegel's Phenomenology,* pp. 57–70.

Derrida, Jacques. "But, beyond . . . (Open Letter to Anne McClintock and Rob Nixon)." In Gates, ed., *"Race," Writing, and Difference,* pp. 354–369.

———. "Edmond Jabès and the Question of the Book." In *Writing and Difference,* trans. Alan Bass, pp. 64–78. Chicago: University of Chicago Press, 1978.

———. *Glas.* Paris: Galilée, 1974. Translated into English by John P. Leavey, Jr., and Richard Rand as *Glas.* Lincoln and London: University of Nebraska Press, 1986.

———. "The Pit and the Pyramid: Introduction to Hegel's Semiology." In *Margins of Philosophy,* trans. Alan Bass, pp. 69–108. Chicago: University of Chicago Press, 1982.

———. "Structure, Sign, and Play in the Discourse of the Human Sciences." In *Writing and Difference,* trans. Alan Bass, pp. 278–293. Chicago: University of Chicago Press, 1978.

Descartes, René. *Meditations on First Philosophy.* In *The Philosophical Works of Des-*

cartes, vol. 1, trans. Elizabeth S. Haldane and G. R. T Ross, pp. 131–199. Cambridge: Cambridge University Press, 1931 (corrected edition).

———. *Principles of Philosophy*. In *The Philosophical Works of Descartes*, vol. 1, trans. Elizabeth S. Haldane and G. R. T Ross, pp. 201–302. Cambridge: Cambridge University Press, 1931 (corrected edition).

Diogenes Laertius. *Lives of the Eminent Philosophers*. Vol. 2. Trans. R.D. Hicks. London: William Heinemann, 1925.

Dodd, James. "The Body as 'Sign and Tool' in Hegel's *Encyclopaedia*." *International Studies in Philosophy* 27 (1995): 21–32.

Donougho, Martin. "The Woman in White: On the Reception of Hegel's Antigone." *Owl of Minerva* 21 (1988): 65–89.

Dove, Kenley. "Phenomenology and Systematic Philosophy." In Westphal, ed., *Method and Speculation in Hegel's Phenomenology*, pp. 27–39.

Düsing, Klaus, "Hegels Theorie der Einbildungskraft." In *Psychologie und Anthropologie oder Philosophie des Geistes: Beiträge zu einer Hegel-Tagung in Marburg 1989*, hrsg. v. Franz Hespe und Burkhard Tuschling, pp. 297–320. Stuttgart-Bad Cannstatt: Frommann-holzboog, 1991.

Elder, Crawford L. "Hegel's Teleology and the Relation between Mind and Brain." *Southern Journal of Philosophy* 17 (1979): 27–45.

Epictetus. *Discourses, Manual and Fragments*. 2 vols. Trans. W. A. Oldfather. Cambridge, Mass.: Harvard University Press, 1925.

Fackenheim, Emil L. *The Religious Dimension in Hegel's Thought*. 1967. Reprint, Chicago: University of Chicago Press, 1982.

Fagan, Patricia. "Philosophical History and the Roman Empire." In Baur and Russon, eds., *Hegel and the Tradition*, pp. 17–39.

Fichte, J. G. *Science of Knowledge*. Ed. and trans. Peter Heath and John Lachs. Cambridge: Cambridge University Press, 1982.

———. *Science of Rights*. Trans. A. E. Kroger. London: Routledge and Kagan Paul, 1970.

———. *The Vocation of Man*. Trans. Peter Preuss. Indianapolis: Hackett Publishing, 1987.

Findlay, J. N. *Hegel: A Re-examination*. London: George Allen and Unwin, 1958.

Flay, Joseph C. "The Dialectic of Irony and the Irony of Dialectic." *Owl of Minerva* 25 (1994): 209–214.

———. "Essence and Time in Hegel." *Owl of Minerva* 20 (1989): 183–192.

———. "Hegel and Merleau-Ponty: Radical Essentialism." In Galen A. Johnson and Michael B. Smith, eds., *Ontology and Alterity in Merleau-Ponty*, pp. 142–157. Evanston, Ill.: Northwestern University Press, 1990.

———. "Hegel's Inverted World." *Review of Metaphysics* 23 (1970): 662–678.

———. *Hegel's Quest for Certainty*. Albany: State University of New York Press, 1987.

———. "Hegel's *Science of Logic*: Ironies of the Understanding." In George di Giovanni, ed., *Essays on Hegel's Logic*, pp. 153–169. Albany: SUNY Press, 1990.

———. "Pragmatic Presuppositions and the Dialectics of Hegel's *Phenomenology*." In Westphal, ed., *Method and Speculation in Hegel's Phenomenology*, pp. 15–26.

———. "Time in Hegel's *Phenomenology of Spirit*." *International Philosophical Quarterly* 31 (1991): 259–273.

Forster, Michael N. *Hegel and Skepticism*. Cambridge, Mass.: Harvard University Press, 1989.

Frame, Douglas. *The Myth of Return in Early Greek Epic*. New Haven, Conn.: Yale University Press, 1978.

Freud, Sigmund. *Civilization and Its Discontents* New York: W.W. Norton, 1961.

———. *Three Essays on the Theory of Sexuality*. Trans. James Strachey. New York: Harper Collins, 1975.

———. "The Unconscious." In James Strachey et al., eds., *The Standard Edition of the Complete Works of Sigmund Freud*, pp. 159–215. London: Hogarth Press, 1957.

Friedman, R. Z. "Hypocrisy and the Highest Good: Hegel on Kant's Transition from Morality to Religion." *Journal of the History of Philosophy* 24 (1986): 503–522.

Fulda, H. F. *Das Problem einer Einleitung in Hegels Wissenschaft der Logik*. Frankfurt am Main: Vittorio Klostermann, 1975.

———. "Zur Logik der *Phänomenologie* von 1807." *Hegel-Studien*, Beiheft 3 (1966): 75–101.

Gadamer, Hans-Georg. "Aesthetics and Hermeneutics." In David Linge, ed. and trans., *Philosophical Hermeneutics*, pp. 95–104. Berkeley: University of California Press, 1976.

———. *Hegels Dialektik: Sechs Hermeneutische Studien*. Tübingen: Mohr, 1980. Translated into English (excluding one essay) by P. Christopher Smith as *Hegel's Dialectic: Five Hermeneutical Studies*. New Haven, Conn.: Yale University Press, 1976.

———. "Man and Language." In David Linge, ed. and trans., *Philosophical Hermeneutics*, pp. 59–68. Berkeley: University of California Press, 1976.

———. *Reason in the Age of Science*. Trans. F. G. Lawrence. Cambridge, Mass.: MIT Press, 1981.

———. *Wahrheit und Methode*. 2. Aufl. Tübingen: J. C. B. Mohr, 1965. Translated into English as *Truth and Method*, ed. G. Barden and J. Cumming. New York: Crossroad Publishing, 1985.

Gates, Henry Louis Jr., ed. *"Race," Writing and Difference*. Chicago: University of Chicago Press, 1986.

Geertz, Clifford. *The Interpretation of Cultures*. New York: Basic Books, 1973.

Glazer, Nathan, and Daniel P. Moynihan, eds. *Ethnicity: Theory and Experience*. Cambridge, Mass.: Harvard University Press, 1975.

Greene, Murray. *Hegel on the Soul: A Speculative Anthropology*. The Hague: Martinus Nijhoff, 1972.

———. "Natural Life and Subjectivity." In Stillman, ed., *Hegel's Philosophy of Spirit*, pp. 94–117.

Grimmlinger, Friedrich. "Zum Begriff des Absoluten Wissens in Hegels 'Phänomenologie.' " In *Geschichte und System*, hrsg. v. Hans-Dieter Klein und Erhard Oeser, pp. 279–300. Wien/München: R. Oldenbourg Verlag, 1972.

Guignon, Charles B. "Heidegger's 'Authenticity' Revisited." *Review of Metaphysics* 38 (1984): 321–339.

———. "Moods in Heidegger's *Being and Time*." In Cheshire Calhoun and Robert C. Solomon, eds., *What Is an Emotion? Classic Readings in Philosophical Psychology*, pp. 230–243. New York: Oxford University Press, 1984).

Hanna, Robert. Review of Michael N. Forster, *Hegel and Skepticism*. *Review of Metaphysics* 43 (1990): 630–631.

Harris, H. S. "Comment on Phenomenology as Systematic Philosophy." In Westphal, ed., *Method and Speculation in Hegel's Phenomenology*, pp. 41–46.

——. "The Concept of Recognition in Hegel's Jena Manuscripts." *Hegel-Studien Beiheft* 20 (1979): 229–248.

——. "Hegel and Antigone's Unwritten Laws," Lecture 1 of *Literature and Religion in Hegel's Phenomenology*. Unpublished.

——. *Hegel's Development: Toward the Sunlight (1770–1801)*. Oxford: Clarendon Press, 1972.

——. *Hegel's Development: Night Thoughts (Jena 1801–1806)*. Oxford: Clarendon Press, 1983.

——. *Hegel's Ladder*. 2 vols. Indianapolis: Hackett, 1998.

——. *Hegel: Phenomenology and System*. Indianapolis: Hackett, 1995.

——. "Skepticism, Dogmatism and Speculation in the Critical Journal." In George di Giovanni and H. S. Harris, eds., *Between Kant and Hegel: Texts in the Development of Post-Kantian Idealism*, pp. 252–271. Albany: SUNY Press, 1985

Heidegger, Martin. "Brief über den Humanismus." In *Wegmarken*, 2. Aufl., pp. 311–360. Frankfurt: Vittorio Klostermann, 1978. Translated into English by Frank A. Capuzzi and J. Glenn Gray as "Letter on Humanism." In *Basic Writings*, ed. David Farrell Krell, pp. 193–242. New York: Harper and Row, 1977.

——. *Contributions to Philosophy*. Trans. Parvis Emad and Kenneth Maly. Bloomington: Indiana University Press, 2000.

——. "Der Ursprung des Kunstwerkes." In *Holzwege*, 6. Aufl., pp. 1–72. Frankfurt: Vittorio Klostermann, 1980. Translated into English by Albert Hofstadter as "The Origin of the Work of Art," in *Poetry, Language, Thought*, pp. 17–87. New York: Harper and Row, 1971.

——. "A Dialogue on Language." In *On the Way to Language*, trans. Peter D. Hertz, pp. 1–54. New York: Harper and Row, 1971.

——. *Die Grundprobleme der Phänomenologie*. Frankfurt: Vittorio Klostermann, 1975. Translated into English by Albert Hofstadter as *The Basic Problems of Phenomenology*. Bloomington: Indiana University Press, 1982.

——. *Hegels Phänomenologie des Geistes, Gesamtausgabe*. Bd. 32. Frankfurt am Main: Vittorio Klosterman, 1980. Translated into English by Parvis Emad and Kenneth Maly as *Hegel's Phenomenology of Spirit*. Bloomington: Indiana University Press, 1988.

——. *Sein und Zeit*. 7. Aufl. Tübingen: Max Niemeyer Verlag, 1953. Translated into English by John Macquarrie and Edward Robinson as *Being and Time*. New York: Harper and Row, 1962.

Heidegren, Carl-Göran. "Hegels Nürnberger Propädeutik—eine wichtige Phase in der Entstehung der 'Rechtsphilosophie'." *Archiv für Geschichte der Philosophie* 70 (1988): 179–211.

Henrich, Dieter. *Aesthetic Judgment and the Moral Image of the World: Studies in Kant*. Stanford, Calif.: Stanford University Press, 1992.

——. "Anfang und Methode der Logik." *Hegel-Studien* 1 (1964): 19–35.

——. "Fichte's Original Insight." Trans. David R. Lachterman. In D. E. Christensen, Manfred Reidel, Robert Spaemann, Reiner Wiehl, and Wolfgang Wieland, eds., *Contemporary German Philosophy*, vol. 1, pp. 15–53. University Park: Pennsylvania State University Press, 1982.

——. "Hegels Logik der Reflexion: Neue Fassung." *Hegel-Studien* 18 (1978): 219–231.

——. Hrsg. *Hegels Philosophische Psychologie. Hegel-Studien* 19 (1979).

Herbenick, Raymond M. "Hegel's Concept of Embodiment." *Philosophical Studies* (Dublin) 20 (1972): 109–112.

Hinchman, Lewis P. *Hegel's Critique of the Enlightenment.* Gainesville and Tampa: University of Florida/University of South Florida Press, 1984.

Holmes, Richard. "The World According to Husserl and Heidegger." *Man and World* 18 (1985): 373–387.

Horowitz, Donald L. "Ethnic Identity." In Glazer and Moynihan, eds., *Ethnicity: Theory and Experience,* pp. 111–140.

Hösle, Vittorio. *Hegels System. Der Idealismus der Subjektivität und das Problem der Intersubjektivität.* Bd. 2. Hamburg: Felix Meiner, 1987.

Houlgate, Steven. *Freedom, Truth and History: An Introduction to Hegel's Philosophy.* London and New York: Routledge, 1991.

——. "Necessity and Contingency in Hegel's *Science of Logic.*" *Owl of Minerva* 27 (1995): 37–49.

——. "World History as the Progress of Consciousness: An Interpretation of Hegel's Philosophy of History." *Owl of Minerva* 22 (1990): 69–80.

Hume, David. *A Treatise of Human Nature.* Ed. L.A. Selby-Bigge. Oxford: Clarendon Press, 1888.

Husserl, Edmund. *Cartesianische Meditationen.* 2. Aufl. Hamburg: Felix Meiner, 1987. Translated into English by Dorion Cairns as *Cartesian Meditations.* The Hague: Martinus Nijhoff, 1960.

——. *Encyclopaedia Brittanica* article, "Phenomenology," trans. Richard E. Palmer. *British Journal of Phenomenology,* May 1971.

——. *Logical Investigations.* 2 vols. Trans. J. N. Findlay. Atlantic Highlands, N.J.: Humanities Press, 1970.

Hyppolite, Jean. *Genèse et Structure de la Phénoménologie de l'Esprit de Hegel.* 2 vols. Paris: Éditions Montaigne, 1946. Translated into English by Samuel Cherniak and John Heckman as *Genesis and Structure of Hegel's Phenomenology.* Evanston, Ill.: Northwestern University Press, 1974.

Kalenberg, Thomas. *Die Befreiung der Natur. Natur und Selbstbewusstsein in der Philosophie Hegels.* Hamburg: Felix Meiner, 1997.

Kant, Immanuel. *Critique of Judgment.* Trans. Werner S. Pluhar. Indianapolis: Hackett Publishing, 1987.

——. *Critique of Practical Reason.* Trans. Lewis White Beck. Indianapolis: Bobbs-Merrill Educational Publishing, 1956.

——. *Critique of Pure Reason.* Trans. Norman Kemp Smith. New York: St. Martin's Press, 1929.

——. *Groundwork of the Metaphysics of Morals.* Trans. H. J. Paton. New York: Harper Torchbooks, 1964.

Kelly, George Armstrong. *Hegel's Retreat from Eleusis: Studies in Political Thought.* Princeton, N.J.: Princeton University Press, 1978.

Kline, George L. "The Dialectic of Action and Passion in Hegel's *Phenomenology of Spirit.*" *Review of Metaphysics* 23 (1969–70): 679–689.

Knox, T. M. "Hegel's Attitude to Kant's Ethics." *Kant-Studien* 49 (1957–58): 70–81.

Kojève, Alexandre. *Introduction à la Lecture de Hegel.* Paris: Gallimard, 1947. Partially translated into English by James H. Nichols, Jr., and edited by Allan Bloom as *Introduction to the Reading of Hegel.* New York: Basic Books, 1969.

Kolb, David. *The Critique of Pure Modernity: Hegel, Heidegger and After.* Chicago: University of Chicago Press, 1986.

——. "The Final Name of God." In Baur and Russon, eds., *Hegel and the Tradition,* pp. 162–175.

Kristeva, Julia. *The Revolution in Poetic Language.* Trans. Margaret Waller. New York: Columbia University Press, 1984.

Labarriere, Pierre-Jean. "La *Phénoménologie de l'Esprit* comme Discours Systématique: Histoire, Religion et Science." *Hegel-Studien* 9 (1974): 131–153.

Lamb, David, and Lawrence S. Stepelevich, eds. *Hegel's Philosophy of Action.* Atlantic Highlands N.J.: Humanities Press, 1983.

Lampert, Jay. "Hegel and Ancient Egypt: History and Becoming." *International Philosophical Quarterly* 35 (1995): 21–32.

——. "Hegel in the Future." Unpublished.

——. "Husserl and Hegel on the Logic of Subjectivity." *Man and World* 21 (1988): 363–393.

——. "Husserl's Account of Syncategorematic Terms: The Problem of Representing the Synthetic Connections that Underlie Meanings." *Southern Journal of Philosophy* 30 (1992): 67–94

——. "Leaving the System As Is." In D. Goicoechea and M. Zlomislic, eds., *Joyful Wisdom,* vol. 5, pp. 37–51. Ontario: Thought House Press, 1997.

——. "Locke, Fichte and Hegel on the Right to Property." In Baur and Russon, eds., *Hegel and the Tradition,* pp. 40–73.

——. *Synthesis and Backwards Reference in Husserl's Logical Investigations.* Dordrecht: Kluwer, 1995.

Lauer, Quentin. "Commentary on 'The Birth of Spirit for Hegel out of the Travesty of Medicine." In Stillman, ed., *Hegel's Philosophy of Spirit,* pp. 43–46.

——. *A Reading of Hegel's Phenomenology of Spirit.* New York: Fordham University Press, 1976.

Leibniz, G. W. *Discourse on Metaphysics.* Trans. Peter G. Lucas and Leslie Grant. Manchester: Manchester University Press, 1961 (corrected edition).

Lewis, Charlton T., and Charles Short, eds. *A Latin Dictionary.* New York: Oxford University Press, 1984.

Liddell, Henry George, and Robert Scott, eds. *Greek-English Lexicon.* Oxford University Press, 1968.

Locke, John. *An Essay Concerning Human Understanding.* Oxford: Clarendon Press, 1975.

Löwith, Karl. *From Hegel to Nietzsche: The Revolution in Nineteenth-Century Thought.* Trans. David. E. Green. Garden City, N.Y.: Anchor Books, 1967.

Ludwig, Walter D. "Hegel's Conception of Absolute Knowing." *Owl of Minerva* 21 (1989): 5–19.

MacGregor, David. "The State at Dusk." *Owl of Minerva* 21 (1989): 51–64.

MacIntyre, Alasdair, ed. *Hegel: A Collection of Critical Essays.* Notre Dame: University of Notre Dame Press, 1976.

——. "Hegel on Faces and Skulls." In MacIntyre, ed., *Hegel: A Collection of Critical Essays,* pp. 219–236.

Mackintosh, Brian K. "From Reason to History in the *Phenomenology of Spirit.*" Unpublished.

Maker, William. "Does Hegel Have a 'Dialectical Method'?" *Southern Journal of Philosophy* 20 (1982): 75–96.

Malabou, Catherine, *L'Avenir de Hegel: Plasticité, temporalité, dialectique*. Paris: Librairie philosophique J. Vrin, 1996.

Marcuse, Herbert. *Hegels Ontologie und die Theorie der Geschichtlichkeit*. 1932. Reprint, Frankfurt am Main: Vittorio Klosterman, 1968. Translated into English by Seyla Benhabib as *Hegel's Ontology and the Theory of Historicity*. Cambridge, Mass.: MIT Press, 1987.

———. *Reason and Revolution: Hegel and the Rise of Social Theory*. Boston: Beacon Press, 1960 (paperback).

McCarthy, Vincent A. *Quest for a Philosophical Jesus: Christianity and Philosophy in Rousseau, Kant, Hegel, and Schelling*. Macon, Ga.: Mercer University Press, 1986.

McCumber, John. *The Company of Words: Hegel, Language and Systematic Philosophy*. Evanston, Ill.: Northwestern University Press, 1993.

———. "Hegel and Hamann: Ideas and Life." In Baur and Russon, eds., *Hegel and the Tradition*, pp. 77–92.

———. "Hegel on Habit." *Owl of Minerva* 21 (1990): 155–165.

McDowell, John. *Mind and World*. Cambridge, Mass.: Harvard University Press, 1996.

Merleau-Ponty, Maurice. "The Child's Relations with Others." In *The Primacy of Perception*, ed. James M. Edie, pp. 100–108. Evanston, Ill.: Northwestern University Press, 1964.

———. *Phenomenology of Perception*. Trans. Colin Smith. New York: Routledge, 1999.

———. *The Visible and the Invisible*. Trans. Alphonso Lingis. Evanston, Ill.: Northwestern University Press, 1969.

Miller, Arnold V. "Absolute Knowing and the Destiny of the Individual." *Owl of Minerva* 15 (1984): 45–50.

Morris, David. "Lived Time and Absolute Knowing: Habit and Addiction from *Infinite Jest* to the *Phenomenology of Spirit*." *Clio* 30 (2001): 375–415.

Morriston, W. "Heidegger on the World." *Man and World* 5 (1972): 455–456.

Mure, G. R. G. *A Study of Hegel's Logic*. Oxford: Oxford University Press, 1950.

Nagel, Thomas. "Sexual Perversion." *Journal of Philosophy* 66, no. 1 (1969): 5–17.

Nicolin, Friedhelm. "Zum Titelproblem der *Phänomenologie des Geistes*." *Hegel-Studien* 4 (1967): 113–123.

Nicholson, Graeme. "The Politics of Heidegger's Rectoral Address." *Man and World* 20 (1987): 171–18.

Nietzsche, Friedrich, *On the Genealogy of Morals*. Trans. Walter Kaufmann and R. J. Hollingdale. New York: Vintage Books, 1967.

Otto, Rudolph. *The Idea of the Holy: An Inquiry into the Non-rational Factor in the Idea of the Divine and Its Relation to the Rational*. Trans. John W. Harvey. London: Oxford University Press, 1950.

Owens, Wayne D. "The Way-Making Movement of Thinking: Heidegger and George's 'The Word.'" *Southern Journal of Philosophy* 26 (1988): 135–151.

Paci, Enzo. *Relazioni e Significati*. Vol. 3. Milan, 1966. Translated in part as "Anthropology, Dialectics and Phenomenology in Hegel," *Radical America* 4, no. 7 (1970): 33–53.

Partridge, Eric, ed. *Origins: A Short Etymological Dictionary of Modern English*. New York: Greenwich House, 1983.

Patterson, Orlando. "Context and Choice in Ethnic Allegiance: A Theoretical Framework and Caribbean Case Study." In Glazer and Moynihan, eds., *Ethnicity: Theory and Experience*, pp. 305–349.

Peperzak, Adriaan. *Autoconoscenza dell'assoluto: Lineamenti della filosofia dello spirito hegeliana*. Napoli: Istituto Italiano per gli Studi Filosofici, 1988.

Petry, M. J. Review of Murray Greene, *Hegel on the Soul: A Speculative Anthropology*. *Hegel-Studien* 9 (1974): 290–295.

Pinkard, Terry. "Freedom and Social Categories in Hegel's Ethics." *Philosophy and Phenomenological Research* 47 (1986–87): 209–232.

———. *Hegel's Phenomenology: The Sociality of Reason*. Cambridge: Cambridge University Press, 1996.

Pippin, Robert B. *Hegel's Idealism: the Satisfactions of Self-Consciousness*. Cambridge: Cambridge University Press, 1989.

Plato. *The Collected Dialogues of Plato*. Ed. Edith Hamilton and Huntingdon Cairns. Princeton, N.J.: Princeton University Press, 1961.

Plotinus. *Enneads*. Vol. 3. Trans. A. H. Armstrong. Cambridge, Mass.: Harvard University Press, 1980.

Pöggeler, Otto. "Die Komposition der *Phänomenologie des Geistes*." *Hegel-Studien* 3 (1966): 27–74.

———. "Zur Deutung der *Phänomenologie des Geistes*." *Hegel-Studien* 1 (1961): 255–294.

Preuss, Peter. "Selfhood and the Battle: The Second Beginning of the Phenomenology." In Westphal, ed., *Method and Speculation in Hegel's Phenomenology*, pp. 71–83.

Ravven, Heidi M. "Has Hegel Anything to Say to Feminists?" *Owl of Minerva* 19 (1988): 149–168.

Recco, Gregory. "The Experience of Analogy." Unpublished.

Reyburn, Hugh A. *The Ethical Theory of Hegel*. Oxford: Clarendon Press, 1921.

Ripstein, Arthur. "Universal and General Wills: Hegel and Rousseau." *Political Theory* 22 (1994): 444–467.

Ritter, Joachim. *Hegel and the French Revolution: Essays on the Philosophy of Right*. Trans. Richard Dien Winfield. Cambridge, Mass.: MIT Press, 1982.

Robinson, Jonathan. *Duty and Hypocrisy in Hegel's Phenomenology of Mind: An Essay in the Real and Ideal*. Toronto and Buffalo: University of Toronto Press, 1977.

Rockmore, Tom. *Cognition: An Introduction to Hegel's Phenomenology of Spirit*. Berkeley: University of California Press, 1997.

———. "Foundationalism and Hegelian Logic." *Owl of Minerva* 21 (1989): 41–50.

Rosen, Michael. *Hegel's Dialectic and its Criticism*. Cambridge: Cambridge University Press, 1982.

Rosen, Stanley. "*Sophrosune* and *Selbstbewusstsein*." *Review of Metaphysics* 26 (1972–73): 617–642.

Rotenstreich, Nathan. "Hegel's Concept of Mind." *Revue Internationale de Philosophie* 6 (1952): 27–34.

Russon, John. "Aristotle's Animative Epistemology." *Idealistic Studies* 25 (1995): 241–253.

———. "Embodiment and Responsibility: Merleau-Ponty and the Ontology of Nature." *Man and World* 27 (1994): 291–308.

———. "Eros and Education: Plato's Transformative Epistemology." *Laval Theologique et Philosophique* 56 (2000): 113–125.

——. *Human Experience: Philosophy, Neurosis and the Elements of Everyday Life*. Albany: State University of New York Press, 2003.

——. "Reading Derrida in Hegel's Understanding." Unpublished.

——. Review of Steven Houlgate, *Freedom Truth and History: An Introduction to Hegel's Philosophy*. *Hegel-Studien* 27 (1992): 192–195.

——. *The Self and Its Body in Hegel's Phenomenology of Spirit*. Toronto: University of Toronto Press, 1997.

——. "Self-Consciousness and the Tradition in Aristotle's Psychology." *Laval Théologique et Philosophique* 52 (1996): 777–803.

——. "We Sense That They Strive: How to Read (The Theory of the Forms)." In John Russon and John Sallis, eds., *Retracing the Platonic Text*, pp. 70–84. Evanston, Ill.: Northwestern University Press, 2000.

Sallis, John. *Chorology: On Beginning in Plato's Timaeus*. Bloomington: Indiana University Press, 1999.

——. "Hegel's Concept of Presentation: Its Determination in the Preface to the Phenomenology of Spirit." *Hegel-Studien* 12 (1977): 129–156.

——. "Imagination and Presentation in Hegel's Philosophy of Spirit." In Peter G. Stillman, ed., *Hegel's Philosophy of Spirit*, pp. 66–88. Albany: State University of New York Press, 1987.

Sambursky, S., and S. Pines. *The Concept of Time in Late Neoplatonism*. Jerusalem: Israel Academy of Sciences and Humanities, 1971.

Sartre, Jean-Paul. *Being and Nothingness*. Trans. Hazel Barnes. New York: Washington Square Press, 1956.

Sax, Benjamin C. "Active Individuality and the Language of Confession: The Figure of the Beautiful Soul in the *Lehrjahre* and the *Phänomenologie*." *Journal of the History of Philosophy* 21 (1983): 437–466.

Schalow, Frank. "Re-opening the Issue of World: Heidegger and Kant." *Man and World* 20 (1987): 189–203.

——. "The Anomaly of World: From Scheler to Heidegger." *Man and World* 24 (1991): 75–87.

Scheiber, Wolfgang. "'Habitus' als Schlüssel zu Hegels Daseinslogik." *Hegel-Studien* 20 (1985): 125–144.

Schelling, F. W. J. *System of Transcendental Idealism*. Trans. Peter Heath. Charlottesville: University Press of Virginia, 1978.

——. *System des transzendentalen Idealismus*. Hrsg. V. H. D. Brandt und P. Miller. Hamburg: Felix Meiner, 1992.

Schiller, Friedrich, *On the Aesthetic Education of Man*. Ed. and trans. Elizabeth M. Wilkinson and L. A. Willoughby. Oxford: Calrendon Press, 1967.

Schmidt, Dennis J. "Circles—Hermeneutic and Otherwise: On Various Senses of the Future as 'Not Yet.'" In David Wood, ed., *Writing the Future*, pp. 67–77. London: Routledge, 1990.

Schmitz, Hermann. Review of Jan van der Meulen, *Hegel. Die gebrochene Mitte*. *Hegel-Studien* 1 (1961): 318–326.

Schmitz, Kenneth L. "Enriching the Copula." *Review of Metaphysics* 27 (1973–74): 492–512.

——. "Hegel's Assessment of Spinoza." In Richard Kennington, ed., *Studies in Philosophy and the History of Philosophy*, vol. 7, pp. 211–236. Washington, D.C.: Catholic University of America Press, 1980.

——. "Hegel on Kant: Being-in-Itself and the Thing-in-Itself." In Richard Kennington, ed., *Studies in Philosophy and the History of Philosophy*, vol. 12, pp. 229–251. Washington, D.C.: Catholic University of America Press, 1985.

——. "Hegel's Philosophy of Religion: Typology and Strategy." *Review of Metaphysics* 23 (1969–70): 717–736.

——. "Metaphysics: Radical, Comprehensive, Determinate Discourse." *Review of Metaphysics* 39 (1986): 675–694.

——. "Philosophy of Religion and the Redefinition of Philosophy." *Man and World* 3, no. 2 (1970): 54–82.

——. "Purity of Soul and Immortality." *Monist* 69 (1986): 396–415.

Schoener, Abraham. "Heraclitus on War." Unpublished dissertation, University of Toronto, 1993.

Schrader, George A. "Hegel's Contribution to Phenomenology." *Monist* 48 (1964): 18–33.

Scott, Charles. "The De-Struction of Being and Time in *Being and Time*." *Man and World* 21 (1988): 91–106.

Sedgwick, Sally. "Metaphysics and Morality in Kant and Hegel." In Sally Sedgwick, ed., *The Reception of Kant's Critical Philosophy: Fichte, Schelling and Hegel*, pp. 306–323. Cambridge: Cambridge University Press, 2000.

Sellars, Wilfrid. "Empiricism and the Philosophy of Mind." *Minnesota Studies in the Philosophy of Science* 1 (1956): 253–329.

Shannon, Daniel Edward. "Hegel's Criticism of Analogical Procedure and the Search for Final Purpose." *Owl of Minerva* 19 (1988): 169–182.

——. "The Question Concerning the Factum of Experience: The Ontological Dimensions of Hegel's Thought." Dissertation, University of Toronto, 1989.

Shklar, Judith N. *Freedom and Independence: A Study of the Political Ideas of Hegel's Phenomenology of Mind*. Cambridge: Cambridge University Press, 1976.

Siep, Ludwig. "The 'Aufhebung' of Morality in Ethical Life." In Lamb and Stepelevich, eds., *Hegel's Philosophy of Action*, pp. 137–155.

——. "Zur Dialectik der Anerkennung bei Hegel." *Hegel-Jahrbuch* (1975): 366–373.

Sills, Chip. "Is Hegel's Logic a Speculative Tropology?" *Owl of Minerva* 21 (1989): 21–40.

Simpson, Peter. *Hegel's Transcendental Induction*. Albany: SUNY Press, 1998.

Sollors, Werner. "Introduction: The Invention of Ethnicity." In Werner Sollors, ed., *The Invention of Ethnicity*, pp. ix–xx. New York: Oxford University Press, 1989.

Solomon, Robert C. "Hegel's Concept of *Geist*." In MacIntyre, ed., *Hegel: A Collection of Critical Essays*, pp. 125–149.

——. "Hegel's Epistemology." *American Philosophical Quarterly* 2 (1974): pp. 277–289.

Smith, P. Christopher. "Heidegger's Criticism of Absolute Knowledge." *New Scholasticism* 45 (1971): 56–86.

Sparshott, Francis. *Taking Life Seriously*. Toronto: University of Toronto Press, 1994.

Speight, C. Allen. "The Metaphysics of Morals and Hegel's Critique of Kantian Ethics." *History of Philosophy Quarterly* 14 (1997): 379–402.

Spinoza, Baruch. *The Ethics: The Treatise on the Emendation of the Intellect and Selected Letters*. Trans. Samuel Shirley. Indianapolis: Hackett, 1995.

Stambaugh, Joan. "An Inquiry into Authenticity and Inauthenticity in *Being and Time*." *Research in Phenomenology* 7 (1977): 153–161.

———. "Time and Dialectic in Hegel and Heidegger." *Research in Phenomenology* 4 (1974): 87–97.

Stegmaier, Werner. "Leib und Leben: zum Hegel-Nietzsche-Problem." *Hegel-Studien* 20 (1985): 173–198.

Stern, David S. Review of David Kolb, *The Critique of Pure Modernity: Hegel, Heidegger and After. Owl of Minerva* 21 (1990): 185–190.

Stillman, Peter G., ed. *Hegel's Philosophy of Spirit.* Albany: State University of New York Press, 1987.

Styranko, Cory. "Architecture and Philosophy in German Idealism." Dissertation, Pennsylvania State University, 2004.

Taylor, Charles. *Hegel.* Cambridge: Cambridge University Press, 1975.

———. "Hegel and the Philosophy of Action." In Lamb and Stepelevich, eds., *Hegel's Philosophy of Action*, pp. 1–18.

———. "The Opening Arguments of the *Phenomenology.*" In MacIntyre, ed., *Hegel: A Collection of Critical Essays*, pp. 151–187.

———. "Understanding and Ethnocentricity." In *Philosophy and the Human Sciences: The Collected Papers of Charles Taylor*, pp. 116–133. Cambridge: Cambridge University Press, 1985.

Tedlock, Barbara. "The New Anthropology of Dreaming." *Dreaming* 1 (1991): 161–178.

Theweleit, Klaus. *Male Fantasies.* 2 vols. Trans. Erica Carter and Chris Turner. Minneapolis: University of Minnesota Press, 1987 and 1989.

van der Meulen, Jan. "Hegels Lehre von Leib, Seele und Geist." *Hegel-Studien* 2 (1963): 251–274.

van Roden Allen, Robert. "Hegelian Beginning and Resolve: A View of the Relationship between the *Phenomenology* and the *Logic.*" *Idealistic Studies* 13 (1983): 249–265.

Varela, Francisco, Adrian Palacios, and Evan Thompson. "Ways of Coloring: Comparative Color Vision as a Case-Study for Cognitive Science." *Behavioral and Brain Sciences* 15 (1992): 1–74..

Verene, Donald Phillip. *Hegel's Recollection: A Study of Images in the Phenomenology of Spirit.* Albany: SUNY Press, 1985.

von der Luft, Eric. "The Birth of Spirit for Hegel out of the Travesty of Medicine." In Stillman, ed., *Hegel's Philosophy of Spirit*, pp. 25–42.

———. "Would Hegel Have Liked to Burn Down All the Churches and Replace Them with Philosophical Academies?" *Modern Schoolman* 68 (Nov. 1990): 41–56.

Warminski, Andrej. "Reading, for Example: 'Sense-Certainty' in Hegel's *Phenomenology of Spirit.*" *Diacritics* 11, no. 2 (1981): 83–94.

Watkins, Calvert, ed. *The American Heritage Dictionary of Indo-European Roots.* Boston: Houghton Mifflin, 1985.

Westphal, Merold, ed. *Method and Speculation in Hegel's Phenomenology.* Atlantic Highlands, N.J.: Humanities Press, 1982.

Wilcocks, R. W. *Zur Erkenntnistheorie Hegels in der Phänomenologie des Geistes.* 1917. Reprint, Hildesheim: Georg Olms Verlag, 1981.

Wildt, Andreas. *Autonomie und Anerkennung: Hegels Moralitätskritik im Lichte seiner Fichte-Rezeption.* Stuttgart: Klett-Cotta, 1982.

Williams, Robert R. *Recognition: Fichte and Hegel on the Other.* Albany: SUNY Press, 1992.

———. "Hegel and Skepticism." *Owl of Minerva* 24 (1992): 71–82.

———. "Hegel's Concept of *Geist*." In Stillman, ed., *Hegel's Philosophy of Spirit*, pp. 1–20.

———. Review of Michael Forster, *Hegel and Skepticism*. *Owl of Minerva* 25 (1993): 84–88.

Winfield, Richard Dien. "Commentary on 'Hegel's Concept of *Geist*.'" In Stillman, ed., *Hegel's Philosophy of Spirit*, pp. 21–24.

Wittig, Monique. "One Is Not Born a Woman." In *The Straight Mind and Other Essays*, pp. 9–20. Boston: Beacon Press, 1992.

Wood, Allen W. *Hegel's Ethical Thought*. Cambridge: Cambridge University Press, 1990.

INDEX

Index

Index

Index

John Russon teaches in the Department of Philosophy
at the University of Guelph, Ontario, Canada.